ECONOMIC DECISION MODELS
for engineers and managers

New York   San Francisco   St. Louis   London   Toronto   Sydney   **McGRAW-HILL BOOK COMPANY**

The diagram on the facing page represents an economic decision. The three linked circles in the center show the interdependent relationship of *men*, *machines*, and *materials*. These physical resources are bounded by the modern philosopher's stone, *money*. The potential transmutation of money into services or products allows each factor in the decision environment to be expressed in common terms. The outer circle suggests ways for the engineer or manager, acting in his capacity as decision-maker, to evaluate the core values. Depending on the amount and type of information available, the decision may be treated under assumed *certainty*, with recognition of *risk*, or by admitting *uncertainty*. A detailed explanation of this model and other economic decision models is the content and purpose of this book.

ECONOMIC
DECISION
MODELS
for engineers and managers

JAMES L. RIGGS Professor of Industrial Engineering, Oregon State University

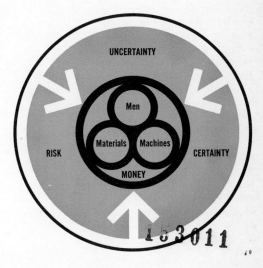

ECONOMIC DECISION MODELS
FOR ENGINEERS AND MANAGERS

Library of Congress catalog card number: 67-26885

234567890 STCZ 7543210

5286

"Economic Decision Models" is a title that could be applied to a broad range of topics. It is so intended for this book. The content is essentially a quantitative approach to practical engineering and management problems, but many theoretical considerations and nonquantitative aspects are necessarily included. The types of models offered range from the fashionably new management tool of critical path scheduling to the traditional, but ever applicable, time-value-of-money concepts from engineering economy. To accommodate a broad coverage of concepts within a reasonable number of pages, mathematical rigor is sacrificed. A heavy reliance is placed on examples and explanations to develop the rationale of solution methods. References are provided at the end of each chapter for students seeking greater depth for particular subjects.

The format of the book proceeds from an introductory section to deterministic models and closes with probabilistic models. A knowledge of algebra is sufficient mathematical sophistication, although rudimentary calculus and a familiarity with probability would help in some sections. Some business students find the basic economics redundant for their training and engineers are already acquainted with certain solution techniques. However, there should be enough new material remaining for either group to easily sustain a one-semester course.

The blend of typical quantitative business subjects and traditional engineering economy topics is intentional. In this era of high-speed data processing, more versatile computers, and interdisciplinary task force operations, it is difficult to distinguish between the responsibilities of engineers and managers. Both rely on many of the same analytical tools. These tools are the polished problem-solving techniques borrowed from operations research, systems engineering, statistics, econometrics and other disciplines. In this book, emphasis is placed on the use of tools, not their source or proof. This approach characterizes the objective of the text: A concise introductory presentation of a wide range of practical decision models. Hopefully, the material will at a minimum provide a better understanding of today's industrial problems, and will lead to more confident decision-making.

Major acknowledgement is owed to the many students who struggled through earlier drafts of this book. Their comments, corrections, and suggestions helped immeasurably. Further gratitude is extended to Professors Bill Boore, Kostas Dervitsiotis, and Mike Inoue for their generous contribution of advice. Any additional comments, corrections, or suggestions from the readers will also be appreciated.

Preface

James L. Riggs
Corvallis, Oregon

Contents

ECONOMIC DECISION MODELS
for engineers and managers

Section One
Introduction

Only the very brash or very naïve would enter a chess competition without knowing the language and rules of chess. Similar inadequacies fail to bar the unprepared or unsuspecting from entering the arena of economic competition. Many are lulled into complacency by an honest but often erroneous belief that they possess an innate money sense which will carry them through. Common sense by itself affords only a vague guideline for most economic decisions expected from engineers and managers. The odds favor the competitor who knows the language and the rules. In this section we will consider some quantitative guidelines for economic decisions.

Many decisions are of a brushfire nature; immediate answers are required for day-to-day problems. The approach to such primary decisions is less sophisticated than those to other types of decisions, but no less important. The familiarity with primary decisions offered in this section lays the groundwork for refined models introduced in later chapters.

Chapter One
Concepts
of
Economic
Decisions

A decision is simply a selection from two or more courses of action. Yet decision-making can be an exciting, traumatic, fascinating experience. Some choices are trivial or largely automatic; others have far-reaching effects. Most major decisions have overtones of economy. Either on a personal basis or on behalf of an organization, we are constantly called upon to judge the most advantageous use for limited resources.

A *fisherman* stands in his crowded cabin and studies a map. Three fishing grounds are circled on the map. He mentally compares the reports and gossip he has heard recently about the grounds. He also considers the market demands, the weather forecasts, the condition of his ship, and the supplies on board. He has to decide where to fish.

An *engineer* contemplates the bulging walls of a large concrete culvert under an interstate highway. The collapsing culvert is the result of thousands of tons of rock recently stockpiled on the roadbed above in preparation for new construction. In a few days the spring thaw will soak the ground and send torrents of water through the culvert. He speculates on possible designs in terms of the conditions and the restrictions imposed by available equipment, materials, and time.

The *owner* of a wholesale distribution center seeks to improve his delivery service in order to meet competition. To do so he can buy or rent more trucks, subcontract his deliveries, open additional outlets, and/or improve his handling facilities. His capital is limited and the outlook for increased volume is uncertain. First he must decide if any action is needed. If it is, he must select the most suitable alternative.

The *manager* of a large manufacturing company surveys a collection of proposals laid out neatly on the long table in the board room. Each proposal represents many hours of staff work. Each is a detailed plan for the development of a new product. He must select the proposal which best serves the interests of the company within the constraints of restricted physical and human resources, competition, legal requirements, available capital, and corporate objectives. His decision will affect the activities of hundreds of people.

Each of the above situations is unique to the participants, but they all possess related basic elements of economic decision-making. Each decision-maker has several alternatives from which to choose. His resources are limited. His objective is to select the most profitable course of action.

A manager is a person skilled in administration. A major part of this skill is necessarily applied to financial matters. Industrial managers seek a practical and economical adjustment of means to ends that benefits production. Production may take the form of information, physical products, or ideas. The output is a function of how successfully a manager's economic decisions lead to feasible, cost-conscious solutions to operational problems.

The concept of "engineering" warrants special atten-

THE ECONOMIC ROLE OF ENGINEERS AND MANAGERS

tion. A narrow view of engineering would limit its application to the designing, building, and operation of machines and operations. The yardstick of performance would be physical efficiency. This ratio of output to input units (foot-pounds, BTUs, minutes, etc.) is certainly important, but it is not the sole objective of engineering effort.

A more widely held definition of engineering reveals its intimate link with industrial economy. "Engineering is the art of organizing men and of directing the forces and materials of nature for the benefit of the human race." Here we can observe a broad responsibility. The "art of organizing" implies management; the "forces and materials of nature" include resources from nuts and bolts to information and energy; "for the benefit of the human race" dictates economy.

With the broader definition goes an expanded interpretation of efficiency. The formula is the same — output over input — but the units differ. By converting physical units to monetary values and by including related operational activities, we get financial efficiency. A high physical efficiency is no guarantee of high financial efficiency. A low physical efficiency is an insufficient reason for deleting an alternative from consideration. There may be other economic circumstances which compensate for lower standards of performance.

Financial efficiency is a composite of many factors. Consider the task of the wholesale distributor described previously. Assume that he has decided to purchase additional trucks. His choice of trucks could be based on the mechanical efficiency of each type. More likely, the selection will depend on economic criteria. This evaluation could take the form

$$\text{Financial efficiency} = \frac{\text{output}}{\text{input}} = \frac{\text{worth}}{\text{cost}}$$

where the output or worth is the revenue received from the services of the trucks and the input or cost includes operating costs, depreciation expense, interest on invested capital, taxes, and other associated expenses. A careful review of the receipts and disbursements involved in the financial efficiency shows typical engineering attributes such as reliability, proper design, accuracy, and safety. It is this feature, plus the inclusion of other economic factors, that makes financial efficiency a realistic and representative method of evaluation.

Thus the objective of engineering and management is to maximize service. The level of service can usually be expressed in monetary terms, with the result that *economic criteria are the basis for evaluation and profit maximization is the goal.*

A casual familiarity with financial efficiency may impart the fallacious idea that decisions for economy are trivial. Just plug into the equation and grind out an answer; if it is a winner, use it. In some situations such a blasé attitude might work. Spectacular discoveries and overnight fortunes attest to the fact that plungers sometimes win. There are also innumerable instances in which spur-of-the-moment, rule-of-thumb decisions failed to pay off.

In an effort to improve the hunch approach to decision-making, popularly termed "scientific management" methods have been developed. The impact of this approach has been impressive. In part its recognition is due to the sincere need of engineers, scientists, and managers for a logical, systematic method of analysis. Another part of its attraction stems from an aura of the divine created by its emphasis on prediction; a focus on the future has always had a special and irresistible appeal.

INTUITION OR ANALYSIS As represented in Fig. 1.1, a decision made at the present time is based on data from past performances and establishes a course of action that will result in some future outcome. *The analytical approach* to decision-making entails a systematic study and quantitative evaluation of the past and future. *Intuition* is oriented in the present but informally embraces memories of the past and estimates of what may happen in the future. Both methods produce verdicts, and both have a place in decision-making.

It is a reasonable assumption that the analytical approach is more reliable, if for no other reason, because more effort is required to conduct it. This required effort is one reason that many decisions are still made by hunches. Effort costs money, and some minor decisions may not warrant the expense. Even major decisions have hunch aspects. Intricate situations generally possess factors beyond the ken of current analytical tech-

Figure 1.1 Decision-making sequence

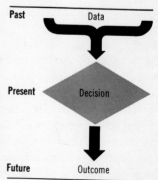

Past	Data
Present	Decision
Future	Outcome

niques. The analyst can go only so far before he must resort to judgment.

Intuition is liberally spiced with instinctive judgment. As such, it is a valid tool in the decision-maker's repertoire, provided the logic is not dulled by fad rules-of-thumb or unrecognized bias. Confidence generated by industrial applications indicates that analytical decision-making tools are also needed. We can set the two approaches in perspective by stating that *analytical methods should be employed whenever they are technically feasible and economically warranted.* Outside these limits, intuition and judgment are necessary and legitimate recourses.

TACTICS AND STRATEGY The decision-making process is accelerated by identifying descriptive characteristics within a decision environment. Four decision situations were described earlier in the chapter: the fisherman, the engineer, the owner, and the manager. We will use these situations to illustrate some environmental patterns.

"Tactics" and "strategy" are familiar military terms. We associate strategic decisions with the High Command and tactical decisions with field operations. Strategy sets broad objectives, and the associated tactics define the multiple maneuvers required to achieve the objectives. The tactical-strategic division of decision areas is as valid in industry as in military operations.

Strategy The aim of industry and engineering is to satisfy human wants. The wants are identified through surveys, polls, and market-research studies. When a specific want is identified and singled out for special attention, a strategy begins to take shape. Further study to determine how the want can be satisfied within the resources available crystallizes strategic objectives.

There are usually several acceptable strategic objectives. A strategic decision ideally selects the objective that makes the best use of the organization's resources in accordance with its long-range goals. The measure of this type of decision is *effectiveness* — the degree to which a strategic objective meets the economic targets of the organization or system.

The *manager* of the manufacturing company faces a strategic decision. Each of the plans for a new product represents a course of action which will commit a significant portion of his company's resources. Will it succeed competitively? Does it suit the company's growth pattern? Is it compatible with the risk policy of the company? All these questions play a part in the effectiveness rating of each plan.

The *owner* of the distribution center has concluded that the purchase of more trucks will best satisfy his strategic objectives. He wants his business to grow. He is willing to gamble that new trucks will shorten his delivery time and thereby increase his market share. Renting or subcontracting would have been only a holding gesture. New outlets are beyond his funding ability. He expects the return on the trucks to exceed an investment in new material-handling facilities. Now he has to make tactical decisions as to size, make, color, and model of trucks to buy; hiring operators; making maintenance provisions; purchasing insurance; and arranging other details to carry out the strategic decision.

Tactics   A strategic plan can usually be conducted in a number of different ways. These operational-level alternatives are tactics. The relative value of tactical choices are rated according to their *efficiency* — the degree to which an operation accomplishes the intended economic effort.

The relationship between strategies and tactics offers some constructive insights. The effectiveness of each strategy is initially estimated from the effect it will have on system objectives. It thus serves as a guide to the area in which tactics will produce the highest efficiency. The actual efficiency of each tactic is determined from a study of the activities required to conduct the tactical operation.

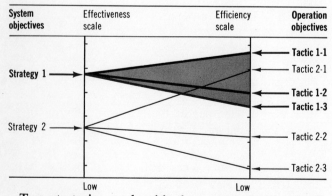

Figure 1.2   Relationship of tactics and strategies

Two strategies, each with three apparent means of accomplishment, are depicted in Fig. 1.2 The average efficiency for the tactics associated with strategy 1 (tactics 1-1, 1-2, and 1-3) has a higher average value than those for strategy 2. However, it could happen that a strategy with a lower effectiveness possesses the tactic with the highest efficiency. Tactic 2-1 is close to the most efficient tactic of strategy 1. If it had been the highest on the efficiency scale, it would be the leading candidate for selection regardless of its strategic origin.

Sensitivity   The decision situation depicted in Fig. 1.2 has high sensitivity; that is, it is vulnerable to small changes in the controlling conditions. With tactics 1-1 and 2-1 so close on the efficiency scale, a slight change in operating conditions or external influencing factors could switch the positions of the top tactics, or even the strategies. An insensitive situation occurs when all the tactics for a given strategy have a higher efficiency than the best tactic of any other strategy. The consequence of high sensitivity is to force a complete investigation to assure the validity of data being evaluated. (Other aspects of sensitivity are included in later discussions of risk.)

The *fisherman* faces a tactical decision as to which of the three fishing grounds to select. His strategic decision to be in the fishing industry with certain equipment operating from a certain port has already been made. Now he must implement this decision by selecting the tactic which best utilizes his resources. Each tactic is a composite of several factors. The economic efficiency of each results from the value of the catch in relation to the supplies expended, the time consumed, and the wear incurred during the trip. In turn, these factors could be subdivided into innumerable smaller accounts. If he tried to consider all the aspects, his decision task would be overwhelming. His logical recourse is to give prime consideration to the most sensitive factors. From experience he knows which factors are most sensitive to unexpected changes in environmental conditions, such as weather. By concentrating his attention on sensitive factors, he sidesteps the issue of extreme detail in his analysis. This approach is not only methodologically sound, it is a natural routine.

The *engineer* with the task of repairing the damaged culvert is contemplating a tactical decision. The causal decision on the strategic level to reconstruct that portion of the state highway system was made by the state highway engineer and his staff. All the activities required to carry out this decision are tactical operations as far as the state highway engineer is concerned. Yet the project engineer for the reconstruction makes his strategic decisions in dealing with gross operations such as right-of-ways, structures, rockwork, grading, and paving. He considers the daily problems of breakdown, maintenance, accidents, work assignments, and so forth to be the tactical operations. Finally, the engineer on the job might consider his strategic decisions to be the scheduling of men and machines to complete the grading and surfacing. All other hourly decisions made to keep the work progressing are tactical. The danger in this "cascade" effect is that a consuming interest in operational efficiency could lead to a chain of events that detracts from the overall project effectiveness.

Suboptimization   In the preceding highway illustration we were exposed to a concept termed *suboptimization* — an attempt to optimize a tactical segment of a problem with little or no regard to the strategic effectiveness of the solution. Whenever multiple objectives are present in a decision situation, it is probable that there is no single course of action that will optimize all the objectives. Therefore the aim must be to select an alternative that achieves the best possible balance between the conflicting objectives. The important point is to recognize when all the notable objectives of a system are *not* being simultaneously maximized.

Most problems are first approached from the suboptimal viewpoint. The primary reason is that analyzing a portion of a system allows the analyst to make some tentative conclusions without being bogged down in a deluge of details. The collection of suboptimal alternatives can then be modified to integrate the parts into an optimal whole. Advances in computer science and operations research may ultimately allow us to readily analyze the complex whole in one evaluation. Until then, we should be aware of the areas in which suboptimization is most likely to occur.

Organization effect   In larger organizations the various operations incident to the accomplishment of a strategic objective are performed by different departments. Each department strives to keep its costs to a minimum. In doing so, the cost-minimization procedures of one department could cause an exorbitant cost increase in another department. A typical example is the desire of the production department to have long production runs for a given type of product in order to reduce setup costs, while the inventory department wants shorter runs so that the inventory level and storage costs of the part will be reduced. The interdependency becomes more complex when the sales department adds its request for larger inventories to avoid unfilled orders and the facilities department warns that storage space should be restricted because warehousing is limited. It is a strategic management function to orient these potentially inconsistent subobjectives toward an optimal system objective.

Time effect   Tactics based on a planning horizon of 1 or 2 years will not necessarily have the same efficiency as those based on a longer span of years. Suppose a manufacturer anticipates using a fixed number of specially designed containers each year. He can purchase the containers or he can make them. If he makes them he will have to buy some new equipment. The economy of the choices is depicted in Fig. 1.3. A planning horizon of 1 or 2 years would indicate that a purchasing plan is preferable; beyond 2 years it is more attractive to make the containers.

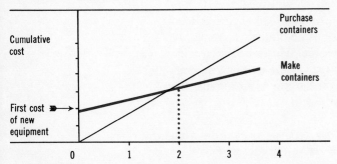

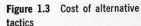

Figure 1.3 Cost of alternative tactics

While too short a planning horizon can severely distort the values, a longer period tends to introduce uncertainties. As we reach further into the future for estimates, the predictions suffer in credibility. This condition is acknowledged by the treatment given to decisions with different amounts of risk.

DEGREE OF CERTAINTY   We can classify engineering and managerial decisions into three broad categories which characterize the environmental conditions of the decision situation and suggest a means of analysis.

Decisions assuming certainty include most traditional approaches to economy. It is often convenient and feasible to consider all the conditions of a problem as known with surety. Actually, in assuming certainty we are basing the analysis on a set of assumptions which we believe have a high expectation of occurring. This expectation can be fully warranted in many instances — stated interest on a high-grade bond, established production patterns, proven designs, quality-inspected materials, respected reputations, etc. Even in situations where risk is known to exist, it is often practical to assume a certain set of conditions. If it is impossible or too expensive to quantify the levels of risk with respect to different alternatives, an assumption of certainty offers a workable means of analysis.

Decisions recognizing risk are appropriate whenever the analyst can obtain good estimates of the probability of future conditions and the economic effect of these conditions. Costly research and experimentation may be required. If the expense is not prohibitive, the reward of a glimpse at the future may be well worth the effort and expense. As an example, assume that an architect is considering submission of a design for a new structure on speculation. He knows that if he wins the commission to do the final design he will receive $10,000. If he fails, he will lose an estimated $800, the cost of preparing the rejected designs. Nothing is gained or lost if he makes no submission. He knows that nine other architects of ability equal to his own are submitting designs. The matrix format for determining the amount of risk is as shown:

	Win [P (W) = 0.1]	Lose [P (L) = 0.9]
Submit	$10,000	−$800
Do not submit	0	0

The columns in the matrix represent possible futures. The probability of these futures (win or lose) was estimated from the number of expected submissions (his own and nine others). The entries in the rows are the expected returns from each future in relation to alternative courses of action. Once we have complete information, as depicted above, the analysis is largely routine.

Decisions admitting uncertainty are necessary when the

analyst wishes to include the effect of different futures in his evaluation but finds it impossible to predict the likelihood of each future. If the architect in the previous example had been únable to estimate the probability of winning the commission, the decision would be made under uncertainty with the format shown on the right. The meagerness of this information makes a quantitative evaluation difficult, but fortunately there are principles of choice available to guide the decision-maker. As in any judgment situation, dependability improves with the acquisition of reliable information.

	Win	Lose
Submit	$10,000	−$800
Do not submit	0	0

Using these classifications for the degree of risk in decision-making, we will consider quantitative measures for determining optimal solutions in each class. The first six chapters of the text deal with conditions of certainty. Risk is considered in Chaps. 8 and 9. The last chapter views uncertainty.

Decision-making is anchored in two worlds: the real, everyday working world and the symbolic, scientifically oriented world. As depicted in Fig. 1.4, *problems* in engineering and managerial economy originate in the real world of economic planning, management, and control. The problem is defined and clarified by *data* from the problem environment. This information allows the analyst to formulate a *hypothesis* in symbolic terms. The symbolic language helps him convert the information to its most usable form. By manipulating and *experimenting* with his abstraction of the real world, he can simulate multiple configurations of reality which otherwise would be too costly or inconvenient to investigate. From this activity a *prediction* hopefully emerges.

The predicted behavior is converted back to reality for testing in the form of hardware or commands. If it is valid, the problem is solved. If not, the cycle is repeated with the added information that the previous approach was unsuccessful.

There is no way to guarantee a workable solution. Some problems defy collection of data. Others seem too complex to offer even a starting point. Yet decision-makers are expected to make decisions. The best defense against being backed into a corner without a rebuttal is a systematic attack on the problem. By "systematic" we mean a step-by-step logical procedure. The

DECISION-MAKING PROCEDURES

Figure 1.4 Decision process

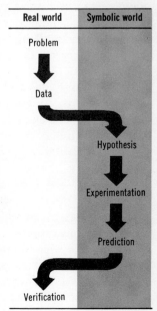

phases of the attack are shown in the flow chart of Fig. 1.5.

DEFINITION OF THE PROBLEM   Defining the problem starts with a frame of mind. The decision-maker must consciously prepare himself to make a decision. He should be aware that explicit measures are required: an exact statement of objectives, information in the greatest quantity and of the best possible quality, correct application of appropriate analytical tools, and the determination to conduct the analysis expeditiously. This is an impressive task, but when exciting decisions are undertaken there never seems to be enough time to do all the desired investigating. A careful definition of the problem is a good relief valve for decision-making under pressure.

The decision environment provides most of the clues for a good definition. We have already observed the nature of strategic and tactical objectives, the sensitivity of alternatives, and the effects of suboptimality. The outgrowth of these considerations is the identification of pertinent objectives and alternative courses of action.

Objectives   If a single objective satisfies the problem, a precise statement is relatively easy. As the ramifications of a problem become more numerous, the goals become more difficult to define. For instance, there is seldom a situation in which it is sufficient to state that the objective is to cut costs. Cost cutting may be subject to a maximum expenditure, a time limit, scheduling restrictions, resource availability, or other less apparent factors. Such factors, or constraints, are also objective criteria.

Contradictory aims and nebulous goals result in confusing objectives. An assignment to get the "finest equipment for the least amount of money" is bewildering. It may be possible to decide what is the "finest" equipment, but it is unlikely to be the least expensive. In a similar vein, a charge to get the "best equipment for our purposes" is too broad to be useful. Double standards and indefinite objectives lead to second-guessing. A precise statement of realistic goals simplifies the entire decision-making process.

Alternatives   In a preliminary search for a solution it may be useful to list all possible courses of action. The goal of such a free-wheeling approach is to identify alternatives that might otherwise be overlooked. "Brain-

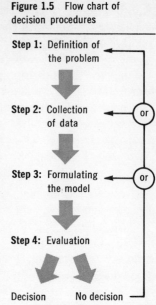

Figure 1.5 Flow chart of decision procedures

Step 1: Definition of the problem

Step 2: Collection of data   or

Step 3: Formulating the model   or

Step 4: Evaluation

Decision   No decision

storming" and "skull sessions" are descriptive names for wholesale idea-accumulation methods which encourage creative effort. While it is important to search for the novel means of accomplishing something, it is just as important to recognize practical limitations. It is a personal and often troublesome question for each individual to decide whether the restrictions he imposes are real or imagined.

COLLECTION OF DATA   Data act as the fuel for decision-making and must be of good quality if the process is to function smoothly. All the steps in decision making rely on data collection. None of the steps can compensate for poor data.

Sources of data are plentiful. Nearly everyone is willing to give an opinion about someone else's problem. Reliable sources of data are less plentiful. Subjective opinions certainly have a part in information collection, but other sources should be thoroughly exploited. The huge list of potential sources includes digested data in handbooks, public records, government bulletins, trade journals, applicable reference books, company production records, accounting data, suppliers' information services, recorded experiments, special reports, and many other works.

Outcomes   Current data are used to predict the outcomes of alternative courses of action. In decisions assuming certainty the outcomes are calculated directly from the input data. When risk is included, current data are extrapolated into the future to provide estimates of what could happen if a given course of action were followed. These estimates are called *payoffs*. The outcomes for the architect considering a design submission were payoffs — $10,000 gain if he won and an $800 loss if he failed to win the competition. As objectives stretch further into hazy uncertainty, the estimation of outcomes is proportionately more demanding. The demand is for high-quality data and its careful inferential treatment.

Intangibles   There are often factors in a decision situation that cannot be translated into dollars and cents with any pretense of accuracy. These factors are called *intangibles*. The distinction between tangible and intangible factors is the ease and accuracy by which data are quantitatively expressed. By applying enough resources, some sort of figure can be imposed on most factors. The question then becomes one of balancing the effort against the worth.

All decisions have some intangible aspects — emotional gratification engendered by a certain course of action, safety considerations, the influence on personnel, reputations, friendships, public relations, and so forth. These aspects are bound to enter the decision process either as identified intangibles or as vague impressions. Thus the question of whether to attempt to quantify the intangibles can be answered only after they have been identified. Regardless of the answer, it is the decision-maker's duty to recognize that intangibles influence a decision just as persuasively as tangible factors.

FORMULATING THE MODEL   A model is a representation of the real world. We begin to formulate our model when we develop objectives and alternatives. The model shows the relationship between cause and effect, between objectives and constraints. It is manipulated to show the end product we can expect from following a given course of action. Because decision situations vary so widely, different types of models are necessary. We will consider three classes: physical, schematic, and mathematical. While we are primarily interested in mathematical models for economy studies, the other classes are also effective aids in special situations.

Physical models   Scale-model cars closely resemble the real-world cars they represent. Some model cars even run on race tracks. Such models not only look like their real-world counterparts, but in some ways they function like real cars. Model cars can be made to collide. If the models are realistic representations, the effects of the collision can be evaluated. A similar real-world collision would entail a major financial outlay and the even greater detractor of danger to human life.

Physical models may be life size or smaller or larger. They may be used for demonstration or experimentation. A globe demonstrates the orientation of one geographical area to another. A two- or three-dimensional model layout of a plant is used to judge the effect of changes in equipment locations on work flow. A layout focuses attention on distance. Other effects such as noise and vibration are not included. Concentration on one feature is an advantage when other features are considered unimportant; it can be a disadvantage when the neglected features are significant.

Schematic models   Graphical representations or schematic models have many features in common with physical models. They may be any size. They emphasize one aspect and can be used for demonstration or experimentation. A pie chart depicting the portion of a dollar spent on different phases of an operation is a demonstration piece. Organizational charts show the divisions and often the responsibilities of areas within an establishment. In a flow-process chart the elements (operations, delays, transportations, storages, and inspections) of a process can be manipulated to determine the effects of rearranging or altering the work flow. Similar experimentation with actual work flow would be at best inconvenient and at worst crippling. Network analysis, as typified by critical path scheduling (Chap. 4), is used to aid project planning and control.

Mathematical models   Equations and formulas are familiar mathematical models. They are more concise and less likely to be misconstrued than the other classes of models. The use of symbols does not improve the accuracy of an analysis, but it does increase the precision. When everyone concerned is familiar with figures and symbols, they are effective for demonstration. Mathematical models are applicable to a wide range of analysis problems.

In decision-making situations we use mathematical models primarily to predict outcomes and to determine the measure of existing operations. Breakeven and minimum-cost conditions are examined through a combination of schematic and mathematical models (Chap. 2). Linear programming models are used to determine the optimal use of available resources (Chap. 3). Calculations involving interest factors reveal the time value of money (Chaps. 5 to 7). Probability models relate risk to strategic and tactical objectives (Chaps. 8 to 9). In all these applications we are still formulating a model in the abstract world to represent conditions in the real world.

EVALUATION   The merit of a model is determined by how well it represents the real world. The ultimate test of predicted behavior comes when the predictions are exposed to reality. Pretesting an evaluation is a confidence-building precaution. The veracity of a model can be checked initially by applying it to historical data. If the objective is to predict sales, the data from 2 years ago can be used as input to predict last year's sales. An agreement between the forecast and actual sales figures indicates that the model can be used for current predictions, provided the decision environment is essentially unchanged.

Each class of models is evaluated differently. Measurements are taken of physical models operating under controlled conditions. Positions are evaluated in schematic models. Rules, algorithms, and decision criteria establish the means of assessing mathematical models. Any good model of quantified data contributes to a complete analysis by making it easier to see the outcomes resulting from different inputs, and by making more time available for the decision-maker to concentrate on intangibles.

After all the decision-making procedures are accounted for, the final authority is the decision-maker. He must evaluate the accuracy and reliability of his data and model. He must temper the model's prediction with any relevant intangible considerations. Then he has to watch his decision being tested in the unsympathetic real world.

PRIMARY COMPARISONS

Not all the decisions in engineering and management are as complex as intimated in the preceding sections. In addition to the necessary but less significant workaday decisions, there are a number of situations in which a direct evaluation of readily available data will yield a solution. The characteristics of such decisions are inferred by their descriptive title, *primary comparisons*.

"Primary" indicates a condition of immediacy. All the influencing factors of the decision environment are already present. Certainty is assumed. The effect of time, including the time-value of investments, is irrelevant to the decision situation.

"Comparisons" indicates that the value of two or more alternatives is being weighed. A valid comparison is possible only if the outcomes of the alternatives are essentially equivalent.

In summary, *primary comparisons lead to a decision between alternatives with equivalent outcomes which are unaffected by time.*

OUTCOME SCALES   Before we can deliberate on the solution to a problem, we have to be able to express our preferences among outcomes. Some of the mystery associated with outcome anticipation is removed if we look at each alternative as if it had already occurred. Then we rate its effect. Ratings may result from individual subjective estimation, consensus opinion, extrapolation of historical records, correlation, or other means.

The more useful rating scales possess mathematical properties which describe the problem and allow an evaluation. We also know that some intangible factors defy such scaling. Therefore it is important to be aware of both qualitative and quantitative scales.

ORDINAL-SCALE COMPARISONS   Each item in a *simple order scale* ranks above or below every other item. After such an ordering has been arranged under conditions of assumed certainty, we have a solution. Where intangibles are significant, an orderly ranking of outcomes is a convenient means of comparison. The decision-maker just lists the alternatives according to his preference of outcomes. He can compare all the outcomes to a common attribute or compare every pair of outcomes. To illustrate the latter case, suppose we have four alternatives which lead to outcomes W, X, Y, and Z. Pairing the results gives

$$W > Y \qquad X > Z$$
$$X > W \qquad Z > W$$
$$X > Y \qquad Z > Y$$

where the symbol $>$ is read "preferred to." By counting the number of times each outcome occurs on the left of the pairings, it is a simple matter to discover the order of preference to be $X > Z > W > Y$ (X is on the left three times, Z two times, and W once; since Y is preferred to none of the other outcomes, it does not occur on the "preferred" side of any preferential pairing).

An evaluation that sets two or more outcomes equal to each other leads to a *weak-order scale*. This condition occurs commonly in "human engineering" or psychological measurements. If we let W, X, Y, and Z represent four levels of illumination, the pairings might reveal

$$W > Y \qquad X > Z$$
$$X > W \qquad Z = W$$
$$X > Y \qquad Z > Y$$

where the symbol $=$ indicates no recognizable difference. The resulting order, $X > (Z = W) > Y$, shows that there is a noticeable difference between only three levels of illumination. Level X is preferred to the others, level Y is the least desirable, and no distinction is possible between Z and W.

Two issues occasionally confuse ordinal scaling. The first is called *intransivity*. This condition occurs when pairings show a relationship such as

$$A > B \qquad B > C \qquad C > A$$

This circular rating might be attributed to the rater's incompetence, but in nature it is not at all unusual. Any sports buff can recall times when team A beat team B which beat team C which won over team A. To resolve the circular conflict into a meaningful order scale we need more information, such as scores from additional contests between teams A, B, and C.

The other issue is the temptation to read into an order a certain numerical spacing between items. The simple order $X > Z > W > Y$ could represent number sets of $100 > 99 > 98 > 2$ or $41 > 10 > 2 > 1$. The lack of specific intervals rules out any arithmetical or statistical operations.

INTERVAL-SCALE COMPARISONS   The next step in scaling is to assign numbers to preferences. We start with an arbitrary zero point and express outcomes according to a constant unit of measurement. The Fahrenheit or centigrade scales of temperature measurement are interval scales. The difference between degrees for each temperature scale is constant, but the two scales have different zero points. This means that the ratio of temperature measurements on one scale is different from the same ratio on the other scale (compare a change in temperature from 10 to 100° on the Fahrenheit scale to the same change on the centigrade scale). Standardized units of measurements must be used to make valid comparisons.

Outcome ratings   Several methods have been suggested to measure values on an interval scale. Churchman and Ackoff offer a method where the values are assumed to be additive. The decision-maker is asked to assign numbers between 1.00 and 0.00 to alternative outcomes according to his approximate intensity of preference. Thus a rating for outcomes W, X, Y, and Z might appear as

X	Z	W	Y
1.00	0.80	0.40	0.30

Now the sum of the values for Z, W, and Y, $0.80 +$ $0.40 + 0.30$, is compared with the ratings for X (1.00). *In order to show a preference for X its rating must exceed the combination of other values $(X > Z + W + Y)$.*[1] New ratings could be assigned, such as

X	Z	W	Y
1.00	0.60	0.20	0.10

where $1.00 > (0.60 + 0.20 + 0.10)$.[1] Next the value for Z is compared to the sum of W and Y. The values above confirm a preference for Z, $0.60 > 0.20 + 0.10$. The sequence ends with a preference shown for W over Y, $0.20 > 0.10$.

There are many sets of numbers that show the same preferential ratings:

X	Z	W	Y
1.00	0.97	0.02	0.01
1.00	0.34	0.32	0.01
1.00	0.04	0.02	0.01

The method by itself does not assure that a legitimate interval scale has been developed. It systematizes the judgment process, but accuracy is still a function of the decision-maker's opinions and effort.

Conditional decisions   The decision situations considered thus far have been independent selections; that is, the decision situations have been self-contained and not dependent on previous or related outcomes. When a decision necessarily includes attention to prior alternatives, it is called a *conditional decision*.

Most design and development problems are conditional in nature. Several alternatives are available at each stage of development or in each area of design. Preliminary evaluations of various combinations of methods or components are particularly suitable to evaluation by interval scales. This approach acts as a filter. The most promising designs are identified for a more thorough examination.

A "decision tree" format is helpful in making conditional decisions. All the alternatives being considered are shown graphically as branches of a tree. Under primary comparisons we are making a selection from several alternatives or combinations of alternatives without regard to the effect of time. In Chap. 9 we will use the

[1]The symbol $>$ is used here in its usual mathematical sense to indicate a quantity relationship. It is read "greater than."

same format with the addition of time effects and risk.

Figure 1.6 illustrates possible combinations available for the specification of a design component. There are three characteristics to be specified: material, shape, and capacity. The choices within the limits of these characteristics have been narrowed to three types of material, two configurations of shape, and three capacity sizes. The square symbol at the left indicates that a decision is to be made among the paths leading to the right. Each node (circle) represents a design quality. The nodes are grouped in columns according to common characteristics. A complete path from the square to a node in the last column represents one alternative.

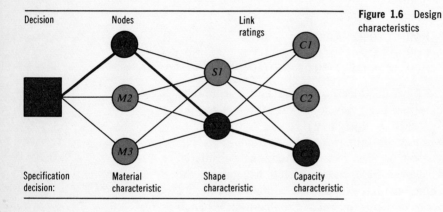

Decision   Nodes   Link ratings

Specification decision: Material characteristic   Shape characteristic   Capacity characteristic

Figure 1.6 Design characteristics

A conditional rating is given to each link between nodes. That is, each characteristic is rated with respect to its value in relation to the other characteristics in its path. One specification for the component could be material 1 ($M1$), shape 2 ($S2$), and capacity 3 ($C3$). The ratings for the material characteristic would depend only on a preference between types $M1$, $M2$, and $M3$, but the link ratings between material and shape would be based on the value of a given shape produced from a given material. Thus the link rating between $M1$ and $S2$ indicates the relative value of shape 2 made from material 1. In turn, the link value between $C3$ and $S2$ is the rating for capacity 3, given that $M1$ and $S2$ are part of the path. There are 18 ($3 \times 2 \times 3$) unique combinations or paths from which to select a specification.

The bold-lined path in Fig. 1.6 represents one design alternative. By rearranging the compact but intertwined branches, we can better recognize other alternatives. Figure 1.7 shows an *extensive* form of the decision tree for the same component with the addition of link ratings. The three characteristics are still segregated by columns, but nodes are provided for each link. This arrangement produces a cluster of nodes for each quality within a characteristic.

Figure 1.7 Extensive decision tree for a design evaluation

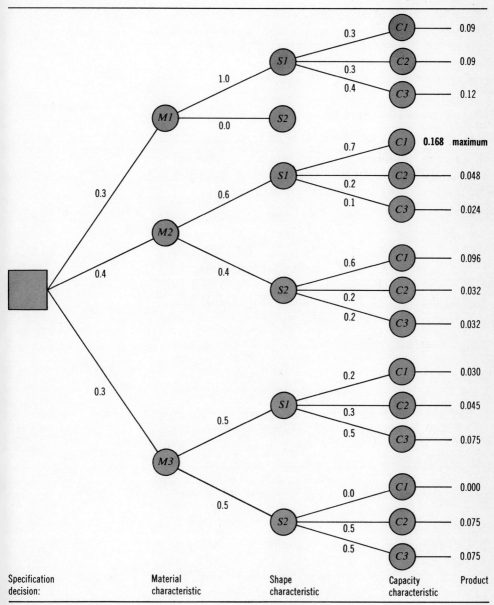

| Specification decision: | Material characteristic | Shape characteristic | Capacity characteristic | Product |

In the example the sum of the link ratings for each cluster is 1.0. This effect could be achieved by dividing each rating in a cluster determined according to the Churchman-Ackoff method by the cluster sum. Thus a cluster's link ratings of

X	Z	W	Y
1.00	0.60	0.20	0.10

would be converted to

$$X = \frac{1.0}{1.0 + 0.6 + 0.2 + 0.1}$$
$$= 1.0/1.9 = 0.53$$
$$Z = 0.6/1.9 = 0.32$$
$$W = 0.2/1.9 = 0.10$$
$$Y = 0.1/1.9 = \underline{0.05}$$
$$\text{Total} \quad 1.00$$

Another, less formal approach is to rate the link outcomes by whole numbers. If there are four alternatives for a cluster, their outcomes might be rated

J	K	L	M
6	2	2	1

which shows a rather strong preference for J, an indifference between K and L, and a slight preference for K or L over M. These ratings can be made to total 1.0 by dividing each by 11 (the sum of the ratings). Thus

$$J = 6/11 = 0.55$$
$$K = 2/11 = 0.18$$
$$L = 2/11 = 0.18$$
$$M = 1/11 = \underline{0.09}$$
$$\text{Total} \quad 1.00$$

The column for the material characteristic has only one cluster, $M1, M2, M3$. For each quality of this characteristic there is a cluster representing two possible shapes, $S1, S2$. The ratings indicate a strong preference for $S1$ with $M1$, a slight preference for $S1$ with $M2$, and an indifference toward shapes for $M3$. Whenever a quality has a zero rating, that path is obviously terminated ($M1-S2$).

The evaluation procedure is simply a forward pass through each branch to determine the path with the largest product. According to the expressed ratings, the path of $M2-S1-C1$ would be the preferred specification, with a product rating of 0.168.

The task of determining the link values is both the main advantage and the main limitation of this approach to primary comparisons. Each conditional rating must reflect the value of that quality in relation to all preceding qualities. Even for a relatively small problem, the rating procedure becomes onerous and complicated. Still, this effort makes the procedure worthwhile, in that it encourages identification and consideration of interdependencies. This close scrutiny may reveal new alternatives or it may eliminate some branches from further consideration. The final evaluation tends to indicate which alternatives warrant further investigation.

RATIO-SCALE COMPARISONS The most useful and widely used rating system is the ratio scale. It has all the properties of the other two scales plus an absolute-zero point and the notable property of additivity. Measurements of weight, length, and money are ratio scales.

Daily exposure to ratio scales makes this means of rating a comfortable experience. Direct measurements of weights and lengths provide the basis for many decisions in both the real world and symbolic world. These direct measures are also used in some economy studies, but the more common practice is to convert all the measures to monetary values whenever possible.

Monetary decisions An adage that is often applicable to primary monetary comparisons is "familiarity breeds contempt." Because it is so customary to make decisions by comparing immediate costs, the more subtle aspects of a problem are sometimes overlooked.

A large family plans to visit relatives on the other side of the country. They plan to drive and are concerned about overnight lodging costs. Motel or hotel accommodations are estimated to cost $30 per night for 5 nights each way. A sleeping trailer can be rented for $65 per week. They will be gone 4 weeks. Other costs associated with pulling the trailer should amount to about $50. The nearly equal cost of the two alternatives ($300 versus $310) makes a decision difficult.

A housewife reads that steak sells for $0.30 per lb less at a market across town from her usual neighborhood shopping area. She spends an additional $1 traveling to and from the distant market to save $0.90 on 3 lb of steak.

A homeowner wants to tear out his present weed-infested yard to start new grass. He can hire a landscape service for $150 to prepare the grounds with their tractor-powered equipment. He can also rent a motorized hand tiller and hire a husky neighbor boy at a total cost of $5 per hour. It should take the boy about 20 to 25 hours to complete the work. This alternative would be at least $25 less than employing the landscape service.

In the decision situations above, the distances traveled and time expended were converted to monetary terms. The conversion makes most of the alternative factors directly comparable, but comparing just the dollars and cents is inadequate unless the outcomes are equivalent. The term "false economy" is a household word that reflects how easy it is to be blinded by "bargains." A comparison between alternatives is valid only when the outcomes of the alternatives are essentially equivalent.

The two modes of lodging for the traveling family should be compared for convenience and comfort as well as price.

The housewife is purchasing quality as well as quantity. If the less expensive meat is of the same quality as regularly priced meat, the monetary comparison is valid.

It is doubtful that the inexperienced operator of a hand tiller can prepare the turf as well as the professional landscape service using customized equipment. If the two alternatives do not produce work of approximately the same caliber, the price comparison is incomplete.

Similar situations occur frequently in all phases of industry. We will consider some of the more common occurrences under the categories of men, methods, materials, and machines.

Evaluation of men   The rewards for extreme proficiency are most apparent in the "star" rating of the entertainment industry. A "name" player receives great remuneration from motion pictures, television, recordings, and book sales. The rewards decrease sharply for supporting players. A major-league ballplayer could expect to earn at least $100,000 a year if his batting average were .400. A proportionate salary would be $50,000 for a .200 hitter, yet a .200 hitter can hardly stay in the league, much less earn $50,000. Similar relationships are not so apparent in production settings.

Assume that a worker receives $3.00 per hour and

that indirect costs of his employment are 50% of his wages. He operates a machine with a burden rate of $13.50 per hour. He typically produces 10 pieces per hour. The cost per piece is

$$\frac{\$3.00 + 0.50 \times \$3.00 + \$13.50}{10} = \$1.80 \text{ per piece}$$

Another worker uses the same type of machine but produces only seven pieces per hour. An equivalent pay-scale calculation would show that his wage W should be

$$\frac{W + 0.50W + \$13.50}{7} = \$1.80 \text{ per piece}$$

$$W = \frac{\$12.60 - \$13.50}{1.5} = -\$0.60 \text{ per hr}$$

which means he would have to pay the company $0.60 per hour for the privilege of working.

While this example is somewhat exaggerated, it does call attention to the vigilance required in determining reasonable wage rates. Bonuses and incentives are methods used to reward proficient workers. It should also be apparent that there is a level of production at which even a minimum wage is undeserved.

Evaluation of methods   Equivalent outcomes are often achieved by entirely different methods or designs. The search for and selection of new means to reduce costs is the forte of a discipline called *value engineering* or *value analysis*. This discipline encourages "a systematic application of recognized techniques which (1) identify the function of a product or service, (2) establish a value for that function, and (3) develop a means to provide value."[1]

Value is established by comparison, and by no other means. It is not an automatic ingredient of any design. Many of today's products and systems are designed by teams. Owing to complexity and the rate of change of technological developments, design groups cannot devote detailed attention to all subassemblies. This leads to suboptimization and subassemblies designated by standard or rote practices. The end result is a decrease in economic value and an increase in unnecessary costs. Figure 1.8 lists four types of economic value, and Fig. 1.9 offers reasons for unnecessary costs.[1]

[1]*Value Engineering Methods Manual*, The Boeing Company, Seattle, Wash., 1962.

Use value	The properties or qualities which accomplish a use, work, or service
Esteem value	The properties of an object which make its ownership desirable
Cost value	The sum of labor, material, overhead, and other costs required to produce economic value
Exchange value	The qualities of an object that make it possible to procure other items in its place

Figure 1.8 Types of economic value

Value engineering emphasizes *use* value. The value of anything can be no more than the value of the function it performs. Unnecessary costs arise when there is a less expensive method that performs the same function without downgrading quality.

Incomplete information	Failure to gather all the facts
Lack of an idea	Failure to explore all possible ways of performing a service or making a product
Honest wrong beliefs	Decisions made on what is believed to be true, and not on the true facts
Habits and attitudes	Habits which take us where we were yesterday and attitudes which tend to keep us there

Figure 1.9 Reasons for unnecessary costs

A value-engineering study starts with the identification of an item's primary function by means of a verb and a noun. According to this technique, the primary function of a table would be to "support weight" and that of a shipping container would be to "provide protection." Any secondary functions are also identified; for example, a shipping container might also "attract sales." All subassemblies, such as a zip-opener for a container, should contribute to the value of either the primary or the secondary function.

Next a value is assigned to the function by comparing it with something else that will do the same task. Areas of costs are evaluated to determine where current quality standards or expenses are excessive. A search is made for alternative methods that preserve the desired quality. For instance, a manufacturer had a contract for engines ranging from 10 to 20 hp. Under the terms of the contract the engines were to be packed in individual crates. This requirement appeared to be unnecessarily costly. After a study of the problem, a proposal was submitted to the buyer to use returnable steel racks in lieu of the crates and to cover the six engines on each rack with a plastic dustcover. The proposal was accepted and significant savings resulted.

If the "noun" in the function description has a measurable parameter, such as weight or length, a mathematical evaluation is feasible. The key to comparison is an assignment of dollar values to the parameters of equivalent quality. When the comparison looks favorable, there is still the problem of implementation. As a rule, any change will meet resistance. The effort required to produce a usable idea often pales into insignificance when compared with the effort required to sell it. In a sound study objections are anticipated and means to overcome them are included.

Another example of value analysis concerns a lock on a small compartment door that appeared unnecessarily expensive. The door was on the outside of a newly designed truck cab and led to a tool compartment. The original design called for a tool-actuated lock which cost $2.27. Its functional description was "secures door." The search for alternatives revealed a spring lock that served the purpose equally well and cost $1.11. A further search led to a clip fastener that cost just $0.21. Finally, the whole assembly was questioned, and it was determined there was no need to have even a door, because the tool storage compartment was readily accessible from inside the cab. The study led to a total saving of $16.42 per truck.

The cost of a value study must be deducted from the savings derived from the study. In order to receive maximum return for the effort expended, studies should be concentrated first on items for which the largest expenditures are planned. There may be many candidates. A selection is made by examining the factors involved in a study by means of the formula

$$\frac{\text{Potential savings}}{\substack{\text{Value study and im-}\\ \text{plementation costs}}} \times \substack{\text{probability of}\\ \text{implementation} } = \substack{\text{rating}\\ \text{factor}}$$

The rating factor helps to establish a precedence list for available study time. Items with the highest potential for cost reduction are given first attention, and studies of items with lower cost-reduction potential are made if time permits.

Evaluation of materials and machines   The selection among types or makes of materials and machines is a commonplace industrial decision. New types of materials which can be processed in different ways on different machines are becoming ever more numerous. Characteristics vary radically from one material or machine to another. The decision-maker has to choose the properties he deems most important for comparison purposes.

Machines, like people, have seemingly individual characteristics. Some machines do more precise work than others. Some take a long period to start or set up. Others have frequent breakdowns and are unreliable. Operating costs vary widely. Because of these diverse characteristics, the assignment of work to different machines can be demanding.

Even the simple question of performing a set of calculations on a hand calculator or on a computer involves several considerations:

What accuracy is needed?	The computer is more accurate.
Is machine time available?	Hand calculations can be performed almost anytime, anywhere.
Is a program available?	It may take as long to write a program for the computer as it would to do the entire problem manually.
Will the problem occur again?	If the answer is yes, it makes writing a program more attractive.
When is the answer needed?	A computer is usually much faster if a program is ready.

Most of the answers to such questions involve time. Machine running time, setup time, checking time, and operator's time are easily converted to monetary terms, but the basis of comparison must still be equivalent outcomes, a solution giving the desired accuracy within the allotted time.

Weight, strength, machinability, and appearance are typical selection alternatives for materials. Again, the decision-maker must decide what he wants for an outcome and evaluate the alternatives accordingly. A building contractor comparing galvanized steel gutters with aluminum gutters faces a material-selection decision. Both materials are adequately strong and rust or corrosion resistant. The desired box-type gutter is available in both materials. Appearance is less important because the gutters will be painted. The main differences are in weight and price. Weight affects installation and shipping costs. On-site costs for a 10-ft trough section would amount to

	Basic cost	Weight, lb	Difference in cost due to weight	Cost comparison
Aluminum	$2.20	4		$2.20
Steel	$1.90	7.5	$0.14	$2.04

This cost comparison could change abruptly if the gutters had to be shipped a greater distance. The 3.5-lb difference per section would be a major cost difference. A building site in Alaska could change the outcome ratings to

	Basic cost		Shipping cost		Installation cost		Total cost
Aluminum	$2.20	+	$0.32	+	$0.41	=	$2.93
Steel	$1.90	+	$0.60	+	$0.51	=	$3.01

MIXED-RATING COMPARISONS   A legitimate question at this stage of rating discussion is "What do we do if some of the ratings are on an interval scale and others are on a ratio scale?" A corollary to this question is "How are alternatives compared when there are several bases for equivalent outcomes?" The answers are found through dimensionless numbers.

Consider the comparison of two prototypes of a new bumper-jack design. Five criteria have been selected for evaluation: safety, cost, appearance, weight, and reliability. The first step is to rate the value of each criterion. Cost and weight are ratio scales, and safety, appearance, and reliability would probabily be rated on an interval scale. Since lower costs and weight are desirable, we can rate the remaining criteria so that lower ratings also indicate a preference. These ratings could be:

	Safety	Appearance	Cost	Weight	Reliability
Jack 1	1	4	$6.27	9.7	1
Jack 2	2	2	$3.86	6.2	3

According to the above ratings, Jack 1 is preferred with respect to safety and reliability, while Jack 2 excels in appearance, cost, and weight.

The next step is to rate the relative importance of each of the criteria. The accorded weights reflect the importance placed on outcomes of the alternatives. *Larger numbers (weights) show a preference.* According to the weighting in the accompanying table,

	Safety	Appearance	Cost	Weight	Reliability
Jack 1	1	4	$6.27	9.7	1
Jack 2	2	2	$3.86	6.2	3
Importance	3	2	4	1	2

cost is deemed the most important criterion and weight is the least important.

With the amount of information now available we can conduct the evaluation. A ratio is formed from the outcomes for each pair of alternatives. Safety ratio is 1/2. The same alternative (jack 1 in this example) is always represented in the numerator. The ratio assures a dimensionless number. Next each ratio is raised to a power corresponding to its rated importance. Thus the cost ratio is treated as

$$\left(\frac{6.27}{3.86}\right)^4 = (1.624)^4 = 6.956$$

and the safety ratio is

$$\left(\frac{1}{2}\right)^3 = (0.50)^3 = 0.125$$

Then all the raised ratios are multiplied. The complete comparison appears as

$$\frac{\text{Jack 1}}{\text{Jack 2}} = \left(\frac{1}{2}\right)^3 \left(\frac{4}{2}\right)^2 \left(\frac{6.27}{3.86}\right)^4 \left(\frac{9.7}{6.2}\right)^1 \left(\frac{1}{3}\right)^2$$
$$= 0.125 \times 4 \times 6.956 \times 1.565 \times 0.111$$
$$= 0.6042$$

The product of less than 1.0 indicates a preference for jack 1 because the denominator (jack 2) is larger than the numerator (jack 1), and we have indicated a preference for low numbers. Expressed another way, the ratio appears as

$$\frac{\text{Jack 1}}{\text{Jack 2}} = \frac{(1)^3 \times (4)^2 \times (6.27)^4 \times (9.7)^1 \times (1)^2}{(2)^3 \times (2)^2 \times (3.86)^4 \times (6.2)^1 \times (3)^2}$$

$$= \frac{1 \times 16 \times 1532 \times 9.7 \times 1}{8 \times 4 \times 221 \times 6.2 \times 9}$$

$$= \frac{237,776}{394,618}$$

$$= 0.604$$

and produces the same quotient. However, the above expression clearly shows the relationship of the numerator and denominator. Remembering that lower numbers in the rating system express a preference, we can observe that jack 1 has the lowest product and is therefore the preferred alternative.

SELECTED REFERENCES

Bridgman, P. W.: *Dimensional Analysis*, Yale University Press, New Haven, Conn., 1922.

Bross, I. D.: *Design for Decision*, The Macmillan Company, New York, 1957.

Churchman, C. W., and R. L. Ackoff: "An Approximate Measure of Value," *Operations Research*, 2, 1954.

————, ————, and E. L. Arnoff: *Introduction to Operations Research*, John Wiley & Sons, Inc., New York, 1957.

Hall, A. D.: *A Methodology for Systems Engineering*, D. Van Nostrand Company, Inc., Princeton, N.J., 1962.

Miles L. D.: *Techniques of Value Analysis and Engineering*, McGraw-Hill Book Company, New York, 1961.

Starr, K. L.: *Product Design and Decision Theory*, Prentice-Hall, Inc., Englewood Cliffs, N.J., 1963.

Thrall, R. M., C. H. Coombs, and R. L. Davis: *Decision Processes*, John Wiley & Sons, Inc., New York, 1954.

Value Engineering Methods Manual, The Boeing Company, Aerospace Division, Seattle, Wash., 1962.

PROBLEMS

1.1 An architect is preparing plans for a prefabricated vacation home. The decision tree below shows the ratings he has placed on the characteristics of two tentative roof and ceiling designs. Ratings are based on expected consumer preferences as to simplicity of do-it-yourself construction, ease of maintenance, and final appearance. A rating of 1.0 is the highest possible. Which combination of design, structural, and finish materials are preferred?

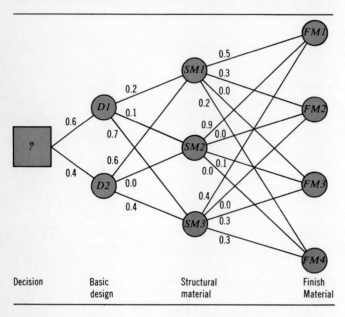

Decision	Basic design	Structural material	Finish Material

1.2 A portable concrete batching plant is to be set up near a bridge construction site. Two sand sources which provide sand of the same fineness modulus are available. One source is 2 miles south of the bridge site and the other is 4 miles north of the site. Coarse aggregate can be obtained from a pit 3 miles north of the bridge site. The design mix calls for twice as many pounds of coarse aggregate as sand for 1 cu yd of mixed concrete. Dump trucks haul rock and sand from their source to the batching plant, and mixer trucks haul the mixed concrete from the plant to the bridge site. The cost of hauling mixed concrete is twice the cost of hauling a similar weight of sand or coarse aggregate in a dump truck. There is room to set up the batching plant anywhere between the two sand sources. Where is the most economical location for the plant, and which sand source should be used?

1.3 An appliance store has received a franchise to distribute a new type of recorder. Plans are being made to advertise the recorder by a direct-mail campaign of at least 14,000 flyers. A mimeograph machine is available at the store. If it is used, the flyers can be produced for $0.01 apiece. However, an artist will have to be employed to make line drawings of the recorder and to do the lettering.

His charge is $195. Franked envelopes can be purchased for $30.00 per thousand.

Another alternative is to have the flyers printed. Plates are supplied by the manufacturer, but printing costs will still amount to $414.00. A slight change in the format will allow the flyers to be sent without envelopes. The alteration will cost $40 and mailing expense will be $0.02 per flyer.

A suitable and equivalent advertisement will result from either method. The addressing costs will be the same for both alternatives. Which one should be selected?

1.4 During the winter many culverts and ditches along a section of forest service road became clogged and damaged. It is estimated that it will take 1000 man-hours of labor to make repairs. It takes 1 hour each way from the nearest station to reach the damaged section. Crew carriers hold a maximum of seven men and can make the round trip for $8. Only four carriers are available, but more can be rented for $16 each per round trip. The road workers receive $15 for an 8-hour day which includes travel time. Power equipment for the job will cost $40 per day regardless of crew size. If there is no shortage of workers, what is the most economical crew size? Should this size crew be used?

1.5 A tie clasp issued to all new recruits in a branch of the Armed Forces is chrome plated, has a pivoted clasp, and contains a replica of the insignia of the service branch in the center. The description of the working function of the clasp could be "holds parts," where the parts are the tie and shirt. A secondary (or perhaps the basic) function is "creates impression." Show how the creation of substitute means and the method of evaluation depend on the functional description of the item. If the present tie clasp costs $0.93, determine a less expensive alternative based on the "holds parts" function. How does this alternative satisfy the function "creates impression"?

1.6 Four items have been singled out by the Communications Department as possibilities for value-engineering studies. The data accumulated for these items are shown in the accompanying table.

Item	Estimated yearly savings	Estimated study and implementation cost	Probability of implementation
1	$14,000	$4000	0.9
2	6,500	1000	0.6
3	41,000	9000	0.7
4	3,300	600	0.8

According to the rating-factor formula, which alternative should be selected? What are some other considerations that are not included in the data that could influence the decision?

1.7 The most widely used mousetrap is the spring-operated type that uses impact to kill the mouse. This kind has been used for many years and is quite efficient. Both the spring and triggering systems are almost the ultimate in simplicity and economy. However, there are certain disadvantages to this type of trap. It is dangerous because it is not selective. It can kill kittens and puppies, and it can hurt babies or adults who happen to touch the sensitive bait device. It can make quite a mess if the mouse bleeds or is cut in half. Setting the trap and removing the dead is not to the liking of most housewives and some men.

In an attempt to produce a better mousetrap, the following three designs have been selected for evaluation.

a List the criteria for evaluating the designs.

b Determine a rating for each outcome of the criteria.

c Weight the importance of the criteria.

d Decide which design is the most promising.

Mousylinder

Operation:
1. Mouse enters cylinder seeking bait.
2. Mouse cannot leave cylinder.
3. Mouse dies from hunger or poisoned bait.

Material as shown

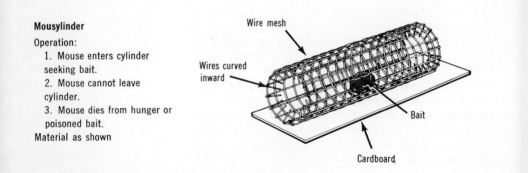

Multicatch Mousetrap

Operation:
1. Mouse goes up ramp.
2. Jumps into recessed section after bait.
3. Trap door sprung by mouse's weight.
4. Mouse caught in well.
5. Slaked lime in well destroys mouse.

Material as shown

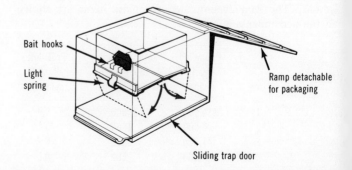

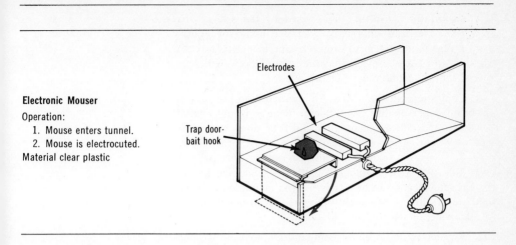

Electronic Mouser

Operation:
1. Mouse enters tunnel.
2. Mouse is electrocuted.

Material clear plastic

Electrodes

Trap door-
bait hook

1.8 The sites for a chemical plant have been narrowed to three locations. The criteria for the final selections, estimates of the outcomes for each alternative, and the importance of the criteria are shown in the accompanying table. Lower outcome ratings and higher importance weights show a preference. Which site appears more attractive? What are the rating ratios of the other sites to the preferred site?

Outcome	Alternative			Importance
	Site 1	Site 2	Site 3	
Labor supply	8	2	1	4
Raw materials	7	1	4	4
Transportation	3	3	1	3
Cost of land	$120,000	$400,000	$300,000	2
Building costs	$1,000,000	$1,200,000	$900,000	2
Annual taxes and utility costs	$20,000	$40,000	$60,000	2
Climate	2	1	4	1

1.9 A concrete contractor uses different-size crews for commercial and residential work. A typical residential job requires 3 hours on site and ½ hour travel each way with a minimum-sized crew of two, a finisher and a laborer. A finisher is paid $3.50 per hour and laborers get $2.00 per hour.

Adding another pair (finisher and laborer) to the minimum crew cuts the working time required for a typical job by 60%. Adding just one laborer to the minimum crew reduces the time by 30%, and adding two laborers cuts it by 50%. Because of the sequence of work and space limitations, the maximum crew size is four.

Transportation costs are unchanged by the size of the crew. An overhead charge of $10 per hour for equipment is also independent of crew size and is levied for both working and travel time. What makeup of crew will provide the most economical performance?

1.10 Contestants in the "Miss All" competition are judged on beauty, personality, and talent. Beauty is considered twice as important as personality and four times as important as talent. Girls are rated on a simple order scale $(1, 2, 3, \ldots, n)$, with 1 the highest rating. One girl has been judged first in beauty but tenth in talent. She knows the girl rated second in beauty is sixth in talent. What is the minimum rating in personality the girl first in beauty needs to assure being selected as "Miss All"?

1.11 An electronic specialty company employs 60 women to fabricate miniature resistor assemblies. The women average 2000 hours of work per year, with an average production of 16.2 assemblies per hour, of which 6% are defective. The top third of this group produce 19.1 assemblies an hour with only 3.4% defective. The cost to the company to rework each defective unit is $0.30.

All work is paid at a straight piecework rate of $0.15 per assembly. Each woman uses a scope and special equipment which has an annual fixed cost of $612. Indirect costs and supervision amount to $740 per year per worker.

For the same total production, how much could be spent per year to select, train, and motivate the women so that all of them would produce at the level of the top 20?

Section Two
Decisions Assuming Certainty

Most traditional decision models treat the future as a known quantity. This assumption of certainty implies neither gullibility nor laziness. A decision environment contains both relevant and irrelevant data. Sorting fact from fiction and the pertinent from the plausible is often difficult enough without encumbering the filtered data with requirements of applicability to every conceivable future. Narrowing the spectrum of possible outcomes to a single value is commonly the most practical approach to a solution.

The assumption of certainty is a matter of judgment. If risk is insignificant or its inclusion will not alter the alternatives, the assumption is justified. Including risk and uncertainty in an analysis adds cost. Where the consequences of a mistake are relatively small, the assumption is also warranted. The availability of data, the time allowed for a decision, the nature of the alternatives, and the importance of the problem all contribute to the evaluation. In this section we will consider the allocation, scheduling, utilization, and time analysis of resources under assumed certainty.

Chapter Two
Breakeven
and
Minimum-cost
Analysis

Breakeven and minimum-cost analyses are extensions of primary-cost comparisons. Both assume a condition of certainty and both deal with short-range cost relationships. The difference between the two lies in the treatment of costs. In primary comparisons specific costs (a burden rate for a certain machine, an hourly wage of a given employee, etc.) were directly compared for different courses of action. In a breakeven or minimum-cost analysis, the variables which produce the specific cost functions (number of units produced, percent of capacity utilized, etc.) are evaluated.

Most organizations strive for profits. They do so through a close scrutiny of their internal operating costs and strict attention to their competitive position. Even intentionally nonprofit organizations must follow the same policy if they are to achieve excellence. We can investigate the revenue-costs-profit relationship by breaking down a unit of output into its component dollar values.

The rectangular block in Fig. 2.1a represents a unit of output. This output can be a product, such as an automobile, or it can be a service, such as collecting garbage from a subscriber. The unit is divided into three segments which broadly classify the producer's interests. The overall height or price for which it can be sold is a function of the consumer's regard for the item.

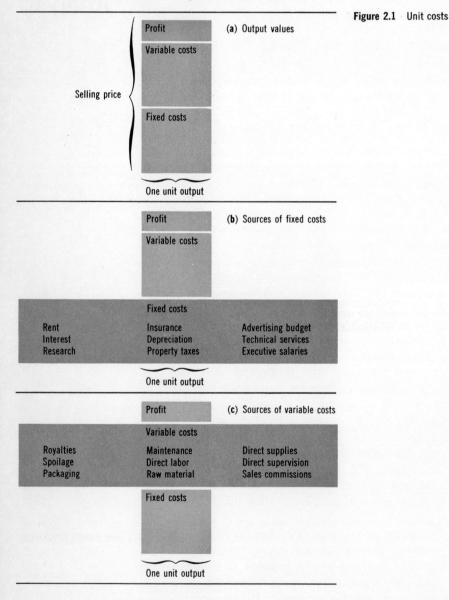

Figure 2.1 Unit costs

FIXED COSTS   Those costs which remain relatively constant regardless of the level of activity are known as *fixed costs* or *indirect costs*. This description implies that the fixed level is maintained whether output is nil or at 100% capacity. In some cases this assumption is not valid; fixed costs may tend to increase as output increases, and they can vary with time. However, the change is usually not significant in short-range studies.

Some of an organization's expenditures which can be considered as fixed are shown in Fig. 2.1*b*. These costs may be thought of as "preparation" expenses. They arise from measures taken to provide the means to produce a product or service. Before a painter can paint a house, he has to have a brush. Whether he paints one house or a dozen with it, the expense has already been incurred and shows as a fixed cost. His insurance and advertisements for work would also be indirect costs.

VARIABLE COSTS   Those costs which are generally proportional to output are called *variable costs* or *direct costs*. Such costs are relatively easy to determine, because they are directly associated with a specific product or service. When there is no output, variable costs are zero. The input material and time required to make a unit give rise to variable costs. For example, the specific type and quantity of paint a painter uses in painting a house is a variable cost. The more houses he paints, the more paint he uses. The quantity used is a function of his output. In a similar manner, the time he spends painting is a direct cost.

PROFIT   In order to examine the competitive aspects of profit we have to add the dimension of quantity. A single unit of output is relatively immune to competition. In isolated instances, a fair-sized output distributed in a local area to satisfy a peculiar need is also shielded from competition. However, as output quantity expands, competition is an increasingly apparent factor. Profit is the cause and effect of competitiveness.

A profit (or a loss) figure attracts a great amount of attention. It is a handy yardstick of success. Like a thermometer, it only measures the level achieved; it does not control the source it measures. Unlike a thermometer, however, continued low-profit readings can eliminate the source.

There are basically three ways to increase profit: (1) increase the selling price, (2) increase the value to increase sales, and (3) decrease the selling price to increase sales. The profit-expansion descriptions are oriented to consumers' interests. The issues become more complicated when we look at them from the producer's viewpoint. Figure 2.2 shows some of the consequences of selling-price manipulations.

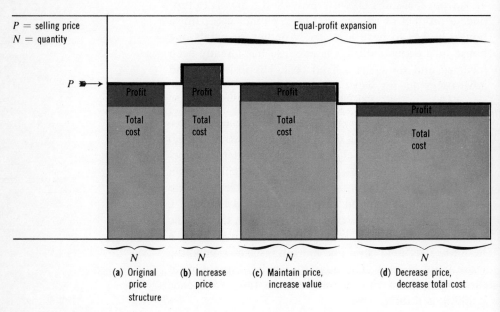

Figure 2.2 Methods for expanding profit

The original price-cost-quantity conditions are shown in Fig. 2.2*a*. *Total revenue* is the product of *N* units sold at selling price *P*. *Total cost* is the sum of variable and fixed costs incurred in producing *N* units. *Profit* is the difference between revenue and total cost (when revenue exceeds costs).

Figures 2.2*b*, *c*, and *d* show increased profit. The colored profit areas of *b*, *c*, and *d* are equal and are larger than the profit in *a*. The dangers and limitations of profit-expansion methods are as follows:

Increased selling price   Competing products or services set an upper limit to price increases.[1] Ultimately, this limit is controlled by the consumer. His willingness to pay is a function of the value he expects to receive and his loyalty to a product. Prices higher than competing products of equivalent value will reduce the number of units sold. The shrinking share of the market eventually causes a decline in total profit.

Unchanged selling price   One way to increase profit without changing the selling price is to sell more units by increasing the value. The greater value perceived by the consumer can result from better quality, more quantity, or more effective advertising. All these measures increase the total cost for the producer. Higher total cost leads to a lower margin of profit per unit sold. If the market is unstable, a very low profit margin can seriously limit recuperative powers during market fluctuations.

A straightforward means to increase profit while holding prices constant is to reduce total costs. Such a task is the continuous aim of industrial engineers and managers. The obstacle is that it becomes increasingly difficult to make more and more savings in an established operation. At first it is easy. When a product or service is new, it meets a high current demand which compensates for operational inefficiencies. As competition forces the price down, the "fat" is removed from operations. Further effort to reduce costs meets diminishing returns. It is like trying to make a horse run faster. A small whip may help at first, but using ever larger whips fails to force proportional returns in greater speed.

Reduced selling price   New areas of cost reduction are exposed by changing the level of operation or capacity. A greater output often allows new methods to be incorporated. Some of the savings resulting from the new meth-

---

[1]Conditions of *free competition* are assumed; similar products or services are available from a number of vendors. In a *monopoly* a single vendor has a unique product and is, temporarily at least, in a position to ignore competition. An *oligopoly* exists when there are so few vendors that an action by one generally forces similar actions by the others. Actual competition is usually a blend of free competition, monopoly, and oligopoly. A patent or a copyright is a limited monopoly. Government regulations, geographical isolation, or periods of disaster sometimes promote artificial supply-and-demand relationships.

ods are passed on to the consumer in the form of a lower selling price. In theory the decreased price should lead to the sale of more units, which in turn satisfies the conditions for incorporating the new methods.

Limitations are inherent throughout the cost-reduction–lower-price–increased-sales cycle. Cost reductions are limited by minimum levels of quality, maximum levels of expenditure for new equipment, and basic labor or material costs that resist lowering. Reduced prices may be an insufficient incentive to attract enough new sales. However, with reasonable care the cycle rewards the producer and leads to a better standard of living for the consumer.

In the above illustrations, methods of profit expansion were treated as discrete alternatives. A more realistic attitude is to combine appropriate features from different methods to fit a particular situation. The breakeven concept is a means of diagnosing the situations.

LINEAR BREAKEVEN ANALYSIS

A linear breakeven problem was encountered in Chap. 1. Figure 1.3 graphically described a make-or-buy decision. The costs for each alternative (make or buy packaging containers) were plotted as a function of the number of containers required. The format was typical of linear breakeven charts.

The name "breakeven chart" is derived from the concept it depicts, the volume or level at which revenue and total cost of operations exactly break even. At this point, one additional unit made and sold would produce a profit. Until the breakeven point is attained, the producer operates at a loss for the period.

STANDARD FORMAT Properties of a typical breakeven chart are displayed in Fig. 2.3. The vertical scale shows the revenue and costs in monetary units. The horizontal scale indicates the volume of activity during the period pictured. The units of volume can be in sales dollars, number of units produced and sold, or the output quantity expressed as a percentage of total capacity.

The horizontal line in the chart shows the fixed costs F, which are constant throughout the range of volume. The sloping line originating at the intersection of the fixed-cost line and the vertical axis represents variable costs V plus the fixed costs. For linear relationships, variable costs are directly proportional to volume; each additional unit produced adds an identical increment of cost. The sum of variable and fixed costs is the total cost C. The sloping line from the origin (intersection of the vertical and horizontal axes) is the revenue line. Revenue R is also assumed to be directly proportional to the number of units produced and sold.

The breakeven point B occurs at the intersection of the total-cost and revenue lines. It thus specifies the dollar volume of sales and the unit volume of output at which an operation neither makes nor loses money. The vertical distance between the revenue line and the total-cost line indicates a profit to the right of B and a loss to the left of B.

A block cost diagram used in the discussion of profit expansion is shown alongside the breakeven chart in Fig. 2.3. For an output volume of N, the costs, revenue, and profit are the same in both formats. The breakeven chart further indicates the profit or loss expectation at levels of output other than N. This feature helps explain such statements as "A very low profit margin can seriously limit recuperative powers during market fluctuations." "A very low profit margin" means that the output is barely on the profit side of the breakeven point. An unstable market could easily cause sales to fall below point B and show a loss for the period.

Figure 2.3 Standard format for breakeven charts

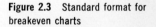
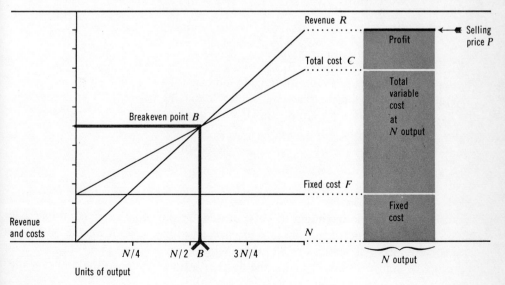

ALGEBRAIC RELATIONSHIPS   The graphic format is convenient for clarifying or presenting economic relationships.
It is possible to obtain quantities for particular conditions by scaling values from the chart. However, the
same conditions can be easily quantified by formulas.
The calculations generally provide greater accuracy.
Letting

B = breakeven volume

R = revenue

Z = gross profit

P = selling price per unit

C = total cost

n = number of units or volume

V = variable cost per unit

F = fixed cost

we have

Revenue per period

$$R = nP$$

Total cost per period

$$C = nV + F$$

Gross profit per period

$$Z = R - C = n(P - V) - F$$

where n can also be a fraction of total capacity when P
and V represent total dollar volume at 100% capacity.

At the breakeven point profit equals zero. To determine the output B at the breakeven point

$$Z = 0 = R - C$$
$$= n(P - V) - F$$

and for $n = B$,

$$B = \frac{F}{P - V}$$

The term $P - V$ is called *contribution*. It indicates the
portion of the selling price that contributes to paying
off the fixed cost. At $n = B$ the sum of contributions
from B units equals the total fixed cost. The contribution of each unit sold beyond $n = B$ is an increment of
profit.

EXAMPLE 2.1 Breakeven point

An airline can carry a maximum of 1000 passengers per month on one of its feeder
routes. The contribution from the fare of each passenger is 75% of the $40 ticket
price. Fixed costs per month are $21,000. What is the average percentage of seats
that must be sold on each flight for the airline to break even on the feeder route?

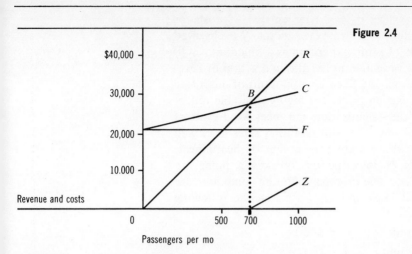

Figure 2.4

SOLUTION The data can be consolidated in a breakeven chart as shown in Fig. 2.4, or the solution can be calculated as

$$\text{Total revenue per month} = nP$$
$$= 1000 \times \$40$$
$$= \$40,000$$

$$\text{Total contribution} = 0.75 \times \$40,000$$
$$= \$30,000$$

$$B\,(\%\text{ of capacity}) = \frac{F \times 100\%}{\text{contribution}}$$
$$= \frac{\$21,000}{\$30,000} \times 100\%$$

or $= 70\%$

$$B\,(\text{passengers}) = \frac{F}{P - V}$$
$$= \frac{\$21,000}{0.75 \times \$40}$$
$$= 700\text{ passengers per mo}$$

Assuming a tax rate of 40%, we could also calculate the net profit at full capacity:

$$\text{Net profit} = Z\,(1 - t) \qquad \text{where } t = \text{tax rate}$$
$$= (R - C)\,(1 - t)$$
$$= [n\,(P - V) - F]\,(1 - t)$$
$$= [1000 \times (0.75 \times \$40) - \$21,000]\,(0.60)$$
$$= \$9000 \times 0.60$$
$$= \$5400$$

A gross-profit line is shown in the lower right corner of the chart, starting at B. Net profit is a fraction of Z which depends on the tax rate for the total earnings of the organization.

BREAKEVEN-POINT ALTERNATIVES Any change in costs or selling price affects the breakeven point. .We observed the gross effects of profit expansion as a function of selling price. Now we can consider the interaction of revenue, variable costs, and fixed costs in terms of output.

A lower breakeven point is a highly desirable objective. It means the organization can meet fixed costs at a lower level of output or utilization. A sales level well above the breakeven output is a sign of healthiness. Three methods of lowering the breakeven point are shown in Fig. 2.5. The original operating conditions are shown as black lines and are based on the following data:

$V = \$7$ per unit $\qquad F = \$400$

$P = \$12$ per unit $\qquad B = 80$ units

R (at $n = 100$ units) $= \$1200$

C (at $n = 100$ units) $= \$1100$

The colored lines depict the measures necessary to reduce the breakeven point in half, from 80 to 40 units.

Fixed-cost reduction: By reducing the fixed costs by half, B is halved. Therefore the new fixed cost F' is

$$F' = \frac{\$400}{2} = \$200$$

and the new breakeven output B' becomes

$$B' = \frac{F'}{P - V}$$

$$= \frac{\$200}{(\$12 - \$7) \text{ per unit}} = 40 \text{ units}$$

Variable-cost reduction: Knowing that B' should equal 40 units, we can solve for the associated V' by

$$B' = \frac{F}{P - V'}$$

or $\qquad V' = P - \dfrac{F}{B'} = \$12 - \dfrac{\$400}{40}$

$$= \$12 - \$10 = \$2 \text{ per unit}$$

Selling-price increase: Raising the selling price P' increases the slope of the revenue line and augments the contribution. The contribution required for B' to equal 40 units is

$$\text{Contribution} = \frac{F}{B'} = \frac{\$400}{40}$$

$$= \$10 \text{ per unit}$$

which leads to

$$P' = V + \text{contribution}$$

$$= \$7 + \$10 = \$17$$

Figure 2.5

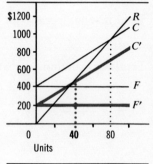

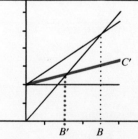

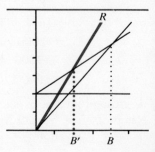

EXAMPLE 2.2 Margin of profit and dumping

A firm producing package-waste-disposal units sells the units for $35,000 each. Variable costs are $20,000 per unit and fixed costs are $600,000. The plant can produce a maximum of 80 units a year. It is currently operating at 60% capacity. The firm is contemplating the effects of reducing the selling price by $2000 per unit, adding a feature to each unit which will increase the variable costs by $1000, and allocating an extra $120,000 per year for advertising. What effect will these measures have on the breakeven point and annual profit if together they cause the plant utilization to climb to 90%?

SOLUTION   Under current conditions,

$$B = \frac{F}{P - V} = \frac{\$600,000}{\$35,000 - \$20,000} = 40 \text{ units}$$

Since the company now sells $0.60 \times 80 = 48$ units per year, the gross annual profit is

$$Z = \text{units sold beyond } B \times \text{contribution per unit}$$
$$= (48 - 40) \times \$15,000 = \$120,000$$

The ratio of gross annual profit to fixed costs is

$$\frac{Z}{F} = \frac{\$120,000}{\$600,000} = 0.20$$

and may be thought of as a margin of profit or safety. The same ratio can be obtained by

$$\text{Margin of profit} = \frac{n - B}{B} = \frac{48 - 40}{40} = 0.20$$

where n is the number sold during the period.

Both the current conditions (dotted lines) and the anticipated conditions (solid lines) are displayed in Fig. 2.6:

We can observe that B has increased as a result of the added expenditures to

$$B' = \frac{\$600,000 + \$120,000}{\$33,000 - \$21,000} = \frac{\$720,000}{\$12,000} = 60 \text{ units}$$

and the gross profit expected at 90% capacity also increased to

$$Z = (0.90 \times 80 - 60) \times (\$33,000 - \$21,000)$$
$$= 12 \text{ units} \times \$12,000 \text{ per unit}$$
$$= \$144,000$$

but the margin of profit has remained unchanged at

$$\frac{Z}{F} = \frac{\$144,000}{\$720,000} = 0.20$$

The firm could also follow a course of action where only one or two of the alternatives are pursued. If the advertising budget is eliminated but the price and

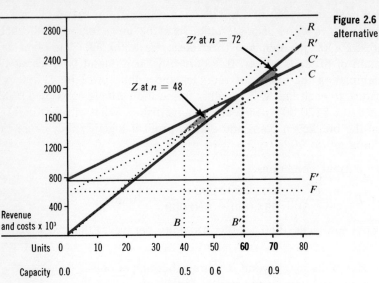

Figure 2.6 Original and alternative conditions

modifications are retained, the same profit ($144,000) would be obtained at an output of

$$n = \frac{Z + F}{P - V}$$

$$= \frac{\$144,000 + \$600,000}{\$33,000 - \$21,000}$$

$$= \frac{\$744,000}{\$12,000 \text{ per unit}} = 62 \text{ units}$$

and

$$B = \frac{\$600,000}{\$12,000 \text{ per unit}} = 50 \text{ units}$$

which makes the margin of safety $(62 - 50)/50$, or 0.24.

There are, of course, many factors to consider in such a decision. If the market is stable, the margin of profit is less important. Some alternatives are easier to implement than others. Some outcomes are more certain than others.

Still another alternative would be to sell a portion of the output at a reduced price. This practice is called *dumping*. It can be accomplished by selling to foreign markets at a lower price or by selling the same product at different prices under different names. There are many dangers in this practice, but if it works, profit will increase because of increased plant utilization.

Figure 2.7 illustrates dumping applied to the original data on waste-disposal unit sales: 48 units are sold at regular prices ($P = \$35,000$) to account for 60% utilization. If 100% utilization could be achieved by "dumping" the remaining capacity at a sales price of $25,000 ($P'$) per unit, the gross profit would increase from $120,000 to $280,000.

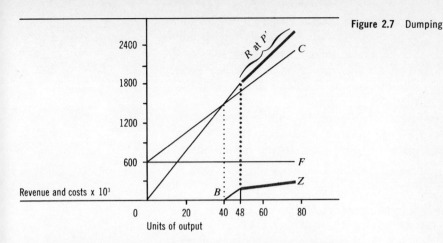

Figure 2.7 Dumping

MULTIPRODUCT BREAKEVEN CHARTS More than one product can be shown on a breakeven chart. Including a whole product line allows the decision-maker to evaluate the combined effect of the product mix on plant utilization, revenue, and costs. A slightly different format for the breakeven chart accentuates the effect of multiple products. This type of graph is shown in Fig. 2.8 and is called a multiproduct profit or contribution chart.

The chart is constructed by plotting fixed costs as a loss on the vertical axis. The horizontal axis denotes sales revenue. At zero sales the only costs associated

Figure 2.8 Multiproduct profit chart

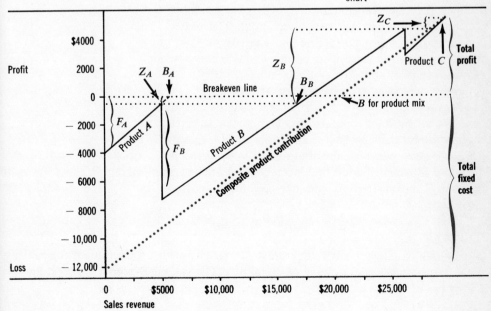

with a product are the negative preparation costs or fixed costs. As production and sales develop, each unit sold makes a contribution toward paying off the fixed costs. When enough units have been sold to pay these costs, the breakeven point is reached and the contribution from further sales is profit.

Three products, A, B, and C, are represented in Fig. 2.8. The plotted values are based on the following assumptions made for the period shown on the chart:

	A	B	C
Selling price per unit	$8	$5	$4
Contribution per unit	$6	$3	$3
Fixed cost	$4000	$7000	$1000
Number of units sold	600	4000	400

Product A is entered in the chart by marking its fixed costs ($4000) on the negative side of the breakeven line at zero sales revenue. The total contribution of A is 600 units $\times$ $6 per unit = $3600. Subtracting the fixed costs from the total contribution leaves a loss of $400 from total sales of $4800.

The remaining products are dealt with in a similar manner. Each fixed cost is entered as a vertical line attached to the highest point on the contribution line for the preceding product. The results are cumulative. The distance the last contribution segment extends above the breakeven line is the total plant profit. The dotted line extending diagonally across the chart is the composite contribution line. The point at which this line crosses the plant breakeven line establishes the sales volume at which fixed costs are exactly covered.

The value of multiproduct breakeven charts lies in their use for product comparisons. The portion of fixed costs borne by each product is easily observed. A product is preferred when its contribution line is steeper than the composite contribution line. Such considerations are important in decisions to add new products or drop old ones.

EXAMPLE 2.3 Multiproduct planning

A fertilizer batching plant is operating at capacity with production of four mixes which have a total sales volume of $2 million. The sales and production-cost figures for mixes W, X, Y, and Z are as shown:

	W	X	Y	Z	Totals
% of total sales	10	20	30	40	100
Contribution (% of P)	45	40	45	35	
Fixed cost charged	$70,000	$180,000	$210,000	$220,000	$680,000
Profit	$20,000	−$20,000	$ 60,000	$ 60,000	$120,000

Recognizing the loss incurred with product X, the company is considering dropping the product or replacing it with another mix. If the product is dropped, the new sales and costs figures are estimated to develop as follows:

	W	Y	Z	Totals
% of total sales	15	35	50	100 (for revenue of $1,800,000)
Contribution (% of P)	45	45	35	
Fixed cost charged	$100,000	$250,000	$290,000	$640,000
Profit	$ 21,500	$ 33,500	$ 15,000	$ 70,000

What course of action should be followed?

SOLUTION   The anticipated and the original conditions are displayed in Fig. 2.9 by a slightly different form of multiproduct breakeven chart. In this version the first entry is made at zero revenue and the point of maximum fixed cost. Then the contributions of each product are plotted progressively to the right. All other interpretations for the two forms of multiproduct charts are the same.

Figure 2.9 Multiproduct contribution chart

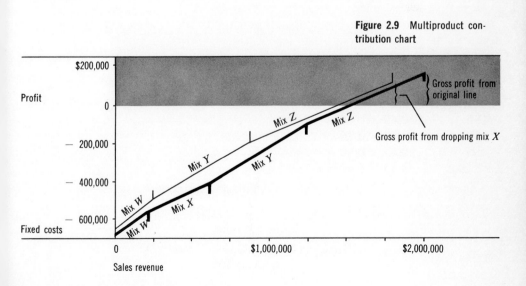

It is apparent from both the chart and the tabulated figures that dropping Mix X is not an attractive course of action. Gross profit will decrease from $120,000 to $70,000. The main reason for the drop is that most of the fixed costs carried by product X did not disappear with its elimination. In addition, the largest increase in sales occurred for Mix Z, which has a lower contribution rate than the product eliminated.

The other alternative mentioned was to replace Mix X with a new product. For this alternative, replacing Mix X with Mix XX, the expected operating figures are as follows:

	W	XX	Y	Z	Totals
% of total sales	10	15	30	45	100
					($2,000,000)
Contribution (% of P)	45	50	45	35	
Fixed cost charged	$70,000	$140,000	$210,000	$275,000	$695,000
Profit	$20,000	$ 10,000	$ 60,000	$ 40,000	$130,000

It is apparent from the above data that altering the mix is a promising possibility — a potential profit increase of $130,000 − $120,000, or $10,000. Another way of making the evaluation is by calculating the total contribution of each line of products. The composite contribution rate (shown in Fig. 2.8) is the sum of each product's contribution weighted according to its percentage of total sales:

$$\text{Weighted contribution} = \text{product contribution} \times \frac{\text{product sales}}{\text{total sales}}$$

then

$$\text{Total contribution} = \text{sum of weighted contributions} \times \text{total sales}$$

and

$$\text{Gross profit} = \text{total contribution} - \text{total fixed cost}$$

Applying this approach to the original product line and the revised line, with Mix XX substituted for Mix X, we have

Original product line:

Mix W	$0.45 \times 0.10 = 0.045$
Mix X	$0.40 \times 0.20 = 0.080$
Mix Y	$0.45 \times 0.30 = 0.135$
Mix Z	$0.35 \times 0.40 = 0.140$
Total	$0.400 = $ composite contribution rate

$$\text{Total contribution} = 0.40 \times \$2,000,000$$
$$= \$800,000$$
$$\text{Gross profit} = \$800,000 - \$680,000$$
$$= \$120,000$$

Revised product line:

Mix W	$0.45 \times 0.10 =$	0.0450
Mix XX	$0.50 \times 0.15 =$	0.0750
Mix Y	$0.45 \times 0.30 =$	0.1350
Mix Z	$0.35 \times 0.45 =$	0.1575

$$\text{Total} \quad 0.4125 = \text{composite contribution rate}$$

$$\begin{aligned} \text{Total contribution} &= 0.4125 \times \$2,000,000 \\ &= \$825,000 \end{aligned}$$

$$\begin{aligned} \text{Gross profit} &= \$825,000 - \$695,000 \\ &= \$130,000 \end{aligned}$$

NONLINEAR BREAKEVEN ANALYSIS

In our considerations of revenue and costs up to this point we have assumed that operating data could be represented by straight lines. In many cases this is a realistic approximation; in other cases it can lead to erroneous conclusions. When linear representations no longer accurately depict a real-world situation, we must turn to nonlinear models for the symbolic world.

A treatment of curved lines requires slightly more sophisticated mathematics than that of straight lines. The actual determination of formulas to represent nonlinear revenue and cost relationships is beyond the scope of this text. However, assuming that we know the curve formulas, their analysis is not much more difficult than the procedures for linear models.

A study of nonlinear relationships leads to a more general examination of revenue and costs as a function of output or plant capacity. An assumption of linearity makes all monetary increments constant over an extended range of output. Nonlinear functions emphasize "marginal value" or rate of change of revenue and costs as a function of output.

MARGINAL REVENUE AND PROFIT *Marginal revenue* is the additional money received from selling one more unit at a specified level of output. For linear revenue functions the marginal revenue is a constant value P. That is, for each additional unit sold, the total revenue is increased by P dollars. Consequently, a greater output automatically increases the total profit.

When the linear relationship is replaced by an expression such as

$$\text{Selling price} = P = 21,000n^{-\frac{1}{2}} \text{ dollars per unit}$$

the price of each unit is not so obvious. Such expressions are evaluated by applying differential calculus.[1] This approach permits us to calculate many points of interest directly, rather than relying on graph readings. The slope of a line, as the change in revenue per unit

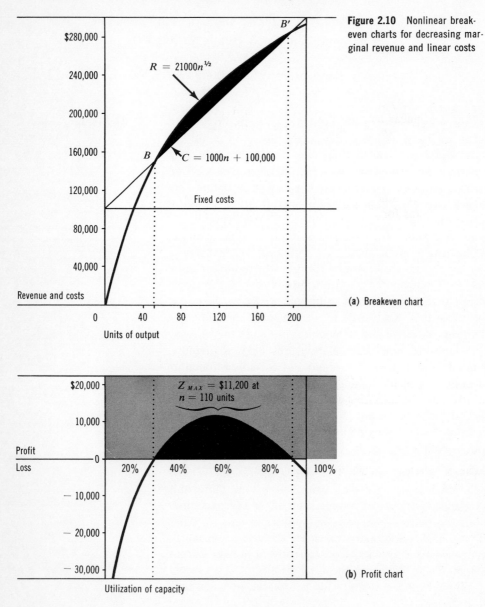

Figure 2.10 Nonlinear breakeven charts for decreasing marginal revenue and linear costs

$R = 21000n^{1/2}$

$C = 1000n + 100,000$

Fixed costs

Revenue and costs

(a) Breakeven chart

Units of output

$Z_{MAX} = \$11,200$ at $n = 110$ units

Profit

Loss

(b) Profit chart

Utilization of capacity

[1]The only differential calculus formula used in this chapter is for the differentiation of a single variable y with respect to x, as in the equation $y = ax^n + b$, where a and b are constants. For this equation, the differentiation formula is $dy/dx = nax^{n-1}$.

output, can be determined for any level of production. For the price function above, the rate of change of revenue with output is

$$\text{Marginal revenue} = \frac{dR}{dn} = \frac{d\,(nP)}{dn} = \frac{d\,(21{,}000n^{1/2})}{dn}$$
$$= 10{,}500n^{-1/2}$$

Figure 2.10a shows a decelerating revenue rate and linear costs. Decreasing marginal revenue could result from a policy of lowering prices in order to achieve a higher plant utilization. The nonlinear total-revenue line in the example fixes two breakeven points. Between these points the firm operates at a profit. Outside the breakeven points a loss is incurred, as shown in the profit chart, Fig. 2.10b. By examining these diagrams, we can observe the effect of a nonlinear relationship. The graphs are based on the following data:

$n = 1$ unit produced and sold per period
$V = 1000$ dollars per unit
$F = 100{,}000$ dollars per period
$P = 21{,}000n^{-1/2}$ dollars per unit

Using the formula for total revenue and the selling-price function, we have

$$R = nP = 21{,}000n^{1/2}$$

and for gross profit

$$Z = R - C$$
$$= R - (nV + F)$$
$$= 21{,}000n^{1/2} - 1000n - 100{,}000$$

Knowing that $Z = 0$ at a breakeven point, we can determine a value or values for B. Rearranging the terms for Z,

$$Z = 0 = -10^3 n - 10^5 + 21 \times 10^3 n^{1/2}$$
$$10^3 n + 10^5 = 21 \times 10^3 n^{1/2}$$

squaring each side of the equation, dividing by 10^6,

$$n^2 + 200n + 10^4 = 441n$$

and collecting terms,

$$n^2 - 241n + 10^4 = 0$$

we have an expression which can be solved with the

quadratic equation[1] to obtain $n = B = 53$ and $n = B' = 187$. These points are marked in Fig. 2.10a.

The point of maximum profit is especially important when two breakeven points are present. The maximum profit point is indicated in Fig. 2.10b. To the left of this point the rate of profit is increasing and to the right it is decreasing. The rate of change of profit with respect to output is called *marginal profit*. At the point of maximum profit, the rate of change (and the marginal profit or slope of the profit line) is zero. Therefore, to find this point we need only differentiate the profit equation, set the derivative equal to zero, and solve for n:

$$\frac{dZ}{dn} = \frac{d\,(21{,}000n^{1/2} - 1000n - 100{,}000)}{dn} = 0$$

$$= 10{,}500n^{-1/2} - 1000 = 0$$

$$n = \left(\frac{10{,}500}{1000}\right)^2$$

$$= 110 \text{ units}$$

MARGINAL COST AND AVERAGE UNIT COST Costs as well as revenue can be nonlinear functions of output. As production increases, the total cost per unit may also increase because of greater maintenance needs, overtime payments to workers, and general inefficiency caused by congestion during stepped-up operation. Under these conditions there are increasing *marginal costs* — the rate of change of total cost with output.

One possible pattern of marginal costs and linear revenue is shown in Fig. 2.11. There could be many patterns — two breakeven points (as in Fig. 2.10), decreasing marginal costs owing to savings realized from quantity purchases or from near-capacity mechanized production, nonlinear functions for both revenue and costs, etc.

The feature points of a breakeven analysis are determined in the manner described previously. To find B, set the profit equation to zero and solve for $n = B$.

Figure 2.11 Increasing marginal cost and linear revenue

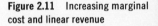
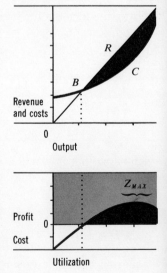

[1]For an equation in the quadratic form $Ax^2 + Bx + C = 0$,

$$x = \frac{-B \pm \sqrt{B^2 - 4AC}}{2A}$$

and for the data given above, this becomes

$$n = \frac{241 \pm \sqrt{241^2 - 4 \times 10^4}}{2} = \frac{241 \pm 134}{2}$$

$$n = 53 \text{ and } 187$$

Differentiate the profit equation and set the derivative equal to zero to solve for the output that produces maximum gross profit. In doing so, it is interesting to note that

$$\frac{dZ}{dn} = \frac{d(nP - nV - F)}{dn} = 0$$

$$= \frac{d(nP)}{dn} - \frac{d(nV + F)}{dn} = 0$$

or

$$\frac{d(nP)}{dn} = \frac{d(nV + F)}{dn}$$

Marginal revenue = marginal cost

This means that when the change in revenue from one additional sale equals the change in cost of producing one more unit, the point of maximum profit is attained. Graphically, this point is at the output where the difference between the total-cost curve and the revenue curve is greatest. If marginal revenue and marginal cost were plotted, the output for maximum profit would be at the intersection of the two curves.

Another interesting statistic associated with a break-even analysis is the *average unit cost*. For linear functions, the average unit cost is

$$\frac{nV + F}{n} = V + \frac{F}{n}$$

where n = a specific output. In the case above the average unit cost continually decreases with increasing output. For nonlinear costs this condition is not necessarily true. We can check by plotting the average unit costs on a graph or by differentiating. If the unit costs go through a minimum point and then increase, the slope of the line will be zero at the output for lowest average unit costs. Thus

$$\frac{d(V + Fn^{-1})}{dn} = 0$$

$$\frac{dV}{dn} - \frac{F}{n^2} = 0$$

$$\frac{dV}{dn} = \frac{F}{n^2}$$

From this equation and the maximum-profit equation we can see that for nonlinear relationships the point of minimum average unit cost does not necessarily coincide with the maximum-profit point.

EXAMPLE 2.4 Nonlinear revenue and costs

A monthly record of operating expenses and revenue for a new manufacturing plant is posted in the manager's office. The purpose is to detect any changes in cost-revenue relationships and to establish the plant's operating pattern.

The graphic result of several months' operations are depicted in Fig. 2.12. The pattern appeared to indicate that as the output became greater, marginal costs increased, and marginal revenue decreased. The belief was confirmed by the formulas developed for the curves that best fit the data.

The selling price of finished units varies according to $P = (100 - 0.001n)$ dollars per unit. The price behavior is attributed to lower per-unit price quotes given

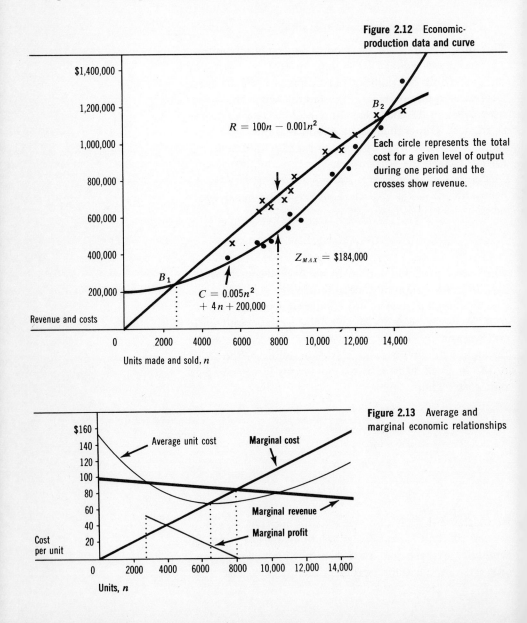

Figure 2.12 Economic-production data and curve

$R = 100n - 0.001n^2$

B_2

Each circle represents the total cost for a given level of output during one period and the crosses show revenue.

$Z_{MAX} = \$184,000$

B_1

$C = 0.005n^2 + 4n + 200,000$

Revenue and costs

Units made and sold, n

Figure 2.13 Average and marginal economic relationships

Average unit cost

Marginal cost

Marginal revenue

Marginal profit

Cost per unit

Units, n

for large orders. Fixed costs are considered reasonable at $200,000 per month. The variable costs, $V = (0.005n + 4)$ dollars per unit, also appear competitive.

The plant was designed to produce 12,000 units per month. Most of the smaller profits and losses occurred when the plant produced beyond its design capacity. Estimates based on the available data are needed for the output which produces the greatest profit, the least average unit cost, and the breakeven points.

SOLUTION   Most of the points are already located on the charts of Fig. 2.12 and 2.13. The following solutions indicate the numerical calculating procedures:

Maximum profit occurs where marginal revenue equals marginal cost, as shown in Fig. 2.13:

$$\text{Marginal revenue} = \frac{d\,(nP)}{dn} = \frac{d\,(100n - 0.001n^2)}{dn} = 100 - 0.002n$$

$$\text{Marginal cost} = \frac{d\,(nV + F)}{dn} = \frac{d\,(0.005n^2 + 4n + 200{,}000)}{dn} = 0.01n + 4$$

At maximum profit

$$100 - 0.002n = 0.01n + 4$$

$$n = \frac{96}{0.012} = 8000 \text{ units}$$

For an output of 8000,

$$Z = R - C = 100n - 0.001n^2 - 0.005n^2 - 4n - 200{,}000$$
$$= -0.006n^2 + 96n - 200{,}000$$
$$Z_{8000} = -0.006 \times (8000)^2 + 96 \times 8000 - 200{,}000$$
$$= \$184{,}000$$

The output for maximum profit is also located by the point at which the marginal profit is zero:

$$\text{Marginal profit} = \frac{dZ}{dn} = \frac{d\,(-0.006n^2 + 96n - 200{,}000)}{dn} = 0$$

$$0 = -0.012n + 96$$

$$n = \frac{96}{0.012} = 8000 \text{ units}$$

The minimum average cost occurs where the output satisfies the relation

$$\frac{dV}{dn} = \frac{F}{n^2}$$

$$\frac{d\,(0.005n + 4)}{dn} = \frac{200{,}000}{n^2}$$

$$0.005n^2 = 200{,}000$$

$$n = 6325$$

At $n = 6325$, the average cost is $67.20, as determined from the average-cost formula, $0.005n + 4 + 200{,}000/n$, and as shown in Fig. 2.13.

The breakeven output is calculated from the gross-profit formula, where $Z = 0$. Thus

$$Z = 0 = -0.006n^2 + 96n - 200,000$$

$$n = \frac{96 \pm \sqrt{(96)^2 - 4 \times 0.006 \times 200,000}}{2 \times 0.006}$$

$$B = n = \frac{96 \pm 66.4}{0.012} = 2477 \text{ units and } 13,533 \text{ units}$$

PRECAUTIONS FOR BREAKEVEN ANALYSES

A breakeven analysis often tends to oversimplify the decision environment. This is an attribute for presentation purposes and for gross evaluations. It can also be a shortcoming for problems where detailed measures are needed. A decision to lower the breakeven point for an operation can result from a study of total revenue and costs, but the study alone seldom reveals the in-plant means to implement the decision. The inability to identify tactical procedures is not really a defect of a breakeven analysis; it merely indicates that the decision-maker should be aware of the limitations of the approach in order to apply it appropriately.

The validity of a breakeven chart is directly proportional to the accuracy of the data incorporated in the chart. The firm must have a good cost-accounting system, and the decision-maker has to identify the pertinency of the costs to the decision situation. When several products are lumped together and represented by one line on a chart, there is a distinct possibility that a poor performance by one product may go undetected. Data from past performances may not be indicative of future performances. More reliable decisions result when the situation is relatively stable and not subject to abrupt changes.

A chart is necessarily limited to a specific time period. A long-range study might show a favorable forecast over a 10-year period, but it would be of little use if the firm did not survive temporary losses in the first few years. This is an example of the time effect of suboptimization considered in Chap. 1. Long-range forecasts are also less credible and are subject to more unexpected difficulties than short-run evaluations. In Chap. 9 we will consider means of evaluating the effects of risk on long-term alternatives.

MINIMUM-COST ANALYSIS

The distinction between a breakeven analysis and a minimum-cost analysis exists more by definition than in solution procedures. As the name implies, a minimum-cost analysis seeks a minimum point on a total-cost curve. No revenue or profit is involved, except as an indirect consequence of reduced costs. In other respects the two types of analysis are very similar. Both require cost data as a function of a design variable, such as units of production or size. Either type can be evaluated by tabular, graphical, and algebraic methods and is adaptable to a wide variety of comparisons under conditions of assumed certainty.

CHARACTERISTICS   Five factors are considered in a minimum-cost analysis. The relationship of these factors to each other is depicted in Fig. 2.14 and is expressed by the formula

$$C = Ax + \frac{B}{x} + K$$

where

Figure 2.14   Minimum-cost factors

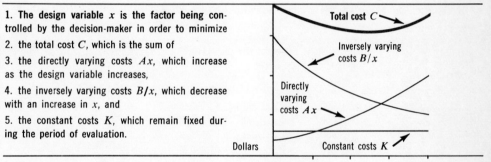

1. The design variable x is the factor being controlled by the decision-maker in order to minimize

2. the total cost C, which is the sum of

3. the directly varying costs Ax, which increase as the design variable increases,

4. the inversely varying costs B/x, which decrease with an increase in x, and

5. the constant costs K, which remain fixed during the period of evaluation.

A surprising number of real-world conditions can be represented by the minimum-cost model. The design variable can have dimensions of money, length, weight, number of parts, time, or combined values such as speed.

METHODS OF SOLUTION   There are three ways to solve minimum-cost problems. The choice largely depends on the type of cost function.

Tabular method   In many practical situations costs are not exactly proportional to the design variable or continuous over the range of the variable. Under such conditions a listing of the outcomes for all the pertinent alternatives is a feasible and time-saving approach.

An appropriate application of the tabular method is in determining the duration of a construction project which will produce minimum total project costs. The total cost for a construction project is the sum of direct and indirect costs. Direct costs of construction vary with time.[1] Direct costs are usually considered constant over short periods of time, but they may vary radically from one period to the next. Indirect costs are relatively fixed from one period to the next, except for bonus or penalty payments, which become due during specified periods.

A contractor is relatively free to choose his own project duration. His selection is influenced by factors such as crew availability, equipment utilization, expected weather, and material procurement. All these factors can be included in the contractor's estimated costs for alternative durations. Therefore his goal of minimizing total project cost is an attempt to optimize the conglomerate influencing factors.

Table 2.1 is a typical tabular approach to identify the optimal duration for a construction project. It reveals that a duration of 40 weeks has the lowest total cost.

Table 2.1 Expected costs for a construction project

Project duration, wk	Cumulative indirect costs	Cumulative direct costs	Total project cost
37	$200,000	$1,200,000	$1,400,000
38	204,000	1,191,000	1,395,000
39	208,000	1,183,000	1,391,000
40*	217,000	1,173,000	1,390,000
41*	226,000	1,167,000	1,393,000
42*	235,000	1,162,000	1,397,000

*A late completion penalty of $5000 is charged to the contractor for each week the project extends beyond week 39.

Graphical method   A graph normally provides a less precise solution than the other methods, but it excels for explanation and discussion purposes. Situations are vividly depicted, and the effect of alternate courses of action is readily observed.

For problems like the construction project described in Table 2.1 and graphed in Fig. 2.15, a graphical solution is more appropriate than an algebraic approach, because costs are not a constant function of the duration. In such cases a "stepwise linear distribution" is

[1]The relationship and composition of direct and indirect construction costs is treated in more detail in Chap. 4.

plotted on the graph; for each duration the exact cost is entered and a linear relationship between plotted points is assumed. The solution in Fig. 2.15 agrees with the tabular solution of 40 weeks.

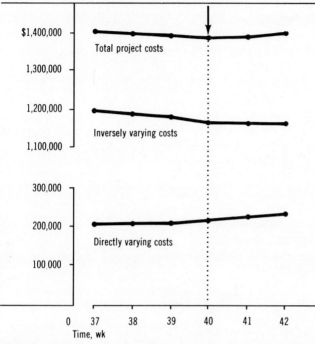

Figure 2.15 Project construction costs

Algebraic method An algebraic solution is based on the formula

$$C = Ax + \frac{B}{x} + K$$

When the direct cost Ax and the inverse cost B/x are exactly proportional to the design variable, we can find the minimum-cost value of x by the same techniques used in nonlinear breakeven analyses. Figure 2.14 showed that the minimum-cost point occurs where the slope of the total-cost line is zero. Therefore we can differentiate the total-cost formula to find the slope and set the derivative equal to zero to solve for x:

$$\frac{dC}{dx} = \frac{d\,(Ax + Bx^{-1} + K)}{dx} = 0$$

$$= A - \frac{B}{x^2} = 0$$

and $$x = \sqrt{\frac{B}{A}}$$

At the minimum-cost point the directly varying costs are equal to the inversely varying costs. This equality is apparent when the minimum-cost value is substituted into the total-cost formula:

$$C = Ax' + \frac{B}{x'} + K \qquad x' = \text{minimum-cost point} = \sqrt{\frac{B}{A}}$$

$$= A\sqrt{\frac{B}{A}} + \frac{B}{\sqrt{B/A}} + K$$

$$= \sqrt{AB} + \sqrt{AB} + K$$

Every organization needs supplies in order to operate. This is equally true for a family unit or a government agency, for a one-man private company or a general corporation.[1] The procurement of supplies and control of inventory amounts to a major expense. Two important questions are

How often should supplies be replenished?

What amount should be replenished each time?

These two questions are related, and the model for their solution is the total cost formula.

INVENTORY FACTORS An organization orders, receives, stores, and uses a great variety of supplies. Typically, there are a relatively few classes of supplies that account for most of the inventory costs. Following the principles of value engineering, most attention should be directed to the key classes where close control will promote the most savings. The potential savings make it advisable to collect the data needed for a minimum-cost study.

After an inventory item has been selected for investigation, the following information is needed:

D = annual demand or usage for the item

M = annual manufacturing rate for the organization producing the item

O = order cost or setup cost to procure the item

H = holding cost for keeping each item in storage one year

i = interest rate for money invested in inventory stock

P = price of the item

---

[1] A larger business organization such as General Motors, General Foods, General Electric, General Dynamics, etc.

This information establishes the five factors for a minimum-cost analysis.

Design variable   The number of items procured for each inventory replenishment is the design variable denoted as Q. If all the items needed for an entire year are procured at one time, then $Q = D$. When inventory is replenished more than once a year,

$$Q = \frac{D}{N}$$

where N is the number of procurement periods per year, or

$$N = \frac{D}{Q}$$

Directly varying costs   The cost of holding items in storage, H, and the interest on money invested in stored items are directly proportional to the inventory level. Immediately after a procurement is made there are Q units in storage. If we assume a constant usage rate and that all the items in storage are depleted before another procurement is received, the average inventory stored is $Q/2$. Then the total annual holding cost[1] is

$$\text{Holding cost} = \frac{HQ}{2}$$

and the annual interest charge is the value of the average inventory, $PQ/2$, times the interest rate i, or

$$\text{Interest charge} = \frac{iPQ}{2}$$

which makes the total carrying cost

$$\text{Carrying cost} = (H + iP)\frac{Q}{2}$$

Inversely varying costs   The costs associated with placing an order or preparing to produce an order, O, occur once each procurement period. Therefore the total annual preparation cost is the order cost for each procurement period, O, times the number of periods per year, N, or

$$\text{Procurement cost} = \frac{OD}{Q}$$

---

[1]"Holding cost" encompasses such diverse expenses as all the costs of providing storage space (rent, lights, heat, maintenance, etc.); keeping records of inventory transactions; protection and insurance for stored inventory; and damage, pilferage, or obsolescence of inventory during the storage period.

Constant costs   It is assumed that the value of each item, P, remains unchanged during a storage period. If P is also assumed constant throughout a year, the total annual purchase cost is

$$\text{Purchase cost} = DP$$

Total cost   The sum of the above costs is the total inventory cost C, or

$$C = \frac{OD}{Q} + \frac{(H + iP)Q}{2} + DP$$

$$\begin{array}{ccccc}\text{Total} \\ \text{cost}\end{array} = \begin{array}{c}\text{procurement} \\ \text{cost}\end{array} + \begin{array}{c}\text{carrying} \\ \text{cost}\end{array} + \begin{array}{c}\text{purchase} \\ \text{cost}\end{array}$$

The total-cost formula can now be adapted to represent different real-world inventory situations. The terms in the formula are changed to fit specific inventory patterns, but the enduring objective is to minimize C by identifying the optimal quantity Q.

ECONOMIC ORDER QUANTITY   An organization ordering items from an internal or external source can usually minimize its costs by adhering to the economic order quantity Q. The calculations for Q are based on the assumptions and inventory pattern shown in Fig. 2.16.

Figure 2.16 Inventory order-quantity pattern

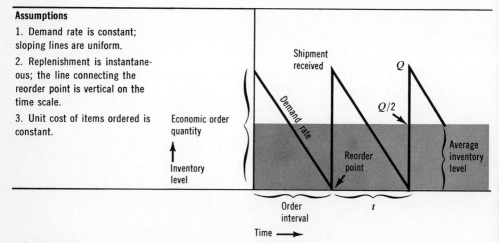

Assumptions

1. Demand rate is constant; sloping lines are uniform.

2. Replenishment is instantaneous; the line connecting the reorder point is vertical on the time scale.

3. Unit cost of items ordered is constant.

Under the stated assumptions we can employ the previously encountered minimum-cost formula to solve for the economic order quantity as

$$\text{Design variable} = Q = \sqrt{\frac{\text{inversely varying costs}}{\text{directly varying costs}}}$$

$$= \sqrt{\frac{2OD}{H + iP}}$$

When the interest charge is included as part of the total holding cost, as is often the case, the order-size formula reduces to

$$Q = \sqrt{\frac{2OD}{H}}$$

and related inventory values based upon Q are

$$\text{Number of orders per year} = N = \frac{D}{Q} = \sqrt{\frac{HD}{2O}}$$

$$\text{Order interval} = t = \frac{\text{working time per year}}{N}$$

$$\text{Total annual cost} = \frac{OD}{\sqrt{2OD/H}} + \frac{H}{2}\sqrt{\frac{2OD}{H}} + DP$$

$$= \sqrt{2ODH} + (DP)$$

EXAMPLE 2.5 Economic order size

A retail paint distributor with several outlets in a large city annually sells 8000 gal of Deep-brand stain. The costs of determining the order amount of each shade of stain, preparing the order forms, and bulk delivery amount to $150. The firm has its own warehouse, which is used to store only its own merchandise. Warehousing and handling costs are prorated at $0.21 per gal per year. The average price paid to the stain manufacturer is $3.15 per gal. Insurance and interest charges amount to 12%. What is the economic order quantity for Deep stain and how often should orders be placed?

SOLUTION   Relating the costs in the problem to our formula symbols, we have

$D = 8000$ gal per yr

$O = \$150$ per order

$H = \$0.21$ per gal per yr on maximum inventory

$P = \$3.15$ per gal wholesale price

$i = 12\%$ of P on the average inventory level

The statement of the problem indicates that the storage space allowed for paint and stain is not used for any other purpose. This means space is provided for the maximum number of gallons received in an order. As the stain is sold, less space is occupied, but the total cost for having the space available is constant. Therefore the directly varying costs are

$$\text{Carrying costs} = HQ + \frac{iPQ}{2} = \frac{(2H + iP)Q}{2}$$

Then the economic lot size formula is

$$Q = \sqrt{\frac{2OD}{2H + iP}}$$

and substituting figures into the formula, we get

$$Q = \sqrt{\frac{2 \times \$150 \times 8000}{2 \times \$0.21 + 0.12 \times \$3.15}}$$

$$= \sqrt{\frac{\$2,400,000}{\$0.798}}$$

$$= 1732 \text{ gal per order}$$

The number of orders per year is

$$N = \frac{8000}{1408} = 4.6 \text{ orders per yr}$$

which makes the order interval in weeks

$$t = \frac{\text{wk per yr}}{N} = \frac{52}{4.6}$$

or about 11 weeks between orders.

QUANTITY DISCOUNTS   Many vendors allow a discount on purchases exceeding a specified amount. "Cheaper by the dozen" is a household slogan which reflects quantity discounts in grocery stores. Freight rates, rental plans, and "three for the price of two" bargains are also familiar examples. Such "bargains" may be a lure to false economy and should be evaluated in terms of total inventory cost before being accepted.

The most direct approach is a comparison of total cost with and without quantity discounts. The procedure as outlined by the flow chart in Fig. 2.17 is a series of total-cost comparisons starting from the lowest possible unit cost. Successive calculations determine the economic order quantity (EOQ) that produces the lowest annual total cost.

To amplify the quantity-discount procedure, consider the following costs for a product with a large annual demand:

$D = 400,000$ units per yr

$O = \$25.00$ per order

$H = \$0.06 + 0.20P$ per unit based on average inventory

$P1 = \$0.50$ per unit on orders up to 9999

$P2 = \$0.47$ per unit on orders from 10,000 to 24,999

$P3 = \$0.45$ per unit on orders above 24,999

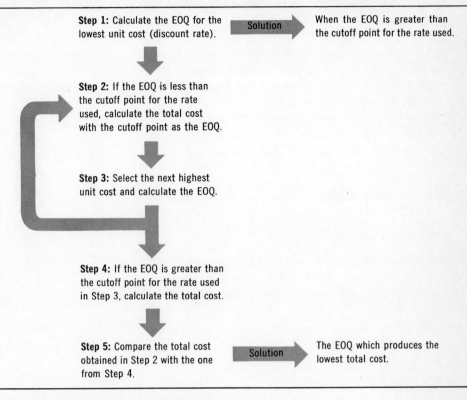

Figure 2.17 Flow chart for order-size calculations with quantity discounts

Step 1: Calculate the EOQ for the lowest unit cost (discount rate).

Solution → When the EOQ is greater than the cutoff point for the rate used.

Step 2: If the EOQ is less than the cutoff point for the rate used, calculate the total cost with the cutoff point as the EOQ.

Step 3: Select the next highest unit cost and calculate the EOQ.

Step 4: If the EOQ is greater than the cutoff point for the rate used in Step 3, calculate the total cost.

Step 5: Compare the total cost obtained in Step 2 with the one from Step 4.

Solution → The EOQ which produces the lowest total cost.

For the lowest rate of $0.45 per unit,

$$Q1 = \sqrt{\frac{2 \times 25 \times 400,000}{0.06 + 0.20 \times 0.45}} = 11,532 \text{ units}$$

Since $Q1$ is less than the quantity needed (25,000) for the price break, the next-higher price level is used:

$$Q2 = \sqrt{\frac{2 \times 25 \times 400,000}{0.06 + 0.20 \times 0.47}} = 11,323 \text{ units}$$

Now the economic lot size ($Q2$) is greater than the cutoff point (10,000) for the discount rate ($0.47 per unit) used to calculate Q. A total-cost comparison is made for $Q2 = 11,323$ and $Q1 = 25,000$ (the cutoff point for the lowest rate):

$$C(Q1) = \frac{25 \times 400,000}{25,000} + (0.06 + 0.2 \times 0.45)$$

$$\times \frac{25,000}{2} + 400,000 \times 0.45$$

$$= \$400 + 1875 + \$180,000 = \$182,275$$

$$C(Q2) = \frac{25 \times 400,000}{11,323} + (0.06 + 0.2 \times 0.47)$$

$$\times \frac{11,323}{2} + 400,000 \times 0.47$$

$$= \$883 + \$872 + \$188,000 = \$189,755$$

The total-cost calculations disclose the advantage of an order size that allows the lowest possible rate. In this example a solution was obtained by passing once through the five steps outlined in Fig. 2.17. If $Q2$ had been less than 10,000 units, it would have been necessary to pass through Steps 2 and 3 again, using the next higher rate. Regardless of the number of cycles required, total cost is the basis of comparison.

ECONOMIC PRODUCTION QUANTITY An economic production quantity (EPQ) is associated with a manufacturing environment, while the economic order quantity (EOQ) is more common in retail situations. The difference between the two quantities is due to delivery time. EOQ calculations are based on an assumption of instantaneous delivery time. EPQ calculations realistically show that inventory is gradually built over a period of time, as illustrated in Fig. 2.18.

Figure 2.18 Inventory-production quantity pattern

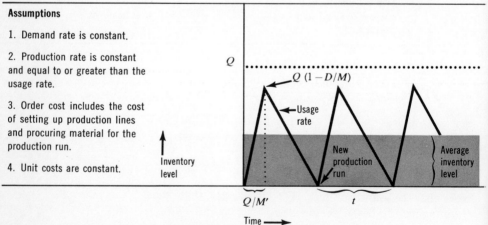

Assumptions

1. Demand rate is constant.

2. Production rate is constant and equal to or greater than the usage rate.

3. Order cost includes the cost of setting up production lines and procuring material for the production run.

4. Unit costs are constant.

Q

$Q(1 - D/M)$

←Usage rate

New production run

Average inventory level

Inventory level

Q/M'

t

Time ⟶

If the manufacturing rate M is just equal to the usage rate D, the items will be used as fast as they are produced. If M is greater than D, inventory is accumulated at the daily rate of $(M - D)$/days per year. The inventory level reaches a maximum after Q/M' days, where M' is the daily production rate. This level is equal to $(M - D)Q/M$, and the average inventory is half this amount, or $(Q/2)(1 - D/M)$. Thus the total cost for a production situation is

$$C = \frac{OD}{Q} + \frac{HQ}{2}\left(1 - \frac{D}{M}\right) + DP$$

and the economic production quantity is

$$Q = \sqrt{\frac{2OD}{H(1 - D/M)}}$$

EXAMPLE 2.6 Economic production-batch size

One department of a plant produces switchplates which are used in the assembly department of the same plant. Switchplates can be produced at the rate of 4000 units per day. The assembly department needs only 182,000 units per year. The cost of authorizing switchplate production and setting up the machines is $300.00 for each production run. The plant operates 260 days per year. The annual cost of holding one unit in storage is $0.10. How many switchplate production runs should be scheduled each year?

SOLUTION

$D = 182,000$ units per yr

$O = \$300$ per production run

$H = \$0.10$ per unit per yr

$M = 4000 \times 260 = 1,040,000$ units per yr

$$Q = \sqrt{\frac{2 \times 300 \times 182,000}{0.10 \times [1 - (182,000/1,040,000)]}}$$

$= 36,400$ switchplates per production run

$$N = \frac{182,000}{36,400} = 5 \text{ production runs per yr}$$

PRECAUTIONS FOR MINIMUM-COST ANALYSES

The main precautions for minimum-cost analyses are shared by all economy studies: the model used in the evaluation should closely approximate the real world, and the data used in the model should be as accurate as possible. Some of the more subtle considerations are difficult to include in the cost equations. For instance, holding a large inventory decreases the chance of running out of stock and thereby reduces potential customer complaints owing to late deliveries or unfilled orders. How do you measure the wrath of disgruntled customers? On the other hand, holding a smaller inventory decreases the chance of being stuck with obsolete or deteriorated stock. How do you measure the fads that make a style obsolete or the many factors that can cause the value of stock to deteriorate? A percentage charge based on judgment and handled like an interest charge is one way to include less tangible cost factors.

The inventory patterns and formulas we have considered are subject to distinct limitations. Where demand and manufacturing rates are essentially constant and lead time is negligible or unimportant, they provide acceptable solutions. When these factors are subject to variation, more demanding analysis techniques, as described in Chap. 9, are required. The decision-maker has to weigh the cost of a rigorous analysis against the value gained by the more realistic evaluation. Economy principles apply even to economy studies.

SELECTED REFERENCES
Biegel, J. E.: *Production Control: A Quantitative Approach*, Prentice-Hall, Inc., Englewood Cliffs, N.J., 1963.
Bowman, E. H., and R. B. Fetter: *Analysis for Production Management*, Richard D. Irwin, Inc., Homewood, Ill., 1961.
Davis, R. C.: *Industrial Organization and Management*, Harper & Brothers, New York, 1957.
Eilon, S.: *Elements of Production Planning and Control*, The Macmillan Company, New York, 1962.
Greene, J. H.: *Production Control*, Richard D. Irwin, Inc., Homewood, Ill., 1965.
Hodges, H. G., and R. J. Ziegler: *Managing the Industrial Concern*, Houghton Mifflin Company, Boston, Mass., 1961.
Magee, J. F.: *Production Control*, Richard D. Irwin, Inc., Homewood, Ill., 1958.
Moore, F. G.: *Manufacturing Management*, Richard D. Irwin, Inc., Homewood, Ill., 1961.
Schweyer, H. E.: *Analytic Models for Managerial and Engineering Economics,* Reinhold Publishing Corporation, New York, 1964.

PROBLEMS
2.1 An import company buys foreign-made sewing machines for $12.50 per unit. Fixed costs of the operation are $21,000 per year. The sewing machines are sold on commission by door-to-door salesmen who receive 40% of the selling price for each machine sold. At what price should the machines be sold to allow the importers to break even on a shipment of 5000 sewing machines?

2.2 A privately owned summer camp for youngsters has the following operating data for a 12-week season:

Charge per camper	$40 per wk
Variable cost per camper	$22 per wk
Fixed costs	$20,000 per season
Capacity per wk	120 campers

a What is the total number of campers that will allow the camp to break even?

b What is the profit for the 12-week season if the camp operates at 90% of capacity?

c What profit would result if the camp stayed open 2 weeks longer and averaged 70 campers paying a reduced rate of $32 per week during the extended season?

2.3 List the costs associated with owning an automobile which should be classified as fixed and those which are variable.

2.4 Estimate dollar values for the costs identified in Prob. 2.3. Assume the annual depreciation is one-fourth of a new car price and the car is driven an average of 15,000 miles per year. Would it be more economical to rent a "fleet" car for $0.10 per mile (the only extra charge is for gasoline) or to operate an owned car? About what percentage of total ownership costs are fixed costs?

2.5 A manufacturer of hand-operated power tools can produce a convenient attachment for use with his line of tools at an estimated annual fixed cost of $3000.00 and variable costs of $1.25 per attachment. He can also buy the complete attachment custom made for his line of tools at a price of $2.00 per attachment for the first 5000 and $1.05 for all units purchased beyond the 5000 breakoff point. At what increments of unit sales should he purchase or manufacture the attachment? What are some factors other than cost that might influence the decision?

2.6 A lake resort includes 5 three-bedroom cabins which rent for $45 a night, and 25 two-bedroom cabins which rent for $35 a night, plus 15 single and 15 double rooms in the lodge which rent for $15 and $25 a night, respectively. The cost of cleaning a rental and preparing for new occupants is $10 for a cabin and $6 for a room. Annual fixed costs for operating the resort are $188,000 for the 200-day season. The average stay at the resort is 2 days, and utilization closely follows the proportion of available rooms and cabins.

a What percentage of resort capacity must be rented each night to break even?

b How many rooms and cabins must be rented each day to make an annual profit of $32,000?

2.7 Sales of a desk lamp which wholesales at $4.00 per lamp have been disappointing. The contribution of each lamp sold is $1.50. It is planned to increase the advertising budget by $0.22 per lamp and reduce the price to spur sales. Twice as much will be allocated for advertising as for price reductions. Current gross profit is $50,000 on sales of 100,000 lamps per year. How many lamps must be sold under the proposed conditions to double the profit?

2.8 A product currently sells for $12. The fixed costs are $4 per unit and 10,000 units are sold annually for a gross profit of $30,000. A new design will increase variable costs by 20% and fixed costs by 10%, but sales should increase to 12,000 units per year. What should the selling price be to keep the same profit ($30,000)?

2.9 A boat marina now sells motor boats of only one make. The boats are divided into classes by size: A, B, and C. With an average value placed on the accessories sold with each boat, the accounting figures for annual turnover are

Type	Average P	Average V	Number sold
A	$ 200	$150	300
B	450	250	175
C	1100	600	100

Adding a new, fancier line of boats, enlarging the display area, and increasing the sales staff could change the cost and sales to

Type	Average P	Average V	Number sold
A	$ 225	$ 175	425
B	500	300	200
C	1200	600	75
D	1800	1000	50

The additional expense of carrying the extra line of boats would double the present $50,000 fixed-cost charge for the original line.
a What is the composite contribution for each line?
b Should the new line be added?

2.10 A consulting engineer was asked by some of his clients to produce a book on "tilt-up" construction. His costs for preparation — artwork, typesetting, plates, etc. — came to $6000. For each 1000 books printed the variable costs — paper, printing, binding, etc. — will be $2000. He believes the number of books he will sell depends on the price he lists for the book. His estimates show that the following number of books would sell at the price shown:

Number of books sold	Price per book
2,000	$10.00
4,000	7.00
10,000	3.50

a What price will give him the greatest profit?
b An advertising agency claims that a $10,000 promotion plan for the book would double the sales at any of the prices listed above. If the engineer accepts their forecast, what price should he use?

2.11 A plant produces products 1, 2, and 3 at annual rates of 10,000, 7000, and 5000 units, respectively. Product 1 accounts for 30% of the plant's revenue, with a 40% contribution on its selling price. Product 2 has fixed costs of $35,000 and a contribution rate of 0.5 P where P is the purchase price. The fixed costs for product 3 are $20,000, while it accounts for 30% of the total sales revenue, with the same contribution rate as the composite contribution rate. Total fixed costs for the plant are $80,000 and total sales amount to $250,000.
a What is the plant breakeven revenue?
b What is the profit for each product?

2.12 Assuming that fixed costs are constant, prove that for a product the marginal-cost curve intersects the average-cost curve at the minimum value for average unit cost.

2.13 A company manufactures industrial clips for assembly work. The marginal revenue has been determined to be

$$\text{Marginal revenue} = 100 - 0.02n$$

where n is the number of clips produced. Variable costs plus fixed costs are calculated from the formula

$$\text{Total cost} = 2n^2 \times 10^{-4} + 10,000$$

Compute the production in clips per year for the following:
a Minimum unit cost of sales
b Production for maximum profit
c Breakeven volume

2.14 Lord Kelvin developed a classic minimum-cost analysis for the most economical wire size to conduct electricity. He proposed that the investment cost in wire diameter (directly varying cost) should be equal to the energy loss due to wire resistance (inversely varying cost). The energy loss in watts is equal to I^2R, where I is the current to be conducted and R is the electrical resistance which is inversely proportional to the cross-sectional area of the wire. Using the following symbols for the cost factors, determine the formula for the wire size which produces the minimum total cost:

A = cross-sectional area of the wire

I = current conducted

R = resistance of the wire

C_c = rate charged for the use of invested capital, %

C_t = rate charged to cover taxes and insurance, %

C_A = cost of wire

C_I = cost of energy

2.15 During fruit harvest a group of orchard growers estimate they can reduce the number of culls sent to the packing plant by hiring field inspectors. Their crop averages 16% culls without inspection on 80 tons picked per day. They expect that for every two inspectors hired the percentage of culls would be cut in half (that is, two inspectors, 8% culls; four inspectors, 4% culls; etc.). An inspector would be paid $14.00 per day. The growers will save $0.20 per ton for each percent the culls are reduced. How many inspectors should be hired?

2.16 A company buys $100,000 worth of a certain material each year. Order costs are 10% of the amount of each order and carrying costs are 20% of the average inventory. How many weeks of supply should be ordered at one time?

2.17 Determine the economic production quantity for the following conditions:

Setup costs per production run	$80.00
Variable production costs per unit produced	$0.30
Percentage charge for interest and insurance	25
Selling price per finished unit	$0.60
Manufacturing rate per yr, units	110,000
Usage rate per yr, units	20,000

2.18 A manufacturer of children's toys uses approximately 200,000 nuts and bolts of one size each year. The nuts and bolts are purchased in standard package quantities of 5000 at a cost of $50.00 per package. The storage costs of $0.001 per year to hold one bolt and matching nut are based on the maximum expected inventory level. Interest and insurance charges are 13% of the average value of inventory on hand. Typical order costs for preparing a purchase order, mailing, receiving, inspecting, and transporting are $25.00 for each purchase. The company operates 250 days per year.

a What is the economic order quantity?

b What is the time interval between orders?

2.19 A type of raw material is used at the rate of 80,000 lb per year. The current price is $1.00 per lb. Storage costs are estimated at $0.09 per lb per year on the maximum inventory value. The cost of placing an order is $10.00 and the lead time is negligible. What is the EOQ?

2.20 The vendor supplying the raw material described in Prob. 2.19 has offered a price reduction of $0.03 per lb on orders over 3000 lb and an additional reduction of $0.05 per lb on orders over 5000 lb. Do these quantity discounts change the EOQ from the original conditions in Prob. 2.19? If so, what should be the new order size?

2.21 Determine the economic order size for the following conditions, where n refers to the number of units and holding costs are based on the average inventory size:

$$O = \$10 + \$0.01n$$
$$H = \$2n + \frac{0.01P}{n^2}$$
$$P = \$40 \text{ per unit}$$
$$D = 800 \text{ units per yr}$$

2.22 Determine the economic lot size under the following conditions:

Annual usage rate 3000 units

Cost of acquisition $8.00 per order

Interest, insurance, and damage 12% of the value of the average inventory

Annual warehousing cost $0.08 per unit, based on the maximum inventory level of 500; if the inventory level exceeds the 500 limit, an additional warehouse must be leased to make the cost $0.12 per unit for the maximum number of units stored

Purchase price $3.00 per unit subject to

4% discount on orders of 200 or over
7% discount on orders of 400 or over
9% discount on orders of 500 or over
10% discount on orders of 600 or over

Chapter Three
Allocation
of Resources

More effective utilization of available resources often creates a narrow margin of competitive advantage:

Limiting resources		Effective utilization
Men		In the right amount
Money	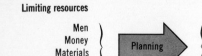	at the right place
Materials		
Machines		at the right time

How many times has a plea been uttered for an extra pair of hands when the available pair would easily have been adequate if the work had been planned properly? The value of such planning may be less obvious in an industrial setting than for personal problems, but it is no less important.

Costs associated with lack of planning are often difficult to detect. Systems that work may remain unquestioned even though a probe could reveal wasted resources. Hidden costs are still costs; unobtained profits are opportunities lost. Part of the solution in recognizing inefficient resource expenditures is knowing what data are required for an analysis and what methods of analysis are available.

One method of dealing with the utilization of resources is through linear programming. We can apply this type of analysis when there are a number of variables linked by linear relationships. The variables are evaluated according to a linear economic function to select the most appropriate resource allocation.

Three applications of linear programming are illustrated in this chapter. A product-mix problem is employed to show a graphical solution. A machine-assignment problem illustrates a simple but useful tabular technique for relating operations. A material-transportation problem offers a technique for minimizing distribution costs. The type of resource being considered is of less interest than the method used. Problems involving men, machines, materials, money, and other factors may be subjected to the systematic linear-programming approach to arrive at an optimal solution.

GRAPHICAL METHOD

The product-mix problem is to determine the most profitable combination of products to produce within the limitation of available production facilities. The mix can be obtained by graphical methods when the number of products is three or fewer.

Consider a firm which must decide the proportion of two products, $P1$ and $P2$, to manufacture for maximum profit. The products are processed through three work stations, $WS1$, $WS2$, and $WS3$, one after the other but in any order. Each work station has a limited number of hours available owing to other production commitments. The processing time required by the products at each station and the total available time at each station is indicated in Table 3.1; the unit profit expected from each product is shown on the bottom line.

Work station	Unit processing time, min		Total work-station time available, min
	$P1$	$P2$	
$WS1$	8	3	3600
$WS2$	5	6	4500
$WS3$	4	3	2400
Unit profit	$0.60	$0.40	

Table 3.1 Production data for products $P1$ and $P2$

LINEAR PROGRAMMING CHARACTERISTICS From the brief description of the problem above we can observe several characteristics of a linear programming routine. The firm desires maximum dollar profits. This goal is stated in the form of an *objective function*, which shows the relationship of profit to units produced. Letting Z equal the profit, the objective function is

$$Z = \$0.60\, P1 + \$0.40\, P2$$

where $P1$ = units produced of
product 1

$P2$ = units produced of
product 2

There are any number of solutions to this equation, including the one the firm seeks, which maximizes the profit Z.

The other values in Table 3.1 establish the conditions which limit production. If resources were not limited, any number of both products could be produced. Unfortunately, such freedom of action is rare. Most production decisions are governed by strict attention to resource availability. These restrictions, called *constraints*, define the boundaries of possible solutions. They may result from internal conditions, such as ready facilities, or they may result from external considerations, such as potential markets.

In the time available at $WS1$ production could be $3600/8 = 450$ units of $P1$, $3600/3 = 1200$ units of $P2$, or some combination of $P1$ and $P2$. The limiting condition is that the sum of production time for the combination of products is less than or equal to the time available at the work station. This constraint is stated mathematically in the form of an *inequation* as

$$8P1 + 3P2 \leq 3600 \qquad \text{for } WS1$$

where the symbol $\leq$ is read "less than or equal to."

The other constraints are

$$5P1 + 6P2 \leq 4500 \qquad \text{for } WS2$$
$$4P1 + 3P2 \leq 2400 \qquad \text{for } WS3$$

In addition, we should note that a negative value for the production of either product is meaningless within the context of practical considerations. Therefore further constraints are

$$P1 \geq 0$$
$$P2 \geq 0$$

where the symbol $\geq$ is read "more than or equal to." This confirms that the number of either product produced must be positive. It also means that the graphical solution must be in the positive xy quadrant.

SOLUTION PROCEDURE Figure 3.1 indicates the steps required for a graphical solution to a product-mix problem. The first step involves the identification of resource limitations and the expected unit profit. After this basic information has been obtained, the remaining steps are largely routine. They are illustrated by application to the two-product mix already described.

Constraints The restriction imposed by the time available in $WS1$ is plotted in Fig. 3.2a. The x axis represents $P1$ and the y axis shows $P2$. The scale must extend far enough to show the maximum amount of either product that could be produced in a work station if it is the exclusive output of that station. The entry on the x axis is the number of $P1$ units that would be produced in $WS1$ if all the time at the station were devoted to $P1$ production. Thus

$$8P1 + 3 \times 0 \leq 3600$$
$$P1 \leq 450$$

or $\qquad P1_1 = 450$ units

Similarly, $P2_1$ is found from

$$8 \times 0 + 3P2 \leq 3600$$
$$P2 \leq 1200$$

or $\qquad P2_1 = 1200$ units

The straight line connecting the two limiting points ($P1_1$ and $P2_1$) joins all combinations of $P1$ and $P2$ which utilize the entire time available (3600 minutes) in $WS1$. For instance, point $WS1_a$ shows production of 225 units of $P1$ and 600 units of $P2$. The time con-

Figure 3.1 Flow chart for the graphical solution of product-mix problems

Step 1: Determine the objective function and constraints.

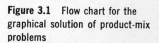

Step 2: Set up a graph and plot constraints.

Step 3: Obtain the slope of the objective function.

Step 4: Test the vertices to find the most profitable mix.

sumed at $WS1$ for this mix is

$$8 \times 225 + 3 \times 600 = 3600 \text{ min}$$

which is, as expected, the total available production time.

It can easily be surmised that any point to the left of line $P1_1P2_1$ denotes a mix which does not require

Figure 3.2 Work-station constraints

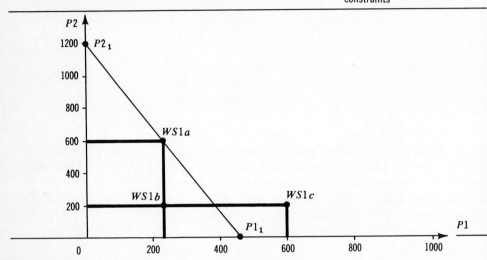

(a) $WS1$ constraint

all the time available at $WS1$. A combination of 225 units of $P1$ and 200 units of $P2$ as depicted by point $WS1_b$ uses only

$$8 \times 225 + 3 \times 200 = 2400 \text{ min}$$

of the available 3600 minutes.

Similar reasoning suggests the area to the right of line $P1_1P2_1$ should include all the combinations of $P1$ and $P2$ which exceed the time limitations of $WS1$. Checking arbitrarily selected points within this region confirms the suspicion. A typical point $WS1_c$ shows a combination of 600 units of $P1$ and 200 units of $P2$. The time required to produce this mix at $WS1$ is

$$8 \times 600 + 3 \times 200 = 5400 \text{ min}$$

which violates our constraint that

$$8P1 + 3P2 \leq 3600 \text{ min}$$

The graphical interpretation of this constraint limits the area of feasible combinations to the space enclosed by the axes and line $P1_1P2_1$. The same relationship exists for the other time constraints imposed by $WS2$ and $WS3$.

Figure 3.2b shows all three work-station constraints. Each of the lines was obtained by the same procedure as was applied to *WS1*, and each one supplies a unique restriction, as did *WS1*. Since the area to the left of each line is the only portion that conforms to the stated restriction, the feasible solution space is confined to the shaded polygon. Any point within the shaded area represents a product mix that can be produced without violating the time limits of the work stations.

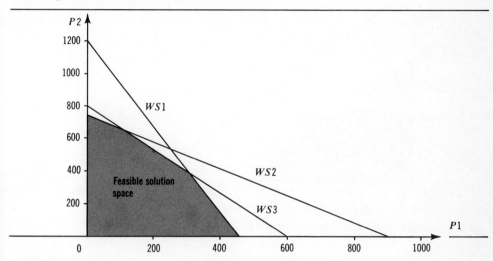

(b) Constraints for *WS1*, *WS2*, and *WS3*

Objective function   The next step is to introduce the objective function. The function can be represented on the graph just like the constraints. If we let the profit Z equal any reasonable value, we can determine the terminal points on the axes. For example, let the profit level be set at $120. Then, from the objective function,

$$\$120 = X = \$0.6\,P1 + \$0.4\,P2$$

When $P1 = 0$ we have

$$\$120 = \$0.6 \times 0 + \$0.4\,P2$$
$$P2 = 300 \text{ units}$$

and when $P2 = 0$ we get

$$P1 = \frac{\$120}{\$0.6} = 200 \text{ units}$$

These two points are shown in Fig. 3.3 as A and B. The segment connecting them, AB, shows all the combinations of $P1$ and $P2$ which yield a profit of $120.

A choice of $Z = \$480$ results in the isoprofit line CD. Since this segment occurs outside the feasible solution space, we can assume that no allowable product combination will permit so much profit. It can also be observed that lines AB and CD are parallel. Between these two lines is another parallel line which represents the most profitable mix that conforms to the facility constraints.

Figure 3.3 Objective function

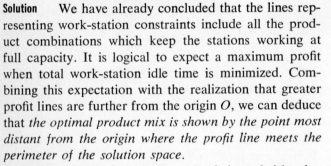

Solution   We have already concluded that the lines representing work-station constraints include all the product combinations which keep the stations working at full capacity. It is logical to expect a maximum profit when total work-station idle time is minimized. Combining this expectation with the realization that greater profit lines are further from the origin O, we can deduce that *the optimal product mix is shown by the point most distant from the origin where the profit line meets the perimeter of the solution space.*

In our example the solution space is bounded by the polygon labeled $OWXYV$ in Fig. 3.4. Each extreme

Figure 3.4 Optimum solution

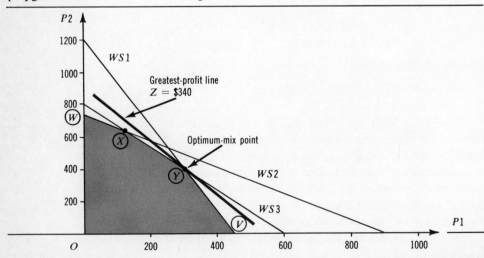

point (O, W, X, Y, or V) is called a *vertex*. The geometry of the polygon indicates the best mix will occur at one of the vertices. Point O can be eliminated immediately; no production permits no profit. Point W would be the best mix only if $P1$ offered no additional profit, and the reverse is true for point V. With only points X and Y left, we see that Y provides the maximum return.

Now the problem is to identify the mix. If the graph were accurately drawn to a large scale, perhaps we could read the mix directly. Another method is to observe which constraints intersect at the selected vertex and solve for the coordinates algebraically. At point Y the constraints are $WS1$ and $WS3$. Then the equations to be solved are

$$8P1 + 3P2 = 3600$$
$$4P1 + 3P2 = 2400$$

Subtracting the first equation from the second, we get

$$4P1 = 1200$$
$$P1 = 300$$

and substituting $P1$ in the first equation,

$$8 \cdot \times 300 + 3P2 = 3600$$
$$3P2 = 3600 - 2400$$
$$P2 = 400$$

which makes the maximum profit

$$Z = \$0.6 \times 300 + \$0.4 \times 400$$
$$= \$180 + \$160 = \$340$$

A close examination of Fig. 3.4 reveals that $WS2$ is partially idle. Checking this by formula, the time consumed in producing the most profitable mix is

$$8 \times 300 + 3 \times 400 = 3600 \text{ min} \qquad \text{for } WS1$$
$$5 \times 300 + 6 \times 400 = 3900 \text{ min} \qquad \text{for } WS2$$
$$4 \times 300 + 3 \times 400 = 2400 \text{ min} \qquad \text{for } WS3$$

Since the time available at $WS2$ is 4500 minutes, the station is idle $4500 - 3900 = 600$ minutes. All three stations would be used to capacity only if the three constraint lines intersected at a single point.

The number of constraints that can be included in a graphical solution is limited only by the drawing space, but the number of products cannot exceed three because we can draw in no more than three dimensions. With three candidates for limited resources, we would have to work with planes and the intersection of planes instead of lines and intersection of lines. For multidimensional problems other methods of solution are available. The *simplex method* is the most widely accepted.[1] We will not pursue this method but will consider special cases of its application in following sections.

The assignment method is employed when a number of operations are to be assigned to an *equal* number of operators with the restriction that *each operator performs only one operation*. The objective is to determine the assignments which maximize the effectiveness of the total allocation. The measure of effectiveness is usually minimum cost or highest profit for a given set of assignments.

The characteristic that one operator is assigned to one operation allows the problem to be stated in the form of a square matrix. If we have three operations (tasks 1, 2, and 3) to be performed and there are three operators available (man 1, man 2, and man 3), we start by delegating the time for each man to perform each task. Assuming that the men are more proficient at some tasks than others, the possible assignments and their respective durations are illustrated in the accompanying table.

	Performance times, min		
Operation	Man 1	Man 2	Man 3
Task 1	20	14	13
Task 2	8	12	9
Task 3	12	8	9

Eliminating the titles and abbreviating the headings from the table above, we have the square matrix shown where the number of rows $(T1, T2, T3)$ equals the number of columns $(M1, M2, M3)$.

SOLUTION PROCEDURE   There are nine cells in the 3×3 matrix above. A matrix of this size allows $3! (1 \times 2 \times 3 = 6)$ possible assignments. We could determine the assignment which takes the least total time by enumer-

	$M1$	$M2$	$M3$
$T1$	20	14	13
$T2$	8	12	9
$T3$	12	8	9

[1]The simplex method was developed by G. B. Danzig in 1947. In no way should "simple" be inferred from "simplex." It is a powerful but complicated tool. Recommended books on the subject are included in the selected references at the end of the chapter.

ating all the possibilities and adding the times for each, as shown in Table 3.2. Enumeration is fairly practical for a problem of this size, but visualize the effort required to solve all the combinations for a 10×10 matrix: $10! = 3,628,800$. Fortunately, there is a much more rapid method of obtaining a solution.

Table 3.2

Number	Assignment (task to man)	Time, min
1	$T1$ to $M1$, $T2$ to $M3$, $T3$ to $M2$	$20 + 9 + 8 = 37$
2	$T1$ to $M1$, $T2$ to $M2$, $T3$ to $M3$	$20 + 12 + 9 = 41$
3	$T1$ to $M2$, $T2$ to $M1$, $T3$ to $M3$	$14 + 8 + 9 = 31$
4	$T1$ to $M2$, $T2$ to $M3$, $T3$ to $M1$	$14 + 9 + 12 = 35$
5	$T1$ to $M3$, $T2$ to $M2$, $T3$ to $M1$	$13 + 12 + 12 = 37$
6	$T1$ to $M3$, $T2$ to $M1$, $T3$ to $M2$	$13 + 8 + 8 = 29$ minimum time

Two-step application   An intuitive approach to an assignment problem is to first check the most attractive allocation for each operation. This natural step is also part of the formal approach to the problem. It is accomplished by subtracting the smallest entry in each row of the matrix from the other entries in the same row. This procedure creates a zero in each row, as illustrated in the sequential steps of Fig. 3.5.

The zeroes show which assignments make the most effective use of resources. Stated another way, the values resulting from the subtraction step represent the difference between the cost that would be realized by utilizing the best assignment and the cost that is obtained by some other assignment. This is called *opportunity cost*. Thus a zero indicates *no* opportunity cost for a specific assignment, because that assignment is the best operation-operator combination that conforms to the constraints of the problem. All other values represent the relative opportunity costs for nonoptimal assignments.

The location of the zeroes in the example matrix immediately discloses the solution. There is one and only one zero in each row and each column. Therefore the opportunity costs are minimum if the tasks are matched to the men in accordance with the zero indicators:

Zero at $T1, M3$ indicates task 1 to man 3

Zero at $T2, M1$ indicates task 2 to man 1

Zero at $T3, M2$ indicates task 3 to man 2

This allocation of work is, of course, the same as that obtained by enumeration.

Figure 3.5   Row opportunity costs

	M1	M2	M3
$T1$	20	14	**13**
$T2$	**8**	12	9
$T3$	12	**8**	9

(a) Smallest entry in each row

	M1	M2	M3
$T1$	7	1	0
$T2$	0	4	1
$T3$	4	0	1

(b) Difference after subtracting smallest entry in each row

Four-step application   Now we will make the problem a little less obvious by designating different wages for the men involved. By pegging the hourly wages at $1.50, $2.00, and $3.00 for $M1$, $M2$, and $M3$, respectively, the time matrix becomes the cost matrix shown in Fig. 3.6. The conversion results from multiplying the time required for each task by the appropriate wage of the operator.

When we compare the relative advantages of different men for the different tasks, we see that $M2$ is the least expensive operator for both $T1$ and $T3$. This conflict means no assignments are apparent after the first row subtraction (Fig. 3.7a).

The next step is to subtract the smallest value in each column from all other values in the column. This step is equivalent to finding the opportunity costs for the men not assigned to their "best"| task. It results in a zero appearing in each column, as well as the zero in each row from the previous step (Fig. 3.7b).

At this stage we can again check the matrix to see if we have a solution. This is accomplished by drawing and counting the *minimum* number of lines necessary to cover all the zeroes in the matrix. The lines may be either horizontal or vertical, but not diagonal. There are usually several ways the same number of lines can be drawn to cover all the zeroes. The placement is unimportant as long as the minimum number are employed. When the total number of lines is equal to the number of rows or columns, an optimal assignment can be made. Figure 3.7c shows this condition to be true for the example.

Having an optimal solution does not imply that there is only one possible way to make the assignment. There may be a choice of several alternatives, each one resulting in a minimum opportunity cost. When multiple equal-cost alternatives are available, the question becomes which one to select. It may be that there are influencing factors which were not included in the cost entries of the initial matrix, such as seniority, personality traits, prestige, quality, convenience, or coordination with other activities. To decide the final assignment, first assign the facilities for which there is no choice, and then randomly or selectively make the remaining allocations until each row and column has one and only one assignment.

In Fig. 3.7b there is a single zero in the $M1$ column

Figure 3.6   3 × 3 cost matrix

	M1	M2	M3
T1	$0.50	$0.47	$0.65
T2	$0.20	$0.40	$0.45
T3	$0.30	$0.27	$0.45

Figure 3.7   Solution procedures and check

	M1	M2	M3
T1	.03	0	.18
T2	0	.20	.25
T3	.03	0	.18

(a)   Row subtraction

	M1	M2	M3
T1	.03	0	0
T2	0	.20	.07
T3	.03	0	0

(b)   Column subtraction

	M1	M2	M3
T1	.03	0	0
T2	0	.20	.07
T3	.03	0	0

(c)   Minimum lines

Figure 3.8   Reduced matrix

	M2	M3
T1	0	0
T3	0	0

(a)   Zero indicators

	M2	M3
T1	$0.47	$0.65
T3	$0.27	$0.45

(b)   Initial costs

at $T2$. Therefore $T2$ and $M1$ must be matched. Removing the column ($M1$) and row ($T2$) corresponding to this assignment, we have the reduced matrix of Fig. 3.8. Since both the remaining rows and columns contain more than one zero, we have a choice of assignments. Regardless of which task is assigned to which man, the total cost will be the same. Other factors can sway the choice of alternatives in Table 3.3 without affecting the optimal solution. The minimum cost for the problem is $0.20 + $0.92 = $1.12.

Table 3.3

Assignment	Cost
$T1$ to $M2$, $T3$ to $M3$	$0.47 + $0.45 = $0.92
$T1$ to $M3$, $T3$ to $M2$	$0.27 + $0.65 = $0.92

The complete procedure for the assignment method is outlined in the flow chart of Fig. 3.9. A solution was obtained for the 3×3 problem just completed at Step 4 because three lines were required to cover all the zeroes.

Figure 3.9 Flow chart of solution steps for the assignment method

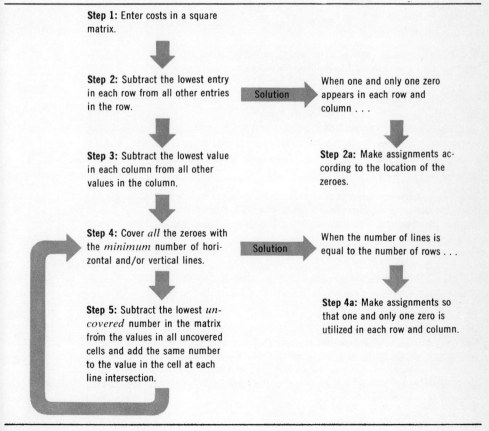

Step 1: Enter costs in a square matrix.

Step 2: Subtract the lowest entry in each row from all other entries in the row.

Solution → When one and only one zero appears in each row and column . . .

Step 2a: Make assignments according to the location of the zeroes.

Step 3: Subtract the lowest value in each column from all other values in the column.

Step 4: Cover *all* the zeroes with the *minimum* number of horizontal and/or vertical lines.

Solution → When the number of lines is equal to the number of rows . . .

Step 4a: Make assignments so that one and only one zero is utilized in each row and column.

Step 5: Subtract the lowest *uncovered* number in the matrix from the values in all uncovered cells and add the same number to the value in the cell at each line intersection.

When fewer zero-covering lines are necessary than there are rows in the matrix, the solution must be carried through Step 5. After conducting the program for this step, the matrix is again checked to see if the number of lines is equal to the number of rows. If not, the cycle Step 4–Step 5–Step 4 is repeated until the conditions for a final solution are obtained.

Five-step application   Another example will be used to illustrate all the solution steps.

Figure 3.10

	M1	M2	M3	M4
J1	12	9	11	13
J2	8	8	9	6
J3	14	16	21	13
J4	14	15	17	12

(a)

Step 1: The initial costs are displayed in Fig. 3.10a. There are four jobs with four machines capable of handling any one of them.

	M1	M2	M3	M4
J1	3	0	2	4
J2	2	2	3	0
J3	1	3	8	0
J4	2	3	5	0

(b)

Step 2: Row subtraction in Fig. 3.10b reveals that three of the jobs are most suitable for machine 4. This conflict eliminates a solution at Step 2.

	M1	M2	M3	M4
J1	2	0	0	4
J2	1	2	1	0
J3	0	3	6	0
J4	1	3	3	0

(c)

Step 3: Subtracting the lowest value in each column gives the opportunity costs with respect to the machines. All columns and rows contain at least one zero after Step 3 is completed.

	M1	M2	M3	M4
J1	2	0	0	4
J2	1	2	1	0
J3	0	3	6	0
J4	1	3	3	0

(d)

Step 4: A check is made in Fig. 3.10d to see if a solution has been obtained. Only three lines are required to cover all the zeroes. Because it is a 4 × 4 matrix, no solution has been obtained. We can verify this conclusion by trying to make an assignment. M4 is indicated as the "best" machine for both J2 and J4. Since no alternatives are available, we must proceed to Step 5.

	M1	M2	M3	M4
J1	3	0	0	5
J2	1	1	0	0
J3	0	2	5	0
J4	1	2	2	0

(e)

Step 5: The smallest uncovered value in the matrix is number 1 at J2, M3. This number, 1, is subtracted from all uncovered numbers including itself. Then 1 is added to all values that appear at line intersections. In the top left cell, number 2 is changed to 3, and in the top right cell number 4 goes to 5.

	M1	M2	M3	M4
J1	3	0	0	5
J2	1	1	0	0
J3	0	2	5	0
J4	1	2	2	0

(f)

Step 4 (repeated): Again a check is made to see if the manipulations of Step 5 have resulted in a solution. Step 4 is repeated. Now there is no way to cover all the zeroes with less than four lines.

	M1	M2	M3
J1	3	0	0
J2	1	1	0
J3	0	2	5

(g)

Step 4a: The final solution is obtained by making specific assignments. In Fig. 3.10f there is only one line (J4) that has just one zero. (We could also have investigated the columns and found unique assignments in columns M1 and M2; the order in which assignments are made does not affect the final solution.) This means that job 4 must be assigned to machine 4. With J4 and M4 eliminated from the problem, the matrix is reduced to 3 × 3, as shown in Fig. 3.10g.

	M1	M2
J1	3	0
J3	0	2

(h)

Here there are two lines with only one zero. Choosing line 2, we can assign J2 to M3. This assignment reduces the matrix to 2 × 2 where the apparent assignments are J1 to M2 and J3 to M1.

In this problem there is only one optimal assignment. No other allocation of jobs to machines can minimize costs. The total opportunity cost associated with an optimal assignment is, of course, zero. From the original cost matrix we can calculate the total cost to be

Assignment	J1 to M2	J2 to M3	J3 to M1	J4 to M4	
Total cost	$9	$9	$14	$12	= $44

In practice it is not necessary to rewrite the matrix repeatedly or to develop reduced matrices; this was done in the examples to give clarity to the presentation. **Additional alternatives** Occasionally a situation arises in which there are more facilities or operators than there are operations to be performed. The assignment method may be used to determine which facilities should be utilized.

Assume that an extra machine is added to the four available for the situation illustrated in Fig. 3.10. We will designate the new machine as $M5$. This machine could represent an anticipated purchase, the expected performance of an old machine after an extensive overhaul, or other special circumstances. The cost of completing each task on the new machine must either be known or estimated.

With five machines and only four jobs, the matrix is no longer square. This condition is alleviated by introducing a "dummy" job called JD. The dummy is an artificial device required to balance allocations — one job to one machine. We can force an assignment to the dummy job by using all zero costs for its row in the matrix. By this maneuver we regain a square matrix and express our indifference as to which machine is assigned to the dummy job. The machine thus assigned is clearly the least desirable for the given tasks. Figure 3.11 shows the matrix of Fig. 3.10 revised to include the new machine $M5$ and the dummy job JD.

Progressing through Step 5 of the solution steps, we find the optimal solution shown in Fig. 3.11b; machine 3 is eliminated. The total cost for the four jobs becomes $9 + 6 + 14 + 10 = 39$. This cost is a reduction of \$5 from the previous assignment based on the original four machines. The next step would be to decide if the required investment for $M5$ is justified in terms of the savings for the current and expected work.

SPECIAL CASES OF THE ASSIGNMENT METHOD A problem involving profits instead of costs is easily transformed to a cost matrix by subtracting all the numbers in the payoff matrix from the largest profit in any cell. The net effect is to convert all the entries to "relative costs," and the problem becomes one of minimizing costs. It can then be solved by the procedures already described. After the optimal assignment has been identified, the payoff can be obtained from the original profit entries for the cells to which assignments have been made.

If a given operation should not be assigned to a certain operator for special reasons, the assignment can be blocked by entering a very large cost in the appropriate cell.

Figure 3.11 Assignment method for dummy operators

	M1	M2	M3	M4	M5
J1	12	9	11	13	11
J2	8	8	9	6	7
J3	14	16	21	13	15
J4	14	15	17	12	10
JD	0	0	0	0	0

(a) Original matrix with dummy added

	M1	M2	M3	M4	M5
J1	3	0	2	5	2
J2	1	1	2	0	0
J3	0	2	7	0	1
J4	4	5	7	3	0
JD	0	0	0	1	0

(b) Solution for the added alternative

The assignment method is a special case of the transportation method which will be described in the next section. Some of the restrictions on the assignment method are relaxed in the more general transportation method, but when condtions permit the use of the assignment approach, it can usually be solved with less effort.

A transportation model is used to assign quantities of a *single commodity* from various *origins* to certain *destinations*. The objective is to identify the transportation routes which result in minimum costs or maximum profit. To achieve this objective we must know the amount and location of the available supplies and the quantities demanded. In addition, a value (usually a cost) must be determined for the effort required to transport supplies from their origin to their destination. With this information the transportation technique leads to a program which satisfies the supply-and-demand relationships with a minimum expense. It can be applied to the allocation of raw materials, finished products, personnel, capital, or any other resource problem that fits the program.

The solution to a transportation problem involves an iterative routine — repeated calculation cycles which lead to an optimal solution. This routine is shown in Fig. 3.12. After developing a feasible solution in Step 3,

Figure 3.12 Flow chart for the transportation method

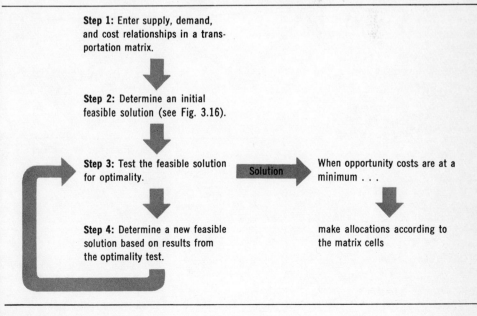

Step 1: Enter supply, demand, and cost relationships in a transportation matrix.

Step 2: Determine an initial feasible solution (see Fig. 3.16).

Step 3: Test the feasible solution for optimality.

Solution

When opportunity costs are at a minimum . . .

Step 4: Determine a new feasible solution based on results from the optimality test.

make allocations according to the matrix cells

it is tested in Step 4 to see if it is an optimal solution. When no lower cost alternatives are discovered, the problem is completed. But if cost-reduction alternatives are disclosed, a new solution must be developed and tested. The Step 3–Step 4–Step 3 iteration is repeated until the superior supply-demand linkage is identified.

TRANSPORTATION MATRIX   A typical transportation problem is represented in Fig. 3.13. Quantities of a certain commodity are available from three warehouses (origins). Each warehouse can ship to any plant (destination). In this example we will assume that the supply available in the warehouses equals the total demand of the plants. Transportation charges are a function of the distance from an origin to a destination. The objective is to minimize shipping costs.

The information mapped in Fig. 3.13a is displayed in the transportation matrix of Fig. 3.13b. Each row represents an origin and each column a destination. The

Figure 3.13

Origins	Warehouses $W1$, $W2$, $W3$, shown as triangles
Destinations	Plants $P1$, $P2$, $P3$, $P4$, shown as circles
Supply	20 units at $W1$, 14 units at $W2$, 30 units at $W3$
Demand	16 units at $P1$ and $P2$, 24 units at $P3$, 8 units at $P4$
Costs	Transportation charge per unit shown on arrows

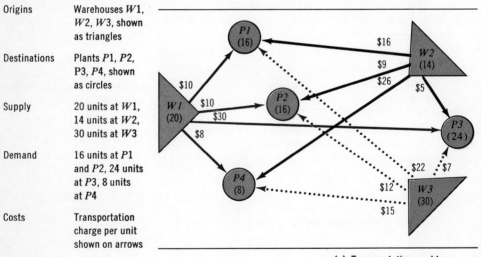

(a) Transportation problem

Destination

Origin	$P1$	$P2$	$P3$	$P4$	Total units avail.
$W1$	10	10	30	8	20
$W2$	16	9	5	26	14
$W3$	22	12	7	15	30
Total units req.	16	16	24	8	64 / 64

(b) Transportation matrix

cell at the intersection of each row and column includes the transportation cost to link that origin-destination. The cost is shown in the upper left corner of the cell. The remaining space in the cell will be utilized to allocate supplies.

Quantities available from the warehouses are shown in the far right column. Plant requirements are noted in the bottom line. These conditions are usually referred to as *rim requirements*. Our problem now crystallizes to the identification of the minimum cost program which satisfies rim requirements.

CONDITIONS FOR A FEASIBLE SOLUTION   The next step (Step 2 from the flow chart) is to develop an initial feasible solution. This is accomplished by allocating quantities in a manner that (1) satisfies the rim requirements, (2) with the number of allocations equal to one less than the number of origins plus the number of destinations $(O + D - 1)$ so that (3) the allocations are in independent positions. The significance of these feasibility conditions will be developed later. In the meantime, we can see how to check a solution to be sure it meets the conditions.

A cell in the transportation matrix is said to be *occupied* if it contains an entry which represents the transfer of a commodity from an origin to a destination. An occupied cell thus shows a quantity which could be shipped from a given supply to satisfy a given demand. The quantity must not exceed either the supply available or the demand requirement. This is checked by summing vertically and horizontally the entries in occupied cells and then comparing the sums to the rim requirements.

Noting the number of occupied cells provides a quick check on whether the total number of entries is exactly one less than the sum of the number of rows and columns.

The independent positions of the entries are tested by attempting a round trip from each allocation back to itself. The trip can be made only by horizontal or vertical movements between occupied cells. If such a round trip is *impossible* without a direct reversal of the traveled route, the positions are independent.

In Fig. 3.14a the occupied cells (denoted by an X) are not in independent positions. The loop $(O2, D2)$-$(O2, D3)$-$(O3, D2)$-$(O3, D3)$ allows an orthogonal passage from a starting cell back to itself. Otherwise, the matrix shows a feasible solution because there are $3 + 4 - 1 = 6$ occupied cells with entries in agreement with the rim requirements.

Altering the allocations to the positions shown in Fig. 3.14b, we have a feasible solution. There are still six allocations in conformance to the rim requirements, and their positions are independent.

Figure 3.14 Test for independent positions

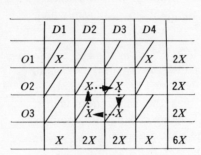

(a) Nonindependent

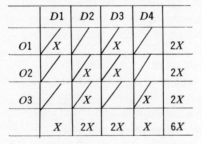

(b) Independent

OBTAINING AN INITIAL FEASIBLE SOLUTION   The intent in formulating an initial allocation is to approach as nearly as possible the optimal solution. The iterative procedure for elevating an initial solution to an optimal solution is often exhausting, hence effort is well spent in bettering the initial solution.

Inspection method   The inspection method is an informal approach based on judgment. It is rapid and works well for problems of limited size. Since the aim is to produce *both* a feasible and a low-cost solution, the first allocation is given to the cell with the lowest transportation cost. This cell is given the largest allocation that adheres to the rim requirements. Then the next-lowest-cost cell is given its maximum allocation, and the procedure is continued until there are $O + D - 1$ occupied cells. In case of a tie between lowest-cost cells, judgment decides the issue.

In applying the inspection method to the sample

problem shown in Fig. 3.13*b*, we see the lowest transportation cost is $5 per unit at cell $W2, P3$. The rim requirements reveal that plant 3 requires 24 units, but warehouse 2 has only 14 units available. Consequently, an entry of 14 units is placed in the cell to allocate all the capacity of $W2$ to $P3$.

The next lowest cost is $7 per unit at cell $W3, P3$. With 30 units available from $W3$ and $24 - 14 = 10$ units still required for plant 3, 10 units are allocated to the cell. At this point the supply from $W2$ is exhausted and the demand from $P3$ is satiated.

Eight units are allocated to cell $W1, P4$, where the unit shipping cost is $8 per unit. Now the lowest cost for an unoccupied cell is $9 per unit at $W2, P2$, but we cannot take advantage of it because there are no units left in $W2$.

A choice is available for the next allocation. A $10-per-unit cost is apparent in cells $W1, P1$ and $W1, P2$. The choice is resolved by looking ahead to the remaining requirements. The last allocations must come from $W3$ to fulfill the demands from $P1$ and $P2$. Since $W3, P2$ has a lower cost per unit than $W3, P1$, the current allocation should go to $W1, P1$.

The order of entries are repeated in the matrix shown in Fig. 3.15 as boldface numbers in the occupied cells. Entries 5 and 6 were largely routine, as there was little choice left for fulfilling the rim requirements. The six entries ($3 + 4 - 1 = 6$) in independent positions make it a feasible solution.

The shipping costs are shown as an extra rim on the bottom and right of the matrix. These costs are the product of the number of units shipped and the charge per unit. The total shipping cost for this initial solution is $604.

Figure 3.15 Initial feasible solution by inspection

	P1	P2	P3	P4		Shipping costs
W1	10 / **4** / 12	10	30	8 / **3** / 8	20	$184 = 12 × $10 + 8 × $8
W2	16	9	5 / **1** / 14	26	14	$ 70 = 14 × $5
W3	22 / **6** / 4	12 / **5** / 16	7 / **2** / 10	15	30	$350 = 4 × $22 + 10 × $7 + 16 × $12
	16	16	24	8		

$208 + $192 + $140 + $64 = $604   total cost

Vogel's approximation method   Vogel's approximation method (VAM) is a more formal approach to an initial solution than the inspection method. It is based on the concept of assigning a penalty for *not* selecting the lowest-cost routes. The goal is to make allocations in a manner that avoids the greatest penalties.

The mechanics for VAM are shown in the procedure steps of Fig. 3.16. After setting up the transportation matrix, the difference between the smallest and the second-smallest cost in each row and each column is calculated. The differences are the penalties. To avoid the heaviest penalty, we make an allocation to the row or column which shows the greatest difference. The allocation is made to the cell that has the lowest cost in that row or column. This procedure is repeated until a feasible initial solution is obtained.

Figure 3.16 Steps for applying Vogel's approximation method

Step 1: Determine the difference between the two smallest costs in each row and column.

Step 2: Select the row or column with the greatest difference (penalty).

Step 3: Make a maximum allocation to the lowest cost cell in the selected row or column.

Step 4: Eliminate the row or column when allocations meet rim requirements.

Solution

When rim requirements are satisfied.

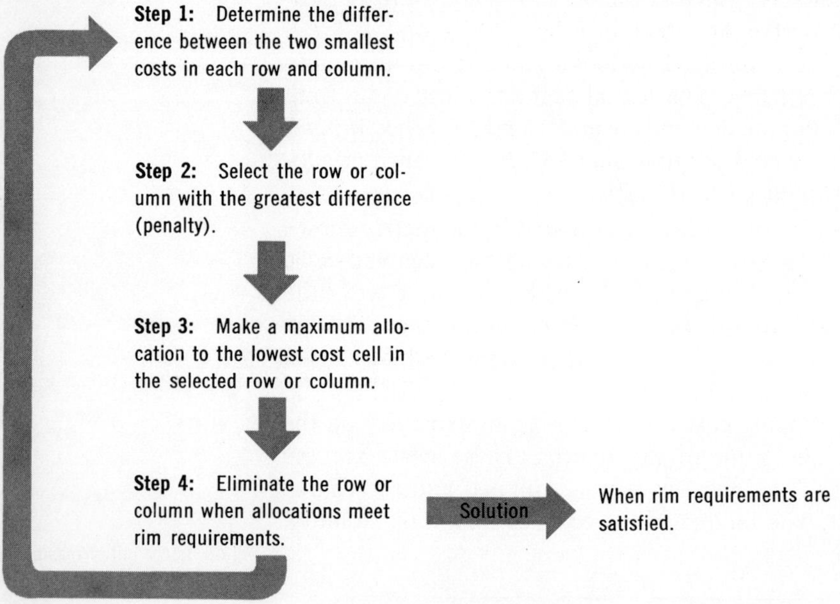

A detailed application of VAM is given in Fig. 3.17. Two matrices are shown for each step in the procedure: a penalty matrix and an allocation matrix. As the solution develops, the penalty matrix is reduced in size, and entries in the allocation matrix approach rim requirements. Repeated drawings of the matrices are not necessary; they are presented here for clarity of application. The same results can be obtained by crossing off columns or rows as they meet rim requirements and

(a) First penalty and first allocation (* represents greatest penalty)

	P1	P2	P3	P4	Pen.
W1	10	10	30	8	2
W2	16	9	5	26	4
W3	22	12	7	15	5
Pen.	6	1	2	7*	

Figure 3.17 Initial feasible solution by VAM

	P1	P2	P3	P4	Avail.
W1				8	20/12
W2					14
W3					30
Req.	16	16	24	8/0	

(b) Reduced penalty matrix and second allocation

	P1	P2	P3	Pen.
W1	10	10	30	0
W2	16	9	5	4
W3	22	12	7	5
Pen.	6*	1	2	

	P1	P2	P3	P4	Avail.
W1	12			8	12/0
W2					14
W3					30
Req.	16/4	16	24		

(c) Reduced penalty matrix and third allocation

	P1	P2	P3	Pen.
W2	16	9	5	4
W3	22	12	7	5
Pen.	6*	3	2	

	P1	P2	P3	P4	Avail.
W1	12			8	0
W2	4				14/10
W3					30
Req.	4/0	16	24	0	

(d) Reduced penalty matrix and fourth allocation

	P2	P3	Pen.
W2	9	5	4
W3	12	7	5*
Pen.	3	2	

	P1	P2	P3	P4	Avail.
W1	12			8	0
W2	4				10
W3			24		30/6
Req.	0	16	24/0	0	

(e) Final allocations and shipping costs

	P1	P2	P3	P4		Shipping costs
W1	10/12	10/	30/	8/8	20	$184 = 12 × $10 + 8 × $8
W2	16/4	9/10	5/	26/	14	$154 = 4 × $16 + 9 × $10
W3	22/	12/6	7/24	15/	30	$240 = 6 × $12 + 24 × $7
	16	16	24	8		

$184 + $162 + $168 + $64 = $578   total cost

reworking penalty calculations to conform to the remaining costs for supplies and demands.

In the example problem only one penalty was maximum at each stage of the reduced matrices. When two or more penalties tie for the maximum rating, an arbitrary selection breaks the tie. The final reduction results in a 1×2 matrix (not shown in Fig. 3.17). The allocations at this stage must complete the rim requirements. In our problem $P2$ still required 16 units. This demand was met by shipping as many units as possible at $10 per unit from $W2$ and allocating the remainder $(16 - 10 = 6)$ to $W3$. The resulting six allocations are in independent positions.

The initial solution developed by VAM is slightly different from the one made by inspection. The total shipping cost of $578 is an improvement of $604 − $578 = $26 over the inspection method. Now we must test this improved feasible solution to see if it is an optimal allocation.

TEST FOR AN OPTIMAL SOLUTION   Step 3 of the transportation method is to test the feasible solution obtained in Step 2 to see if it is the least-cost allocation. A secondary function of the test is to indicate where the allocation can be improved if the solution is not optimal. This information is obtained by determining an opportunity cost for each of the unoccupied cells.

An unoccupied cell represents a routing which is not being used in the solution. If a unit is transferred to this cell and the transfer results in a positive opportunity cost, an optimal solution has not yet been obtained. A lower-cost allocation will result from including this cell in a revised solution. When an opportunity cost is zero, it means there is an equal-cost alternative solution.

A choice of routes then depends on other management considerations which may not have been included in the original statement of the problem.

Let us now test the initial solution of the example problem for optimality. We can begin with any unoccupied cell. Choosing cell $W1, P2$, one unit is allocated as shown in Fig. 3.18. This allocation violates the rim requirements, so we must deduct one unit from the original allocations in row $W1$ and column $P2$. Subtracting one unit from $W2, P2$ adjusts the demand for $P2$ but causes a shortage in row $W2$. Adding one unit to $W2, P1$ puts $W2$ in balance and causes a surplus in column $P1$. By deducting one unit from $W1, P1$, we close the loop which compensates for the unit added at $W1, P2$ and maintains the rim requirements.

A transportation cost is associated with each shift of a unit. The cost effect of the shifts is noted in Fig. 3.19. The net cost of all the shifts around the loop is $7 per unit. This increase in cost is a *negative* opportunity cost. Therefore -7 is entered in cell $W1, P2$ to indicate that a loss of $7 would result from shipping one unit by this route compared to the existing allocations.

Figure 3.18 Closed loop for a one-unit shift

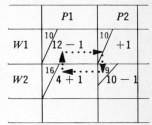

Figure 3.19 Cost of adding one unit to $W1, P2$

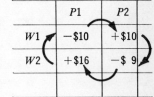

	P1	P2
Adding 1 unit to $W1, P2$		+$10
Deducting 1 unit from $W2, P2$		$-$ 9
Adding 1 unit to $W2, P1$		$+$ 16
Deducting 1 unit from $W1, P2$		$-$ 10
Net cost of change		+$ 7

The procedure for checking the remaining cells is to identify a closed loop from an unoccupied cell back to itself, where right-angle turns are permitted only at occupied cells. Units or their respective costs are alternately added and subtracted at each turn. It is permissible to skip over occupied cells in completing a loop. The resulting one-unit shifts must maintain the rim requirements. The cost of transferring a unit to an unoccupied cell is then the sum of the costs for all units shifted in the loop.

The importance of independent positions for initial allocations should now be apparent. A closed loop of occupied cells (dependent positions) would make it impossible to construct a closed loop from certain unoccupied cells (for instance, try to construct closed loops for any of the unoccupied cells in Fig. 3.14a). No opportunity costs can be calculated for the cells where closed loops are unavailable.

The opportunity costs for all the unoccupied cells in the VAM initial solution are shown in Fig. 3.20. The cells in the closed loops for each opportunity cost are identified in Table 3.4.

	P1	P2	P3	P4	
W1	10 / **12**	10 / −7	30 / −32	8 / **8**	20
W2	16 / **4**	9 / **10**	5 / −1	26 / −12	14
W3	22 / −3	12 / **6**	7 / **24**	15 / +2	30
	16	16	24	8	

Figure 3.20 Opportunity costs for the initial solution

Table 3.4

Unoccupied cell	Closed loop connecting occupied cells	Cost of shifting one unit in the loop	Opportunity cost
$W1, P2$	$W1, P2 - W2, P2 + W2, P1 - W1, P1$	$\$10 - 9 + 16 - 10 = \$7$	− 7
$W1, P3$	$W1, P3 - W3, P3 + W3, P2$ $- W2, P2 + W2, P1 - W1, P1$	$\$30 - 7 + 12 - 9 + 16$ $- 10 = \$32$	−32
$W2, P3$	$W2, P3 - W3, P3 + W3, P2 - W2, P2$	$\$5 - 7 + 12 - 9 = \$1$	− 1
$W2, P4$	$W2, P4 - W2, P1 + W1, P1 - W1, P4$	$\$26 - 16 + 10 - 8 = \$12$	−12
$W3, P1$	$W3, P1 - W2, P1 + W2, P2 - W3, P2$	$\$22 - 16 + 9 - 12 = \$3$	− 3
$W3, P4$	$W3, P4 - W3, P2 + W2, P2$ $- W2, P1, + W1, P1 - W1, P4$	$\$15 - 12 + 9 - 16 + 10$ $- 8 = -\$2$	+ 2

REVISING AND RETESTING THE SOLUTION The positive opportunity cost in cell $W3, P4$ indicates that the initial solution is not optimal. We must revise the solution to include an allocation to this cell. A revised program always includes the cell with the highest opportunity cost.

We know costs can be reduced $2 per unit by involving cell $W3, P4$ in the solution. It is logical to take full advantage of this cost reduction by allocating as many units as possible to $W3, P4$. The maximum number possible is revealed by the closed loop from which the opportunity cost was derived (shown in Fig. 3.21).

The smallest allocation in a negative cell is the limiting number for altering the solution. This number is entered in the unoccupied cell. Then the other alloca-

Figure 3.21 Allocations within a closed loop

	P1	P2	P3	P4	
W1	⊕ 12			⊖ 8	20
W2	⊖ 4	⊕ 10			14
W3		⊖ 6	24	⊕	30
	16	16	24	8	

tions in the loop are changed to conform to the new entry and the rim requirements. The negative cell $W2, P1$ contains the smallest allocation, four units. Therefore, four units are added to the positive cells in the loop and subtracted from the negative cells. The resulting solution is given in Fig. 3.22.

Again it is necessary to test the current solution for optimality. The same procedure as described previously is appropriate. A practical shortcut is to bypass the check for very-high-cost routes. However, any cells with borderline or questionable costs should be tested to assure that no cost-reducing routes are overlooked.

The opportunity costs included in Fig. 3.22 show that the solution obtained by allocating four units to $W3, P4$ is the optimal solution: none of the unoccupied cells has positive opportunity costs. Shipping costs have been reduced by $578 - $570 = $8 through the four-unit shift.

Figure 3.22 Optimal solution and shipping costs

	P1	P2	P3	P4		Shipping costs
W1	10/ 16	10/ −5	30/ −30	8/ 4	20	$192 = 16 × $10 + 4 × $8
W2	16/ −2	9/ 14	5/ −1	26/ −14	14	126 = 14 × $9
W3	22/ −5	12/ 2	7/ 24	15/ 4	30	252 = 2 × $12 + 24 × $7 + 4 × $15
	16	16	24	8		
	$160 +	$150 +	$168 +	$92	= $570	total cost

SPECIAL CONDITIONS **Degeneracy** One of the requirements for a feasible solution is that the occupied cells number one less than the sum of the rows and columns. When this requirement is not met we term the solution *degenerate*.

Degeneracy can occur in an initial solution or in subsequent solutions. In Fig. 3.23 the initial allocation by inspection has resulted in a degenerate solution; there are only three allocations instead of the four $(2 + 3 - 1)$ required. Because there are only three occupied cells, we cannot obtain opportunity costs for the unoccupied cells. No closed loops can be established.

	D1	D2	D3	
O1	3 / 400	4 /	3 /	400
O2	4 /	6 / 300	2 / 300	600
	400	300	300	

Figure 3.23 Degenerate initial solution

We can alleviate this condition by adding an infinitesimal quantity to an unoccupied cell in an independent position with respect to the occupied cells. The quantity, denoted by the Greek letter ε (epsilon), is assumed to be so small that adding or subtracting it from a number does not change that number. Thus

$$1 + \varepsilon = 1 = 1 - \varepsilon$$

However, a cell is treated as occupied when allocated an ε quantity even though the rim requirements do not reflect its presence.

An infinitesimal quantity has been added to cell $O1, D2$ in Fig. 3.24a. When this feasible solution (four occupied cells in independent positions) is tested, the closed loop from $O2, D1$ reveals a positive opportunity cost. Shifting 300 units to this cell provides the optimal solution shown in Fig. 3.24b.

Figure 3.24 Degenerate to feasible to optimal solution

	D1	D2	D3	
O1	3 / 400 ⊖	4 / ε ⊕	3 / −3	400
O2	4 / ⊕	6 / 300 ⊖	2 / 300	600
	400	300	300	

(a) Feasible initial solution by adding ε

	D1	D2	D3	
O1	3 / 100	4 / 300	3 / −2	400
O2	4 / 300	6 / −1	2 / 300	600
	400	300	300	

(b) Revised and tested solution

Unequal supply and demand   It is quite possible that the quantities available in a transportation model do not equal the quantities required. This situation is handled by adding a dummy origin or destination. The optimal solution identifies the requirement which cannot be satisfied or the location of available supplies which remain unused.

When supply is greater than demand, a *dummy destination* is included in the matrix. The cost of shipping from each origin to this destination is zero. The excess supply is entered as a rim requirement for the dummy destination.

A *dummy origin* is added to the matrix when requirements are greater than the supplies available. Again the costs associated with dummy shipments are assumed to be zero. The rim quantity assigned to the dummy origin balances total supply to total demand.

Maximization   Profit maximization for the transportation method is conducted in the same manner as the assignment method. "Relative costs" are calculated by subtracting the payoff (profit received by shipping from a given origin to a given destination) for every cell from the largest payoff in the matrix. Then the solution is determined by finding the optimal allocations for minimizing relative costs. The total profit from the allocations is calculated by transforming the relative costs back to their original payoff values.

SELECTED REFERENCES

Chung, A. M.: *Linear Programming*, Charles E. Merril Books, Inc., Columbus, Ohio, 1963.

Dantzig, G. B.: *Linear Programming and Extensions*, Princeton University Press, Princeton, N.J., 1963.

Ferguson, R. O., and L. F. Sargent: *Linear Programming: Fundamentals and Applications*, McGraw-Hill Book Company, New York, 1958.

Garvin, W. W.: *Introduction to Linear Programming*, McGraw-Hill Book Company, New York, 1960.

Graves, R. L., and P. Wolfe: *Recent Advances in Mathematical Programming*, McGraw-Hill Book Company, New York, 1963.

Loomba, N. P.: *Linear Programming: An Introductory Analysis*, McGraw-Hill Book Company, New York, 1964.

Saaty, T. L.: *Mathematical Methods of Operations Research*, McGraw-Hill Book Company, New York, 1959.

Sasieni, M., A. Yaspan and L. Friedman: *Operations Research: Methods and Problems*, John Wiley & Sons., Inc., New York, 1960.

Shuchman, A.: *Scientific Decision-making in Business*, Holt, Rinehart and Winston, Inc., New York, 1963.

PROBLEMS

3.1 The *XYZ* company makes two models of a certain product, *M*1 and *M*2. Each *M*1 contributes a $90 profit and each *M*2 contributes $70. Both models pass through the same assembly areas, *A*1 and *A*2, where 200 hours are available in each. *M*1 requires 40 hours in each assembly area. *M*2 requires 20 hours in *A*1 and 50 hours in *A*2. What is the optimum product mix?

3.2 A firm is faced with a shortage of raw materials. It has 1 ton of material *A* on hand, 3 tons of material *B*, and 4 tons of material *C*. All materials have the same cost. The two products produced which require these raw materials are *P*1 and *P*2. The requirement and profit associated with one unit of each product are shown in the following table:

| Product | Profit | Lb of material per unit | | |
		A	*B*	*C*
*P*1	$4	2	3	4
*P*2	$7	1.5	6	10

What is the best combination to produce and how much profit will the mix provide?

3.3 What mixture of the two types of livestock feed shown in the following table should be purchased to provide the least expensive blend that will satisfy minimum daily requirements of the animals?

Ingredients	% ingredient per lb of feed		Minimal daily requirement, lb
	F1	F2	
I1	20	15	2
I2	0	25	1
I3	25	0	1.5
I4	20	30	3
Cost per lb	$0.15	$0.40	

3.4 Given the matrix below, obtain an optimal assignment:

	C1	C2	C3	C4	C5	C6	C7
R1			0		0		
R2			0			0	
R3	0	0	0				0
R4					0		
R5		0			0	0	
R6	0	0					
R7		0		0			0

3.5 Five workers $(W1, \ldots, W5)$ are available to work with the machines given in the matrix below. The entries in the matrix indicate the costs associated with each worker-machine assignment. X indicates that a worker cannot work on the indicated machine. Mn is a machine designed to replace one of the existing machines. The problem is to find the best combination of machines and the optimal worker assignment. What is the total cost of this assignment?

	M1	M2	M3	M4	M5	Mn
W1	12	3	6	X	5	9
W2	4	11	X	5	X	3
W3	8	2	10	9	7	5
W4	X	7	8	6	12	10
W5	5	8	9	4	6	X

3.6 A new office building has been constructed to allow centralization of administrative functions. Six regional managers will be moved to the new central location. All the offices for the managers are on the same floor. Each office has the same room area and furnishings, but the exposures and views differ. In order to please as many of the managers as possible, the managers were asked to rank their preferences for offices, with 6 being the most desirable and 1 the least desirable. The following rankings were submitted:

Office

Manager		A	B	C	D	E	F
	P	4	2	5	1	3	6
	Q	1	3	5	2	4	6
	R	3	5	6	2	1	4
	S	2	4	6	1	3	5
	T	5	2	6	4	1	3
	U	1	6	3	5	2	4

Determine the assignment which will provide the most overall satisfaction.

3.7 The cell entries in three transportation problems below represent shipping costs per unit transported. Determine the optimal allocations.

a

	D1	D2	D3	D4	D5	D6	
O1	2	1	4	0	1	2	18
O2	3	2	0	4	2	5	23
O3	1	3	3	5	3	0	6
	8	6	6	10	7	10	

b

	D1	D2	D3	D4	
O1	80	120	60	30	290
O2	40	80	80	110	480
O3	120	20	40	50	180
O4	20	60	70	40	350
O5	30	50	70	30	200
	400	200	800	100	

c	D1	D2	D3	
O1	1	4	2	6
O2	2	1	3	4
O3	2	2	2	7
O4	4	3	1	5
O5	5	4	1	6
O6	1	3	5	7
	11	9	10	

3.8 A fishing fleet has four different types of boats. One boat will be assigned to each of four fishing areas. The expected catch (in tons) during a limited season is shown below for boats 1, 2, 3, and 4 in areas A, B, C, and D. What should the assignment be to maximize profit? For this assignment, what is the expected total catch?

Area

Boat		A	B	C	D
	1	60	90	40	100
	2	120	100	80	110
	3	50	70	40	60
	4	180	100	110	140

3.9 Orders for crates of produce have been received by a wholesaler from markets in the five cities shown below:

Cities	Number of crates ordered
Centerville	95
Podunk	65
Riverside	80
Webster City	195
Johnstown	135

The wholesaler has produce available at these locations:

Locations	L1	L2	L3
Crates available	200	115	255

The produce is to be hauled in the wholesaler's trucks. Adequate trucks are available at each storage location. The distance in miles between the markets and storage locations are shown in the matrix below. What shipping program should be used?

	L1	L2	L3
Centerville	50	46	58
Podunk	85	64	69
Riverside	100	120	95
Webster City	95	55	80
Johnstown	95	65	75

3.10 An airline operating in Alaska has several types of planes at its disposal from which to choose. Present demands require the delivery of freight to the following locations:

Location	L1	L2	L3	L4
Tonnage	13	9	6	21

The matrix below gives tonnage capacity of each plane and the expected profit per ton carried to the given location. X indicates it is not possible for that plane to fly to that particular location owing to runway size. What is the maximum profit?

	L1	L2	L3	L4	
P1	X	7	60	40	10
P2	30	50	50	0	8
P3	40	50	50	20	9
P4	−20	0	X	−20	15
P5	50	60	50	30	7

3.11 Four factories supply five market areas. The annual capacities of the factories and the yearly expected demands from each of the market areas are as noted:

Factory	F1	F2	F3	F4	
Capacity	2000	1500	3000	1500	

Market	M1	M2	M3	M4	M5
Demand	700	1200	2000	1800	500

The cost of shipping one unit to each of the market areas is shown in the following cost matrix in cents per unit:

	F1	F2	F3	F4
M1	6	7	6	9
M2	8	7	6	7
M3	7	8	5	6
M4	10	9	6	6
M5	5	8	7	5

What percent of capacity should be utilized in each of the factories to provide the lowest-cost satisfaction of market demands? Where should the products from each factory be sent? What is the total shipping cost?

Chapter Four
Scheduling
of
Resources

After resources have been allocated to specific operations, the next step is coordination. Resources (men,
money, materials, and machines) are required to perform an activity. Activities follow each other in some
sequence set by constraints of the work environment.
For the work to be completed economically and on
time, the resources have to be matched to the activities.
The coordination of resource availability with a set
sequence for the activities to which the resources have
been allocated is the art of scheduling.

Industrial scheduling has received a lot of attention
in recent years. Many new techniques have been developed, but it is well recognized that much more work is
needed before the "art" is converted to a "science." We
will consider two categories of scheduling: project and
job shop. *Project scheduling* involves a large number
of activities which are related by a required order of

completion. Complications result from limited resource availability and the need to monitor progress for control of the project duration. *Job-shop scheduling* is concerned with the routing of jobs in a certain order through a series of work centers. Elapsed time is the measure of effectiveness in job sequencing.

The transformation of raw materials into finished products usually entails several operations. These operations must follow a given sequence. Because of limited resources, similar operations required for several products may be performed at the same work station. This condition imposes the problem of selecting a preferred order for products passing through the station. The magnitude of the problem becomes truly impressive when there are several work stations serving many products.

Consider a case in which there are five work stations (A, B, C, D, and E) and five products (1, 2, 3, 4, and 5) which are processed in the stations. Each product has a set order for processing, such as

Product 1	A-B-C-D-E
Product 2	B-E-D-C-A
Product 3	B-A-D-C-A
Product 4	D-B-E-A-C
Product 5	A-E-C-B-D

The time required by each product in each work station is known and is independent of the work-station–product sequence. The criterion is to select the sequence of products through the work stations that minimizes the total processing time. If we were to solve this problem by enumeration, we would have to evaluate $(5!)^5 = 25,000,000,000$ sequences. The time required prohibits this approach. Many special routines have been developed to deal with specific conditions, but unfortunately, sequencing models have not been generalized to the extent of other models we have encountered. We will explore two cases in which satisfactory solution techniques are currently available.

PROCESSING n JOBS THROUGH TWO FACILITIES The solution method for this sequencing situation is often referred to as Johnson's rule.[1] Specifically, it applies to a situation in which there are any number of jobs, n, which are

[1] S. M. Johnson, "Optimal Two- and Three-stage Production Schedules with Setup Times Included," *Naval Research Logistics Quarterly*, vol. 1, March, 1954.

processed by only two work stations. All jobs follow the same order from the first facility to the second. The processing time for each job in each facility is assumed to be known and is not affected by jobs which follow it or precede it. The sequence which minimizes the elapsed time from the beginning of the first job to the end of the last job is identified by the procedure shown in Fig. 4.1.

Figure 4.1 Flow chart for processing n jobs through two facilities

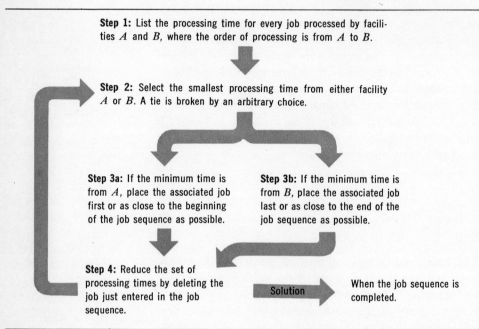

Step 1: List the processing time for every job processed by facilities A and B, where the order of processing is from A to B.

Step 2: Select the smallest processing time from either facility A or B. A tie is broken by an arbitrary choice.

Step 3a: If the minimum time is from A, place the associated job first or as close to the beginning of the job sequence as possible.

Step 3b: If the minimum time is from B, place the associated job last or as close to the end of the job sequence as possible.

Step 4: Reduce the set of processing times by deleting the job just entered in the job sequence.

Solution

When the job sequence is completed.

EXAMPLE 4.1 Application of Johnson's rule

Four reports are to be prepared for reproduction in the typing pool and then sent to the printing plant. The report preparation time varies according to length and content. Printing time is a function of the number of copies printed. Processing times, in hours, are as follows:

Report	A	B	C	D
Typing	6	5	4	10
Printing	2	6	8	5

SOLUTION   Step 1 of the procedure outlined in Fig. 4.1 is included in the statement of the problem. Applying Steps 2 and 3, we find that the smallest processing time is 2 hours for job A in the printing facility. Since it occurs in the second processing stage (printing), we enter the job last in the sequence as

Job sequence | | | A |

The reduced set of processing times becomes

Report	B	C	D
Typing	5	4	10
Printing	6	8	5

from which the smallest processing time is 4 hours occurring in the first facility. Therefore the associated job C is entered first in the job sequence,

Job sequence | C | | | A |

which reduces the remaining process times to

Report	B	D
Typing	5	10
Printing	6	5

The tie between the smallest processing times (5) is broken by an arbitrary choice of job B in the first facility, to give

Job sequence | C | B | D | A |

In this example the same job sequence results from breaking the tie between B and D in favor of D rather than B. In any case, the way a tie is broken will not alter the total elapsed time, although it can produce alternative optimal sequences. A detailed schedule for this problem is given in Table 4.1. The minimum elapsed time for completing the reports is 27 hours. If the facilities have no work other than the reports, the idle time would be $27 - 25 = 2$ hours for the typing pool, and $(4 - 0) + (19 - 18) + (25 - 24) = 6$ hours for the printing plant.

Table 4.1 Total elapsed time for an optimal sequence

	Typing			Printing		
Report	Total time	Time in	Time out	Total time	Time in	Time out
C	4	0	4	8	4	12
B	5	4	9	6	12	18
D	10	9	19	5	19	24
A	6	19	25	2	25	27

PROCESSING TWO JOBS THROUGH n FACILITIES A slightly different twist in sequencing exposes the problem of routing two jobs through a series of n facilities when each job has its own processing order. For this situation we will use a graphical method of analysis.[1] The criterion

[1] S. B. Akers, Jr., "A Graphical Approach to Production Scheduling Problems," *Operations Research*, vol. 4, 1956.

is again to minimize the elapsed time from the beginning of the first job to the end of the last job.

The steps for obtaining a graphical solution are outlined in Fig. 4.2. Details of the method will be developed by examining the following job-machine sequencing situation, where letters indicate facilities and numbers show the associated processing times:

Job 1 A-4 to C-2 to D-6 to E-3 to B-2
Job 2 C-8 to A-3 to D-4 to B-2 to E-3

Step 1: Obtain the processing times and order for two jobs.

Step 2: Draw a set of orthogonal axes and set a time scale.

Step 3: Letting each axis represent one job, from the origin mark the processing times in the given order along each axis.

Step 4: Block off the rectangular areas in the chart where a common facility is indicated on both axes.

Step 5: Draw a continuous line from the origin to the upper right corner using only horizontal, vertical, and 45° movements while avoiding the blocked-off areas.

Step 6: Determine the idle time for one job by adding the vertical or horizontal line increments to the job time.

Step 7: Select the sequence which has the least total elapsed time.

Figure 4.2 Flow chart for processing two jobs through n facilities

These data fulfill the requirements of Step 1, the order in which each job passes through the facilities and the time required in each facility. Processing times in the given order are laid out on orthogonal axes, as shown in Fig. 4.3. The horizontal axis represents job 1 and the vertical axis job 2. Processing times progress in order from the origin outward.

The coordinates of any point in the chart show a state of completion for the jobs. At the origin neither job has started. At the point marked P in Fig. 4.3, job 1 has passed through facilities A, C, and D, while job 2 has been processed through A and C. The top right point in the chart marked "completion" indicates that both jobs have been completely processed. The rectangular blocks represent impossible operating conditions: both jobs are being processed at the same time in one facility. Consequently, the shaded blocks in the chart represent forbidden schedules.

Figure 4.3 Graphical solution for processing two jobs through five facilities

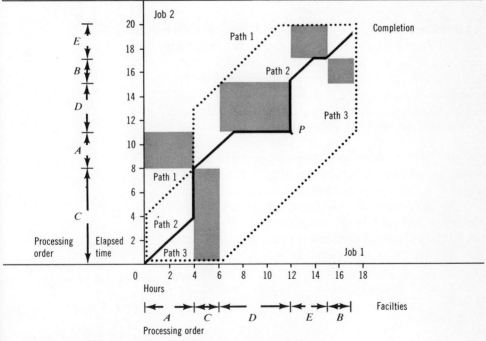

A line passing from the origin to the "completion" point is actually a time schedule for processing. This line must avoid the blocked areas and can make only horizontal, vertical, and 45° diagonal movements. A horizontal portion shows that only job 1 is being processed at the time. Equivalently, a vertical movement means that job 1 is idle while job 2 is being processed. A diagonal movement represents simultaneous processing of both jobs. Since our aim is to minimize idle time, we apparently want to choose a path with as much diagonal travel as possible.

There are many possible paths from zero to completion. Three are shown. None of them are necessarily optimal, but the effectiveness of each can be measured by the total elapsed time it requires. Elapsed time is easily determined by adding the idle time, identified by horizontal or vertical movements on the chart, to the job processing time. Either job will show the same elapsed time for a given path. Thus the elapsed times for the three paths are

	Job 1		Job 2	
Path 1	$17 + 4 + 5$	$= 26$	$20 + 6$	$= 26$
Path 2	$17 + 4 + 4 + 1$	$= 26$	$20 + 5 + 1$	$= 26$
Path 3	$17 + 9$	$= 26$	$20 + 6$	$= 26$

All three paths have the same elapsed time, but each has a different schedule. In such cases the choice can be based on coordination with other jobs. By generating a number of paths and getting the elapsed time for each, we are reasonably sure to identify a path which will yield an optimal or near-optimal schedule that synchronizes with other on-going activities.

Probably the most common form of schedule is a simple listing of events and the times they are expected to occur. For small projects of short duration this approach is adequate. About the only drawback is the temptation to "carry it in your head" without benefit of a critique. As projects become larger lists become longer. It is difficult to relate numerous events to overall project objectives. Many graphical or semigraphical techniques have been devised to overcome this obstacle. We will look into three methods of analyzing schedules for different-sized projects.

MAN-MACHINE CHARTS   At the micro end of the project scale is a work situation in which a man or a crew operates a machine or a battery of machines. The operations required to keep the machines producing form a repetitive cycle. Each cycle can be represented by a schedule of operations for the operators and the machines. A chart of these schedules is logically called a *man-machine chart*. It encourages visual analysis and serves as a check on economy calculations.

EXAMPLE 4.2 Optimum man-machine ratio

A large number of semiautomatic machines produce identical products. Time studies reveal the following standard times, in minutes, for one operator to service one machine:

Load machine	1.2
Remove finished unit	0.4
Inspect finished unit	2.3
Package finished unit	3.1
Walk to next machine	0.3
Machine running time per unit	17.4

One unit is produced during each machine cycle of 17.4 minutes. The machine burden rate is $10.00 per hour and the labor rate for an operator is $4.20 per hour. How many machines should one operator service?

SOLUTION The most economical man-machine ratio is the one that minimizes the cost per unit produced. As shown in the one-man-per-machine chart of Fig. 4.4a,

Figure 4.4 Man-machine charts

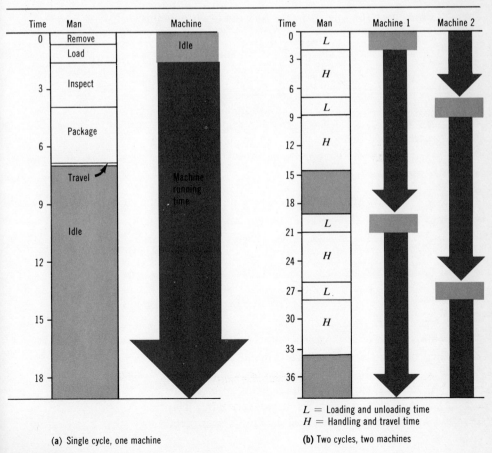

L = Loading and unloading time
H = Handling and travel time

(a) Single cycle, one machine

(b) Two cycles, two machines

the machine is idle while the operator removes the finished piece and loads in new stock. While the machine is running the operator can inspect, package, and travel to the next machine, but he also has idle time. Ideally, we would like to eliminate unproductive time for both the man and the machine. When this is not possible, as is the usual case, we must strike a balance between the higher cost for idle machine time and the lower cost for idle operator time.

A graphical solution is shown in Fig. 4.4b, where one operator services two machines. By studying the arrangement we can observe that with one operator the idle machine time is minimized, and that increasing the number of machines will introduce unproductive machine time.

A numerical solution starts with the calculation

Minimum machine-cycle time = loading-unloading time + running time
$$= 1.6 + 17.4 = 19 \text{ min}$$

Minimum operator-cycle time = loading-unloading time + handling and travel time
$$= 1.6 + 5.7 = 7.3 \text{ min}$$

which can be used to roughly fix the solution area:

$$\text{Approximate number of machines} = \frac{19}{7.3} = 2.6$$

Then the unit cost for one operator servicing two machines is

Labor: $19 \text{ min} \times \dfrac{\$4.20}{60 \text{ min}} = \$1.33$

Burden: $19 \times 2 \times \dfrac{\$10.00}{60} = \underline{6.33}$

Total cost per cycle $\$7.66$

Unit cost: $\dfrac{\$7.66}{2} = \$3.83$

For three machines it is

Labor: $(3 \times 7.3) \times \dfrac{\$4.20}{60} = \$1.53$

Burden: $21.9 \times 3 \times \dfrac{\$10.00}{60} = \underline{10.50}$

Total cost per cycle $\$12.03$

Unit cost: $\dfrac{\$12.03}{3} = \$4.01$

GANTT CHARTS   The charts named after Harry L. Gantt (also called bar charts) are well-known and widely used scheduling models. In their most common form they have a horizontal scale for time increments or calendar dates. Divisions of a project are listed vertically. The operations required to conduct each portion of a project show as horizontal bars which relate performance to the time scale. A typical Gantt chart format is shown in Fig. 4.5. It shows the same information as given in Table 4.1 plus a work-progress scale. The mark "Now" shows the present time, and the shaded portions of the bars indicate the amount of work accomplished up to "Now." The printing plant is on schedule, and the typing pool is 1 hour behind schedule. By this means the chart is used to monitor progress. Lagging portions of a project are identified. Corrective action can be initiated before the troubled activities throw subsequent dependent activities behind schedule. Control is vital for project economy.

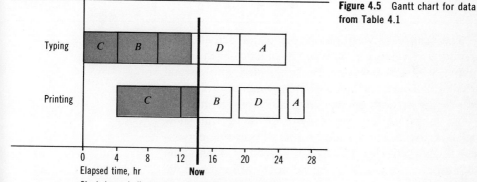

Figure 4.5 Gantt chart for data from Table 4.1

Gantt charts are applicable to small or large projects. Simplicity is their greatest virtue. As a communication tool or for presentation purposes they are excellent. On the other hand, their simplicity limits their use in analyzing complex projects. Many users have modified or customized bar charts to allow more information to be shown. Such modifications often clutter the chart to the extent that it is little better than a listing. For complex, interrelated projects, networks are a more adequate approach.

NETWORKS Network diagrams are found everywhere: road maps are geographical networks, wiring diagrams are electrical networks, flow charts are organizational networks. A scheduling network is shown in Fig. 4.6. It has roughly the same format as other networks. Different routes are shown, as on a road map; nodes (circles) indicate junction points, as in wiring diagrams; and arrows show the direction of flow, as in flow charts. An important addition to the scheduling network is the expected completion time shown for each segment (durations are shown below each arrow).

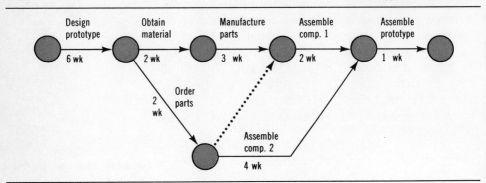

Figure 4.6 Network schedule for a prototype development

The sample network shows the major activities required to develop a prototype. In practice each of the activities would probably be subdivided into several smaller activities for better planning and control. As it stands, the network offers a gross timetable for management consideration. An analysis of times will show which activities are the most critical. Assigning personnel to the activities will fix responsibility. Identifying the resources required for each activity will indicate the adequacy of preparation. By monitoring progress, potential trouble areas will be anticipated. All these objectives are pursued by a network approach known as critical path scheduling.

CRITICAL PATH SCHEDULING

We will consider critical path scheduling (CPS) as a representative name for the many network-analysis techniques that have been developed in recent years. Since 1958, when the program evaluation and review technique (PERT) and the critical path method (CPM) were introduced, few, if any, management tools have received such wide new acclaim. The most distinguishing feature between the program evaluation and review approach and the CPM approach is that the former employs probabilistic time estimates (a range of possible activity completion times), while the latter uses deterministic times (a single, most likely time estimate for each activity). We will consider only deterministic times, because most industrial projects, with the exception of research and development work, can be accurately defined by a single duration.

Within the framework of CPS the analysis of schedules will be extended to include resource assignments and minimum-cost calculations, as well as the traditional planning and control aspects. Thus CPS is a management-control tool for defining, integrating, and analyzing what must be done to complete a project economically and on time.

ARROW NETWORKS   The network phase of CPS has two parts: the collection of data and the graphical representation of the data. The former part is by far the more difficult, and its importance cannot be overemphasized. There is a computer slogan which fits the facts nicely — GIGO — if you put Garbage In, you get Garbage Out. The activities required to complete a project must be identified accurately and completely, the order of completion must be defined carefully, and the estimated activity durations must be as realistic as possible. If these initial objectives are not attained, any further effort is essentially wasted.

The graphical-representation phase is largely a mechanical procedure. Network construction is not easy at first. There are a number of conventions to master. After the terminology and rules become familiar, however, the work is almost automatic.

Activity list   An *activity* is a time-consuming effort required to perform part of a project. A list of all the activities required to complete a project is called the *activity list*.

The way a project is broken down into its component activities depends on the nature of the project and the purpose of the network analysis. Natural divisions include the type of work, type of labor needed, responsibility for work, location of work, financial or accounting categories, equipment or material required, or structural elements. Activity definitions describe one or more of these divisions.

It is important to be able to identify the beginning and end points of each activity. The end of one activity and the beginning of the subsequent activity is a distinct point in time called an *event*. Thus an event is a point of accomplishment and/or a decision.

Restriction list   When one activity must be completed before another can begin, a constraint or *restriction* exists. A restriction list establishes the constraint relationships for all the activities in a project. There are three questions that determine the constraints of each activity:

What immediately precedes this activity?

What immediately follows this activity?

What other activity can be done during the same time?

A restriction list normally shows only prerequisite-postrequisite relationships. That is, each activity is shown to restrict only those activities which *immediately* follow it. For this condition, the event that marks the end of a prerequisite also denotes the beginning of any postrequisite activities. The shorthand notation $A < B, C$ indicates activity A is a prerequisite to activities B and C, or B and C are postrequisites of A. The symbol $<$ in this case is read "precedes": A precedes B and C.

EXAMPLE 4.3 Activity and restriction lists for building a patio

A vacation cabin is situated 100 miles from the owner's home. He plans to build a protected covered patio at the cabin. In order to make the best use of his time and any handyman labor he hires, he has decided to put the project on a critical-path schedule. Determine the activity and restriction lists.

SOLUTION   Before an activity list can be made, all available information should be collected. Assuming that the owner has in mind the style, type of construction, his source of labor and materials, and a knowledge of any peculiarities he is likely to encounter, his activity list might appear as follows:

Symbol	Activity description	Estimated time, hr
A	Order and deliver lumber, fiberglass, nails, etc.	2
B	Order and deliver concrete blocks, mortar, etc.	2
C	Excavate for foundation	10
D	Erect block foundation	6
E	Frame roof and deck	8
F	Lay decking	6
G	Place roofing	2
H	Build windbreak	6
I	Clean up	2

It is sometimes convenient to estimate durations as the activity list is completed. Here the durations are in hours for one man to complete each activity.

The corresponding restriction list would be

$$A < E \qquad D < E \qquad G < I$$
$$B < D, H \qquad E < F, G \qquad H < I$$
$$C < D \qquad F < I$$

Network construction   An arrow network is a graphical expression of the activity list and the restriction list. It faithfully portrays the logic and information from the lists in a more digestible form. Some conventions used in arrow networks are shown in Fig. 4.7. An activity is expressed by an arrow. The description or symbol can be placed above the arrow and the number of hours of duration below. Nodes (circles) represent the events that begin and end each activity. After a network has been drawn, the nodes are numbered to facilitate computer or manual analyses.

A single event can denote the beginning or ending of any number of activities. When two or more activities start from one event, the configuration is called a *burst* (Fig. 4.7b). Conversely, a *merge* occurs when two or more activities have the same ending event (Fig. 4.7c).

An event is sometimes dependent on another event even though the two are not linked together by an activity. This relationship is shown by a dummy arrow. A *dummy* is a dotted arrow drawn from the end of a prerequisite activity to the beginning of the postrequisite activity. It shows a restriction between two events (or activities), but implies no elapsed time.

In Fig. 4.7d activities A and B must be completed before activity D can begin. The restriction of A on D is apparent from the direct connection of the two activities. The restriction of B on D is shown by a dummy from the end of B to the beginning of D. The dummy shows a one-way, zero-time constraint. That is, A in no way restricts C, and the restriction of B on D ends immediately with the completion of B.

A dummy is also used to avoid confusion in node numbering. For calculation purposes, nodes are numbered to identify the activities. In order to differentiate between activities, each must have a unique set of node numbers, because numbers replace letters for activity designation. Observe the confusion in Fig. 4.8a; both

Figure 4.7 Network configurations

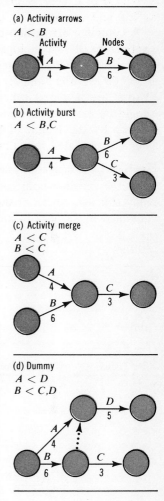

(a) Activity arrows
A < B

(b) Activity burst
A < B,C

(c) Activity merge
A < C
B < C

(d) Dummy
A < D
B < C,D

Figure 4.8 Artificial-dummy convention

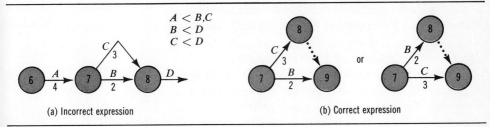

A < B,C
B < D
C < D

(a) Incorrect expression

or

(b) Correct expression

activities B and C have the same node numbers, and both would be designated as activity 7, 8. The problem is resolved by introducing an artificial dummy for either activity B or C (Fig. 4.8b). Thus one activity is denoted as 7, 8 and the other as 7, 9.

A complete arrow network is just a collection of the expressions shown in Figs. 4.7 and 4.8 which depicts the entire project. The network is easier to understand if all the arrows flow from left to right and crossed arrows are avoided wherever possible. No attempt should be made to indicate the relative duration of an activity by the length of its arrow. The network can later be translated to a time scale if desired.

EXAMPLE 4.4 An arrow network for building a patio

After the vacation-home owner has compiled his activity and restriction lists, he is ready to construct an arrow network for his patio project. Convert the information contained in the lists to an arrow network.

SOLUTION

Figure 4.9 Arrow network for the patio project

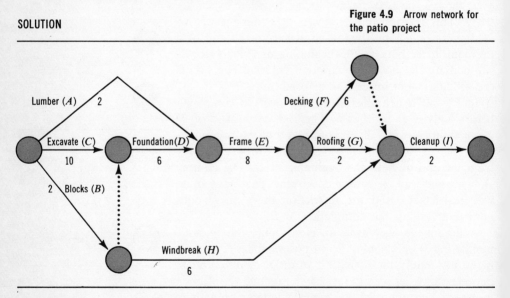

TIME CALCULATIONS   Drawing a network provides a check on the basic logic of a project plan. Any serious omissions, overambitious inclusions, and contradictory assignments can be corrected before schedule times are calculated. Errors discovered at the network stage pay high dividends in avoiding later wasted effort.

Time estimates   An estimated duration is needed for every activity. It would be ideal for the estimator to be completely familiar with all aspects of the project and to have a reliable crystal ball to predict future contingencies. Unfortunately, neither of these conditions often occurs. As a substitute, records of past performances on similar undertakings are a prime source of information for estimating current projects. Company files, work logs, project reports, consultants, general literature from agencies and suppliers, and other company personnel are potential estimating aids. Precautions should be taken to assure that the current working and technological conditions are equivalent to those in effect for past performances.

The critical path   Through each project runs a chain of operations which have no schedule leeway. These are called *critical activities*. A change in the duration of a critical activity will equally alter the total project duration. The chain of critical activities is called the *critical path*, and is the sequence which results in the longest completion time for the project.

Boundary times   The critical path sets a rigid schedule for critical activities, but all noncritical activities have a certain leeway in scheduling called *float*. In general, *total float* may be thought of as the difference between the time that is available to do an activity and the time required for that activity. Leeway in the starting and completion dates for an activity is defined by its boundary times:

Earliest start (ES)
: The earliest time all related activities preceding the chosen activity can be completed

Earliest finish (EF)
: The estimated activity time (ET) added to that activity's ES time

Latest start (LS)
: The latest time an activity may be started in order not to cause a delay in the project completion date

Latest finish (LF)
: The estimated activity time ET added to that activity's LS time; the same as the ES of the postrequisite activity

From the definitions of the boundary times, it is apparent that any surplus time is found between the earliest and latest start or finish times. Therefore the total float (TF) is

$$TF = LS - ES = LF - EF$$

Calculation of boundary times by the matrix method   A nodal-numbered network is required for the matrix method of boundary-time calculations. The node at the beginning of an activity is the *i node* for that activity, and the node at the end is its *j node* (Fig. 4.10*a*). To simplify the matrix calculations, every *i* node should be smaller than the corresponding *j* node. This condition applies to dummy numbering as well as to activities.

Figure 4.10

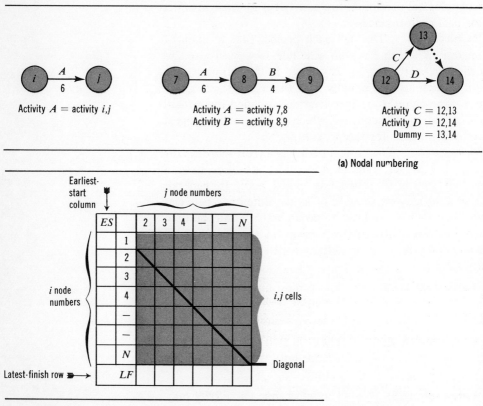

Activity A = activity i,j

Activity A = activity 7,8
Activity B = activity 8,9

Activity C = 12,13
Activity D = 12,14
Dummy = 13,14

(a) Nodal numbering

(b) Matrix format

A matrix format is shown in Fig. 4.10*b*. Each column represents a *j* node from the network, and each line represents an *i* node. With the first node (*i*) in the network numbered 1 and the last node numbered *N*, the columns are numbered 2 to *N* and the rows are numbered 1 to *N*. Every activity and dummy in the network has a unique cell in the matrix. The duration of each activity is entered in the upper left corner of the *i,j* cell for the activity. Dummies are treated like activities with a zero duration. If all the activities have *i* nodes smaller than *j* nodes, no durations will be entered below the diagonal line in the matrix.

The procedure for calculating the boundary times and total float is shown in the flow chart of Fig. 4.11. A very small network will be used to illustrate the calculation steps.

Figure 4.11 Flow chart for matrix boundary-time calculations

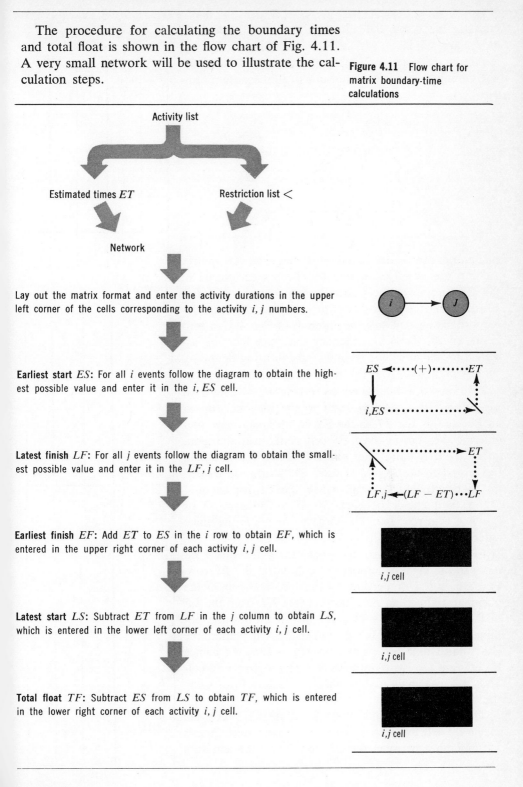

Activity list

Estimated times ET

Restriction list $<$

Network

Lay out the matrix format and enter the activity durations in the upper left corner of the cells corresponding to the activity i, j numbers.

Earliest start ES: For all i events follow the diagram to obtain the highest possible value and enter it in the i, ES cell.

$$ES \blacktriangleleft \cdots (+) \cdots ET$$
$$i, ES \cdots \blacktriangleright$$

Latest finish LF: For all j events follow the diagram to obtain the smallest possible value and enter it in the LF, j cell.

$$\cdots \blacktriangleright ET$$
$$LF, j \blacktriangleleft (LF - ET) \cdots LF$$

Earliest finish EF: Add ET to ES in the i row to obtain EF, which is entered in the upper right corner of each activity i, j cell.

i,j cell

Latest start LS: Subtract ET from LF in the j column to obtain LS, which is entered in the lower left corner of each activity i, j cell.

i,j cell

Total float TF: Subtract ES from LS to obtain TF, which is entered in the lower right corner of each activity i, j cell.

i,j cell

After the network is checked for accuracy and the nodes are numbered, the activity and dummy times are transcribed to appropriate cells in the matrix. Note that the dummy's zero is centered in its cell, because no fur-

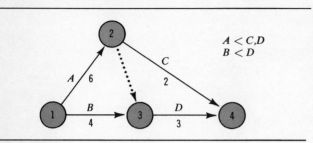

$A < C,D$
$B < D$

ther entries are needed in a dummy cell. The next matrix entry is the initial start time for the project placed in the ES column at the i row for the first event, $1, ES$. Normally a zero is used, but any number that signifies a coordinating time may be entered. In Fig. 4.12 a zero is shown for $1, ES$. A calendar date can later be assigned to the zero time to make all following boundary times cumulative from the assigned date.

ES times are calculated by taking the i events in ascending order, reading right to the diagonal, up to an ET, adding the ET to the ES in the same i row, and entering the sum in the i, ES cell under consideration. When there is more than one ET above the diagonal, the largest resulting sum is used. Dummies are treated just like activities. In Fig. 4.13a the ES for event 4 $(4, ES)$ is a choice between $3 + 6 = 9$ in row i-3 or $2 + 6 = 8$ in row 1-2. The largest sum, 9, is the value entered in $4, ES$.

LF calculations start by transcribing the last i, ES entry to the highest numbered j column in the LF row. For each LF, j proceeding to the left, read up to the diagonal, right to an ET, subtract that ET from the LF in the same column, and enter the smallest value obtained for the LF, j being sought. In calculating the latest finish time for event 2 in Fig. 4.13b, the choice is between $9 - 2 = 7$ in column 4 or $6 - 0 = 6$ in column 3. The smallest difference, 6, results from using the dummy zero.

The remaining boundary times and float are recorded in the i, j cell for each activity. The latest start time is the difference between the LF and ET in the activity's

Figure 4.12 Sample network and corresponding matrix

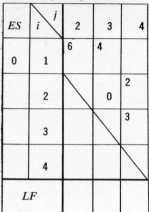

Figure 4.13
a ES calculations

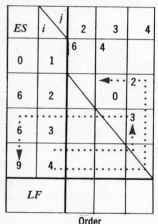

Order

b LF calculations

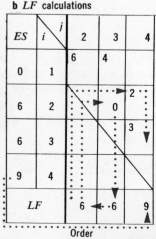

Order

j column. *LS* is entered in the lower left corner of the cell. The sum of $ET + ES$ in the activity's *i* row is the earliest finish and is entered in the upper right corner. $LS - ES = TF$ for an activity and is entered in the lower right corner. Total float can also be determined from $LF - EF = TF$ for a check on calculations. The completed matrix for the sample problem is given in Fig. 4.13c.

Critical activities are easy to identify because their total float must be zero. To obtain the sequence of critical activities through the project (the critical path), simply mark the *j* nodes where an activity in the column shows no *TF*. Combine these nodes with the first *i* node, and the entire path is delineated. In the sample problem the sequence is 1-2-4 and means activities 1, 2 and 3, 4 are critical.

c Completed matrix

ES	i \ j	2	3	4
0	1	6 6 / 0 0	4 4 / 2 2	
6	2		0	2 8 / 7 1
6	3			3 9 / 6 0
9	4			
LF		6	6	9

EXAMPLE 4.5   Matrix calculations for building a patio

Calculate the boundary times for the patio project.

SOLUTION   The nodal-numbered network and the associated matrix are shown in Fig. 4.14. The critical path, as revealed by the matrix calculations, is shown by double arrows in the network.

Computer calculations   Without computer applications it is highly doubtful that CPS would be as widely used as it is today. Computers perform the boundary times and float calculations accurately and rapidly. In addition, computer programs are available for resource-leveling and cost-minimization procedures which will be considered later in this chapter.

Computers cannot make an activity list, restriction list, or time estimates. For most CPS programs it is necessary to construct a network in order to determine the i, j numbers for the activities. When these preliminaries have been accomplished, the data from the network are punched on cards, and the appropriate computer program to process the data is selected. When costs and resources are not formally evaluated, the computer output is usually in the form of a *boundary timetable* similar to the one shown in Table 4.2.

With the exception of the last column, the information in the boundary timetable is the same as that recorded in the matrix of Fig. 4.14. The last column is free float, abbreviated as *FF*. *Free float* is the difference between the *EF* of an activity and the smallest *ES* of any postrequisite activities. It may be thought of as the

136

time by which the latest finish of an activity can exceed its earliest finish without affecting any other activity. It has little practical use in scheduling but is mentioned because it is characteristically included in computer programs.

The choice between using a computer and manual methods is mainly a question of cost and convenience. Each method has its advantages. Some merits of computer methods are speed, accuracy, and capacity; some

Figure 4.14 Matrix calculations for the patio project

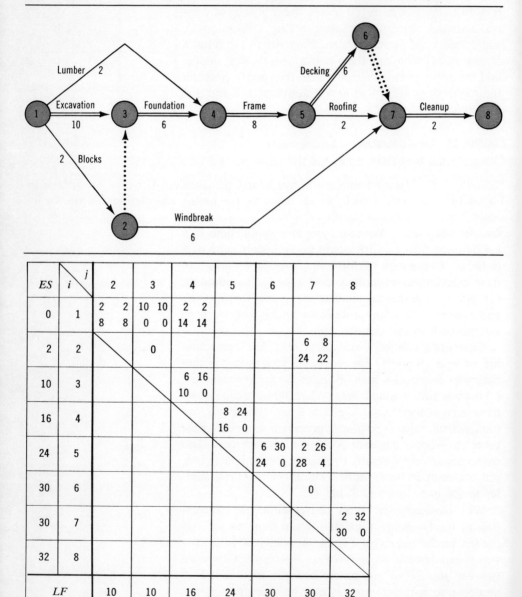

ES	i \ j	2	3	4	5	6	7	8
0	1	2 2 / 8 8	10 10 / 0 0	2 2 / 14 14				
2	2		0				6 8 / 24 22	
10	3			6 16 / 10 0				
16	4				8 24 / 16 0			
24	5					6 30 / 24 0	2 26 / 28 4	
30	6						0	
30	7							2 32 / 30 0
32	8							
LF		10	10	16	24	30	30	32

merits of manual methods are availability, flexibility, and familiarity. Relative costs are not included in either list because they are a function of individual project requirements. Very large projects with extensive cost and resource analyses are obvious candidates for electronic assistance. At the other extreme, it would be absurd to use a computer for an informal project plan. Between such limits personal judgment of cost and convenience decides the issue.

Table 4.2 Boundary timetable for the patio project

I	J	ET	ACTIVITY DESCRIPTION	ES	EF	LS	**LF**	TF	FF
1	2	2	BLOCKS	0	2	8	10	8	0
1	3	10	EXCAVATION	0	10	0	10	0	0
1	4	2	LUMBER	0	2	14	16	14	14
2	3	0	DUMMY						
2	7	6	WINDBREAK	2	8	24	30	22	22
3	4	6	FOUNDATION	10	16	10	16	0	0
4	5	8	FRAME	16	24	16	24	0	0
5	6	6	DECKING	24	30	24	30	0	0
5	7	2	ROOFING	24	26	28	30	4	4
6	7	0	DUMMY						
7	8	2	CLEANUP	30	32	30	32	0	0

TIME CHARTS A graphical expression of a boundary timetable is called a *time chart*. It is a cross between an arrow network and a bar graph. As such, it displays complex interrelationships found in arrow networks with the easy readability of a bar graph.

Conventions Basically, the conversion of a network to a time chart amounts to making the network conform to a rectangular coordinate system. The horizontal axis indicates time, and the vertical axis represents activity chains. The conversion process is largely a mechanical effort, since the basic data are already tabulated in the network and the matrix or boundary timetable.

Each symbol used in a network has its counterpart in a time chart, as shown in Fig. 4.15*a*. Solid vertical lines indicate restrictions in both directions, and dotted vertical lines indicate restrictions only in the direction of the arrow. A horizontal line corresponds to the duration of the activity, and double lines indicate the critical path or paths. Activity descriptions are noted, but no *ET*'s are required because cumulative time is shown in time carets at both ends of the activity line. Carets indicate the *ES* and *EF* for each activity. Other information such as the costs or resources required by an activity can be inserted below the activity line.

Total float is also represented on a time chart. It is shown as a horizontal dotted line following the last activity in a chain of activities. When there are several activities in the chain, all the activities share the indicated float. If all the scheduling leeway is utilized to postpone one activity in the chain, the following activities can have no float time. The start of a project is shown in the network of Fig. 4.15*b* and the associated time-chart segment is shown in Fig. 4.15*c*. Activities *B*, *C*, and *D* all share the 3 days of float in the *B-C-D* chain. If the start of *B* is postponed until day 3, the starting times for *C* and *D* are fixed, respectively, at 6 and 8. Any later start would extend the total project duration, because the critical activity *E* could not start at day 10.

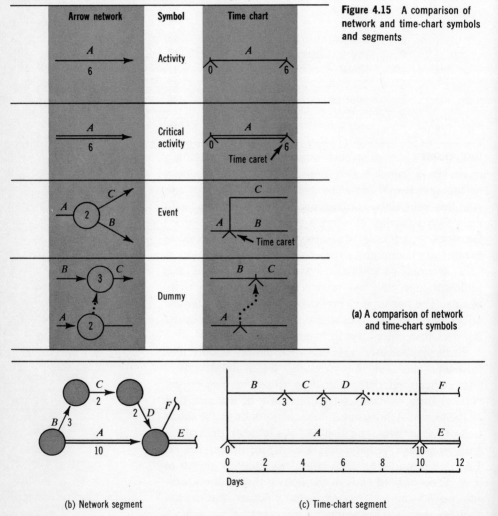

Figure 4.15 A comparison of network and time-chart symbols and segments

(a) A comparison of network and time-chart symbols

(b) Network segment

(c) Time-chart segment

EXAMPLE 4.6 Time chart for building a patio

Construct a time chart according to conventions for the patio construction project.

SOLUTION   Utilize the information from the matrix and network in Fig. 4.16.

Figure 4.16 Conventional time chart for the patio project

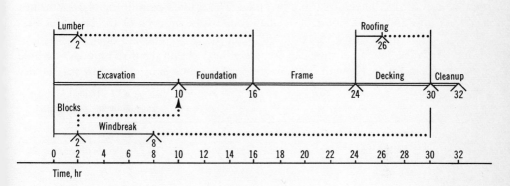

A time chart drawn according to conventions is *not* a schedule; it is a starting point for a schedule. The float lines point out areas of schedule flexibility, while the critical path sets limits to schedule juggling. Additional restrictions can be added by including manpower, cash, equipment, or other resource constraints associated with particular activities. A working schedule evolves when float time is employed to improve resource utilization.

Applications   A graphical approach to problem solution is a basic tool. It has long been recognized as an aid in scheduling. Nearly all products and projects pass through a graphic stage in their development. Almost every manager and engineer depends in part on charts for his information.

Charting can be divided into three broad areas of usefulness:

1. Survey, or analysis of a present situation
2. Design, or development of a new or revised solution
3. Presentation, or display of the solution

As applied to CPS, networks are useful for surveys and time charts are more suitable for design and presentation. The value of the charts lies in their concise but complete pictorial representation, which allows the decision-maker to see the outcomes of alternative courses of action.

EXAMPLE 4.7 A schedule for building a patio

The patio builder has decided to try to complete the construction over a weekend. He plans to work two 8-hour days. Hired help is available. Since there are no space or tool limitations, he believes he can complete actual construction work in half the estimated time by using two workers instead of one. Determine a 16-hour schedule for completion of the patio.

SOLUTION   All the activity times except the order and delivery of lumber and concrete blocks can be halved by using two men. The critical path in Fig. 4.16 indicates a project duration of 32 hours. Two men must work on each of the critical activities to cut the project time to 16 hours. Since there is adequate float for the noncritical activities, one other man can complete them within the time limit. A schedule is presented in Fig. 4.17, with specific work assignments indicated below the activity lines.

Figure 4.17   16-hour-completion schedule for the patio project

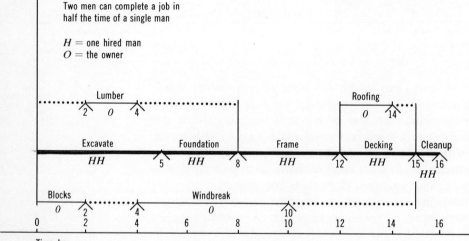

RESOURCE SCHEDULING   The allocation of resources for nonrepetitive projects is an exercise in coordination. Resources are usually limited in quantity. The activities in a project have constraints for sequential order and completion times. Resource scheduling coordinates the assignment of resources to activities within stated limitations.

Single-resource scheduling   A certain piece of equipment or a production machine might warrant special attention because of its high cost or limited availability. A cursory check of the time chart reveals whether or not it is scheduled to be in two places at the same time. If it is scheduled for two activities at the same time, it may be possible to avoid overlapping assignments by taking advantage of existing float time. When no usable float exists, a decision has to be made between acquiring more of the limiting resource or altering activity times. Alterations could take one or more of the following forms:

1. Working overtime to shorten the duration of one or more of the activities requiring limited resources
2. Shortening the duration of prerequisite or postrequisite activities to allow float time for rescheduling the key activities
3. Changing the resource requirements; a substitute resource may change the duration of the activity involved
4. Extending the total project duration

The criterion for selecting from the above alternatives will probably be cost, but less tangible factors such as goodwill or convenience may also influence the decision.

Multiple-resource scheduling When several types of resource are included, the analysis becomes more complicated. The complexity is a function of the number of resources considered critical, the degree of their criticality, and the frequency with which these resources occur in the project plan.

A manual approach to leveling multiple resources is the use of a *resource grid*. The grid is drawn to the same scale as the time chart. Columns represent time units and the rows represent resource units. Thus, if the time scale is in hours and each resource unit is one man, a cell in the grid would represent 1 man-hour (see Fig. 4.19).

There is no set procedure for manually obtaining an optimum resource-leveled schedule. The steps in Fig. 4.18 suggest a convenient approach. Each activity using the resource is represented by a rectangle with dimensions of resource increments and time. The rectangles are adjusted in the grid to conform to the resource limits of the grid and the sequential order of the time chart. If all the rectangles do not fit into the grid, the measures suggested for single resource scheduling can be utilized. These measures either change the shape of the rectangles or extend the grid.

In Fig. 4.19 the problem is to complete the given project with a four-man crew. The number of men required for each activity is displayed on the time chart. The first activity entered in the grid is A. This activity

Figure 4.18 Steps for manual resource leveling

Step 1: Lay out a resource grid to the same scale as the time chart. Allow one line for each increment of the resource being allocated.

Step 2: Label the anticipated resource requirement for each activity in the time chart.

Step 3: Fit the rectangles representing the resource requirements for each activity into the grid. Give priority to the activities with the greatest usage and least amount of float while adhering to sequential relationships.

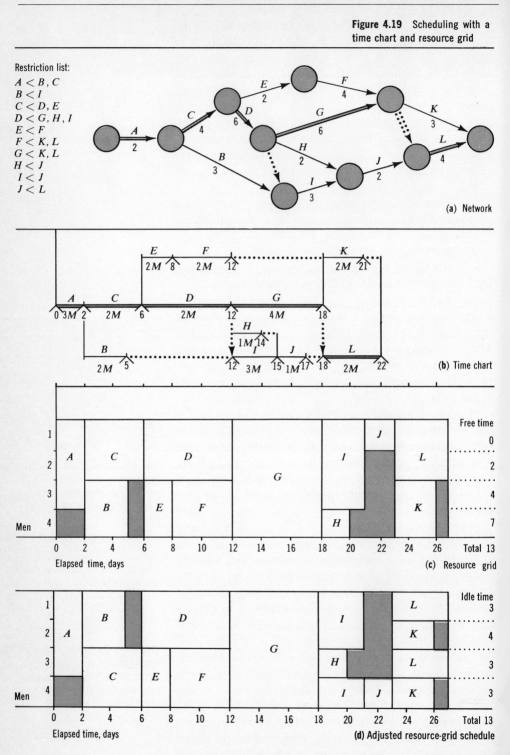

Figure 4.19 Scheduling with a time chart and resource grid

Restriction list:
$A < B, C$
$B < I$
$C < D, E$
$D < G, H, I$
$E < F$
$F < K, L$
$G < K, L$
$H < J$
$I < J$
$J < L$

(a) Network

(b) Time chart

(c) Resource grid

(d) Adjusted resource-grid schedule

forms a rectangle three resource units (men) tall and two time units (days) wide. The result is a block representing six man-days.

As the remaining activities are placed in the chart, it becomes apparent that the project cannot be completed with four men in the 22 days indicated on the time chart. The grid has to extend to 27 days to accommodate all the work. The completed grid sets a working schedule. Some manipulations can still be made to redistribute idle time (shown shaded in the figure). By sliding segments of activity blocks vertically, the idle time is relocated to prorate it among the crew as shown in the final portion of the figure. By the same means each worker could be given special attention. Job assignments might reflect the fact that a certain worker is better on one type of job than another, is going to night school, or cannot stand heights.

The schedule in the grid supersedes the conventional time chart from which it evolved. It may be used as it stands, redrawn in the form of a time chart, or put into bar-graph form. The same format is appropriate for other types of resources, such as materials and money. It may be amended slightly to serve as an assignment sheet or a record-keeping form.

COST ANALYSIS The purpose of a CPS cost analysis is to determine the most practical, economical schedule that adheres to a project's time constraints. In an informal manner, economic efficiency is a consideration in the identification, makeup, and time estimation of each activity. However, total project costs are more than the sum of individual activity costs, and there may be time constraints other than those imposed by the activity relationships. Factors outside the project, as well as those within, must be included in a formal analysis.

The buying or selling of time is the fundamental concept of a cost analysis. If conditions appear to favor a shorter project duration, time segments along the critical path which cut the project duration are "purchased" by increasing the direct costs. After each purchase the new "economic" position is evaluated by including indirect costs.

Project direct costs The direct cost of an activity is the sum of direct labor, material, and equipment charges required to complete it. When a separate agency such as a consulting firm or subcontractor undertakes the entire activity, direct cost is the amount paid to that agency. Thus activity time-cost relationships take a variety of forms. Several of the more common configurations are shown in Fig. 4.20. Any of these cost relationships may be used in a cost analysis.

Figure 4.20 Activity direct-time-cost patterns

Linear increase of cost with decreasing time: a job that can be efficiently implemented by increasing resources

Constant cost which does not vary with time: a subcontracted job with an established minimum time

A distinct step increase of direct cost at a point in time: a job where a major cost rise occurs if the duration is to be shortened, due to an incremental resource charge

A concave cost-time relationship: a job where some limitation prevents an increasing resource application from showing a proportionate return. This very common pattern is represented by a piecewise linear approximation

A noncontinuous time-cost relationship: an activity, such as delivery time, where there is only a normal time cost and a crash time cost

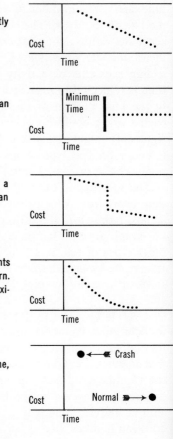

Project indirect costs   Supervision and other customary overhead charges are the principal sources of indirect costs. Interest on funds invested in a project, liquidated damages, and bonuses are additional indirect costs primarily associated with construction. The relationship of indirect, direct, and total costs was shown in Fig. 2.15.

Project total-cost analysis   A semigraphical approach as outlined in Fig. 4.21 is used for a CPS cost analysis. Athough the procedure is rather time consuming, the redeeming feature is that only a portion of most projects benefit from cost analysis. Times and costs for many activities are fixed. Certain sections of a project may be considered more important and therefore should be subjected to close cost scrutiny. This condition often occurs after a project is partially completed but behind schedule. A careful cost examination reveals the most economical measures to speed up the progress.

Figure 4.21 Flow chart for minimum-project-cost calculations using primal and dual charts

Step 1: Draw an arrow network for the project. Obtain direct-cost estimates for different activity durations and the indirect-cost information for different project durations.

Step 2: Draw a "primal" time chart for the project based on the least-cost (longest) schedule. Label the priority of the cutting-time segments for each activity.

Step 3: On an overlay of the primal chart draw lines perpendicular to the cut segments and restriction lines to form a "dual" network for cash flow.

Step 4: Label the paths through the dual network to conform to cost estimates in Step 1 and the priorities in Step 3. Float segments have zero cutting costs.

Step 5: Select the least expensive unused path passing completely through the project which cuts one time unit from the project duration. Add the cost of cutting the time unit to the project's direct cost before the cut.

Step 6: Add the indirect cost to the direct cost to obtain the total cost for that duration.

Solution ➡

When the total project costs reach a minimum value.

We will apply the cost-analysis procedure to the project introduced in Fig. 4.19. With the network already developed, we can start with the cost data in Step 1. The estimated direct costs for each activity are shown in Table 4.3. In this example estimates have been secured for three activity durations called least cost, normal cost, and crash cost. A linear approximation of costs is used for durations between the three estimates. Exact cost increments should be used when available.

Primal chart   A primal time chart based on the least-cost activity times is shown at the top of Fig. 4.22. Each time increment beyond the crash-cost minimum time is labeled for every activity. The labels establish the order in which the time increments are used for cutting time from that activity. The more expensive cuts are given higher numbers, which indicate less desirability or a low priority. Float is unlabeled, but it is utilized wherever possible because it costs nothing to eliminate a unit of float.

Intermediate durations are calculated by the formula

$$\frac{Cost_{ET1} - Cost_{ET2}}{ET2 - ET1}$$

Thus to cut B from 7 to 6 days costs

$$\frac{\$1200 - \$800}{7 - 3} = \$100 \text{ per day}$$

and to cut B from 3 to 2 days costs

$$\frac{\$1410 - \$1200}{3 - 2} = \$210 \text{ per day}$$

Table 4.3 Estimated direct costs for three activity durations

Activity	Least		Normal		Crash	
	ET	Cost	ET	Cost	ET	Cost
A	2	$ 300	2	$ 300	2	$ 300
B	7	800	3	1200	2	1410
C	5	800	4	880	3	1000
D	8	3200	6	3420	4	3620
E	6	320	2	440	2	440
F	8	240	4	320	3	470
G	8	1160	6	1260	4	1600
H	4	170	2	190	2	190
I	6	360	3	510	3	510
J	2	210	2	210	2	210
K	5	330	3	410	3	410
L	5	460	4	540	2	560
		$8350		$9680		$10,720

Dual network   The next step is to construct the dual network. The term "dual" is borrowed from electrical circuit theory to indicate a network based on arcs obtained by "cuts" of the primal time chart. The lower portion of Fig. 4.22 shows how a dual and a primal are related. The dual is superimposed on the primal chart to illustrate how arcs of the dual represent cutting paths in the primal. The cutting arcs are bounded by restriction lines. Vertical restriction lines in the primal are horizontal arrows in the dual which restrict horizontal movements to the direction of the arrows. Each arc corresponds to one potential cut of a primal time segment. Essentially all the elements of the primal are perpendicular in the dual. Thus the cash flow in the dual is perpendicular to the time flow of the primal.

The working version of a dual network is shown in Fig. 4.23. This is the same network depicted in Fig. 4.22, except that the primal chart has been removed, priorities and costs have been added, and it has been turned 90° to make it easier to read. Now the problem is to select the lowest-cost paths through the project in the direction of the dual cash flow. Each path selected reduces the project duration by one time unit. A path can jog along solid vertical lines in either direction, but it can go only in the direction of the arrowhead when the lines are dotted. No horizontal portion of the same line (an arc) may be used more than once. The process is trial and error to arrive at the least-cost path for each cut, but the open display of all the pertinent information makes the process relatively easy. Paths are numbered in the order of least cost. Thus path $P1$ cuts through

Figure 4.22 Construction of primal time chart and dual network

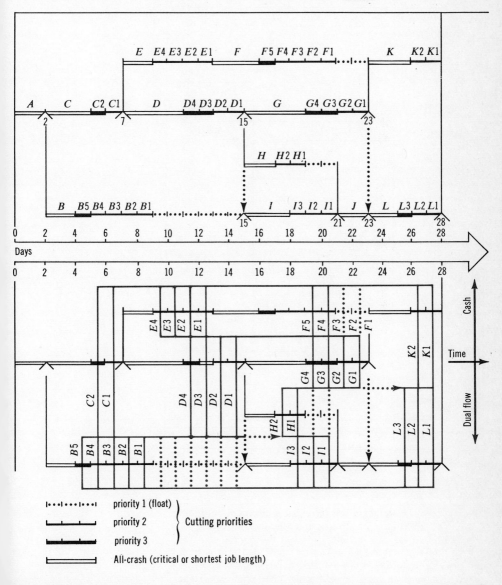

the float for B and reduces activity C by one day ($C1$) at a cost of \$80 to shorten the project duration from 28 to 27 days. The new direct cost for the project is \$8350 + \$80 = \$8430.

Total cost   The final step is to calculate the total cost for the different project durations. Direct costs increase progressively as each cut is made. The lowest-direct-cost

Figure 4.23 Dual network with the cutting order indicated

B5-$210		
B4-$100	C2-$120 (P6)	
B3-$100	C1-$80 (P1 and P4)	
B2-$100		
B1-$100		
P10		E4-$30
P9		E3-$30
P8	D4-$100 (P10)	E2-$30
P7	D3-$100 (P9)	E1-$30 (P11)
P6	D2-$110 (P8)	
P1 and P4*	D1-$110 (P7)	

H2-$10

I3-$50 (P12)	H1-$10 (P12)		F3-$20 (P9)	
I2-$50 (P11)	(P11)	G4-$170 (P12)	F2-$20 (P8)	
I2-$50 (P5)	(P5)	G3-$170 (P11)	F1-$20 (P7)	
		G2-$50 (P5)	(P5)	
		G1-$50 (P3)	(P3)	

F5-$150
F4-$20 (P10)

L3-$80 (P2)*		
L2-$10 (P2)*	K2-$40 (P2)	
L1-$10 (P3)	K1-$40 (P2)	

Flow

'Each path is the least-cost route for a given cut duration. Thus $P1$ costs the least for cutting one day, but $P2$ — two paths that do not include $P1$ — has the lowest cost for cutting two days. The cost of $P3$ is added to the total direct cost for $P2$. Then $P4$, which is the same as $P1$, is utilized when the fourth day is cut. Thereafter each additional cut cost is added to the previous total direct cost.

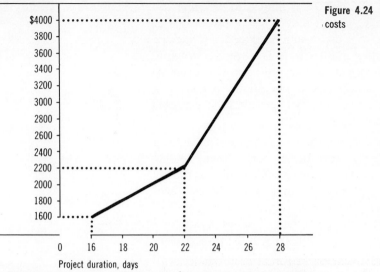

Figure 4.24 Project indirect costs

schedule is determined from the list of least-cost-activity estimates. The costs of successive cuts are added to the lowest project cost to obtain direct project costs for various durations. Associated with each of these durations is an indirect cost. For this example we will assume that the indirect costs follow the pattern shown in Fig. 4.24, which is typical of indirect costs entailing a penalty for completing a project beyond a certain limit. The steeper slope after 22 days represents penalty payments added to regular indirect costs beyond the penalty limit (22 days).

The total-cost figures resulting from the analysis are tabulated in Table 4.4. They reveal that a duration of 22 days offers the lowest-cost schedule.

Table 4.4 Total costs for different project durations

Cut no.	Days	Cost calculations	Direct cost	Indirect cost	Total cost
0	28	$8350	$8350	$4000	$12350
1	27	8350 + 80 + 0	8430	3700	12130
2	26	8350 + 40 + 80 + 40 + 10	8520	3400	11920
3	25	8520 + 50 + 10 + 0	8580	3100	11680
4	24	8580 + 80 + 0	8660	2800	11460
5	23	8660 + 50 + 50 + 0	8760	2500	11240
6	22	8760 + 120 + 0	8880	2200	11080
7	21	8880 + 110 + 20 + 0	9010	2100	11110
8	20	9010 + 110 + 20 + 0	9140	2000	11140
9	19	9140 + 100 + 20 + 0	9260	1900	11160
10	18	9260 + 100 + 20 + 0	9380	1800	11180
11	17	9380 + 170 + 50 + 30 + 0	9630	1700	11330
12	16	9630 + 170 + 50 + 30 + 10	9890	1600	11590

PROJECT CONTROL   When CPS is limited to planning and analysis only, management fails to make use of one of its principal assets; its use should be extended to include project coordination and control. The specific structure of a control system will vary according to the organization of the firm and the type of operation it is undertaking. Nevertheless, we can identify certain basic elements that exist in every control system.

Sensor   It is necessary to have a method of measuring performance. The sensory device for a home heating system is a thermostat; in project scheduling it is usually a man or a group of men. As applied to CPS, the function of a sensor includes observing, measuring, and reporting the types and quantities of times, costs, and resources consumed by each activity in the project plan.

Monitor   A monitor compares actual performance with a set of predetermined standards. Just as a thermostat compares the actual room temperature with the setting for the desired temperature, a schedule monitor compares the actual use of resources with those anticipated in the project plan. This feedback function is necessary for a continuous evaluation of the status of a project that identifies trouble areas.

Controller   A controller is an activating mechanism, such as a switch that turns on a heater. Its function is to initiate corrective action whenever actual performance is below standard. One of the main decisions is how far to allow performance to fall below standard before initiating remedial action.

Objectives   The unifying measure of a control system is the purpose it serves. The intent of a heating system is to provide a comfortable temperature. The objective of project control is generally the conservation of time, costs, and resources.

SELECTED REFERENCES

CPM in Construction, Associated General Contractors of America, Washington, D.C., 1962.

Evarts, H. F.: *Introduction to PERT*, Allyn and Bacon, Inc., Boston, Mass., 1964.

Fondahl, J. W.: *A Non-computer Approach to the Critical Path Method for the Construction Industry*, Stanford University Press, Stanford, Calif., 1962.

Ford, L. R., and D. R. Fulkerson: *Flows in Networks*, Princeton University Press, Princeton, N.J., 1962.

Miller, D. W., and M. K. Starr: *Executive Decision and Operations Research*, Prentice-Hall, Inc., Englewood Cliffs, N.J., 1960.

Moder, J. J., and C. R. Phillips: *Project Management with CPM and PERT*, Reinhold Publishing Corporation, New York, 1964.

Muth, J. F., and G. L. Thompson: *Industrial Scheduling*, Prentice-Hall, Inc., Englewood Cliffs, N.J., 1963.

Riggs, J. L., and C. O. Heath: *Guide to Cost Reduction through Critical Path Scheduling*, Prentice-Hall, Inc., Englewood Cliffs, N.J., 1966.

Shaffer, L. R., J. B. Ritter, and W. L. Meyer: *The Critical-path Method*, McGraw-Hill Book Company, New York, 1965.

PROBLEMS

4.1 A testing laboratory has seven samples to test for the same properties. Each test is in two parts which must follow the same order, because the samples are destroyed during the tests. A sample is always subjected to test 1 first. The laboratory has only one machine of the type required for each part of a test. Based on the testing times below for each test, determine the order in which the samples should be tested to minimize the total time to complete all seven tests.

Sample	Test 1	Test 2
1	2	3
2	7	9
3	10	8
4	5	2
5	6	11
6	4	3
7	8	11

4.2 Two jobs are to be processed through five machines, A, B, C, D, and E. The order of processing and the times, in hours, required by each machine are as noted:

	1	2	3	4	5
Job 1	C-2	D-5	E-4	A-1	B-9
Job 2	A-3	C-2	D-3	B-11	E-5

What is the minimum elapsed time required to complete both jobs?

4.3 A company received four rush orders to be processed through two departments. All other work for the departments is stopped while the rush orders are being completed. Each order passes from Department A to Department B with the following expected processing times in hours:

a Draw a Gantt chart for the optimal schedule.

b What would the elapsed time be if Department A actually took 10 hours to complete order 2 and Department B finished order 2 in 2 hours?

	1	2	3	4
Department A	3	7	6	6
Department B	2	5	10	4

4.4 An operator earning $3.00 per hour runs a machine with a burden rate of $4.80 per hour. What is the unit cost when he operates two and three machines? The activity times, in minutes, for producing one piece are as given:

Insert piece in machine	0.60
Remove finished piece	0.30
Inspect piece	0.50
File burr and set aside	0.20
Walk to next machine	0.05
Machine running time	3.95

4.5 Two operators, each paid $2.75 per hour, operate two semiautomatic machines. Both operators must work together at all times. The element times, in minutes, for the work cycle are as follows:

Load	1.2
Run	3.4
Unload	0.7
Inspect prior to loading	0.4 (part is on worktable during inspection)
Inspect after completed	0.8 (done while machine is running)

The machines are located next to each other, and transportation times are included in the above elements. If material costs $15.80 per part, direct machine cost is $24.00 per hour, and overhead is calculated to be 25% of labor, materials, and machine costs, what is the cost of each completed part?

4.6 Construct an arrow network segment for each set of restrictions:

a	b	c	d
$A < C$	$A < D$	$A < C$	$A < C, D$
$B < C$	$B < D, E$	$B < D, E$	$B < C, D$
$C < E$	$C < E$	$C < D$	$C < E$
$D < E$	$D < F$	$D < F$	$D < E$
	$E < F$	$E < F$	

4.7 During a slack period part of an assembly line is to be shut down for the repair of a certain machine. While the machine is torn down the area will be painted. Construct a network for this machine-rebuilding project based on the following activity list furnished by the line foreman (activities are not in order of accomplishment):

A	Order new parts	*F*	Deliver parts to be
B	Reassemble machine		repaired
C	Tear out old foundation	*G*	Build new foundation
D	Dismantle machine	*H*	Pick up repaired parts
E	Paint area	*I*	Clean up

4.8 A driver pulls into a service station and tells the attendants to fill up the car and a 5-gal gas can for his power mower. He uses a credit card. Draw a network for the service he should obtain, assuming that there are several attendants and they provide complete service: check oil, wash windows, check tires and battery, etc.

4.9 Transcribe the information from the network shown below to a matrix and calculate all five boundary conditions:

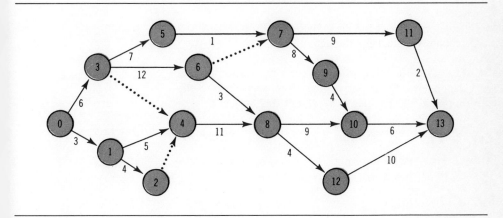

4.10 Develop a matrix for the following nodal-numbered activity list. From the matrix determine only *ES* and *LF* times. How can the critical path be identified in the matrix by using only these two boundary times?

i	*j*	Duration
0	1	8
0	2	4
0	4	14
1	2	6
2	3	5
2	5	7
3	4	0
3	6	1
4	6	3
5	6	3

4.11 Given the following activity list, time estimates, and restrictions, draw an arrow network and complete a boundary timetable (do not include free float):

Activity	Duration	Postrequisites	Activity	Duration	Postrequisites
A	2	B	H	6	M
B	4	G, F, L	I	11	K
C	3	E, I, J	J	7	K
D	4	I, J	K	12	M
E	7	G, F, L	L	9	K
F	16	M	M	5	
G	6	H			

4.12 Free float can easily be calculated from the matrix. Assuming that the other five boundary times have already been entered in the matrix, determine the procedure for calculating free float.
a Show the steps for calculating free float by a flow-chart format.
b Calculate free float for the activities in Prob. 4.10.
c Calculate free float for the activities in Prob. 4.11.

4.13 The activities and restrictions for a fabrication project are given below. Construct a time chart according to the conventions in the chapter to represent this project.

Activity	Description	ET	Restrictions
A	Make parts list	2	$A < B, C$
B	Prepare routings	3	$B < D$
C	Order and procure material	4	$C < E, F$
D	Make schedule	3	$D < E, F$
E	Process parts for subassembly 1	3	$E < G$
F	Process parts for subassembly 2	2	$F < H$
G	Assemble S. A. 1	2	$G < I$
H	Assemble S. A. 2	4	$H < I$
I	Final assembly	1	. . .

4.14 Construct a conventional time chart based on the activity information given in Prob. 4.11.

4.15 Construct a bar graph based on *ES* times for the fabrication project described in Prob. 4.13. Show the activity duration as a solid bar and the float associated with each activity as a hollow bar attached to the end of the solid portion. Explain how the graph could be used to make men or machine assignments for the project.

4.16 A conventional time chart has been developed for a project. The resources are indicated below the activity lines and represent the manpower required to conduct the activities. Assume that each activity must be completed once it is started.

a Construct a resource-time grid for an available crew size of five men. Distribute the idle time as evenly as possible.
b Construct a resource grid for a crew size limited to three men. Do not change the shape of the activity blocks even if the project duration has to be extended.

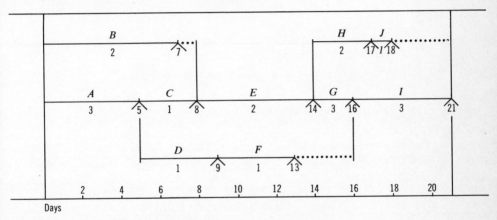

Days

4.17 Three carpenters and five laborers are available for the project described by the network below. Symbols for the activities and their duration times are shown above the arrows. Complete a resource-time grid with an even work distribution for each type of worker. Laborers L must work at the same time as carpenters C when both are assigned to the same activity.

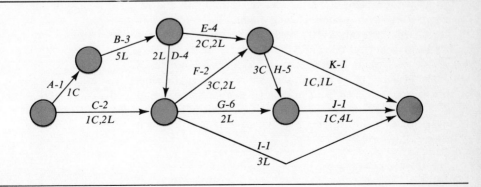

4.18 A project arrow network is shown below. Above each arrow is the letter symbol for the activity and the time of its duration. Below each arrow is the crew size required to perform the activity. A boldface number means that the crew must employ a certain piece of equipment called "machine X."

a Determine the schedule duration for the minimum cost, and schedule the project so that only one machine X is needed. Keep the crew size constant. Direct labor costs are $40 per day per man. Indirect costs total $200 per day.
b After the project has been analyzed for cost and resource expenditures, construct a bar chart to show the actual schedule for minimum costs. Indicate which activities require machine X.

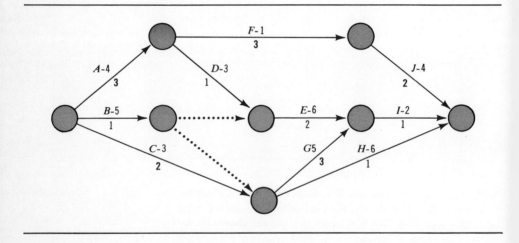

4.19 Plans are being made to remodel a shipping and receiving area in a manufacturing plant. The remodeling project will have an $1100 basic burden cost and other incremental indirect costs of $100 per day. The $1100 base indirect cost results from overhead and supervision charges for the project. The $100-per-day indirect-cost increments are due to extra help and additional storage-space rental while the old area is torn up. The activities, restrictions, and direct-cost estimates for three activity durations are shown in the following table:

Activity	Least time	Least cost	Normal time	Normal cost	Crash time	Crash cost	Restrictions
A	4	$ 200	4	$ 200	3	$ 250	$A < D, C$
B	7	300	6	350	5	450	$B < F, G$
C	11	800	10	870	8	950	$C < F, G$
D	5	100	3	140	2	180	$D < E$
E	3	300	3	300	3	300	$E < F$
F	6	180	5	210	4	240	
G	6	560	6	560	4	800	
		$2440		$2630		$3170	

a Construct a conventional time chart based on the least-cost activity durations.
b Determine the project duration that yields the minimum total direct cost.
c Determine the project duration that yields the minimum total cost.
d Show the results of part (c) in a time-chart format.

Chapter Five
Concepts
of
Interest

As we investigate different economic situations we continually encounter an uncontrollable factor — time. Thus far we have not directly considered time and its effects. The problems we have dealt with were characterized by either immediate outcomes or alternatives affected similarly by time. Through the use of interest calculations we can evaluate the time value of economic decisions.

Nearly everyone is at least acquainted with the term *interest*, the money paid for the use of borrowed capital or, equivalently, money gained from the use of loaned capital. The practice of charging interest dates back almost to the beginning of recorded history. Today it is an established principle. It is also a concept that is easy to accept without appreciation of its full potential or consequences.

TIME AND MONEY

EXAMPLE 5.1 Time value of money

The famous purchase of Manhattan Island from the Indians for $24 is often referred to as an exceptional bargain. This incident reputedly occurred in 1626, when Peter Minuit of the Dutch West India Company bought the rights to the island from local residents. But was it a bargain?

SOLUTION   Suppose the Indians had invested the money received from Minuit at a reasonable interest rate of 6% compounded annually. Over the years the original investment would have increased to the following proportions:

Year	Value of the original $24 investment
1626	$24.00
1676	$442.08
1726	$8143.25
1776	$149,999.92
1826	$2,763,021.69
1876	$50,895,285.75
1926	$937,499,015.11
1976	$17,268,876,484.38

REASONS FOR INTEREST   The significance of interest is obvious in the above example. The reasons for this effect become more apparent when we examine the uses of capital. In our economic environment capital is the basic resource. It can be converted to production goods, consumer goods, or services. It has the power to earn and to satisfy wants.

From a lender's viewpoint, capital is a fluid resource. He can spend it on goods expected to produce profit or on personal satisfaction. He can hoard it or give it away. It can also be loaned. If he lends it, he will normally expect some type of compensation. His compensation is interest. Interest pays for the administrative expense of making the loan, for the risk that the loan will not be repaid, and for the loss of earnings which would be obtained if the money had been used for other purposes.

From a borrower's viewpoint, a loan is both an obligation and an opportunity. A borrower must expect to repay the loan. Failure to repay leads to a damaged reputation, loss of possessions, and other consequences. The loan offers an opportunity to do something immediately that would otherwise have to be delayed. In some cases an objective would no longer exist after a delay. In order to take advantage of an existing course of action or to fulfill a current need, the borrower agrees to pay a certain amount in addition to the sum immediately received. This interest is the premium paid to avoid waiting for the money.

INTEREST RATE   An *interest rate* is the ratio of the amount gained from an investment to the amount invested for a specified period (usually 1 year). The level of the interest rate is a function of the borrower's and lender's viewpoints. For the borrower interest paid is a cost which he seeks to minimize; for the lender interest received is a gain which he hopes to maximize. The actual rate for a transaction is a compromise within the broader framework of risk, availability of capital, and investment opportunities.

Simple interest   When a *simple interest rate* is quoted, the interest earned is directly proportional to the capital involved in the loan. Expressed as a formula, the interest earned, I, is calculated by

$$I = Pin$$

where P = present amount or principal

i = interest rate per period

n = number of interest periods

Since the principal or amount borrowed, P, is a fixed value, the annual interest charged is constant. Therefore the total amount a borrower is obligated to pay a lender is

$$F = P + I = P + Pin$$
$$= P(1 + in)$$

where F = a future sum of money. When n is not a full year, there are two ways to calculate the simple interest earned during the period of the loan. Using *ordinary simple interest,* the year is divided into twelve 30-day periods or a year is considered to have 360 days. In *exact simple interest* a year has exactly the calendar number of days.

EXAMPLE 5.2 Simple interest

A loan of $200 is made for a period of 13 months from January 1 to January 31 the following year at a simple interest rate of 8%. What future amount is due at the end of the loan period?

SOLUTION   Using ordinary simple interest, the total amount to be repaid after 13 months is

$$F = P + Pin$$
$$= \$200 + \$200 \times 0.08 \times \left(1 + \frac{1}{12}\right)$$
$$= \$200 + \$16 \times 1.0833$$
$$= \$200 + \$17.33 = \$217.33$$

If exact simple interest is used, the future value (assuming the year in question is not a leap year) would be

$$F = P + Pin$$
$$= \$200 + \$200 \times 0.08 \times \left(1 + \frac{31}{365}\right)$$
$$= \$200 + \$16 \times 1.0849$$
$$= \$200 + \$17.36 = \$217.36$$

Compound interest rate Most economy studies are based on *compound interest*. With simple interest the amount of interest earned is based on the initial value of the loan and is due at the end of the loan period. With compound interest the life of a loan is divided into a number of interest periods. At the end of the first period the earned interest is calculated and added to the initial value of the loan. The sum of $P + I$ is then considered to be the value of the loan for the second period. In this way the interest earned during each period in turn earns interest during the following periods. *All* the money, both return and investment (or, in banking terms, accrued interest and principal) has earning power when interest is compounded.

EXAMPLE 5.3 Compound interest

A sum of $200 is deposited in an account where the interest rate is 8% compounded annually. What is the future value of the deposit if it is left for 2 years?

SOLUTION The interest period is given as 1 year. The amount due at the end of the first year and from which the second year's return will be calculated is

$$F1 = P + Pi$$
$$= \$200 + \$200 \times 0.08$$
$$= \$200 + \$16 = \$216$$

In the second year interest is due on both the initial investment and the first year's return.

$$F2 = P + Pi + (P + Pi)i$$
$$= P(1 + i + i + i^2)$$
$$= P(1 + i)^2$$
$$= \$200 \times (1 + 0.08)^2$$
$$= \$200 \times 1.1664 = \$233.28$$

From the example it is apparent that compound interest increases the future value of an account faster than simple interest; $200 invested for 2 years at 8% simple interest would have a future sum of $200 + $200 \times 0.08 \times 2 = $232. Tables are available to make the calculation of compound interest as easy as simple interest. The present value P is multiplied by a *compound-inter-*

est factor, $(1 + i)^n$, to obtain the future sum F. Compound-interest factors are tabulated in Appendix A for different interest rates per period, i, and the number of periods n.

Nominal interest rate A year is often divided into several interest periods. Interest is earned and compounded during each period. One way of expressing this condition is to quote the total interest figure as an annual rate and designate the number of periods per year by which it is divided. For instance, a year divided into four periods with interest at 2% per quarter may be quoted as "8% compounded quarterly." Stated in this fashion it is called a *nominal interest rate*. The future value at the end of 1 year for $200 earning interest at 8% compounded quarterly is

$$F\,(3\,\text{mo}) = P + Pi = \$200 + \$200 \times 0.02$$
$$= \$200 + \$4 = \$204$$

$$F\,(6\,\text{mo}) = \$204 + \$204 \times 0.02$$
$$= \$204 + \$4.08 = \$208.08$$

$$F\,(9\,\text{mo}) = \$208.08 + \$208.08 \times 0.02$$
$$= \$208.08 + \$4.16 = \$212.24$$

$$F\,(12\,\text{mo}) = \$212.24 + \$212.24 \times 0.02$$
$$= \$212.24 + \$4.24 = \$216.48$$

Effective interest rate Comparing the future value of $200 after 1 year compounded at 8% annually ($216) and at 8% compounded quarterly ($216.48) clearly reveals that the way interest rates are quoted affects the return. Nominal interest rates are compared by calculating the *effective interest rate*, the ratio of the annual return to the amount invested. For the $200 invested at 8% compounded annually,

$$\text{Effective interest rate} = \frac{F - P}{P}$$
$$= \frac{\$216 - \$200}{\$200}$$
$$= \frac{\$16}{\$200} = 0.08$$

At 8% compounded quarterly,

$$\text{Effective interest rate} = \frac{F - P}{P}$$
$$= \frac{\$216.48 - \$200}{\$200}$$
$$= \frac{\$16.48}{\$200} = 0.0824$$

The effective interest rate can also be obtained without reference to the amount invested. Letting m be the number of interest periods per year and j be the quoted nominal interest rate, then

$$\text{Effective interest rate} = \left(1 + \frac{j}{m}\right)^m - 1$$

Again using 8% compounded quarterly as an illustration, $j = 0.08$ and $m = 4$ and

$$\text{Effective interest rate} = \left(1 + \frac{0.08}{4}\right)^4 - 1$$
$$= (1.02)^4 - 1$$
$$= 1.0824 - 1 = 0.0824$$

EXAMPLE 5.4 Nominal and effective interest rates

A loan can be arranged at a nominal rate of 12% compounded monthly or 13% compounded semiannually. Which arrangement provides the lower debt at the end of the loan period?

SOLUTION   The more attractive arrangement is the one with the lowest effective interest rate. At 12% compounded monthly $j = 0.12$ and $m = 12$ and

$$\text{Effective interest rate} = \left(1 + \frac{0.12}{12}\right)^{12} - 1$$
$$= (1.01)^{12} - 1$$
$$= 1.127 - 1 = 0.127$$

At 13% compounded semiannually $j = 0.13$ and $m = 2$ and

$$\text{Effective interest rate} = \left(1 + \frac{0.13}{2}\right)^2 - 1$$
$$= (1.065)^2 - 1$$
$$= 1.134 - 1 = 0.134$$

The loan at 12% compounded monthly will have the lower F value.

EQUIVALENCE   Two things are equivalent when they produce the same effect. From Example 5.4 we could say that an effective interest rate of 13.4% is equivalent to a nominal interest rate of 13% compounded semiannually. Both interest calculations produce the same effect on an investment.

If $200 were sealed and buried today, it would have a cash value of $200 when it was dug up 2 years from now. Disregarding any change in the buying power of money, the value is constant. We have already observed that $200 deposited at 8% compounded annually has a value of $200 × (1 + 0.08)^2 = $233.28 after 2 years. Therefore $200 today is equivalent to $233.28 two years from now if it earns 8% compounded yearly. Similarly,

164

to plan on having $200 in 2 years from now, only

$$\$200 \times \frac{1}{(1 + 0.08)^2} = \$171.46$$

has to be deposited today.

The $200 could also be used to pay two equal annual $100 installments. The buried $200 could be retrieved after 1 year, an installment paid, and the remaining $100 interred again until the second payment was due. If instead the $200 is deposited at 8%, there would be $216 available at the end of the first year. After paying the first $100 installment, the remaining $116 would draw interest until the next payment. Paying the second $100 installment would leave

$$\$116 \times 1.08 - \$100 = \$125.28 - \$100 = \$25.28$$

in the account. Because of the earning power of money, the initial deposit could have been reduced to $180.80 to pay out $100 at the end of each of the 2 years. Thus $180.80 is equivalent to $100 received 1 year from now, plus another $100 received 2 years from now.

The concept of equivalence is the cornerstone for time value of money comparisons. To have a precise meaning, income and expenditures must be identified with time as well as with amount. A decision between alternatives having receipts and disbursements spread over a period of time is made by comparing the equivalent outcomes of the alternatives at a given date.

EXAMPLE 5.5 Equivalent values

How can $1000 today be translated into equivalent alternative expressions of cash flow?

SOLUTION

$1000 today is equivalent to $1791 received 10 years from now.

$1000 today is equivalent to $237.40 received at the end of each year for the next 5 years.

$1000 today is equivalent to $317.70 received at the end of years 6, 7, 8, 9, and 10.

$237.40 received at the end of each year for the next 5 years is equivalent to a lump sum of $1791 received 10 years from now.

$317.70 received at the end of years 6, 7, 8, 9, and 10 is equivalent to $1791 received 10 years from now.

$237.40 received at the end of each year for the next 5 years is equivalent to $317.70 received at the end of years 6, 7, 8, 9, and 10.

Figure 5.1 Equivalent outcomes with an interest rate of 6% compounded annually

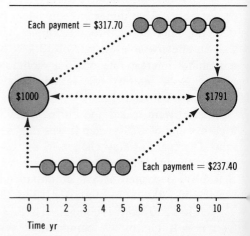

Cash flow is translated to a given point in time by determining either its present worth or its future worth. A present-worth calculation converts a single future sum or a series of future values to an equivalent amount at an earlier date. This date is not necessarily the present time. Future-worth calculations convert values occurring at any time to an equivalent amount at a later date.

Equivalent values could be determined by calculating the compound amount of each sum for each period. This tedious routine is avoided by using compound-interest tables for different present- and future-worth factors. There are two basic types of factors. The one we have already considered converts a single amount to a present or future value. The other type is for a series of uniform values called an *annuity*. In the tables we will use an annuity is characterized by (1) *equal payments*, (2) *equal periods between payments*, and (3) *the first payment occurring at the end of the first period*. Annuity factors are used to convert a series of payments to a single future or present sum and to translate single sums into a series of payments occurring in the past or future.

CONVERSION SYMBOLS   Before studying the development of compound-interest factors, we will consider their abbreviations and relationships. The six most commonly used time-value conversions are

To find	Given	Symbol
Future worth	Present amount	$(f/p)_n^i$
Present worth	Future amount	$(p/f)_n^i$
Future worth	Annuity of A amounts	$(f/a)_n^i$
Worth of annuity A	Future amount	$(a/f)_n^i$
Present worth	Annuity of A amounts	$(p/a)_n^i$
Worth of annuity A	Present amount	$(a/p)_n^i$

The symbol for each time-value conversion is an abbreviation for the function performed.[1] The first letter indicates the quantity being sought and the second letter is the known amount. The superscript shows the applicable interest rate per period, i (%), and the subscript

[1] For the sake of standardization, the symbols adopted for interest factors in this text are those used by the American Telephone and Telegraph Company in their text *Engineering Economy*, 2nd ed., 1963.

is the number of interest periods n involved in the conversion. In the equation

$$F = \$200 \, (f/p)_2^8$$

$200 is the known present amount P, the interest rate is 0.08 per period ($i = 8$), and F is the equivalent future worth f after two periods ($n = 2$). The numerical value of $(f/p)_2^8$, found from a table, is 1.166 and would yield the same solution as in Example 5.3.

The conversion descriptions and symbols connote that certain factors are reciprocals of one another. Other relationships are not apparent from the abbreviations but are useful in conversion calculations. The following equalities are verified during the development of the conversion formulas:

$$(f/p)_n^i = \frac{1}{(p/f)_n^i} \qquad (f/p)_n^i \times (p/a)_n^i = (f/a)_n^i$$

$$(f/a)_n^i = \frac{1}{(a/f)_n^i} \qquad (f/a)_n^i \times (a/p)_n^i = (f/p)_n^i$$

$$(p/a)_n^i = \frac{1}{(a/p)_n^i} \qquad (a/f)_n^i + i = (a/p)_n^i$$

DEVELOPMENT OF INTEREST FORMULAS A better understanding of the conversion process is achieved by studying the development of interest formulas. The symbols employed are the same as those described previously. The numerical values of the formulas for different interest rates and compounding periods are tabulated in Appendix A.

Single-payment future-worth factor The effect of compound interest on an investment was demonstrated in previous examples. The future worth of a present amount when interest is accumulated at a specific rate i for a given number of periods n, where $F1$ is the future worth at the end of the first period and Fn is the future worth at the end of n years, is

Use: To find F, given P
Expression: $(1 + i)^n$
Symbol: $(f/p)_n^i$
Formula: $F = P(1 + i)^n$
$F = P(f/p)_n^i$

$$F1 = P + Pi = P(1 + i)$$
$$F2 = P[(1 + i) + (1 + i)\,i]$$
$$\quad = P[(1 + i)(1 + i)] = P(1 + i)^2$$
$$F3 = P[(1 + i)^2 + (1 + i)^2\,i]$$
$$\quad = P[(1 + i)^2(1 + i)] = P(1 + i)^3$$
$$Fn = P(1 + i)^n$$

The ratio of future worth to present amount is then

expressed as

$$\frac{F}{P} = (f/p)_n^i = (1 + i)^n$$

Single-payment present-worth factor P is the present worth of a sum n periods in the future. Rearranging the single-amount future-value formula $F = P(1 + i)^n$ to express P in terms of F,

$$P = F\frac{1}{(1 + i)^n}$$

we have the ratio of present worth to future value:

$$\frac{P}{F} = (p/f)_n^i = \frac{1}{(1 + i)^n}$$

Use: To find P, given F

Expression: $\dfrac{1}{(1 + i)^n}$

Symbol: $(p/f)_n^i$

Formula: $P = F\dfrac{1}{(1 + i)^n}$

$P = F(p/f)_n^i$

Sinking-fund factor   A fund established to accumulate a given future amount through the collection of a uniform series of payments is called a *sinking fund*. Each payment has a constant value A and is made at the end of an interest period.

The growth pattern of a sinking fund is illustrated in Table 5.1. Each end-of-year payment A is equal to $1000 and continues for 5 years. Interest is 8% compounded annually. It is assumed that each payment begins to draw interest as soon as it is deposited in the sinking-fund account. Thus the first payment draws interest for 4 years and the last payment receives no interest.

Use: To find A, given F

Expression: $\dfrac{i}{(1 + i)^n - 1}$

Symbol: $(a/f)_n^i$

Formula: $A = F\dfrac{i}{(1 + i)^n - 1}$

$A = F(a/f)_n^i$

Table 5.1 Compound amount of a uniform series of payments

Time of payment (end of year)	Amount of payment A	Future worth at end of 5 yr
1	$1000	$1000 \times (1.08)^4 = $1360
2	1000	$1000 \times (1.08)^3 = 1260$
3	1000	$1000 \times (1.08)^2 = 1166$
4	1000	$1000 \times (1.08)^1 = 1080$
5	1000	$1000 \times (1.08)^0 = 1000$
		Annuity value F at the end of year 5 $= $5866

A more general expression for the future worth of an annuity develops from the use of symbols to represent the values in Table 5.1. The first payment, earning interest for $n - 1$ periods, increases to a future worth of

$$F = A(1 + i)^{n-1}$$

Each of the payments is treated in the same manner and collected to obtain the total amount F:

$$F = A(1 + i)^{n-1} + A(1 + i)^{n-2} + A(1 + i)^{n-3}$$
$$+ A(1 + i)^{n-4} + A(1 + i)^{n-n}$$

Factoring out A and letting the exponent $n - n = 0$, we have

$$F = A \left[(1 + i)^{n-1} + (1 + i)^{n-2} + (1 + i)^{n-3} \right. $$
$$\left. + (1 + i)^{n-4} + 1 \right]$$

Multiplying this equation by $1 + i$ results in

$$F(1 + i) = A \left[(1 + i)^n + (1 + i)^{n-1} + (1 + i)^{n-2} \right.$$
$$\left. + (1 + i)^{n-3} + (1 + i) \right]$$

Subtracting the original equation from the last equation gives

$$F(1 + i) - F = -A + A(1 + i)^n$$
$$Fi = A \left[(1 + i)^n - 1 \right]$$

and solving for A,

$$A = F \frac{i}{(1 + i)^n - 1}$$

we see the sinking-fund-factor expression is

$$(a/f)_n^i = \frac{i}{(1 - i)^n - 1}$$

Series-payment future-worth factor From the development of the sinking-fund-factor formula,

$$Fi = A(1 + i)^n - 1$$

which, expressed in terms of F, results in

$$F = A \frac{(1 + i)^n - 1}{i}$$

Then the time value for the future worth of the annuity is expressed as

$$(f/a)_n^i = \frac{(1 + i)^n - 1}{i}$$

Use: To find F, given A

Expression: $\dfrac{(1 + i)^n - 1}{i}$

Symbol: $(f/a)_n^i$

Formula: $F = A \dfrac{(1 + i)^n - 1}{i}$

$F = A (f/a)_n^i$

EXAMPLE 5.6 Future worth of a series of payments
A manufacturing firm in a foreign country has agreed to pay \$25,000 in royalties at the end of each year for the next 5 years for the use of a patented product design. If the payments are left with the foreign company, interest on the retained funds will be paid at an annual rate of 15%. What total amount will be available in 5 years under these conditions?

SOLUTION   The annual payments form an annuity. Knowing that $A = \$25,000$ per period, $i = 15\%$ per period, and there are 5 periods, the future worth F is calculated from

$$F = A (f/a)_5^{15}$$

to obtain

$$F = \$25,000 \times 6.742$$
$$= \$168,550$$

If the patent owners insisted on an accumulated value of $175,000, the five end-of-year royalty payments would have to be

$$A = F (a/f)_5^{15} = \$175,000 \times 0.148 = \$25,900$$

Capital-recovery factor   The capital-recovery factor is used to determine the amount of each future annuity payment required to accumulate a given present value when the interest rate and number of payments are known. For instance, the amount of each annual payment made for 5 years in order to repay a debt of $3993 bearing 8% annual interest can be determined through the use of the capital-recovery factor $(a/p)_n^i$. Table 5.2 shows that it would take five $1000 payments to repay the $3993 debt.

Use: To find A, given P

Expression: $\dfrac{i(1 + i)^n}{(1 + i)^n - 1}$

Symbol: $(a/p)_n^i$

Formula: $A = P \dfrac{i(1 + i)^n}{(1 + i)^n - 1}$

$$A = P (a/p)_n^i$$

Table 5.2   Present worth of a uniform series of payments

Time of payment (end of year)	Amount of payment A	Present worth at 8%
1	$1000	$1000 \times (1.08)^{-1} = \$ 926$
2	1000	$1000 \times (1.08)^{-2} = 857$
3	1000	$1000 \times (1.08)^{-3} = 794$
4	1000	$1000 \times (1.08)^{-4} = 735$
5	1000	$1000 \times (1.08)^{-5} = 681$
		Present worth P of the 5-yr annuity $= \$3993$

Using symbols to represent the conversions shown in Table 5.2, the present worth of an annuity is

$$P = A [(1 + i)^{-1} + (1 + i)^{-2} + (1 + i)^{-3} + (1 + i)^{-4} + (1 + i)^{-n}]$$

and multiplying both sides of the equation by $(1 + i)^{-1}$ results in

$$P (1 + i)^{-1} = A [(1 + i)^{-2} + (1 + i)^{-3} + (1 + i)^{-4} + (1 + i)^{-n} + (1 + i)^{-n-1}]$$

Subtracting the first equation from the second equation,

$$P [(1 + i)^{-1} - 1] = A [(1 + i)^{-n-1} - (1 + i)^{-1}]$$

converting $(1 + i)^{-1} - 1$ to $-i/(1 + i)$, multiplying both sides by $-(1 + i)$, and rearranging, we have

$$P \frac{i(1 + i)}{(1 + i)} = A [(1 + i)(1 + i)^{-1} - (1 + i)(1 + i)^{-n-1}]$$

$$Pi = A [1 - (1 + i)^{-n}]$$

$$Pi = A \frac{(1 + i)^n - 1}{(1 + i)^n}$$

This yields

$$A = P \frac{i(1+i)^n}{(1+i)^n - 1}$$

from which comes the expression for the capital-recovery factor,

$$(a/p)_n^i = \frac{i(1+i)^n}{(1+i)^n - 1}$$

The relationship among time-value annuity factors is apparent from the way the capital-recovery factor can be converted to the sinking-fund factor by substituting $P = F(1+i)^{-n}$ in the capital-recovery formula, as

$$A = P(a/p)_n^i = \frac{F}{(1+i)^n}(a/p)_n^i = \frac{F}{(1+i)^n} \frac{i(1+i)^n}{(1+i)^n - 1}$$

$$A = F \frac{i}{(1+i)^n - 1} = F(a/f)_n^i$$

or

$$(a/p)_n^i = (a/f)_n^i + i$$

as indicated by

$$\frac{i(1+i)^n}{(1+i)^n - 1} = \frac{i}{(1+i)^n - 1} + i$$

$$= \frac{i + (1+i)^n - i}{(1+i)^n - 1} = \frac{i(1+i)^n}{(1+i)^n - 1}$$

Series-payment present-worth factor   The present value of a series of uniform end-of-year payments can be calculated in the cumbersome fashion shown in Table 5.2. The present worth is more readily determined by use of the series-payment present-worth factor, $(p/a)_n^i$.

Expressing the known relationship

$$A = P \frac{i(1+i)^n}{(1+i)^n - 1}$$

in terms of P,

$$P = A \frac{(1+i)^n - 1}{i(1+i)^n}$$

we have the time-value expression for the present worth of an annuity,

$$(p/a)_n^i = \frac{(1+i)^n - 1}{i(1+i)^n}$$

Use: To find P, given A

Expression: $\dfrac{(1+i)^n - 1}{i(1+i)^n}$

Symbol: $(p/a)_n^i$

Formula: $P = A \dfrac{(1+i)^n - 1}{i(1+i)^n}$

$P = A(p/a)_n^i$

EXAMPLE 5.7   Present worth of a series of payments

The management of a wearing-apparel firm is considering a proposal from a consulting firm to introduce a new method of training inexperienced sewing-machine operators. The consultants claim that their program will produce savings of $7000 per year over the planned 5-year life of the project. Immediate costs to implement the program are $12,000. Annual training expenses will be $4000. The company uses 6% annual interest for cost comparisons. Do the anticipated savings warrant the expense of hiring the training consultants?

SOLUTION   Assuming that the costs and savings occur at the end of each year,

$$A = \text{annual savings} - \text{annual costs}$$
$$= \$7000 - \$4000$$
$$= \$3000$$

For the proposal to be acceptable, the net return must be greater than the $12,000 initial cost. By translating the 5-year annuity to the present time, the initial cost and the present worth of the gross savings, P, are compared directly.

$$P = A\,(p/a)_5^6$$
$$= \$3000 \times 4.212$$
$$= \$12,636$$

The indicated total net saving exceeds the initial cost by

$$\$12,636 - \$12,000 = \$636$$

which gives very little leeway for any error in the cost estimates.

The same conclusion results from a different approach with the same data. From the capital-recovery formula, the annual return on the gross savings, A, required for 5 years to meet a current obligation of $12,000 is

$$A = P\,(a/p)_5^6$$
$$= \$12,000 \times 0.2374$$
$$= \$2849$$

Comparing the required return to the expected annual gross savings shows annual net savings of

$$\$3000 - \$2849 = \$151$$

CONTINUOUS COMPOUNDING   The interest tables in Appendix A are based on discrete or lump-sum payments. Another way to view cash flow is to assume that it is continuous. This assumption is the basis of *continuous compounding*; earned interest is computed and added to the previous balance at every moment of time.

Both discrete and continuous models of cash flow are approximations of actual transactions. Cash incomes or outlays do not always follow a uniform pattern, nor do they always occur as periodic end-of-period payments. They are often irregular in amount and in timing.

Tables for continuous compounding have been developed for the six interest factors previously described. They are appropriately used when cash flows continuously at a constant rate over a period of time. However, we will focus our attention on discrete compounding because it is more commonly understood, accepted, and used by industry.

Interest problems are solved by translating receipts or disbursements to a desired point in time. The calendar date of this point depends on the type of problem and the time that is most meaningful in terms of analysis objectives.

The notable points in the statement of a problem are the interest elements, P, F, A, n, and i. Generally, three of the elements are known and the problem entails solving for a fourth element. Several money-time conversions may be required in one solution.

The concept of equivalence was introduced earlier in this chapter. Through the use of compound-interest factors equivalent relationships are easily formulated to reflect the time value of money. Because several equivalent conditions may be needed to solve one problem, it is often convenient to draw a rough sketch of cash flow to a time scale. The purpose of a money-time chart is to keep track of cash flow; it does not provide a graphical solution to a problem.

The calculation of equivalent values and the pictorial representation of interest factors are illustrated by the following examples. In each instance the interest is assumed to be compounded annually, and all payments or receipts occur at the end of an interest period. The numerical values for the interest symbols are from Appendix A.

EXAMPLE 5.8 Present worth of a single payment

What is the worth on August 1, 1971, of a $10,000 payment to be received on August 1, 1980, at an interest rate of 4%?

SOLUTION   Find P (1971), given $F = \$10,000$, $n = 9$, and $i = 4\%$:

$$P = F\,(p/f)_9^4$$
$$= \$10,000 \times 0.7026$$
$$= \$7026$$

Figure 5.2

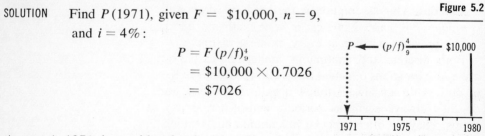

August 1, 1971, is considered to be "now," or the present time P. The $7026 available now is equivalent to $10,000 9 years in the future when the interest rate is 4% compounded annually.

EXAMPLE 5.9 Interest rate for a single payment

At what annual interest rate will $1000 invested today be worth $2000 in 9 years?

SOLUTION   Find i, given $P = \$1000$, $F = \$2000$, and $n = 9$ years:

$$\frac{F}{P} = (f/p)_n^i$$

$$\frac{\$2000}{\$1000} = (f/p)_9^i$$

$$2.0 = (f/p)_9^i$$

$$i = 8\%$$

Figure 5.3

$1000 \cdots (f/p)_9^i \cdots \blacktriangleright \$2000$

0   9

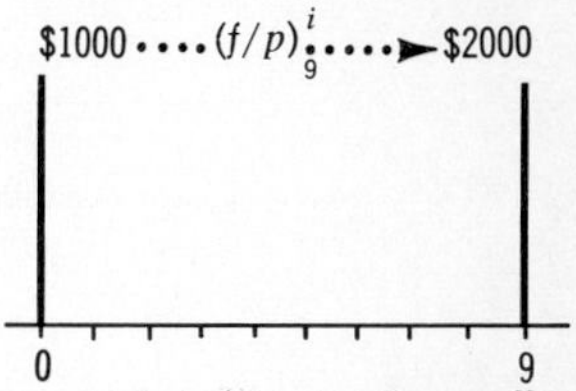

The interest rate i is determined by locating the interest rate at which the single-payment future-worth factor is equal to 2.0 at $n = 9$ (a reciprocal relationship using a present-worth factor could serve just as well). The numerical value of i is found by leafing through the pages of interest rates and noting the appropriate factor values for the given number of periods.

It is usually necessary to interpolate from table values when n or i is unknown. The error introduced by linear interpolation is relatively insignificant for most practical applications. If the investment period for Example 5.9 had been 10 years instead of 9, the interest-rate calculation would be

$$(f/p)_{10}^i = \frac{F}{P} = \frac{\$2000}{\$1000} = 2.0$$

at $i = 7\%$, $(f/p)_{10}^7 = 1.967$; and at $i = 8\%$, $(f/p)_{10}^8 = 2.159$.

Then, by interpolation, we have

$$i = 0.07 + 0.01 \times \frac{2.000 - 1.967}{2.159 - 1.967}$$

$$= 0.07 + 0.01 \times \frac{0.033}{0.192}$$

$$= 0.07 + 0.0017 = 0.0717$$

$$= 7.2\%$$

EXAMPLE 5.10 Annuity due

What is the present worth of a series of 15 year-end payments of $1000 each *beginning today* when the interest rate is 5%?

SOLUTION   Find P, given $A = \$1000$, $n = 15$, and $i = 5\%$. A series of payments made at the beginning instead of the end of each period is sometimes referred to as an *annuity due*. Rather than create a special factor for this annuity pattern, we can break the series of payments into two parts. If the first payment is evaluated separately, the remaining payments fit the pattern for an ordinary annuity beginning at the time of the first payment.

The present worth of $1000 received today is, of course, $1000. Then the total present worth is

$$P = A + A\,(p/a)^5_{14}$$
$$= \$1000 + \$1000 \times 9.899$$
$$= \$1000 + \$9,899$$
$$= \$10,899$$

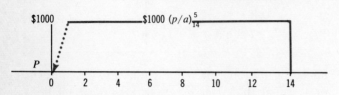

Figure 5.4

Another pattern for a series of payments, where the first payment does not begin until some date later than the end of the first period, is called a *deferred annuity*. Like an annuity due, a deferred annuity is evaluated by dividing the time period into two parts. One portion is the number of payment periods n, plus 1. This portion forms an ordinary annuity of n periods. The second portion is the number of periods left after subtracting $n + 1$ periods. A solution results from determining the present worth of the ordinary annuity and then discounting this value through the deferred period.

EXAMPLE 5.11 Deferred annuity

With interest at 6%, what is the worth on June 30, 1969, of a series of year-end payments of $317.70 made on June 30 from 1975 through 1979?

SOLUTION   For an annuity deferred 5 years, find $P(1969)$, given $A = \$317.70$, $n = 5$, and $i = 6\%$. The value of a money-time chart becomes more apparent as interest problems assume interrelated patterns. The two portions of the problem are apparent in Fig. 5.5. The annuity starts on June 30, 1974, with the first payment due 1 year later. Then the present worth on this date, labeled $P(1974)$, is

$$P(1974) = A\,(p/a)^6_5$$

The present worth of $P(1974)$ on June 30, 1969, is

$$P(1969) = P(1974)\,(p/f)^6_5$$

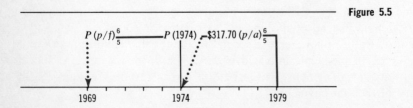

Figure 5.5

Collecting the terms, we have

$$P(1969) = A (p/a)_5^6 (p/f)_5^6$$
$$= \$317.70 \times 4.212 \times 0.7473$$
$$P = \$1000$$

The previous example may be recognized as one of the equivalent outcomes presented without proof in Fig. 5.1. Another of the outcomes from the same figure is shown in Fig. 5.6. The value of the annuity after five

Figure 5.6

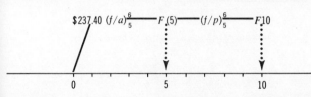

payments of $237.40 is labeled $F5$. Letting the end of the fifth year be "now," $F5$ is treated as a present value and the single-payment future-worth factor is used to find the compound amount at the end of year 10:

$$F5 = A (f/a)_5^6 \quad \text{and} \quad F10 = F5 (f/p)_5^6$$
$$F10 = A (f/a)_5^6 (f/p)_5^6$$
$$= \$237.40 \times 5.637 \times 1.338$$
$$= \$1791$$

More extensive economic situations often include both income and outlay. Such situations are evaluated by calculating the net outcome at a certain point in time. A money-time chart incorporates receipts and disbursements by displaying income above the time-reference line and outlays below the line. Other payment categories can be handled similarly.

EXAMPLE 5.12 Income and outlay

A boy is now 11 years old. On his fifth birthday he received a gift of $4000 from his grandparents which was invested in 10-year bonds bearing interest at 4% compounded semiannually. His father plans to have $3000 available for the boy's nineteenth, twentieth, twenty-first, and twenty-second birthdays to finance a college education. To help the financing the grandparents' gift will be reinvested when the bonds mature. How much should the father allocate to invest each year on the boy's twelfth through eighteenth birthdays to complete the education plan? All future investments will earn 6% annually.

SOLUTION   The money-time chart for the problem is based on an evaluation date of the boy's eighteenth birthday. It would be equally valid to use any of his birthdays for the comparison date. The same value for his father's payments, A, would result for any chosen date, but there is usually one time which reduces the number of required calculations to a minimum.

As shown in Fig. 5.7, there are three payment plans involved: a series of outlays, a lump-sum investment, and a series of annual investments. After we compute the difference between the amount available from the lump-sum investment and the amount required for the education expenses on a common date, we can determine the annual payment necessary to accumulate this difference.

Figure 5.7

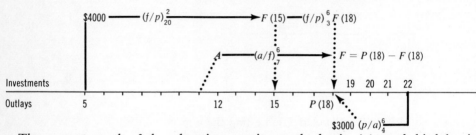

The present worth of the education annuity on the boy's eighteenth birthday is

$$P18 = A \, (p/a)_4^6$$
$$= \$3000 \times 3.465$$
$$= \$10,395$$

The future worth of the grandparent's gift is a function of two investment rates: 2% per period for 20 periods (a nominal interest rate of 4% compounded semiannually for 10 years), followed by 6% per period for three periods:

$$F18 = P \, (f/p)_{20}^2 \, (f/p)_3^6$$
$$= \$4000 \times 1.486 \times 1.191$$
$$= \$7079$$

The difference F between the amount required and the amount available at year 18 is

$$F = P18 - F18$$
$$= \$10,395 - \$7079$$
$$= \$3316$$

which is the required future value for the series of $18 - 11 = 7$ payments A beginning on the boy's twelfth birthday:

$$A = F \, (a/f)_7^6$$
$$= \$3316 \times 0.11914$$
$$= \$395$$

Thus an annual investment of $395 for the next 7 years will assure a contribution of $3000 per year for 4 years beginning on the boy's nineteenth birthday.

Economic decisions with revenue and expenses spread over a span of time are evaluated by comparing the time value of cash flow. Three methods are commonly

TIME COMPARISONS

used to compare outcomes of alternatives on an equivalent basis: (1) the annual-cost method, (2) the present-worth method, and (3) the rate-of-return method. The first two methods compare costs or revenue on the basis of a stipulated minimum acceptable return on invested capital. The alternative with the lowest "equivalent annual expense" or lowest "equivalent present cost" is the economic choice. The rate-of-return method compares alternatives on the basis of the percentage return on increments of investment. The amount that an alternative exceeds a minimum standard return within available investment sources is the criterion for selection.

All three bases of comparison are mathematically compatible. That is, an economic preference for a certain alternative registered by one method will also be indicated by the other methods. All the methods are well established, and each has its champions. With practice an analyst will select the method most suitable for the data, circumstances, and audience in the decision environment.

One set of economic conditions will be used to illustrate the three methods of time comparisons. The problem information given in Table 5.3 is not a complete decision description in that taxes, depreciation, and other practical aspects are ignored. It does, however, provide a sound basis for examining the comparison methods.

ANNUAL-COST METHOD OF COMPARISON With the annual-cost method all the receipts and disbursements occurring over a period of time are converted to an equivalent uniform yearly charge. It is a very popular method because of the widespread inclination to view a year's gains and losses as a yardstick of progress. Cost-accounting procedures, depreciation expenses, tax calculations, and other summary reports are annual in nature. These yearly cost tabulations generally make the annual-cost method easier to apply and comprehend than the other methods.

Equivalent uniform annual costs are calculated by converting nonuniform and sporadic costs to a yearly annuity via interest factors, and then adding any other constant annual costs to obtain one revenue figure. The procedure is repeated for all the alternatives. The alternative with the lowest equivalent revenue requirements is preferred.

BASIC PROBLEM DATA

A certain function is currently being performed at an annual labor expense of $20,000. One alternative, Plan A, is to leave the operation unchanged. In effect, this is the "do-nothing" alternative which is almost always present in a decision situation. A second alternative, Plan B, is to invest $30,000 in layout modifications which will allow the function to be performed at a reduced labor cost of $15,000. The expense of the renovations must be recovered in 10 years according to operating policy. Plan C is a proposal to install a labor-saving device which will cut the labor cost to $12,000. The device will be worn out in 5 years and has no salvage value. Table 5.3 is a year-by-year tabulation of the cash flow for the three plans. If the company's minimum acceptable rate of return is 8%, which plan offers the greatest economic benefit?

Year	Plan A	Plan B	Plan C
19–0	. . .	$30,000	$25,000
19–1	$20,000	15,000	12,000
19–2	20,000	15,000	12,000
19–3	20,000	15,000	12,000
19–4	20,000	15,000	12,000
19–5	20,000	15,000	37,000
19–6	20,000	15,000	12,000
19–7	20,000	15,000	12,000
19–8	20,000	15,000	12,000
19–9	20,000	15,000	12,000
19–10	20,000	15,000	12,000

Table 5.3 Cash flow for alternative operating plans

For the basic problem data, the annual-cost comparison of the three plans is conducted as follows:

Plan A The annual cost can be read directly from Table 5.3, $20,000 per year. Regardless of any required interest rate,

$$\text{Annual cost for Plan } A = \text{labor expense}$$
$$= \$20,000$$

Plan B The first step is to spread the initial $30,000 investment over the 10-year study period. This as accomplished by using the capital-recovery factor to convert the present sum to a series of uniform costs:

$$A = P\,(a/p)_{10}^{8}$$
$$= \$30,000 \times 0.14903$$
$$= \$4471$$

Then the already constant labor expense is added to the computed equivalent uniform costs to get

Annual cost for Plan B

= labor expense + equivalent cost of the modifications

= \$15,000 + \$4471

= \$19,471

which is slightly less than the labor costs without the modifications.

Plan C A comparison of alternatives with different lives is introduced in Plan C. The labor-saving device has a life of 5 years. Since the study period is 10 years, the device goes through two cycles of wear; purchased new at time zero it is worn out at the end of year 5 and is immediately replaced by a new identical device, which in turn is useless at the end of year 10.

In most comparisons of alternatives with different lives the calculations are not so convenient. It is necessary to assume that the annual costs for each life cycle are constant. This means that to compare two alternatives the study period must extend through the lowest common multiple of the estimated lives of the alternatives. For example, if one alternative had an 8-year life and the other a 12-year life, the study period would be 24 years, three life cycles for the first alternative and two for the second.

Since the study period for the three plans is already a common multiple of two 5-year life cycles for Plan C, we only need to calculate the annual cost for one 5-year period, because the second cycle follows the same uniform cost pattern:

Annual cost for Plan C

= labor expense + equivalent cost of the labor-saving device

= labor expense + $P(a/p)_5^8$

= \$12,000 + \$25,000 × 0.25046

$\doteq$ \$12,000 + \$6262

= \$18,262

Conclusion   Summarizing the three plans, we have

	Plan A	Plan B	Plan C
Investment	0	\$30,000	\$25,000
Annual cost	\$20,000	19,471	18,262

These results mean that for the preferred Plan C compared to the currently used Plan A an investment of \$25,000 will yield a return of 8% per year plus the equivalent receipt of $20,000 - $18,262 = $1738 each year from savings in labor expense.

PRESENT-WORTH METHOD OF COMPARISON   Present worth is the value of money at time zero. Any receipts or disbusements which take place on the zero date are incorporated in the analysis at their stated value. To these first costs are added the present worth of future payments. When the payments are in the form of an annuity, the present worth is calculated with the p/a factor. Lump sums are translated to time zero by using the single-payment present-worth factor p/f.

A study period should be the same for two alternatives compared by the present-worth method. For example, a direct comparison of the present worth of an alternative with a life of 12 years to one with a life of 17 years is inconclusive. The results of such a study are not equivalent, because no compensation is allowed for operating conditions during the extra 5 years of activity in the second alternative. Inflation, technological breakthroughs, or many other circumstances could radically affect the economic position of an alternative during the period of additional life expectancy. An assumption that the same costs will be repeated during successive life cycles leads to the use of lowest common multiples of expected life, as described for annual-cost calculations. Another approach, which assumes perpetual life for alternatives, is considered in Chap. 7.

The following calculations reveal the present worth of the three plans at time zero, 19–0.

Plan A The uniform series of payments for labor cost are converted to an equivalent present amount by

$$\text{Present worth of Plan } A = (p/a)^8_{10}$$
$$= \$20,000 \times 6.710$$
$$= \$134,200$$

Plan B The first cost of the modification ($30,000) is already a present value. Adding this initial cost to the present worth of the $15,000 annual labor expense, we have

Present worth of Plan B

$= $ modification cost $+$ present worth of annual labor cost

$= $ first cost $+ A\,(p/a)^8_{10}$

$= \$30,000 + \$15,000 \times 6.710$

$= \$30,000 + \$100,650$

$= \$130,650$

Plan C   Two life cycles of the labor-saving device must be accounted for in Plan *C*. The first cost of $25,000 is added to the replacement cost discounted 5 years and to the present worth of 10 years of annual labor costs to obtain

Present worth of Plan *C*

$= $ first cost $+$ discounted replacement cost $+$ present worth of labor cost

$= \$25,000 + \$25,000\,(p/f)^8_5 + \$12,000\,(p/a)^8_{10}$

$= \$25,000 + \$25,000 \times 0.6806 + \$12,000 \times 6.710$

$= \$25,000 + \$17,015 + \$80,520$

$= \$122,535$

Conclusion   As expected, Plan *C* is again preferred. The results are interpreted as a claim that an investment of $25,000 will return 8% plus the equivalent single payment of $134,200 - $122,535 = $11,665 at time 19–0 from the annual $20,000 - $12,000 = $8000 reduction in labor expense.

The mathematical convertibility of present worths and annual costs is demonstrated by

Present worth of Plan *C*

$$= \text{annual cost for Plan } C \times (p/a)^8_{10}$$

$$\$122,535 = \$18,262 \times 6.710$$

$$\$122,535 = \$122,537$$

(the inequality is due to "rounding off") and

Annual cost for Plan *B*

$$= \text{present worth of Plan } B \times (a/p)^8_{10}$$

$$\$19,471 = \$130,650 \times 0.14903$$

$$\$19,471 = \$19,471$$

Although both methods lead to the same decision, the annual-cost method is more generally recommended. Present-worth calculations do show the magnitude of a decision in terms of today's dollars, but the large values are somewhat difficult to interpret, and the calculations tend to be cumbersome for alternatives with different lives.

RATE-OF-RETURN METHOD OF COMPARISON   A rate-of-return calculation measures the percentage of profit expected from following a certain course of action. Profit may result from the difference between income and costs of producing the income or from savings derived from adopting an alternative means of accomplishing an objective. The basis of comparison is the amount invested to produce the profit. In its most direct form,

$$\text{Rate of return} = \frac{\text{annual profit}}{\text{invested capital}}$$

Used as a method of evaluating alternatives, the rate of return measures the returns from a larger investment against those obtained from a smaller investment to ascertain if the incremental investment earns a stipulated minimum acceptable rate. This is accomplished by equating the present worths or annual costs of two investments. The rate of return is the interest rate that balances the equation. If the rate is greater than the minimum required return, the larger investment is preferred, provided that sufficient capital is available to make the additional increment of investment.

When a single proposal is assessed, only i is unknown. In this case the rate of return can be found directly by interpolation. More often alternatives are compared where the rate of return is determined by trial and error. Two interest rates are assumed, and the rate of return is found by interpolation.

The preferred alternative from the basic problem data has already been calculated, but we will go through the rate-of-return procedure to verify the solution. Any decision situation benefits from additional insights. A rate of return is a universally understood measure of economic success which provides a different viewpoint from the other comparison methods. It gives a decimal rating to opportunities, as shown in the following calculations:

Plan A versus Plan C   Alternatives are usually compared in order of increasing initial investments. Plan A has no initial cost, while Plan C has a first cost of $25,000. Equating the plans in terms of annual costs, we have

Annual cost for Plan A = annual cost for Plan C

$$\$20,000 = \$12,000 + \$25,000\,(a/p)_5^i$$

$$\frac{\$20,000 - \$12,000}{\$25,000} = (a/p)_5^i$$

$$0.320 = (a/p)_5^i$$

From $i = 15\%$, $(a/p)_5^{15} = 0.29832$; from $i = 20\%$, $(a/p)_5^{20} = 0.33438$. Interpolation results in

$$\text{Rate of return} = 0.15 + 0.05 \times \frac{0.32000 - 0.29832}{0.33438 - 0.29832}$$

$$= 0.15 + 0.05 \times 0.601$$

$$= 0.18 = 18\%$$

The results indicate that an investment of $25,000 in the labor-saving device will yield a return of 18% over the study period.

Plan C versus Plan B   The next comparison pits Plan C against Plan B, rather than Plan A against Plan B, because Plan A has been eliminated from further consideration. If Plan C had not shown a return above the minimum acceptable rate (8%), it would have been eliminated instead. Again using annual costs for the evaluation, we have

Annual cost for Plan C = annual cost for Plan B

$$\$12,000 + \$25,000\,(a/p)_5^i = \$15,000 + \$30,000\,(a/p)_{10}^i$$

or, rearranging,

$$\$25,000\,(a/p)_5^i - \$30,000\,(a/p)_{10}^i - \$3000 \neq 0$$

which will equal zero only if we use a negative rate of return. This negative rate arises because Plan C is more economical than Plan B, as was shown in previous calculations. Thus Plan C is again the indicated preference.

To illustrate the use of present-worth equations in determining a rate of return, Plan C is once more compared to Plan A in the following calculations:

Present worth of Plan A = present worth of Plan C

$$\$20,000\,(p/a)_{10}^i$$
$$= \$25,000 + \$25,000\,(p/f)_5^i + \$12,000\,(p/a)_{10}^i$$

Rearranging gives

$$0 = \$25,000 + \$25,000\,(p/f)_5^i - \$8000\,(p/a)_{10}^i$$

Turning to the interest tables, we obtain for $i = 20\%$

Present worth $= \$25,000 + \$25,000 \times 0.4019$
$$- \$8000 \times 4.192$$
$$\$1512 = \$25,000 + \$10,048 - \$33,536$$

and for $i = 15\%$

Present worth $= \$25,000 + \$25,000 \times 0.4972$
$$- \$8000 \times 5.019$$
$$-\$2722 = \$25,000 + \$12,430 - \$40,152$$

Interpolation yields

$$\text{Rate of return} = 15\% + 5\% \times \frac{0 - (-\$2722)}{\$1512 - (-\$2722)}$$
$$= 15\% + 5\% \times \frac{\$2722}{\$4234}$$
$$= 18.2\%$$

which is very close to the return calculated from annual costs in the original equation.

Conclusion   The rate-of-return method yields the same preference (Plan *C*) as the other methods, and the degree of preference is stated in readily understood terms. A rate of return can be compared without interpretation to rates representative of other investment opportunities. The method is well suited for comparisons between investments where absolute amounts are unknown but estimated differences in cash flow are available.

SELECTED REFERENCES

DeGarmo, E. P.: *Engineering Economy*, The Macmillan Company, New York, 1967.

Grant, E. L., and W. G. Ireson: *Principles of Engineering Economy*, The Ronald Press Company, New York, 1960.

Thuesen, H. G., and W. J. Fabrycky: *Engineering Economy*, Prentice-Hall, Inc., Englewood Cliffs, N.J., 1964.

Taylor, G. A.: *Managerial and Engineering Economy*, D. Van Nostrand Company, Inc., New York, 1964.

Tyler, C., and C. H. Winter, Jr.: *Chemical Engineering Economics*, McGraw-Hill Book Company, New York, 1959.

Wellington, A. M.: *The Economic Theory of Railway Location*, John Wiley & Sons, Inc., New York, 1837.

PROBLEMS

5.1   A loan of $400 is made at 7% simple interest for a period of 3 years. What is the total amount to be repaid at the end of the loan period?

5.2   What amount of interest is earned on a deposit of $800 for the last 6 months of a calendar year at the rate of
a   10% ordinary simple interest?
b   10% exact simple interest?

5.3   How much money would have to be invested today to provide a balance of $500 at the end of 4 years if the simple interest rate is 7%?

5.4   What is the ordinary simple interest rate being paid on a loan of $714 that earns $41 interest in 6 months?

5.5 What is the effective interest rate for
a 12% compounded semiannually?
b 12% compounded quarterly?
c 12% compounded monthly?

5.6 What nominal interest, compounded quarterly, is required to provide a 6% effective interest rate? A 12% effective interest rate?

5.7 A personal loan is made at an interest rate of 3/4% per month on the unpaid balance. What is the effective interest rate? How much interest is earned if the duration of the loan is 18 months?

5.8 How long will it take for $1 to double in value (disregarding any change in the buying power of a dollar) if
a The interest rate is 10% compounded annually?
b The interest rate is 10% compounded semiannually?
c The interest rate is 10% ordinary simple interest?

5.9 How is it possible to determine the numerical value of a capital-recovery factor a/p if the only table available is
a p/f?
b a/f?
c f/a?

5.10 Determine the value of $(f/a)_8^4$ using only the table for p/a.

5.11 Develop a formula for the present worth of an annuity due.

5.12 What is the future worth of each of the following investments?
a $6300 in 6 years at 15% compounded annually.
b $2000 in 4 years at 4¼% compounded annually.
c $200 in 27 years at 6% compounded annually.
d $4300 in 6 years at 7% compounded semiannually.
e $500 in 17 years at 9% compounded quarterly.

5.13 What annual interest rate increases an investment of $1400 to $2000 in 9 years?

5.14 How many years will it take for the balance left in a savings account to increase from $1000 to $1500 if interest is received at a nominal rate of 6% compounded semiannually throughout the period?

5.15 Solve the following problems with an annual interest rate of 5%:
a What amount must be invested today to secure a perpetual income of $6000 per year?
b A present expenditure of $50,000 is justified by what annual saving for the next 12 years?
c What is the annual payment that will provide a sum of $20,000 in 20 years?

d How much money can be loaned today on an agreement that $700 will be paid 6 years from now?

e What payment can be made today to prevent a series of year-end expenses of $2800 lasting 15 years?

f If the down payment on a piece of land is $7000 and the annual payments for 8 years are $2000 per year, what is the value of the land now?

g What single payment 10 years from now is equivalent to a payment of $5500 in 3 years?

h If $12,000 must be accumulated by annual payments in 15 years, but the first payment cannot be made until 4 years from now, how much will each payment be?

5.16 What semiannual cost beginning today is equivalent to spending lump sums of $2000 in 2 years, $4000 in 4 years, and $8000 in 8 years if the nominal interest rate is 8% compounded semiannually?

5.17 A small refining company entered into a contract for raw materials with an agreement to pay $60,000 now and $15,000 per year beginning at the end of the fifth year. The contract was made for 10 years. At the end of the third year, because of unexpected profits, the company requested that it be allowed to make a lump-sum payment in advance for the rest of the contract. Both parties agreed that 7% compounded annually was a fair interest rate. What was the amount of the lump sum?

5.18 A construction firm can lease a crane required on a project for 3 years for $180,000 payable now, with maintenance included. The alternative is to buy a crane for $240,000 and sell it at the end of 3 years for $100,000. Annual maintenance costs are expected to be $5000 the first 2 years and $10,000 the third year (payable at the end of each year). At what interest rate would the two alternatives be equivalent?

5.19 A machine can be repaired today for $2000. If repairs are not made, the operating expenses will increase by $200 each year for the next 5 years. Assume that the expenses will occur at the end of each year and the machine will have no value under either alternative at the end of the 5-year period. The minimum acceptable rate of return is 12%.

a Compare the present worth of the two alternatives.

b Compare the annual cost of the two alternatives.

5.20 A family is planning to buy a vacation cabin for $9000. They intend to keep the cabin for 6 years and expect the annual upkeep and taxes to amount to $900 per year. Without any major repairs, the cabin should have a resale price of $6000. What is the equivalent annual cost of owning the cabin if the family's acceptable interest rate is 5%?

5.21 The family depicted in Prob. 5.20 could also do some renovations on the cabin during their vacation periods which would increase the resale value to $17,000. How much could they afford to invest in materials each year if they hope to receive $500 per year for their labor?

5.22 An inventor has been offered $12,000 per year for the next 5 years and $6000 annually for the following 7 years for the exclusive rights to his invention. At what price could he afford to sell his patent rights today to earn 10%, disregarding taxes?

5.23 If investments are made of $2000 now, $1500 in 2 years, and $1000 in 4 years, all at 4% effective interest, what will the total amount be in 10 years?

5.24 Three years ago a student borrowed $4000 to finance his education, agreeing to repay the loan in 100 payments at an interest rate of 12% compounded monthly. He has just received an inheritance and desires to pay the remaining principle in a lump sum. How much does he owe?

5.25 What annual expenditure for 10 years is equivalent to spending $1000 at the end of the first year, $2000 at the end of the fourth year, and $3000 at the end of the eighth year, if interest is at 8% per year?

5.26 The village hotshot borrowed $4000 to buy a chrome-plated peanut stand. He agreed to pay the loan back in 45 equal payments at 18% interest compounded monthly. A year after he took out the loan, he asked you to calculate how much of the $4000 debt he had paid off. Determine not only how much he has paid on the principal, but also how much interest he has paid so far.

5.27 A shady individual engaged in making small loans offers to lend $200 on a contract that the borrower pay $6.80 at the end of each week for 35 weeks in order to pay off his debt. What is
a The nominal interest rate per annum?
b The effective interest rate?

5.28 A teacher wants to accumulate $10,000 in order to take a year off 10 years from now. He now has $4000 in savings certificates which earn interest at 4% compounded semiannually. He plans to invest an equal amount each year in an account that earns 3% annual interest. How large should this amount be to give him $10,000 in 10 years when it is combined with the future value of the savings certificates?

5.29 A grocery store owner is considering the purchase of an adjacent lot to use for customer parking. The lot can be purchased for $6000 cash or on an agreement to make an initial payment of $2000 now and annual payments of $600 for 9 years beginning 1 year from now. At what interest rate are the two alternatives equivalent?

5.30 The following alternatives are available to accomplish an objective:

	Plan A	Plan B	Plan C
Life cycle	6 yr	3 yr	4 yr
First cost	$2000	$8000	$10,000
Annual cost	$3200	$700	$500

a Compare the present worths of the alternatives using an interest rate of 7%.

b Compare the annual costs of the alternatives using an interest rate of 15%.

5.31 Today is January 24, 1972. Suppose that 10 years ago you had started putting $10 per month in the bank. You made payments continually for 6 years and then stopped, but the accumulated deposit was left in the bank. On January 24, 1976, you plan to open a mousetrap factory. The money in the savings account will be used to advertise your new mousetrap. If you use $100 per month in advertising, for how many months can you continue before the fund is exhausted? The money is invested at 6% compounded monthly.

5.32 Assume *Playmate* magazine offers two types of subscriptions, payable in advance, as follows:

$$1 \text{ yr} \quad \$5$$
$$2 \text{ yr} \quad \$8$$

a In comparing the economy of a 1-year subscription with that of a 2-year subscription, what is the rate of return on the extra investment in the 2-year subscription?

b As an added bonus, with each subscription to *Playmate* a nature-lover's calendar is included. However, only one calendar is included, even with a 2-year subscription. If you figure your money is worth 10%, how much could you afford to pay for next year's calendar so that both subscription rates can be considered equal in value?

Chapter Six
Time Evaluation
of
Tactical
Alternatives

The tactical or strategic stature of alternatives is relative to the decision environment. In a one-man printing shop a decision to buy a collator may be a major decision indicative of strategic plans to expand operations. Several years later, after the one-man operation has grown to a large printing enterprise, the purchase of another collator is a routine tactical decision. The relationship of objectives to the system within which the decision is being made determines whether the decision is a tactical or a strategic one.

If we recall from Chap. 1 that tactics are associated with the efficiency of operations, it follows that many decisions to improve operations involve the time value of investments. New machines, process modifications, method improvements, and many other operational decisions have money-time aspects. In this chapter we will consider the influence of time on investments to achieve tactical objectives.

We observed in Chap. 5 how capital can increase as a function of time and the prevailing interest rate. Capital can also be increased by investments in production goods. Such capital equipment is merely a change in the form of the assets of a firm. These facilities are expected to make products which can be sold at a profit. Any earned profit is equivalent to interest obtained by loaning capital. The difference is the intermediate stages between the commitment of capital and the receipt of earnings.

In Chap. 2 we saw that profit accounts for only a small portion of the selling price. Part of the sales price compensates for the fixed costs of production. A major portion of these costs is associated with the capital invested in production facilities. This capital is maintained by charging a *depreciation cost* to the revenue earned through the use of production goods.

Depreciation means a decrease in worth. Most industrial assets are worth less as they get older. Newly purchased production goods have the advantage of latest technical designs, and they operate with less chance of breakdown or need for repairs. Except for possible antique value, production facilities become less valuable as they get older. Eventually they have to be replaced or retired. This change in worth is accounted for by the depreciation charges made during the productive life of an asset.

IMPORTANCE OF DEPRECIATION   The costs of industrial production can be divided into direct money costs — wages, salaries, services, raw materials, etc. — and *imputed costs* — payments not contractually required for production during a short accounting period. In financial accounting, depreciation is an imputed cost. The principal objectives for charging a depreciation cost can be summarized as (1) an effort to recover capital invested in production assets, (2) to accurately determine imputed costs of production for cost records, and (3) to include the cost of depreciation in operating expenses for tax purposes.

To emphasize the importance of depreciation, consider the plight of an individual who used $8500 in

CONCEPTS OF DEPRECIATION

avings and borrowed $10,000 to buy a used tractor, ruck, and hauling rig to start a landscaping service. His business was good. A gross income of $20,000 a year allowed him to meet annual operating and loan-repayment expenses of $9000. After 5 years of comfortable living with good wages, his loan was repaid but his equipment was worn out. The salvage value after the 5 years of use was only $500. When he looked for replacement equipment he realized he no longer had his original $8500 to use as a down payment. His investment had not been recovered from the earnings it afforded.

From the vantage point of hindsight, it is obvious that he should have made provisions to set aside $8500 − $500 = $8000 during the life of his equipment. This would have shown his actual earnings during the period and allowed the capital consumption to be shown as an expense on his tax report.

While the theory of depreciation is completely plausible, converting the concept to practice presents some problems:

What can cause an asset to lose value?

How long is the useful life of an asset?

What salvage value will it have at the end of its useful life?

What is the pattern of its decrease in value?

What method of depreciation is most appropriate? Neatly defined solutions are not available for most of these questions. The exact answers are revealed only by time. After an asset has lost its value we know how, why, and when it happened, but the answers come too late to be useful. Therefore we have to use estimates based on experience, records, guides, and a broad understanding of the principles and practices of depreciation.

CAUSES OF DEPRECIATION Being aware of the potential reasons that assets decrease in value helps to estimate the pattern of the decrease.

Physical depreciation Everyday wear and tear of operation gradually lessens the physical ability of an asset to perform its intended function. A good maintenance program retards the rate of decline, but it seldom maintains the precision expected from a new machine. In addition to the normal wear, accidental physical damage can also impair ability.

Functional depreciation   Demands made on an asset may increase beyond its capacity to produce. A central heating plant unable to meet the increased heat demands of a new building addition no longer serves its intended function. At the other extreme, the demand for services may cease to exist, as with a machine which produces a product no longer in demand.

Technological depreciation   Newly developed means of accomplishing a function may make the present means uneconomical. Steam locomotives lost value rapidly as railroads turned to diesel power. Current product styling, new materials, improved safety, and better quality at lower cost from new developments make old designs obsolete.

Depletion   Consumption of an exhaustible natural resource to produce products or services is termed *depletion*. Removal of oil, timber, rock, or minerals from a site decreases the value of the holding. This decrease is compensated for by a proportionate reduction in earnings derived from the resource. Theoretically, the depreciation charge per unit of the resources removed is

$$\frac{\text{Present value of resource}}{\text{Remaining units of resource}} = \text{depletion rate (dollars per unit)}$$

In practice the depletion rate is largely set by the percentage of a year's income allowed for a depletion charge by the Bureau of Internal Revenue. Allowances for depreciation vary with the type of resource. Highest allowances are theoretically allowed for resources which require greatest expenditures for discovery and development.

Monetary depreciation   A change in price levels is a subtle but troublesome cause of depreciation. Customary accounting practices relate depreciation to the original price of an asset, not to its replacement. If prices rise during the life of an asset, a comparable replacement becomes more expensive. This means that the capital recovered will be insufficient to provide an adequate substitute for the worn-out asset. Because the depreciation is actually happening to the invested capital representing the asset instead of to the asset itself, monetary depreciation is very difficult to estimate.

ECONOMIC LIFE   The great variety of ways an asset can lose value makes the estimation of an accurate life a difficult problem indeed. The *economic life* of an asset is the number of years of use that minimizes the equivalent annual cost of holding the item. This is opposed to *service life* or *ownership life*, which is the actual number of years the asset is kept. Hopefully, the service life equals the economic life. Grossly stated, an asset's life can be estimated from a study of past performances of similar assets with reference to current conditions, and to the suggested life recommended by the Bureau of Internal Revenue.

Depreciation expense is recognized as a legitimate deduction from income. Since taxes are paid on net income, the way in which depreciation charges are spread over the life of an asset has a marked effect on income taxes. Two factors establish the pattern of depreciation deductions: the length of life used in calculating depreciation and the method of prorating year-by-year depreciation charges over the selected life. Acceptable methods of writing off depreciation will be discussed in following sections. Lives considered reasonable by the Bureau of Internal Revenue for assets used in different industries are tabulated in Table 6.1.

The guidelines suggested by the Bureau should be taken as just that — guidelines. There is considerable flexibility allowed for depreciation allowances. If it is apparent that the economic life of a particular asset is longer or shorter than suggested by the composite categories of the guidelines, the best estimate should be used. When the life is shorter than the suggested life, the burden of proof falls on the taxpayer. Therefore a reasonable study should precede the selection.

Many tables and formulas have appeared over the years which set average service lives for various types of assets. Some are well documented. Others appear less valid. In making use of such advice it is important to know the validity and exact description of the asset being evaluated; precise mortality data are of little value if the characteristics of the described asset differ from the one being studied.

When an asset is consumed in large quantities (for example, telephone poles), a thorough study is feasible. For lower-consumption assets, particularly those with high initial costs, attention should be given to broad considerations such as the following:

1. Cost of maintenance as the asset gets older. Loss of revenue arises from lost production during down time as well as from the labor cost of servicing.

Table 6.1 Selected depreciation lives recognized by the Bureau of Internal Revenue

Group	Life, yr	Group	Life, yr
General business			
Office furniture, fixtures, machines, equipment	10	Transportation	
		Aircraft	6
Land and site improvements — not otherwise covered	20	Automobile	3
		Buses	9
Buildings: apartments, banks, factories, hotels, stores, warehouses	40–60	General-purpose trucks	4–6
		Tractor units	4
		Trailers	6
Nonmanufacturing activities			
Agriculture		Logging and sawmilling	6–10
Machinery and equipment	10	Mining, excluding petroleum refining and smelting and refining of minerals	10
Animals	3–10		
Buildings	25	Recreation and amusement	10
Contract construction		Wholesale and retail trade	10
General	5		
Marine	12		
Manufacturing			
Aerospace industry	8	Motor vehicles and parts	12
Apparel and textile products	9	Paper and allied products	
Chemicals and allied products	11	Pulp and paper	16
Electrical equipment		Paper conversion	12
General	12	Plastic products	11
Electronic equipment	8	Printing and publishing	11
Fabricated metal products	12	Rubber products	14
Glass products	14	Ship and shipbuilding	12
Knitwear and knit products	9	Textile-mill products	12–14
Leather products	11	Tobacco products	15
Lumber, wood products, and furniture	10	Other manufacturing in general	12
Machinery unless otherwise listed	12		
Transportation, Communications, and Public Utilities			
Air transport	6	Motor transport	
Central steam production and distribution	28	Freight	8
Electric utilities		Passenger	
Hydraulic	50	Pipeline transportation	2
Nuclear	20	Radio and television broadcasting	
Steam	28	Railroads	
Transmission and distribution	30	Machinery and equipment	1
Gas utilities		Structures and similar improvements	3
Distribution	35	Water utilities	5
Manufacture	30		

Source: *Depreciation: Guidelines and Rules*, publication 456 issued by the U.S. Bureau of Internal Revenue, July, 1962. For details consult the original publication.

2. Decrease in quality or quantity of output with age.

3. Cost comparisons with newer facilities that produce a similar output. This is particularly appropriate when a used machine is purchased.

4. Increased fuel or power consumption owing to lower operating or design efficiency.

5. Comparison of labor cost plus machine cost with the costs of more automated machines. As labor costs increase, an earlier method requiring more workers becomes less attractive.

6. Chance of sudden obsolescence because of a breakthrough in production or product design.

Behind all the guides and suggestions for estimating economic life is a basic management philosophy that often prejudices the actual selection. On one hand is a desire to keep a facility in operation as long as possible because average annual capital recovery costs will be lower. On the other hand is a drive to minimize the chance of losses from inferior quality or inefficient operation due to an overlong life estimate. When these two opposing views are further colored by personal attachments for certain brands of equipment or a wish to always have the most modern facilities, life estimations get very convoluted.

Since an asset has no absolute inherent life, appraisals are bound to vary. For most assets explicit investigations of all the influencing factors are not practical, yet the factors should at least be considered, because the life selected has a major effect on the comparison of alternative asset acquisitions.

DEPRECIATION ACCOUNTING   In making depreciation studies it is convenient to visualize a charge for depreciation as being a series of payments made to a specific fund for the replacement of the asset being studied. While this notion is quite accurate in concept, it is seldom followed in industrial practice. A bookkeeping account shows the annual charge for depreciation; the charge is used for tax purposes, but it will appear in the account as "other assets," such as working capital. The physical form of the "depreciation fund" could be stocks of raw materials or finished products.

An exception to the practice of keeping account of depreciation funds by book entries is the occasionally used sinking-fund-depreciation method. In this method a separate depreciation reserve fund is established by payments invested outside the company. The interest earned by the fund is the interest paid by the organization that holds the investments. The annual payments are determined by the sinking-fund formula $(a/f)_n^i$, where f is the amount needed to replace the asset, n is the economic life, and i is the interest received on the invested funds. Sinking-fund depreciation is not too common, because a company's earning power is usually higher than the interest rate attainable from outside sources. Thus funds kept within the organization for its own operations are more valuable (in essence, they return a higher interest rate) than conservative outside investments.

For depreciation allowances kept within a firm, a charge is made each year against the cost of operations and is credited to the asset's reserve for depreciation. The original cost of the asset minus the accumulated depreciation reserve is called the *book value*. Land is one of the few assets for which no reserve is needed, because land values normally remain constant or appreciate in value. Therefore any portion of an investment representing land is usually deducted from the original cost when making depreciation calculations.

DEPRECIATION METHODS

Concurrent with the identification of an asset's economic life is the choice of a method to determine the annual charge for depreciation. Many methods are available. Certain industries such as the machine-tool interests[1] have developed customized formulas to represent the depreciation patterns peculiar to their trade. From the depreciation methods available, we will investigate four which account for most of the industrial practices:

The *straight-line* method

The *sum-of-digits* method

The *declining-balance* method

The *sinking-fund* method

The above methods are based strictly on time. That is, an asset used every day has the same depreciation charge as one used only once a year. Some advocate that depreciation should be based on the amount of use as well as the economic life. It is possible to combine a usage factor with a time-based method such as straight-line depreciation to reflect the rate of decreasing value

[1]*MAPI Replacement Manual*, Machine and Allied Products Institute, Chicago, 1950.

with use. This approach is acceptable for tax purposes as long as it can definitely be shown that the useful life is a function of the rate of production. However, the Bureau of Internal Revenue states[2] that for most property it is not possible to obtain the necessary use information with any degree of accuracy, and therefore the method is not considered generally applicable.

Each depreciation method has unique features which appeal to different management philosophies. A method by which the bulk of the money invested is recovered early in the life of an asset is a popular conservative view. An early writeoff guards against sudden changes which could make the equipment less valuable. Methods by which the annual charge is constant simplifies the accounting procedure. In general, the desirable features of a depreciation method are that it (1) recovers the capital invested in an asset, (2) maintains a book value close to the actual value of the asset throughout its life, (3) is easy to apply, and (4) is acceptable to the Bureau of Internal Revenue.

The broad patterns of capital recovery for the four methods we will consider are shown in Fig. 6.1. The curves are based on depreciation charges without taxes or profit on the investment. The sinking-fund method has the slowest rate of capital recovery. If the interest rate used for the sinking-fund calculations is zero,

Figure 6.1 Book value of an asset calculated by different depreciation methods

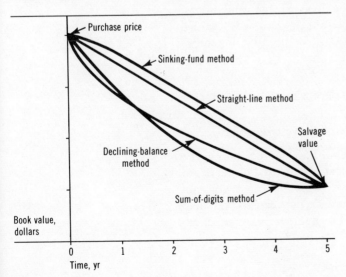

[2]*Bulletin F*, issued by the U.S. Bureau of Internal Revenue, January, 1942.

$(a/f)_n^o$, the sinking-fund curve coincides with the values for the straight-line method. Both the sum-of-digits and the declining-balance methods recover a large share of the initial investment early in the depreciable life. In the first half of an asset's economic life, about three-fourths of the depreciation cost is written off by the sum-of-digits method and two-thirds is written off by the declining-balance method.

All the methods will be illustrated by reference to the problem information shown below:

BASIC PROBLEM DATA

Trucks purchased by a delivery company cost $4000 each. Past records indicate the trucks should have an economic life of 5 years. They can be sold for an average of $800 each after 5 years of use. The company currently receives 7% interest on invested funds. Determine:

a The depreciation charge during year 1
b The depreciation charge during year 2
c The depreciation reserve accumulated by the end of year 2
d The book value at the end of year 3

Capital recovery for the described depreciation methods do not include income-tax considerations. The symbols used in the development of the formulas are

$P =$ purchase price (present worth at time zero) of the asset

$S =$ salvage value or future value at the end of the asset's economic life. The salvage value is positive if the item is resold or scrapped, zero if it is discarded at no cost, or negative if removal costs exceed resale value

$n =$ economic life in years

$N =$ number of years of depreciation or use from the time of purchase

$i =$ interest rate received on invested capital

STRAIGHT-LINE METHOD   Straight-line depreciation is the simplest to apply and the most widely used of the depreciation methods. The annual depreciation is constant. The book value is the difference between the purchase price and the product of the number of years of use times the annual depreciation charge:

$$\text{Annual depreciation charge} = \frac{P - S}{n}$$

$$\text{Book value at end of year } N = P - \frac{N}{n}(P - S)$$

EXAMPLE 6.1 Straight-line depreciation applied to the basic problem data

SOLUTION (a) and (b) Since the annual depreciation cost is constant, the charges for both the first and second year are

$$\text{Depreciation charge} = \frac{P - S}{n} = \frac{\$4000 - \$800}{5}$$

$$= \$640 \text{ per year}$$

(c) The depreciation reserve at the end of year 3 is the sum of the annual depreciation charges for the first 3 years and is equal to $3 \times \$640 = \$1920$.

(d) The book value at the end of 3 years can be determined in two ways: by formula,

$$\text{Book value at the end of year 3} = \$4000 - \frac{3}{5} \times (\$4000 - \$800)$$

$$= \$4000 - 0.6 \times \$3200$$

$$= \$2080$$

or, with the book value considered as the difference between the purchase price and the amount accumulated in the depreciation reserve,

$$\text{Book value at the end of year 3} = \$4000 - \$1920 = \$2080$$

SUM-OF-DIGITS METHOD The sum-of-digits method provides a larger depreciation charge during the early years of ownership than in the later years. The name is taken from the calculation procedure. The annual charge is the ratio of the digit representing the remaining years of life $(n - N + 1)$ to the sum of the digits for the entire life $(1 + 2 + 3 + \cdots + n)$ multiplied by the initial price minus the salvage value $(P - S)$. Thus the annual charge decreases each year from a maximum the first year.

$$\text{Annual depreciation charge} = \frac{n - N + 1}{1 + 2 + 3 + \cdots + n} (P - S)$$

$$= \frac{2(n - N + 1)}{n(n + 1)} (P - S)$$

$$\text{Book value at end of year } N = \frac{2[1 + 2 + \cdots + (n - N)]}{n(n + 1)} (P - S) + S$$

EXAMPLE 6.2 Sum-of-digits depreciation applied to the basic problem data

SOLUTION (a) The sum of digits for the 5-year economic life is

$$1 + 2 + 3 + 4 + 5 = 15$$

or

$$\frac{n(n + 1)}{2} = \frac{5(5 + 1)}{2} = 15$$

which is the denominator of the formula for

$$\text{Depreciation charge during year 1} = \frac{n - N + 1}{15}(P - S)$$

$$= \frac{5 - 1 + 1}{15} \times (\$4000 - \$800)$$

$$= \frac{5}{15} \times \$3200 = \$1067$$

(*b*) After the first year only 4 years remain in the economic life. Therefore, with $n - N + 1 = 5 - 2 + 1 = 4$,

$$\text{Depreciation charge during year 2} = \frac{4}{15} \times \$3200 = \$853$$

(*c*) The ratio for calculating the depreciation reserve has a numerator equal to the sum of the digits representing the years during which the reserve was built up:

$$\text{Depreciation reserve at end of year 3} = \frac{5 + 4 + 3}{15} \times \$3200$$

$$= \$2560$$

(*d*) Book value at the end of year 3 = P − depreciation reserve

$$= \$4000 - \$2560 = \$1440$$

or by formula,

$$= \frac{2[1 + 2 + \cdots + (n - N)]}{n(n + 1)}(P - S) + S$$

$$= \frac{2 \times [1 + (5 - 3)]}{5 \times (5 + 1)} \times \$3200 + \$800$$

$$= \frac{6}{30} \times \$3200 + \$800$$

$$= \$640 + \$800 = \$1440$$

DECLINING-BALANCE METHOD The declining-balance method is another means of amortizing an asset at an accelerated rate early in its life, with corresponding lower annual charges near the end of service. An important point with this method is that the salvage value must be greater than zero. A depreciation rate is calculated from the expression

$$\text{Depreciation rate} = 1 - \left(\frac{S}{P}\right)^{1/n}$$

which requires a positive value for the salvage value S in order to be realistic. This constant rate is applied to the book value for each depreciation period. Since the undepreciated balance decreases each year, the depreciation charge also decreases, and the

Book value at end of year N

$$= P (1 - \text{depreciation rate})^N$$

$$= P \left\{ 1 - \left[1 - \left(\frac{S}{P} \right)^{1/n} \right] \right\}^N$$

$$= P \left(\frac{S}{P} \right)^{N/n}$$

Annual depreciation charge $=$ book value at $N - 1 \times \left(1 - \sqrt[n]{\frac{S}{P}} \right)$

Book value at end of year $N = P \left(\frac{S}{P} \right)^{N/n}$

A form of the declining-balance method allowed by the Income Tax Code since 1954 is based on a depreciation rate which does not depend on the S/P ratio. It is called the *double-declining-balance method*. Its name is derived from the way the depreciation rate is determined. The rate is arbitrarily chosen within the restriction that it cannot exceed double the straight-line rate. Assuming that a maximum rate is desired, the formula would be

$$\text{Depreciation rate} = \frac{200\%}{n}$$

and is used in depreciation calculations like the other declining-balance rate. This arbitrary rate has no relation to an estimated salvage value. For example, applying the double-declining-balance method to the basic problem data, with the maximum rate, we have

$$\text{Depreciation rate} = \frac{200\%}{5} = 40\%$$

which leads to

$$\text{Book value, end of yr 5} = P \left(1 - \frac{200\%}{5} \right)^N$$

$$= \$4000 \times \left(1 - \frac{2.0}{5} \right)^5$$

$$= \$4000 \times (0.6)^5$$

$$= \$4000 \times 0.08776 = \$351$$

This overcompensates for the $800 expected from the salvage value. There is always an undepreciated balance left at the end of the economic life. When the salvage value is less than the book value at the end of an asset's service, tax laws allow the difference to be declared as a loss.

EXAMPLE 6.3 Declining-balance depreciation applied to the basic problem data

SOLUTION (a) Multiplying the purchase price by the depreciation rate gives

$$\text{Depreciation charge, yr 1} = \$4000 \times \left[1 - \left(\frac{\$800}{\$4000}\right)^{1/5}\right]$$

$$= \$4000 \times (1 - \sqrt[5]{0.20})$$

$$= \$4000 \times (1 - 0.724)$$

$$= \$4000 \times 0.276 = \$1104$$

(b) Since the depreciation rate is constant, it is multiplied by the undepreciated balance to produce

$$\text{Depreciation charge, yr 2} = (\$4000 - \$1104) \times 0.276$$

$$= \$2896 \times 0.276 = \$799$$

(c) The accumulated depreciation can be calculated by summing the annual charges to yield

$$\text{Depreciation reserve, end of yr 3} = \$1104 + \$799 + (\$4000 - \$1903) \times 0.276$$

$$= \$1903 + \$2097 \times 0.276$$

$$= \$2482$$

(d) The book value at the end of year 3 is

$$P(1 - \sqrt[N]{S/P})^N = \$4000 \times (1 - 0.276)^3$$

$$= \$4000 \times (0.724)^3$$

$$= \$4000 \times 0.3794 = \$1515$$

Or, when the depreciation rate has not already been calculated, it may be easier to calculate the book value at the end of year 3 as

$$P(S/P)^{N/n} = \$4000 \times \left(\frac{\$800}{\$4000}\right)^{3/5}$$

$$= \$4000 \times (0.20)^{0.6}$$

$$= \$4000 \times 0.3794 = \$1515$$

The depreciation reserve could also be calculated by using the book-value formula as

$$\text{Accumulated depreciation} = P\left[1 - \left(\frac{S}{P}\right)^{N/n}\right]$$

SINKING-FUND METHOD   The sinking-fund concept has already been introduced on page 195 and by the compound-interest calculations. While a firm rarely deposits sinking-fund payments in an outside business, it is a potentially useful model for an asset that loses value slowly during the first years and more rapidly during later years. The annual depreciation charge is constant *if earned interest is not included.* The amount of accumulated depreciation reserve is equal to the future worth of the series of uniform depreciation-charge payments at a given date. Then the book value is the difference between the purchase price and the depreciation reserve. Book values according to the sinking-fund method are greater than they would be by the straight-line method. Increasing the interest rate increases the difference.

$$\text{Annual depreciation charge} = (P - S)(a/f)_n^i$$
$$\text{Book value at the end of year } N = P - (P - S)(a/f)_n^i (f/a)_N^i$$

EXAMPLE 6.4   Sinking-fund depreciation applied to the basic problem data

SOLUTION   (a) and (b) The constant annual charge for depreciation is
$$(P - S)(a/f)_n^i = (\$4000 - \$800)(a/f)_5^7$$
$$= \$3200 \times 0.17389 = \$556$$

However, it should be recognized that when a sinking fund is accumulated within a firm, funds must be allocated to account for the interest earned by depreciation reserve. Thus during the second year the capital recovery includes the depreciation charge ($556) plus the interest earned by the first year's depreciation charge ($556 × 0.07 = $38.92).

(c) The depreciation reserve at the end of year 3 is
$$(P - S)(a/f)_n^i (f/a)_N^i = \$3200\,(a/f)_5^7\,(f/a)_3^7$$
$$= \$556\,(f/a)_3^7$$
$$= \$556 \times 3.215 = \$1782$$

(d) The book value at the end of year 3 is
$$P - \text{accumulated depreciation} = \$4000 - \$1782$$
$$= \$2212$$

TAX EFFECT OF DEPRECIATION METHODS   In selecting a depreciation method, attention should be given to its effect on income taxes. Among the methods approved by the Bureau of Internal Revenue there is a considerable difference in the year-by-year tax pattern. The effect is apparent when after-tax returns from different methods are directly compared.

Let us assume that the trucks described in the basic problem data produce a cash return of $10,000 per year. The costs of annual operation account for $8500 of the revenue. After depreciation expense is deducted, the remaining portion of the revenue is gross profit. Assuming a federal income-tax rate of 50%, half the gross profit is the net profit. Based on these assumptions, the net profit resulting from straight-line and sum-of-digits depreciation during the economic life of one truck is shown in Table 6.2.

The different depreciation methods do not change the total depreciation charge or the total after-tax returns, but the pattern is changed. The more rapid capital recovery by accelerated depreciation methods allows a slightly higher rate of return on invested capital because the present worth of higher early returns is greater than the same total returns spread evenly over the period of service.

In Table 6.2 it is assumed that the annual operating costs are constant. Since it is logical that operating costs for a new machine will be lower than those for an older machine, more gross profit results in the early service years. More rapid writeoff methods provide a higher depreciation charge during the more profitable years, which tends to increase the tax advantages of these methods.

Table 6.2 Comparison of after-tax returns for straight-line and sum-of-digits depreciation methods

		Straight-line depreciation		
Year	Revenue (1)	Annual depreciation (2)	Gross profit (1) − (2) (3)	After-tax return (1) − ½ (3) (4)
1	$1500	$ 640	$ 860	$1070
2	1500	640	860	1070
3	1500	640	860	1070
4	1500	640	860	1070
5	1500	640	860	1070
	$7500	$3200	$4300	$5350

Sum-of-digits depreciation		
Annual depreciation (5)	Gross profit (1) − (5) (6)	After-tax return (1) − ½ (6) (7)
$1067	$ 433	$1284
853	647	1177
640	860	1070
427	1073	963
213	1287	856
$3200	$4300	$5350

EQUIVALENCE OF METHODS WHEN INTEREST CHARGES ARE INCLUDED

The time-value equivalence of different methods is an interesting aspect of depreciation accounting. Interest charges are not formally included in straight-line, sum-of-digits, or declining-balance methods. Even in sinking-fund calculations the interest factor does not account for the return that would be received if the funds were not invested in the depreciable asset. If the return on invested capital is included, the different patterns share a common, equivalent annual cost. The importance of this condition is that it allows one basic formula to represent any depreciation method when alternatives are being compared.

It is possible to derive the equivalent formula from the equations for each depreciation method. Instead of individual derivations, the equivalence is demonstrated by example in Table 6.3. Two depreciation methods, straight-line and sum-of-digits, are compared according to the present worth of annual capital recovery plus a return on the unrecovered balance of the investment. The return may be thought of as the "profit" that would result if the undepreciated portion of the funds for an asset were invested at a given rate of return.

Table 6.3 Capital recovery plus return at 7% interest for straight-line and sum-of-digits depreciation

Year (N)	Book value at beginning of year (1)	Return on unrecovered capital at 7% interest $0.07 \times (1)$ (2)	Depreciation charge in year (3)	Capital recovery plus return $(2)+(3)$ (4)	$(p/f)^7_N$ (5)	Present worth of payments $(4) \times (5)$ (6)
Straight-line depreciation method					
1	$4000	$280	$640	$920	0.9346	$ 860
2	3360	235	640	875	0.8734	764
3	2720	190	640	830	0.8163	678
4	2080	146	640	786	0.7629	600
5	1440	101	640	741	0.7130	528
				Total present worth of straight-line payments		$3430
Sum-of-digits depreciation method					
1	$4000	$280	$1067	$1347	0.9346	$1259
2	2933	205	853	1058	0.8734	923
3	2080	146	640	786	0.8163	642
4	1440	101	427	528	0.7629	403
5	1013	71	213	284	0.7130	203
				Total present worth of sum-of-digits payments		$3430

The asset depicted in Table 6.3 is from the basic problem data used previously. Initial cost is $4000, with the resale value $800 in 5 years. Therefore, using a desired rate of return of 7% on invested capital, the *return* for the first year is $4000 × 0.07 = $280. Subsequent returns are calculated from the book value during each year. Thus, for straight-line depreciation, the book value during year 2 is

Capital unrecovered during yr 2

$$= \text{first cost} - \text{accumulated depreciation}$$

$$= \$4000 - \$640$$

$$= \$3360$$

This is used to calculate the return on unrecovered capital during year 2, $3360 × 0.07 = $235.20. Adding the depreciation charge for each year to the return on unrecovered capital during that year gives the total annual cash flow for capital recovery plus return. The single-payment present-worth factor is used to translate the periodic cash flow to an equivalent single value at time zero.

The present worth by both depreciation methods is $3430. The same value would be obtained if the sinking-fund or the declining-balance method were applied to the basic problem data. It should be recognized that a present worth of $3430 results from a fictitious interest charge on the unrecovered capital. Actual depreciation practices seldom include this charge, but it is applied in the example to show that the different depreciation patterns are equivalent from a time-value standpoint based on investment returns rather than operational considerations.

EQUIVALENT CAPITAL RECOVERY DEPRECIATION   Once we have accepted the time-value equivalency of depreciation methods, we can employ one formula to account for the capital recovery investment returns of any asset:

Capital recovery depreciation $= (P - S)(a/p)_n^i + Si$

The first part of the formula, $(p - S)(a/p)_n^i$, establishes an

  annual payment for the economic life of the asset, n, which recovers the initial investment P
  less the portion that is recovered by the salvage value S
  plus an acceptable rate of return, i.

The second part of the formula, Si, accounts for the annual return that would have been earned by

money represented by the salvage value S,

if this amount had been invested at the acceptable interest rate, i.

Applying the capital-recovery depreciation formula to the basic problem data, we have an equivalent depreciation charge:

$(P - S)(a/p)_n^i + Si$

$$= (\$4000 - \$800) \times (a/p)_5^7 + \$800 \times 0.07$$

$$= \$3200 \times 0.2439 + \$56$$

$$= \$780.48 + \$56$$

$$= \$836.48$$

To show that this annual charge produces an equivalent capital recovery, we can compare the present worth of capital-recovery depreciation,

Annual equivalent depreciation charge $\times (p/a)_5^7$

$$= \$836.48 \times 4.1002$$

$$= \$3430$$

to the present worth of the depreciation methods determined in Table 6.3. As advertised, the results are the same: the present worth of capital-recovery depreciation equals the present worth of capital recovery plus return for straight-line and sum-of-digits depreciation. Thus the one formula for capital-recovery depreciation can be used for comparing the time-value of alternatives, regardless of the method actually employed for depreciation accounting.

REPLACEMENT OF ASSETS

Replacement refers to a broad concept embracing the selection of similar but newer asset substitutes and the evaluation of entirely different ways to perform an asset's function. For example, old trucks could be replaced by newer models that operate similarly but have better performance. They could also be replaced by a conveyor system, an overhead crane, or even manual labor if any of these methods provide more economical performance.

We have already observed how depreciation accounting serves as a preparation for replacement. There are many clues that lead to a replacement investigation — an asset becomes less efficient, operating costs increase, current demands cannot be met, new developments make older methods noncompetitive. Any one of these factors or a combination of them could lead to a decision to replace or retire an asset.

A replacement decision is between the present asset, called the *defender*, and currently available replacement alternatives, called *challengers*. The defender may or may not be at the end of its economic life. The challengers may or may not perform the function of the defender in the same way. The decision environment is bounded by current operating data and estimates of future outcomes based on the latest information. Past performances and previous replacement decisions are not relevant to the decision.

STUDY PERIOD   Comparisons between the defender and its challengers are conducted by determining the time value of receipts and disbursements associated with each alternative. Annual-cost, present-worth, or rate-of-return methods may be used. Annual-cost comparisons are probably the most common. The choice depends largely on the pattern of cash flow and the length of the study period.

A study period ideally extends into the future to a point at which the alternatives exhibit identical operational results. Where this point is extremely difficult to discern, an infinite study period is possible by assuming that the interest periods n extend to infinity. In contrast, an artificially short study period assumes that the economic life of each alternative is minimal. Between these extremes there is usually a realistic study period in which the effects of the alternatives are essentially the same. In general, longer study periods are more realistic, but the cash-flow estimates are less reliable.

IRRELEVANT CONSIDERATIONS   The outcomes of a decision cannot start before the moment a decision is made. Occurrences prior to the decision-making point are common to all the alternatives being compared. That is, any information available up to the moment a decision is made, such as the announcement of a dramatic new method of performing the function of the asset being evaluated, applies to the challengers as well as to the defender. Past events should not influence the choice between alternatives unless they affect future events in different ways for different alternatives.

The most common instance of including irrelevant information in a replacement decision arises from the use of a book value for the present worth of the defender. The book value is a result of a previous decision, made when the present defender was a challenger. As shown in Fig. 6.2, the actual value of an asset may be quite different from the value shown by the depreciation pattern. The difference between the amount an asset is worth today and the worth shown by depreciation records is called a *sunk cost*.[1] Because these sunk costs are the result of past expenditures and policies, they should have no bearing on the current decision.

The mental static generated by sunk costs is hard to comprehend unless there is a personal involvement. Let the asset in Fig. 6.2 represent a production machine with a first cost of $3000. By straight-line depreciation, the book value at the end of the second year is

$$\$3000 - 2 \times \frac{\$3000 - \$600}{4} = \$1800$$

but because of recent design changes the 2-year old machine can be sold for only $1000. The $1800 − $1000 = $800 sunk cost appears as a loss arising from a poor choice in purchasing. Further complications could take the form of recent repairs. The owner's feeling might be, "I've had some bad luck on repairs, but it's running now, and I've got so much in it I can't

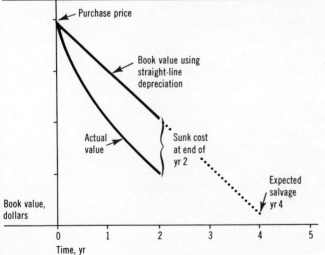

Figure 6.2 Comparison of actual value to book value

[1]To be specific, a sunk cost occurs only when the book value exceeds the present realizable value. Sunk costs arise from overestimation of the salvage value or economic life. An underestimation could result in a book value less than actual value. Such a profit should be handled like sunk costs for replacement studies; both should be ignored.

afford to sell it for what it would bring." The weakness of this argument (as would probably be evident to the owner if he were on the other end of the conversation) is that he should be seeking the alternative that will provide him with the least *future* annual cost, not one that will make his past expenditures look good.

The implications of sunk costs may take different forms. A hesitation to accept an apparently sound replacement may exist because a large sunk cost could cloud the current profit outlook. The usual accounting practice is to write off a reduction in assets when it occurs. The loss is deducted from what would otherwise be profit. Even when a defender has already been completely written off, there may still be reluctance to make a commitment for a challenger. Any loss from continued use of a defender usually causes less censure than similar losses from the acceptance of a new approach. Such considerations stem from a management feeling that a loss caused by a replacement suggests an earlier error in judgment.

RELEVANT CONSIDERATIONS   The cash flow from the retention or replacement of an asset is a composite of many separate cost categories. A challenger characteristically has high capital costs and low operating cost. The reverse is usually true of a defender. Some of the cost considerations which establish the relative value of alternatives are the following:

Present cost or worth of an asset

Resale, salvage, or scrap value of the asset at the end of the study period

Direct material and direct labor costs

Property taxes and insurance

Amount and pattern of maintenance costs

Cost of waste and inefficiency

Differences in indirect costs

Dollar values are estimated for the appropriate categories noted above. When one of them, such as salvage value, results in a return rather than an outlay, it is expressed as a negative cost. A comparison of alternatives summarizes the time value of periodic negative and positive payments over the study period.

Many of the finer points in a replacement study are best amplified by sample applications. Each of the following examples illustrates principles broadly described in the preceding sections.

REPLACEMENT-STUDY PATTERNS

REPLACEMENT BECAUSE OF DETERIORATION   Deterioration may result in excessive operating costs, increased maintenance cost, higher reject rates, or a combination of added costs. As costs climb, it soon becomes apparent a replacement study is warranted. Successive studies may be required to determine when the costs for operating for one more period become greater than the average costs expected from the replacement.

A replacement study which assumes that an asset will be replaced by another asset of the same type leads to a minimum-cost replacement period, as shown in Fig. 6.3.

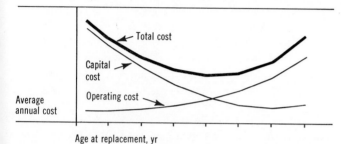

Figure 6.3   Pattern of deterioration costs

Operating costs for most industrial equipment tend to increase with age. At the same time, annual capital-recovery costs decrease because a greater age spreads the charges over a longer period of time. Summing the two types of costs on an annual basis identifies the period between replacements at which the average annual cost is minimized.

The procedure for determining the optimum length of a replacement cycle for assets with identical cost patterns is described in Example 6.5. A zero interest rate is assumed in the solution to simplify the description.

EXAMPLE 6.5   Replacement by a similar asset

A city delivery service with a fleet of panel trucks makes store-to-home deliveries for several merchants. Past records, modified to account for recent price trends, indicate a cost pattern over a 6-year period that is expected to apply to depreciation and maintenance for future truck acquisitions. The purchase price per truck is $3000.

	1	2	3	4	5	6
Operating cost	$800	$1000	$1300	$1600	$2000	$2500
Resale price	$1600	$1000	$600	$500	$400	$300

Assuming a zero interest rate and that all the trucks are going to be replaced at one time, how many years should they be kept in service before replacement?

SOLUTION   The average cost per year is the sum of accumulated capital costs plus operating costs divided by the number of years in the cumulation period. Column (2) of Table 6.4 shows the cumulative operating costs. Column (3) is a tabulation of capital costs obtained by subtracting the resale price at different ages from the original purchase price. The average annual costs in column (5) result from dividing the total costs accumulated during the life of a truck by its age.

Table 6.4   Average annual cost with 0% interest

Age of truck, yr (1)	Cumulative operating costs (2)	Cumulative capital costs (3)	Total costs (2) + (3) (4)	Av annual costs (4) ÷ (1) (5)
1	$ 800	$1400	$2200	$2200
2	1800	2000	3800	1900
3	3100	2400	5500	1833
4	4700	2500	7200	1800
5	6700	2600	9300	1860
6	9200	2700	11900	1983

From the table we conclude that the minimum average cost is obtained by keeping the trucks for 4 years. If interest charges had been included and equivalent annual costs calculated, the values in column (5) would be slightly larger, but the general pattern would remain about the same.

When comparing a challenger which initiates a repeating cycle (as exhibited in Example 6.5) with a present asset, the minimum average cost of the challenger is matched against the cost expected for the defender during the *next* year. If the average cost is less, a replacement is indicated.

REPLACEMENT BECAUSE OF OBSOLESCENCE   Each new development or refinement of an older method makes the previous way of accomplishing an objective less attractive. Improved designs reduce the salvage value of existing assets. The combined effect of lower operating costs for the challenger and greater sunk costs for the defender usually accompany the evaluation of a "modus operandi" challenged by technological improvements.

EXAMPLE 6.6   Sunk cost because of obsolescence

An office copying machine was purchased 2 years ago for $700. Based on an expected economic life of 5 years and a salvage value of $100, the current book value resulting from straight-line depreciation is $460. Operating costs composed of material, labor, and maintenance expenses amount to $4200 per year. Some type of copier will be needed for the next several years.

The same company that manufactured the presently used copying machine has a new model which costs $1000 but will perform the current workload with operating costs of $3500 per year. They are offering $500 for the old model as a trade-in on the new machine. The expected salvage value for the new model is $200 at the end of 10 years.

Another company has a different type of copier which is available only on a lease basis. The company claims that leasing their copier at $750 per year will reduce the operating expense for the present amount of work to $2750. Since they do not accept trade-ins, the machine now in use would have to be sold in the open market, where it is expected to bring only $250.

If the minimum acceptable rate of return is 10% before taxes, should the defending copier be replaced by one of the challengers?

SOLUTION   The salvage value of the present copier depends on the alternative that is chosen, but in either case the remaining period of expected service is 3 years. For the alternative allowing a trade-in, the resale value ($500) is greater than the book value ($460). This bonus may make management happy, but it is just as irrelevant as a sunk cost. The comparison must rely on the current value for the defender and its retained salvage value 3 years from now.

The leased copier has the lower equivalent annual expense, according to the quoted costs. Adopting the leased machine should provide a saving over the operating cost of the present machine of $1450 a year for the next 3 years. It is impossible to know the characteristics of the machine that would have replaced the present copier 3 years hence. Therefore the expedient assumption is that the defender's costs will be repeated and the challenger will continue to show the same advantage.

Annual cost of the defender:

Capital recovery:
$(P - S)(a/p)_3^{10} + 0.1S = (\$500 - \$100) \times 0.40211 + 0.1 \times \$100$ $ 161
Operating costs   4200
                                                                                                                    $4361

Annual cost of the challenger from the same company:

Capital recovery:
$(P - S)(a/p)_{10}^{10} + 0.1S = (\$1000 - \$200) \times 0.16275 + 0.1 \times \$200$ $ 152
Operating costs   3500
                                                                                                                       $3652

The advantage of a challenger from the same company is $4361 − $3652 = $709 per year.

Comparing the present machine with the leased copier, a salvage value of $250 is all that can be allowed, because that is the actual value obtainable under the stated conditions. The leased machine requires no invested capital.

Annual cost of the defender:

Capital recovery:
$(P - S)(a/p)_3^{10} + 0.1S = (\$250 - \$100) \times 0.40211 + 0.1 \times \$100$ $ 70
Operating costs   4200
                                                                                                                    $4270

Annual cost of the challenger from the leasing company:

Capital recovery	0
Lease expense	$ 750
Operating costs	2750
	$3500

The advantage of a challenger from the leasing company is $4270 − $3500 = $770 per year.

Viewing a replacement decision from a stranger's out-look may clarify the situation and provide impartiality. A stranger viewing the choice of a copier described in Example 6.6 could place the decision in the following context: "I need a copying machine. From one manufacturer I can buy a new machine for $1000 which will have a $200 salvage value at the end of 6 years. The annual operating costs for this machine will be $3500. From the same manufacturer I can also get a used copier for $500 which will last 3 years. It will have a $100 salvage value and annual operating expenses of $4200. On the other hand, I can lease a machine for $750 a year, with expected operating costs of $2750, or buy a used machine for $250 which will last 3 years and have annual operating costs of $4200. I will select the alternative which provides the lowest equivalent annual cost."

REPLACEMENT BECAUSE OF INADEQUACY When current operating conditions change, an older asset occasionally lacks the capacity to meet new requirements. Sometimes a similar asset can be purchased to supplement the old asset, as in the case of placing a new generator along-side an old one to meet new power demands. At other times the old asset can be remodeled or renovated until it is capable of meeting the new demands. New layouts, building additions, and design changes are examples of possible modifications.

Alternatives or supplements to an existing asset are usually compared with a challenging new asset which may perform an equivalent function in an entirely different manner. Replacing a wood stove by an oil furnace, for example, provides an entirely different way to heat a home. Even though a challenger is deemed a desirable replacement, the defender may still have value as usable equipment. In such cases it can be sold or retained for standby purposes. It is also possible that secondary uses can be found for assets replaced from their primary function.

EXAMPLE 6.7 Required replacement by dissimilar assets

A small bridge leading to a proposed industrial park has a load limit of 10,000 lb. A manufacturing firm will lease a building site in the park if the capacity of the bridge is raised to 60,000 lb. The developers of the land have two alternatives. They can reinforce the old bridge, or they can tear it out and fill in the low area, leaving a culvert to carry away surface water.

The present bridge has no realizable salvage value. Reinforcement would cost $30,000 and should provide adequate access for 10 years without any major additional work. The salvage value from added materials would be $8000 in 10 years.

A culvert-and-fill approach to the park would cost $60,000 and should meet all requirements for the next 50 years. There would be no salvage value. In addition, it will cost $2000 to remove the old bridge. Maintenance costs are expected to be $2200 per year less than upkeep for a bridge.

Property taxes and insurance on the improvements will be 1% of the first cost. The required return on investments is 8% before taxes. If the developer feels that a new approach to the park is required, which alternative should be selected?

SOLUTION   Since a replacement for the old bridge is definitely necessary, there is no distinct defender-challenger relationship. The lower-initial-cost alternative, reinforcement, would best fit the role of defender. Its equivalent annual cost is the sum of capital recovery, extra maintenance costs, and taxes plus insurance.

Reinforcement:

Capital recovery:
$$(P - S)(a/p)_{10}^8 + 0.08S = (\$30,000 - \$8000)$$

$\times\ 0.14903 + 0.08 \times \$8000$	$3279
Additional maintenance costs	2200
Taxes and insurance: $0.01 \times \$30,000$	300
	$5779

The equivalent annual costs for a culvert-and-fill approach are the total capital-recovery costs for the new construction plus the removal of the old bridge and annual taxes and insurance on the construction cost. The difference in maintenance cost has already been included in the other alternative.

Culvert and fill:

Capital recovery:

$P(a/p)_{50}^8 = (\$60,000 + \$2000) \times 0.08174$	$5068
Taxes and insurance: $0.01 \times \$60,000$	600
	$5668

The advantage of culvert and fill is $5779 - $5668 = $111 per year.

From strictly a cost viewpoint, the culvert and fill has a slight advantage. Other management considerations could influence the final choice. For instance, the developers might be willing to forego the annual $111 benefit in order to be allowed an opportunity to change plans in 10 years when the reinforced bridge will again need a replacement study. They might be short of capital at the present time or have other possible investments with a greater potential rate of return than that earned on the extra increment of investment ($62,000 - $30,000 = $32,000) required for the culvert and fill.

CONCLUSIONS Several salient features are implied by the preceding examples. The value of a replacement study, like other economic evaluations, is directly proportional to the validity of the data. However, some costs have more effect than others. Replacement decisions are very sensitive to operating estimates. Unfortunately, these are also more difficult to estimate than costs such as purchase price, taxes, insurance, etc.

A conservative approach where estimates are highly uncertain is to give every advantage to the defender. This is accomplished by assuming that the present differential between operating costs of the defender and challenger will remain constant during the study period, and that there are no capital-recovery costs for the defender. If a challenger still looks good under these handicaps, it is truly a valid contender.

Salvage values are necessarily subject to question because they occur at the most distant point in a replacement study. The basic principle is to use the best *current* estimate of the future, regardless of previous estimates. Appraisals may change from one study to the next because of price fluctuations, availability, and needs. An often-neglected cost associated with salvage is the expense of getting an old asset ready for the new purchaser. These expenses could include dismantling, overhaul, painting, crating, cartage, and repairs to the area vacated by the disposed asset. When such costs exceed the disposal price, the salvage value is a loss and is treated as a minus quantity (S is negative) in capital-recovery calculations.

Another commonly ignored cost is the expense associated with putting a new asset in operating order. Special wiring, piping, guard rails, foundations, and other facilities may be needed before new equipment can operate. Radically different or complex equipment often requires more "debugging" than is provided by the supplier. In a replacement study these operational-type costs should be treated as capital costs.

The bridge-replacement example demonstrated a case in which there was no choice about making a replacement study. More commonly an asset performs its intended function without obvious financial loss. If an acceptable challenger goes unnoticed, the accumulated yearly losses from failing to recognize the need for a replacement can be substantial. One clue to a replaceable asset is its proximity to its economic life. As an

asset nears the end of its original life estimation, it
becomes a more likely candidate for a replacement
study. Other clues include an awareness of new developments which could lead to asset obsolescence and the
deterioration of performances as indicated by reject
rates or frequent repairs.

SELECTED REFERENCES
Eidmann, F. L.: *Economic Control of Engineering and
Manufacturing*, McGraw-Hill Book Company, New York,
1931.
Kurtz, E. B.: *The Science of Valuation and Depreciation*,
The Ronald Press Company, New York, 1937.
Marston, A., R. Winfrey, and J. C. Hempstead: *Engineer-
ing Valuation and Depreciation*, McGraw-Hill Book Com-
pany, New York, 1953.
Norton, P.: "Engineering Economy," sec. 3 in E. L. Grant
and W. G. Ireson (eds.), *Handbook of Industrial Engineer-
ing and Management*, Prentice-Hall, Englewood Cliffs, N.J.,
1955.
Samuelson, P. A.: *Economics*, 5th ed., McGraw-Hill Book
Company, New York, 1961.
Specthrie, S. W.: *Industrial Accounting*, Prentice-Hall, Inc.,
Englewood Cliffs, N.J., 1959.
Terborgh, G.: *Dynamic Equipment Policy*, McGraw-Hill
Book Company, New York, 1949.

PROBLEMS
6.1 An asset cost $400 when purchased 4 years ago. A
scrap value of $50 was expected at the end of its 7-year
economic life. Determine the depreciation charge during
the coming year and its current book value by
a Straight-line depreciation
b Sum-of-digits depreciation
c Declining-balance depreciation
d Sinking-fund depreciation (6%)

6.2 A production machine with a first cost of $2000 is expected to last 4 years, when it will be worth $200. Tabulate the book value at the end of each year by the declining-balance and double-declining-balance methods of depreciation.

6.3 Show that for the asset described in the basic problem data on page 198 the capital recovery plus return will be equal to $3430 at an interest rate of 7% when depreciation is calculated by
a The sinking-fund method
b The declining-balance method

6.4 A grain elevator was built 15 years ago at a cost of $43,000. It was expected to have a salvage value after 30 years of 10% of its first cost. Depreciation is by a sinking fund held by a local bank which has paid interest during the period at 4% compounded annually. The owners now want to add a second grain elevator which will cost $60,000. How much additional capital will they need if they apply the depreciation reserves from the first elevator toward construction of the second?

6.5 A car owner bought his automobile for $3600 5 years ago. He received $400 when he traded it in on a new one. He had driven it 70,000 miles. His investments earn $3\frac{1}{2}\%$ interest. What was the cost per mile for capital recovery plus return during his period of ownership?

6.6 A standby generator was purchased 6 years ago for $4200. Similar equipment had shown an economic life of 15 years with a salvage value of 15% of the first cost. The generator is no longer needed and is to be sold for $1800. The interest rate is 8%. What is the difference between the actual and anticipated equivalent annual capital recovery costs?

6.7 A salesman made an agreement to purchase a building lot by making six annual payments of $900 each. He was then transferred to a different location before he could build a home. When he returned 2 years later, he found he could buy an equivalent lot for $3000 because land values had decreased during his absence. He now feels that he will lose $1800 if he drops his contract to buy the equivalent lot. Assuming that he will suffer no penalty for reneging, describe the "stranger's viewpoint" to clarify his present position.

6.8 Assume that a minimum rate of return of 10% is required on the delivery truck described in Example 6.5. Does this assumption change the age for replacement?

6.9 A mechanical testing machine with an initial cost of $8000 closely follows the following cost pattern:

Year	Operating costs	Salvage value
1	$3500	$6000
2	3800	5000
3	4200	4300
4	4600	3900
5	5100	3500
6	5800	3200
7	6700	3000

Using 0% interest and assuming that replacement equipment will follow the same cost pattern, determine the economic life.

6.10 A new type of testing machine to perform the same function as that depicted in Prob. 6.9 is now available at a purchase price of $14,000. The new machines cost more, but they have twice the capacity of the older models. A company plans to replace four of the older type with the new design. The four candidates for replacement are now 2 years old. They will be replaced when the expected costs for keeping them in service one more year is greater than the average annual cost (at 0% interest) for challengers with comparable capacity. The expected cost pattern for the new machine is:

Year	Operating costs	Salvage value
1	$ 7,200	$10,800
2	7,600	8,600
3	8,400	7,500
4	9,500	5,500
5	11,000	4,000

When will the replacement occur?

6.11 At the end of half its expected economic life, a 4-year old machine has a book value of $5800 from its original cost of $9200. Estimated operating costs for the next year will amount to $6000. An equipment dealer will allow $3600 if the machine is traded in now and $2800 if it is traded in a year later. The dealer proposes the purchase of a new machine to perform the same function, which will cost $14,000 installed. This machine will have an estimated operating cost of $4500 per year and at the end of 4 years will have a salvage value of $3000. Is it profitable to replace the existing machine now if the minimum return on investment is 15% before taxes?

6.12 Machine A was installed 6 years ago at a total cost of $8400. At that time it was estimated to have a life of 12 years and a salvage value of $1200. Annual operating costs, excluding depreciation and interest charges, have held relatively constant at $2100. The successful marketing of a new product has doubled the demand for parts made by machine A. The new demand can be met by purchasing an identical machine which now costs $9600 installed. The economic life and operating costs for the two machines will be the same. The salvage value for the second A-type machine will be $1600.

A different type of machine, B, costs $17,000 installed but has twice the capacity of machine A. Its annual operating costs will be about $3100, which should be relatively constant throughout its 10-year economic life. Salvage is expected to be $4000. The present machine can be used as a trade-in on the new machine B. It is worth $3000.

Compare the two alternatives on the basis of equivalent annual cost when the interest rate is 10%.

6.13 A machine has a present book value of $400. It cost $1000 new 3 years ago. It can now be sold for $100. A new machine to replace it will cost $1200 and has an expected life of 4 years. Neither machine has any salvage value. Assume straight-line depreciation and a 0% interest rate to determine

a The sunk cost of the old machine

b The depreciation rate for the new machine (dollars per year)

c The depreciation rate for the old machine as it will be used in a comparison for replacement (dollars per year)

d The rate of return for the replacement machine if it could save $200 per year in labor costs.

6.14 An asset has an initial cost of $65,000 and an estimated salvage value of $5000 after 12 years.

a If the company has no established rate for the double-rate declining-balance depreciation method, what rate would provide a salvage value close to the one estimated for the asset?

b What amount is accumulated in a depreciation fund after 5 years if straight-line depreciation is used?

c What would the depreciation charge be in the eighth year by the sinking-fund method if $i = 4\%$?

d If the declining-balance depreciation rate is 10%, what would the book value be after 3 years?

e If the asset had to be sold after 7 years of use for $7000, what would be the sunk cost, by sum-of-digits depreciation?

6.15 A factory uses 11 machines of a special design which are custom made. Each one costs $5000. In operation, maintenance costs are $1000 the first year and increase by

20% each year (i.e., third-year maintenance cost is $1000 \times 1.2 \times 1.2$). Depreciation is straight line, and a machine has no salvage value at any time. Interest for the use of capital is charged at 10%. At what service life will the average annual cost be a minimum?

6.16 An overhead crane was installed in a warehouse 14 years ago at a cost of $38,000. Straight-line depreciation shows a current book value of $14,200 based on a 20-year economic life. Operating costs, including labor and maintenance, are $16,500 a year.

Two lift trucks could handle the same capacity as the crane with a one-third reduction in operating costs. However, 2000 sq ft of storage space valued at $2 per sq ft/yr would be lost in providing lanes for the trucks. Lift trucks can be purchased for $4800 apiece. They have an economic life of 10 years and an expected salvage value of one-tenth their purchase price.

If the trucks are purchased, the crane can be dismantled and sold for a net gain of $7800. Capital is valued at 6%.

a What will be the sunk cost of the crane if the change is made?

b What was the original estimate for the salvage value of the crane?

c What is the annual cost of the defender and the challenger?

Chapter Seven
Time Evaluation
of
Strategic
Alternatives

No strict demarcation exists between tactical and strategic alternatives, but we have designated the evaluation of existing operations as tactical comparisons. Now we will consider the evaluation of proposed system changes as strategic comparisons.

Funds must be available before a proposed project can be initiated. These funds may be obtained from within or outside the firm. Along with funding goes the problem of identifying prospective alternatives for fulfilling the objectives of the project. Limited funding necessarily narrows the choice of alternatives. The selection among the qualifying alternatives depends largely on an evaluation of revenue and expenses expected during the study period. These investment considerations are depicted in Fig. 7.1.

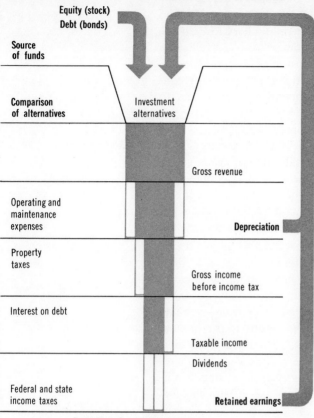

Equity (stock)
Debt (bonds)

Source
of funds

Comparison
of alternatives

Investment
alternatives

Gross revenue

Operating and
maintenance
expenses

Depreciation

Property
taxes

Gross income
before income tax

Interest on debt

Taxable income

Dividends

Federal and state
income taxes

Retained earnings

Evaluation of revenue and expenses

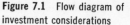

Figure 7.1 Flow diagram of investment considerations

In this chapter we will first give attention to the source of investment funds. Then we will turn to consideration of revenue and expenses which lead to a time evaluation of strategic investments.

SOURCES OF CAPITAL

Industrial funds for capital investments come from (1) depreciation charges, (2) retained earnings, (3) new debt, and (4) equity capital. The first two sources are internally generated, and the last two require outside financing.

INTERNAL FUNDS   Any excess of revenue over total disbursements provides a source of capital for expansion or other new investments. However, this same excess is the source of returns to owners of the capital already invested. Since the money comes from profit, it is subject to income taxes. These two factors — the desire of owners to receive substantial profits when possible and the tax penalty on reinvested capital — tend to limit the use of retained earnings as a source of funds. Still, it is recognized that returning a portion of the profit to the firm through research, acquisitions, or expansion contributes to retention of a competitive position and to growth.

One of the purposes of depreciation charges is to recover capital invested in depreciable assets. Quite often an asset is unable to fulfill current needs at the end of its service life. The accumulated depreciation funds are then available to finance different areas of development and to meet new needs. Provisions for making current essential replacements are necessary, but the remaining funds provide a tax-exempt means to finance worthwhile new ventures.

EXTERNAL FUNDS A firm raises new capital by borrowing or by selling part of its ownership equity. In either case, the new capital is expected to provide adequate returns. To the debt holders its return is the interest charge, and to the new owners it should provide dividends or an increase in the value of the ownership share.

Ownership of a firm may vary from a single individual in a small business to thousands of stockholders in a corporation. Stocks are categorized by two classes, *common* and *preferred*. Both represent a share in ownership, but each has certain privileges and restrictions. A holder of preferred stock is usually guaranteed a definite dividend, an annual percentage return on the amount invested in the corporation, which is payable before common-stock holders may receive any return. Preferred stock also receives a higher priority for the distribution of assets in case the corporation fails. Usually preferred stock carries a vote in company operations, but not always. The preferential treatment on returns is the source of the name "preferred," and tends to stabilize the price of such stocks.

A holder of common stock is in much the same position as an individual owner of a company. He has no contractual guarantee for a fixed return on his investment. He prospers as the company prospers and suffers with its losses. He has a voice in management and reasonable access to corporate records. Since stocks represent ownership in real property, their value is affected by price trends and tend to protect the worth of holdings during inflationary periods.

Most loans obtained by larger companies take the form of bond sales. There are two basic types of bonds, *mortgage* and *debenture*. Mortgage bonds represent a mortgage or claim on the firm's physical assets, while debentures are unsecured obligations to repay. In the event of liquidation of a firm, mortgage bonds are satisfied before any other claim on assets. For his money, a bond holder is further guaranteed a fixed return for the life of his bond as long as the borrower is solvent. This is an advantage during years of declining prices and is a disadvantage during inflation. Moreover, there is no increase in the value of a bond if the company is especially successful, nor is a bond holder allowed a voice in the management of the borrowing firm.

BOND VALUE The owner of a bond receives two types of payments in return for the use of his money. First, the face value is the amount that can be redeemed when the loan is due. This payment is a lump sum F received at a future date. The second type of return is a series of equal payments received at equal intervals until the bond is retired. Each payment A is a percentage of the face value of the bond. Thus the present value of a bond, P, is the present worth of the redemption value and the annuity of periodic interest payments. This relationship expressed as a formula is

$$P = F\,(p/f)_n^i + A\,(p/a)_n^i$$

where P = present worth of the bond

F = face value or redemption value

$A = F \times$ (stated interest rate on the bond)

n = number of interest periods before retirement

i = interest rate received by the bond holder

EXAMPLE 7.1 Present value of a bond

What amount should be paid for a 10-year bond with a face value of $1000 and interest at 5% payable semiannually if the buyer desires to earn 6% compounded semiannually on his investment?

SOLUTION Since interest is payable twice a year, there are 20 periods ($n = 20$) before retirement. Bond interest payments A are a percentage (5%/2) of the face value ($1000) received each period, or

$$A = \frac{0.05}{2} \times \$1000 = \$25$$

Solving for the present worth of the bond, we have

$$P = \$1000\,(p/f)^3_{20} + \$25\,(p/a)^3_{20}$$
$$= \$1000 \times 0.55368 + \$25 \times 14.8775$$
$$= \$553.68 + \$371.94$$
$$= \$925.61$$

which means a buyer would refuse to pay the stated face value of the bond when his desired rate of return is 6%.

EVALUATION OF FUNDING SOURCES   The source of capital for new investments can significantly affect the attractiveness of alternatives. Limited capital tends to increase the minimum demanded rate of return. Only those alternatives with the highest returns will be pursued when funds are not available to invest in ventures that would otherwise qualify. A shortage of equity funds can sometimes be relieved by borrowing. Using debt money to finance alternatives adds the cost of interest to the outcome. It also allows a course of action to be initiated now instead of at some later date when equity funds are available.

Debt financing usually makes a good business better and poor business worse. A thriving business can expand faster with the injection of outside funds. When the earned rate of return clearly tops the rate owed on borrowed funds, the difference is a bonus payment on current equity funds. A sick business may recover with the help of borrowed funds or it may get worse from the added burden of debt interest and repayment. A firm financed entirely by equity funds weathers brief spells of loss much more easily than if it were obligated to large debt payments.

A decision to sell equity in a firm leads to dilution of ownership and control. Individual ownership may divide into a partnership, and a partnership may incorporate to issue stock. The new ownership has a voice in management which usually transmits the message that it expects a decent return on invested capital. While added ownership may be more tolerant than debtors of short-range losses, both debt and equity holders expect a gain from the use of their funds.

EXAMPLE 7.2   Before-tax evaluation of funding

Two brothers own and operate a vegetable cannery valued at $300,000. They have an opportunity to buy a firm which now supplies most of their warehousing and distribution services. An expected annual saving of $16,000, exclusive of financing costs but including costs for a 20-year depreciation schedule, should result from the acquisition. There are insufficient equity funds to meet the $100,000 purchase price.

The needed funds can be secured from a bond issue or by selling 25% control of the firm. The 20-year bonds would carry 6% interest. Which source of funds would provide the greater return to the brothers on their equity?

SOLUTION   The 20-year depreciation schedule for the bond issue will create a depreciation reserve equal to the face value ($100,000) of the bonds by the time of retirement. It would be a mistake to include both depreciation charges and bond-retirement charges in the evaluation, because none of the brothers' capital is invested. The only function of the depreciation charge is recovery of the capital of the bond holders. The annual 6% interest cost is deducted from the expected gross return to yield

$$\text{Net return} = \$16,000 - 0.06 \times \$100,000 = \$10,000$$

which is a rate of return on the $100,000 venture of $10,000/\$100,000 = 0.10$. This means that the brothers would receive a return of 10% on the loan for which they are liable. Looking at it another way, the investment allows an increased return on their original equity of

$$\text{Return on equity} = \frac{\$10,000}{\$300,000} \times 100\% = 3.33\%$$

By selling one-quarter interest in their partnership for $100,000 and investing that amount in the firm, the brothers' equity is still

$$(\$100,000 + \$300,000) \times 0.75 = \$300,000$$

The $16,000 is a net saving when the new investment is made, because the depreciation is already included and there are no additional interest charges. This leads to a total rate of return for the investment of $16,000/\$100,000 = 0.16$. The brothers' share is then $16\% \times 75\% = 12\%$. Or, on the basis of the brothers' equity,

$$\text{Return on equity} = \frac{\$16,000 \times 0.75}{\$300,000} \times 100\% = 4\%$$

A comparison of the two returns on equity indicates that selling an interest in the firm could be advantageous. However, further investigation would better reveal the influence of taxes and the merit of sharing management decisions with a new partner.

Several features of Example 7.2 are worthy of emphasis and extension.

1. Dual charges for the writeoff of depreciation and bond expense are an inaccurate representation of capital recovery. If the investment is composed only of borrowed funds and the life of the debt equals the

life of the capital recovery period, the interest rate for the loan is automatically the minimum required rate of return.

2. An owner's equity may allow him to secure a loan by which he can receive a greater return on his original investment. The debt-ownership ratio for an investment deserves close attention. Debt financing increases the profit-making leverage on equity, but it also increases risks. Fixed obligations could consume all the revenue from a venture that fails to prosper.

3. Comparisons based just on the relative monetary merits of different funding devices are incomplete. For instance, in the situation from Example 7.2 the formation of a larger partnership would increase available capital, but it could also lead to management disagreements. In addition, there is the legal aspect to consider. When any partner dies, the partnership ends and each member is liable for all the debts of the partnership.

The effect of taxes is important in evaluating different sources of funds. As depicted in Fig. 7.1, interest on debt is deductible from income taxes. In effect, the government pays part of the cost of borrowing. Higher tax rates magnify the benefits of using debt instead of equity capital.

EXAMPLE 7.3 After-tax evaluation of debt versus equity funding

The owner of a drive-in restaurant believes there is a good potential for another drive-in at a nearby town. He has $40,000 of owned capital with which to expand his business. Using this amount he can open a new operation which should yield a gross income before taxes of $8000. He feels that a conservative study period of 10 years is reasonable, and he will use straight-line depreciation for tax purposes. The salvage value is expected to be $10,000.

After checking with a bank, he finds that he can borrow $20,000 at 6% interest per year on the unpaid balance. The loan extends for 10 years and would be repaid in 10 annual installments.

If his effective tax rate is 40% for the period, which means of financing is the most attractive?

SOLUTION The relative attractiveness of the two methods of financing the new drive-in is determined by calculating the rate of return after taxes for each. Using his own equity entirely, the amount to be recovered is first cost minus the present worth of the salvage value, or

$$\$40,000 - \$10,000\,(p/f)^i_{10}$$

The straight-line depreciation charge is deductible from revenue for tax purposes.

At a 40% tax rate,

$$\text{Annual income tax} = 0.40 \times \left(\$8000 - \frac{\$40,000 - \$10,000}{10} \right)$$
$$= 0.40 \times \$5000 = \$2000$$

which makes the return for capital recovery

$$A = \$8000 - \$2000 = \$6000$$

Then the rate of return can be calculated from

$$\text{Equity} = \text{present worth of salvage} + \text{present worth of returns}$$
$$\$40,000 = \$10,000 \, (p/f)^i_{10} + \$6000 \, (p/a)^i_{10}$$

At 10%,

$$\text{Return} = \$40,000 - \$10,000 \, (p/f)^{10}_{10} - \$6000 \, (p/a)^{10}_{10}$$
$$= \$40,000 - \$10,000 \times 0.3855 - \$6000 \times 6.144$$
$$= \$40,000 - \$40,719 = -\$719$$

At 12%,

$$\text{Return} = \$40,000 - \$10,000 \times 0.3220 - \$6000 \times 5.650$$
$$= \$40,000 - \$37,120 = \$2880$$

$$\text{Rate of return} = 10\% + 2\% \times \frac{-\$719}{-\$719 - \$2880}$$
$$= 10\% + 2\% \times 0.195 = 10.39\%$$

When part of the expansion fund ($20,000) comes from a loan, the interest expense (6%) is nontaxable. The interest during the first year is $20,000 \times 0.06 =$ $1200 and decreases from this amount each year as the debt is repaid. The net return for the first year is

$$A1 = \text{gross return} - \text{taxes} - \text{debt payments}$$
$$= \$8000 - 0.40 \times \left(\$8000 - \frac{\$30,000}{10} - \$1200 \right) - \$20,000 \, (a/p)^6_{10}$$
$$= \$8000 - 0.40 \times \$3800 - \$20,000 \times 0.13587$$
$$= \$8000 - \$1520 - \$2717 = \$3763$$

Since the return lowers slightly each year because of decreasing deductible interest charges, each year's net return has to be calculated separately.

Equity funds are reduced by half when a loan is utilized. Therefore the capital-recovery formula is

$$\text{Equity} = \text{present worth of salvage} + \text{present worth of returns}$$
$$\$20,000 = \$10,000 \, (p/f)^i_{10} + [\$3763 \, (p/f)^i_1 + A_2 \, (p/f)^i_2 + \cdots + A_{10} \, (p/f)^i_{10}]$$

which yields a rate of return of approximately 15%.

Borrowed funds thus increase the rate of return on equity capital by about one-half. If an amount greater than $20,000 were borrowed, the rate of return on equity would increase proportionately. This condition of high leverage could make a prospective rate of return misleadingly high when compared with an alternative with a lower leverage. The calculated returns should serve as a guide for the drive-in owner. The higher return using borrowed capital is appealing, but the final decision must reflect other investment alternatives available for the owner's capital and his confidence in the proposed undertaking.

An economic study encompasses many elements. Some of these elements combine to produce a specific decision situation. Like a chemist investigating an unknown compound, we seek to identify the elements of cash flow in order to better understand the economic problem. The most common elements include revenue, capital expenditures or first cost, recurring annual expenses, nonrecurring expenses, and salvage values.

REVENUE AND EXPENSE

REVENUE In an industrial setting, revenue is the money received from customers for the services or products sold to them. There are many patterns of revenue flow. A retail store has essentially a continuous influx of revenue during working hours. Plumbers are often paid after each service call. Utility services are paid for by the month. Farmers usually get their money after a crop is harvested. A homebuilder has to wait until a house is sold before he receives revenue. The timing of the revenues associated with an alternative may have a significant bearing on its acceptability. One of the main reasons that new businesses often fail is the time lag between incurred first costs and the establishment of an expected level of revenue.

Revenue is somewhat harder to estimate than costs for many industrial projects. If a new investment is to serve the same purpose as an existing asset, historical data provide a reliable estimate of future revenue. When the investment is destined to satisfy a new function, revenue estimates are less certain. What looks like a sure bet on the drawingboard may end as a miserable flop in the market, where it is exposed to the buying whims of the public.

Occasionally a precise measure of revenue contribution is impossible. Sums spent on customer goodwill and improved employer-employee relationships are at best extremely difficult to measure in terms of revenue increments. Yet there is a demand for such investments. This situation often results in the setting aside of a certain sum for "public relations" or investments with intangible returns. Then the sum is divided between projects rated according to a nonmonetary scale of attractiveness, as described in Chap. 1.

Funds for government or public activities result from various types of taxes and charges for specific services. Everyone is familiar with income taxes and charges for services such as mail delivery. Both of these are revenue sources secured from the public for benefits expected· from the governing agencies. Because of their mandatory nature and long history, they can be estimated quite accurately. However, the portion of revenue justified for a specific public project is as difficult to estimate as industrial projects.

National, state, and local governments engage in numerous activities to benefit their constituents. Budgets set the costs for such services as protection, cultural development, and economic benefits, but the revenue from most of the services is a lump-sum tax payment. Different services make tax payments palatable to different individuals. With the identity of individual benefits lost in the common pool of tax revenues, assignment of an accurate worth to each service is awkward. Yet some kind of assignment must be made in order to evaluate alternatives.[1]

Privately owned public utilities occupy a position midway between government and industry. This position results from the great amount of invested capital required to provide public services such as electricity, water, telephone communication, railroad transportation, etc. Only by developing a high usage factor can an acceptable return on invested capital be obtained from low service rates. In order to assure both reasonable returns and reasonable rates, an exclusive geographical franchise is allotted to a utility company. Coupled with the grant of a monopolistic position are regulations controlling rates and standards of service. A regulatory body seeks to set a quality of service which satisfies the customers while permitting rates that allow the utility to earn an acceptable rate of return. Because of this control, revenue can be accurately forecast.

FIRST COST   The capital expenditure required to start a project and carry it to an operational level is referred to as *first cost*. The estimation of the initial investment required for an alternative is an early phase of an economic study. The factors that set the first cost have a

[1]See page 245 for benefit-to-cost evaluations of public projects.

direct effect on later operating costs. Selection of an automated production line reduces costs for labor. More expensive construction can lower costs for maintenance and repairs. Insurance, interest, and depreciation charges are proportional to initial investments.

After the design conditions have been decided upon, the direct costs of acquisition are readily determined from well-established estimating procedures, such as manufacturers' quotes or competitive bidding. When errors occur, they are usually on the low side and result from an incomplete listing of desired features and less obvious costs. Among the items that may be overlooked are the following:

Materials (freight, sales tax, storage costs, damage)
Installation (extra costs for special arrangements and unconventional designs)
Interest, taxes, salaries, and insurance during a construction phase
Change orders during construction (installation costs for additions or deletions to the original plans)
Investigation, exploratory, and legal fees
Promotional costs
Engineering and associated fees
Debugging and starting-up costs

Although many of these expenses are more difficult to estimate than more conventional costs, they can drain capital just as thoroughly as charges for physical assets.

Current levels of costs used in estimating investments may not be applicable to future conditions. Generally this is not a serious problem, but two situations bear watching. One is when an old alternative is resurrected for reconsideration. Old cost estimates may be outdated by new methods or different price levels. The other condition is when current levels reflect abnormal or temporary prices. If prices are adjusted for first costs, similar adjustments should be investigated for other costs.

First costs of outcomes can immediately eliminate some alternatives. Insufficient capital is a genuine reason to turn down an investment even though it has a handsome rate of return. An investment that would be wise for a firm with adequate capital could be a futile or even disastrous course of action for a firm with limited finances.

RECURRING ANNUAL EXPENSES   Most annual costs are easy to recognize and anticipate. We have already considered interest and depreciation charges. As in the case of first cost, overlooking expenses is an equal or greater danger than errors in estimation.

The cost of labor includes more than direct wages. Among the overhead expenses generally proportional to wages are accident, health, and unemployment insurance; vacation and retirement pay; and costs due to accidents and sickness.

Maintenance costs are the ordinary costs required for the upkeep of property and restoration required when assets are damaged but not replaced. Items under maintenance include the costs of inspecting and locating trouble areas, replacement of minor parts, power, labor, materials, and minor changes or rearrangement of existing facilities for more efficient use. Maintenance costs tend to increase with the age of an asset, because more upkeep is required later in life and the trend of wages and material prices is upward.

Property taxes and insurance are usually expressed as a percentage of first cost in economy studies. Although the value of property decreases with age, taxes and insurance seldom show a corresponding decrease. Therefore a constant annual charge is a realistic appraisal of future expense.

Income taxes   We have already observed how the annual cost of income taxes can vary according to the source of investment funds and the method of depreciation. In many economic studies the alternatives are affected identically by taxes; the same source of funds and the same depreciation methods are used for all the alternatives. In such cases there is no need to include income taxes as part of the study. But when some alternatives have special tax-deductible features, it is prudent to make after-tax evaluations.

A thorough coverage of income taxes would make up a book larger than this text. Since we cannot delve into the many ramifications of personal income deductions, capital gains, depletion rates, investment credits, and other tax situations, we will limit our attention to some basic corporate-tax relationships. For the sake of simplicity, a 50% income-tax rate will be used for illustrative purposes. The actual rate for a study is the tax-rate level at which an alternative will affect taxable income.

Income taxes are due whenever revenue exceeds allowable tax deductions. The surplus over deductions is gross equity return. In order to have \$1 of net equity return, the required revenue R before federal taxes is

$$R - 0.50R = \$1$$
$$R = \$2$$

Since federal taxes result from achieving the goal of an equity return, they are part of the cost of using such capital.

When states also collect income taxes, the federal and state tax rates can be combined to form

Effective tax rate = federal rate + state rate
$$- \text{ federal rate} \times \text{state rate}$$

Using a state income-tax rate of 8% where federal taxes at 50% are deductible from gross revenue for state-tax calculations,

Effective tax rate = $0.50 + 0.08 - 0.50 \times 0.08$
$$= 0.54$$

Assuming that the effective tax rate is known, the annual cost of taxes can be calculated according to

Income tax = taxable income $\times$ tax rate

and

Taxable income = gross income before tax
$$- \text{ interest on debt}$$

Substituting terms, we have

Income tax = (gross income before tax
$$- \text{ interest on debt}) \times \text{tax rate}$$

Recognizing that

Gross income before tax
$$= \text{ return for debt interest and dividends}$$
$$+ \text{ surplus} + \text{ income tax}$$

leads to

Income tax = (return + income tax
$$- \text{ interest on debt}) \times \text{tax rate}$$

Collecting terms and dividing by the tax rate, we have

$$\frac{\text{Income tax}}{\text{Tax rate}} - \text{income tax} = \text{return} - \text{interest on debt}$$

which can take the form

$$\text{Income tax} \times \frac{1 - \text{tax rate}}{\text{tax rate}} = \text{return} - \text{interest on debt}$$

or Income tax = (return for debt interest and dividends

$$+ \text{ surplus } - \text{ interest on debt}) \times \frac{\text{tax rate}}{1 - \text{tax rate}}$$

EXAMPLE 7.4 Income taxes

A corporation has an effective tax rate of 54%. Gross revenue for the past year was $8 million. Operating expenses and depreciation accounted for $6 million. Interest on outstanding debts was $1.2 million. What amount is left for dividends and surplus after taxes?

SOLUTION

Gross income before tax = $8,000,000 − $6,000,000 = $2,000,000

Taxable income   = $2,000,000 − $1,200,000 = $800,000

Income tax   = $800,000 × 0.54 = $432,000

Dividends + surplus   = taxable income − income tax

                       = $800,000 − $432,000

                       = $368,000

Overhead costs   The great variety of expenses described under the heading of fixed or indirect costs in Chap. 2 should be considered while comparing alternatives. *Overhead costs* embrace all the production costs not directly charged to products as direct labor and direct materials. The reason for this catchall cost is the prohibitive expense of assigning and charging to each product a specific proportion of such costs as the wages of supervisors, factory heat and light, janitorial services, secretarial help, shipping and receiving, etc.

Several methods are used to allocate the composite overhead expense to a product. A base such as direct labor, machine rate, or direct material cost is selected. Then the annual overhead is divided by the annual cost or usage time of the base category. The resulting ratio is multiplied by the base cost for producing one unit of a product. This gives the portion of overhead that each product is expected to carry and is included as a cost in determining the sales price. For instance,

$$\text{Direct labor ratio} = \frac{\text{total annual overhead cost}}{\text{total annual direct labor cost}}$$

then

$$\frac{\text{Overhead charges}}{\text{Unit of product } X} = \text{direct labor ratio}$$

$$\times \frac{\text{direct labor cost}}{\text{unit of product } X}$$

Overhead costs, in common with income taxes, often have an identical effect on several alternatives. That is, the same value for overhead costs would apply for different alternatives, making their inclusion redundant in a comparison. Where there is a difference in overhead charges between alternatives, care should be exercised to include them in the correct proportions.

EXAMPLE 7.5 Overhead costs

An equipment salesman claims that the installation of a machine he sells will allow equal quality and quantity of output with one less worker. Using the firm's required rate of return (15%) and overhead–direct-labor ratio (0.6), he substantiates his claim with the following figures:

Annual savings for the elimination of one worker:

Direct labor: 1 man $\times$ $6000 per man-yr	$6000
Overhead: $6000 $\times$ 0.60	3600
Total saving	$9600

Annual cost of new machine ($P = $20,000, $S = 0$, $n = 10$):

Capital recovery:	
($20,000 $-$ 0) $(a/p)_{10}^{15} = $20,000 $\times$ 0.19925	$3985
Operation	3200
Maintenance	600
Taxes and insurance	200
Total cost	$7985
Net saving	$1615

Does the salesman's evaluation appear valid?

SOLUTION   Maybe. Assuming that the estimated life of the machine and its operating costs are accurate, there is still a question whether overhead costs will be reduced by $3600. A one-man reduction in the workforce would probably have little effect on the total overhead costs. Since the main purpose of an overhead ratio is to allocate indirect costs to products, it is not an exact measure of indirect wages. Therefore the quoted savings in overhead should be investigated.

NONRECURRING EXPENSES   Accompanying the acquisition of some assets is an obligation for specific, one-time-only expenditures. Often these nonrecurring expenses occur in the initial stages of acquisition and are lumped together with first costs. Training operators for a new machine is a typical example. In other cases the approximate time for a future expense can be anticipated. A new roof on a warehouse or a major overhaul on a machine falls into this category. These nonrecurring expenses are often of considerable magnitude and should be included in the evaluation.

SALVAGE VALUE   Salvage value is a nonrecurring cost or revenue related to the termination of an asset's service. It is a net value in that it is the sum of all the positive and negative cash transactions associated with the disposal of an asset. Positive cash flow or receipts are realized when the asset is sold for junk, retained for reuse at another location or for a different purpose, or resold to another company. Negative cash flow is usually caused by removal costs.

In comparing an existing asset with a replacement it is usually necessary to establish two salvage values. The first is the worth of the asset if removed today. This is the price that could be obtained for it, less the removal costs. The second salvage value is its worth at the end of the study period, or its remaining life. Normally the second salvage value is less than the first. For equipment with relatively long service life, a salvage based on junk value is a realistic compromise between possible future resale and removal cost.

Every decision situation has quantitative and nonquantitative aspects. In most cases the influence of less tangible considerations is more readily discernible after the quantitative data have been evaluated. First the quantities are converted to monetary receipts and disbursements so far as possible. Then the effect of time on the cash flow is introduced and the alternatives are compared. The bases of comparison for tactical and strategic alternatives are the same: present worth, equivalent annual amounts, and rate of return. The remaining portions of this chapter are devoted to explanations and examples of different evaluation situations.

EVALUATION OF INVESTMENTS IN NEW PROJECTS   New projects are distinguished from on-going or familiar projects by the lack of definitive data. The adjective "new" implies a course of action just lately developed or recently recognized. Anything new tends to be both fascinating and risky. The fascination comes from the unknown potential that may be reaped from a fresh approach. Risk is a handmaiden of the uncertain and unfamiliar. These characteristics lead to the following practical considerations. Some advantages of new projects are:

1. Fresh designs fill current needs.
2. Latest techniques, materials, and methods can be used.

COMPARISON OF STRATEGIC ALTERNATIVES

3. Existing policies and procedures tend to be relaxed for new projects and therefore set fewer restrictions.

4. Enthusiasm is often high for those engaged in a new venture.

New projects also have disadvantages:

1. There are few data available to predict the success or costs for a new project.

2. Many new projects require a major immediate investment which produces no comparable returns for a prolonged time period.

3. Competition and economic cycles tend to limit the choice of initiation and development times.

4. Operational techniques of a new project are not known with certainty, and the management is frequently unproved.

Many of the handicaps and blessings of a new venture defy monetary scaling. When a new project is an extension of an old one, records are generally available for logical estimates. Completely different ventures force the analyst to rely heavily on surveys and interpretations of recent industrial trends. In all cases it is desirable to identify and include as many nonmonetary factors as possible. The actual evaluation of quantifiable cash flow is conducted according to practices already described.

EXAMPLE 7.6 Investment in a completely new venture

A doctor is considering the purchase of a parking lot as part of his retirement preparations. The lot is in a good downtown location. Because of rising land values, he expects the lot to appreciate rather than depreciate with time. His list of expected operating expenses includes the following:

Lot attendants	$900 per mo
Utilities: electricity, water	$80 per mo
Maintenance and supplies	$60 per mo
Taxes	$5 per $100 on the assessed value of $42,000
Insurance	$900 per yr

The price asked for the lot is $48,000. A review of the records reveals that gross earnings from the lot have averaged $19,000 per year for the last 3 years. The doctor believes that a new department store scheduled to be built a block from the lot should increase the lot utilization by 10%. If the purchase is made, the funds will be taken from the doctor's savings account, which is currently earning 4.25% compounded annually. Should he make the investment?

SOLUTION   The need for parking lots in a downtown area is well accepted. There appears to be little need for working capital above the purchase price because the lot is already operating. Since the doctor is not thoroughly familiar with parking-lot operations, he may have overlooked some costs. In addition, there is always the chance that a competing multistory garage could be built nearby or that a buying trend toward suburban shopping centers could siphon off his trade. To compensate for these risks, he should expect a rate of return well above that earned by his savings. The return is calculated as

Annual gross earnings: $19,000 × 1.1		$20,900
Annual costs:		
Wages: $900 × 12	$10,800	
Operating costs: ($80 + $60) × 12	1,680	
Taxes: $42,000 × $5/$100	2,100	
Insurance	900	
Total costs		$15,480
Net earnings		$ 5,520

With depreciation charges assumed to be unnecessary because of rising land values,

$$\text{Rate of return} = \frac{\$5,520}{\$48,000} = 0.115$$

which is greater than his present rate of return of 0.0425 and therefore makes the investment appear feasible and quite attractive.

EVALUATION OF PERPETUAL-SERVICE INVESTMENTS   The sum of first cost plus the present worth of disbursements assumed to last forever is called a *capitalized cost*. This type of evaluation is essentially limited to long-lived assets. It is not used as extensively as it once was, but is still favored by some for studies of dams, railway rights of way, tunnels, and similar structures which provide extended service.

The calculation of capitalized cost is conducted like a present-worth comparison, where *n* equals infinity. This makes the analysis very sensitive to the selected rate of return. Like all present-worth calculations, the final figure is usually an impressive amount. As such, it could appear discouragingly high unless properly interpreted. Expressed as a formula,

$$\text{Capitalized cost} = P + \frac{A}{i}$$

where A is the uniform difference between annual receipts and disbursements. When there is no revenue, the formula becomes

$$\text{Capitalized cost} = P + \frac{\text{disbursements}}{i}$$

EXAMPLE 7.7 Capitalized cost

A $500,000 gift was bequeathed to a city for the construction and continued upkeep of a music hall. Annual maintenance for a hall is estimated at $4000. In addition, $10,000 will be needed every 10 years for painting and major repairs. How much will be left for the initial construction costs after funds are allocated for perpetual upkeep? Deposited funds can earn 4% annual interest, and the returns are not subject to taxes.

SOLUTION   The total capitalized cost is known to be $500,000. From the capitalized-cost formula,

$$\text{First cost} = \text{capitalized cost} - \frac{\text{annual disbursements}}{i}$$

The annual disbursements are $4000 for maintenance plus the annual payments necessary to accumulate $10,000 every 10 years. The funds will earn interest at 4%, so we have

$$\text{First cost} = \$500,000 - \frac{\$4000 + \$10,000\,(a/f)_{10}^4}{0.04}$$

$$= \$500,000 - \frac{\$4000 + \$10,000 \times 0.08329}{0.04}$$

$$= \$500,000 - \frac{\$4833}{0.04}$$

$$= \$500,000 - \$120,825 = \$379,175$$

which means that the interest earned on the amount left after allowing $379,175 for construction will cover all the anticipated upkeep indefinitely, provided the interest rate continues at 4% or more.

EVALUATION OF INCREMENTAL INVESTMENTS   A decision situation usually involves several alternative courses of action. Some of the alternatives may be eliminated by obviously superior similar outcomes of other alternatives. Others are eliminated by lack of funds, personnel, or equipment required to conduct them. If the remaining alternatives possess essentially the same investment level and a similar cash-flow pattern, the one with the lowest equivalent annual cost or present worth is the economic choice. When different capital requirements exist, alternatives should be compared in pairs.

The procedure for comparing alternatives with different investment levels is outlined in Fig. 7.2. It is assumed that alternatives with capital requirements beyond the available investment funds have already been discarded. Following these steps will eliminate two selection criteria which often lead to inaccurate conclusions: (1) the alternative that offers the highest rate of return on total investment and (2) the alternative with the largest investment that meets the required rate of return. The latter choice could lead to a larger investment than desirable, which prevents a portion of the funds from earning higher returns available through substitute investments.

Figure 7.2 Flow chart for the selection of alternative investments where a minimum rate of return is required on unlimited capital

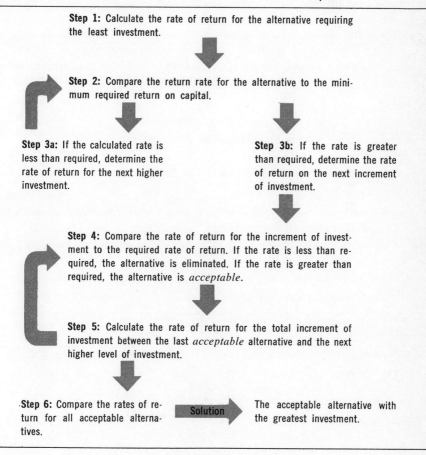

Step 1: Calculate the rate of return for the alternative requiring the least investment.

Step 2: Compare the return rate for the alternative to the minimum required return on capital.

Step 3a: If the calculated rate is less than required, determine the rate of return for the next higher investment.

Step 3b: If the rate is greater than required, determine the rate of return on the next increment of investment.

Step 4: Compare the rate of return for the increment of investment to the required rate of return. If the rate is less than required, the alternative is eliminated. If the rate is greater than required, the alternative is *acceptable*.

Step 5: Calculate the rate of return for the total increment of investment between the last *acceptable* alternative and the next higher level of investment.

Step 6: Compare the rates of return for all acceptable alternatives.

Solution The acceptable alternative with the greatest investment.

EXAMPLE 7.8 Comparison of alternatives requiring different amount of capital

Four designs for a product with the associated revenue and cost estimates have been presented to top management for a decision. A 10-year study period was used. A minimum rate of return of 10% before taxes, a rate expected from other investments with similar risk, is required. Based on the following projected cash flows, which of the four alternative designs appears the most attractive?

	A	B	C	D
Total investment	$170,000	$260,000	$300,000	$330,000
Annual receipts	114,000	120,000	130,000	147,000
Annual disbursements	70,000	71,000	64,000	79,000

SOLUTION   The alternatives are arranged in order of increasing investment requirements. Using the steps from Fig. 7.2, we first consider design A by calculating

$$\text{Capital-recovery factor} = \frac{\text{annual return}}{\text{capital invested}}$$

$$(a/p)^i_{10} = \frac{\$114,000 - \$70,000}{\$170,000} = \frac{\$44,000}{\$170,000} = 0.2588$$

Solving for i, the rate of return for design A is 22.5%. This is greater than the required rate of 10%, which qualifies the design as an acceptable alternative.

The next increment of investment is $\$260,000 - \$170,000 = \$90,000$ for the evaluation of design B. The comparison of this design to the last acceptable design shows

$$\text{Capital recovery factor} = \frac{\text{increase in annual returns}}{\text{next increment of investment}}$$

$$(a/p)^i_{10} = \frac{\$120,000 - \$71,000 - \$44,000}{\$260,000 - \$170,000} = \frac{\$5000}{\$90,000} = 0.055$$

and, from the tables, i is less than ½%, which is well under the required rate. In fact, the annual return of $5000 will not even pay back the initial investment in 10 years. Design B is thus an unacceptable alternative.

Design C is evaluated by comparison with the *last acceptable alternative*, which in this case is design A. Therefore

$$(a/p)^i_{10} = \frac{\$130,000 - \$64,000 - \$44,000}{\$300,000 - \$170,000} = \frac{\$22,000}{\$130,000} = 0.1692$$

$$i = 10\% + 2\% \times \frac{0.1692 - 0.1628}{0.1770 - 0.1628} = 10.9\%$$

With a rate of return of 10.9% on the extra increment of investment needed to use design C, this design becomes an acceptable alternative. Design D shows

$$(a/p)^i_{10} = \frac{\$147,000 - \$79,000 - \$66,000}{\$330,000 - \$300,000}$$

$$(a/p)^i_{10} = \frac{\$2,000}{\$30,000} = 0.0667$$

which makes it an unacceptable alternative. Therefore, assuming that sufficient capital is available, design C appears to be the most attractive with a rate of return on total investment of

$$(a/p)^i_{10} = \frac{\$130,000 - \$64,000}{\$300,000} = \frac{\$66,000}{\$300,000} = 0.22$$

$$i = 0.189 \quad \text{or} \quad 18.9\%$$

To better illustrate the ways by which alternatives can be incorrectly selected, we can again refer to the figures in Example 7.8. This time we will look at only the total investment instead of the increments. The rate of return for each design is calculated from

$$(a/p)^i_{10} = \frac{\text{net returns}}{\text{total investment}}$$

which results in the following values for the four designs:

	A	B	C	D
Net returns	$44.000	$49,000	$66,000	$68,000
Investment	$170,000	$260,000	$300,000	$330,000
Rate of return	22.5%	13.5%	18.9%	15.9%

One type of mistake would be to select design A, which has the greatest rate of return. This would prevent the additional investment of $300,000 − $170,000 = $130,000 in design C, which returns 10.9%. Since 10.9% is higher than the 10% expected from other investments with similar risks, a loss of about 1% on $130,000 would occur.

Another type of error is to select the largest investment that still meets the 10% rate-of-return requirement. In the example, this would be design D. We have already observed the unsatisfactory rate of return for the extra investment in design D over design C. Therefore putting $330,000 − $300,000 = $30,000 into design D forces this amount of capital to earn less than the 10% it would receive if invested elsewhere.

EVALUATION OF INVESTMENTS BY THE "PAYBACK METHOD"   The payback method of analysis draws its name from the criterion of merit for alternatives, the time required for the returns from an investment to pay back the amount invested. It is a crude yardstick of acceptability which is mentioned, not because it is highly recommended, but because it is widely used. By considering the assumptions involved, we can properly interpret the results.

The number of years required for returns from an investment to equal the amount spent is

$$\text{Payback period} = \frac{\text{required investment}}{\text{annual receipts} - \text{annual disbursements}}$$
$$= \frac{\text{first cost}}{\text{annual savings}}$$

Application of these equations can lead to deceptive conclusions, because they give no consideration to returns obtainable beyond the payback period. For example, an investment of $1000 in an asset with a life of 1 year and an associated net return of $1000 would yield

$$\text{Payback period} = \frac{\$1000}{\$1000 \text{ per yr}} = 1 \text{ yr}$$

Another investment of $1000 returns $250 per year during its economic life of 5 years and yields

$$\text{Payback period} = \frac{\$1000}{\$250 \text{ per yr}} = 4 \text{ yr}$$

Favoring the alternative with the shortest payback period would rate the first alternative best, yet this alternative actually earns nothing: $1000 - 1000 = 0$. Meanwhile, the spurned second alternative would have provided an annual return of 8%: $\$1000/\$250 = 4 = (p/a)_5^8$.

If the results of payback calculations are questionable, why are they used? There are at least two apparent reasons. One is simplicity. Since both depreciation and interest effects are ignored, calculations are quick and simple. The other reason stems from a preoccupation with the flexibility of capital. If the money spent on an improvement is recovered rapidly, the funds can be allocated to other desired projects. This concept tends to engender a false sense of security with reasoning such as, "If the project can quickly pay for itself, it must be good" or, "Only the best projects can make our short-payback-period requirement."

While the payback method is not generally appropriate, there are occasions when it can be useful. Alternatives with the same service lives receive a valid comparison by the payback criteria. Where funds are exceptionally limited, cash-flow considerations may be equal to or more important than total earnings. A statement of the period by which invested funds will be returned can be a good auxiliary criterion upon which to judge alternatives. A short payback period guards against the chance of losses owing to new technological developments.

EXAMPLE 7.9 Payback comparisons for alternatives with different lives

The foreman of a small machine works has received three suggestions for reducing production costs. Suggestion A is for new jigs and fixtures, B is to rebuild an existing machine to improve its performance, and C is a new machine to replace some manual labor. The following estimates have been made for the three alternative investments:

	A	B	C
First cost	$1800	$2350	$4200
Economic life, yr	3	5	8
Net annual saving	$645	$840	$1100
Payback period, yr	2.8	2.8	3.8

The foreman selects alternative B. His explanation for the choice is that because of limited capital for investments, shorter payback periods are preferable. With alternatives A and B having the same payback period, B is favored because the annual savings are greater than for A. What are the fallacies in this reasoning?

SOLUTION Based on just the payback period, consistent attention to the condition of limited capital would dictate a preference for alternative A over B because A requires less investment capital. Based on the rate of return on each investment, C is the most attractive, as attested to by

Rate of return for A at $(p/a)_3^i = 2.8$, or $i = 3.5\%$.
Rate of return for B at $(p/a)_5^i = 2.8$, or $i = 13\%$.
Rate of return for C at $(p/a)_8^i = 3.8$, or $i = 20\%$.

The flaws in the foreman's reasoning stem from a strict reliance on the payback criterion. Too short a period can obviously block acceptance of some high-return alternatives. If successive investments in shorter-lived alternatives produce a rate of return less than one longer-lived alternative, flexibility is purchased by the loss of revenue. In the example successive utilization of alternatives A and B limits the maximum investment to $2350, but it also limits the rate of return to less than half that achievable by accepting alternative C.

EVALUATION OF PUBLIC ACTIVITIES BY BENEFIT-TO-COST RATIOS

The difference between public activities and private activities are many. At the outset there is a difference in motives. Private activities are essentially oriented toward profit for owners, while public activities are intended to benefit the general welfare of the population. Profit is easily expressed in monetary terms. General welfare can be very ambiguous and difficult to measure in any precise terms. Some of the factors that contribute to measurements problems are the following:

Financial efficiency is often less important than philosophical reasons for a project.

Many benefits, such as beauty, patriotism, or culture, defy scaling.

Continuity of purpose and planning is often lacking because administrators are subject to election.

Politics, pressure groups, and vociferous minorities can obscure issues and force short-sighted views at the expense of long-term economy.

Putting a public project up to a vote is one of the best ways to evaluate its merit. However, lethargy of voters and the remoteness of a project from the source of its funding (the taxpayers) limits the workability of decisions by vote. The choice between a football stadium and an art museum in a city would probably arouse enough interest by those affected to assure a careful appraisal. Yet an equal expenditure to develop a wildlife refuge might inspire less interest even if the affected voters were known.

From an economy viewpoint, public activities and private activities can be treated similarly. Even though there are many nonmonetary considerations involved, a comparison of the known cash flow aids a decision. Voters in a school-bond election should know the cost of possible alternatives in order to weigh the expense against educational benefits. An economic analysis is warranted whenever suitable monetary estimates are available and an evaluation of these estimates will help decide the degree of general welfare.

A benefit-to-cost ratio is a common method of comparison for federal projects and other multipurpose public activities. All the expected benefits from a course of action are evaluated in monetary terms and totaled in the numerator. The denominator is the sum of all the costs to conduct the project. The ratio of benefits to cost is expected to exceed 1.0 before a project is justified.

Rate-of-return and benefit-to-cost (B/C) calculations are closely related. Benefits are comparable to savings and costs are akin to investment funds prorated on an annual basis. On this basis the minimum required rate of return is 100%. The similarity extends to the handling of incremental values. The increased benefits from each increment of additional cost beyond the last acceptable alternative must exceed 1.0 before it is acceptable.

EXAMPLE 7.10 Benefits-to-costs comparison

A number of small earthen dams are contemplated for the headwaters of a drainage system. Four tributaries originate in a national forest and flow together to form a river which passes through private lands. Each year there is some flooding, and every few years a major inundation occurs. Construction of one or more dams will ease the threat of high water. Dams on all the tributaries would largely eliminate the chance of a major flood.

In addition to the damage to private lands, floods also ruin fire and logging roads in the forest. Other benefits from the dams include the value of the impounded water for fire protection and recreational use. The following benefit and cost estimates have been developed for feasible combinations of dams:

Dam sites	Construction costs	Annual maintenance and operation	Annual flood benefits	Annual fire benefits	Annual recreation benefits
1	$1,200,000	$20,000	$200,000	$20,000	$30,000
1 and 2	1,500,000	35,000	190,000	40,000	$30,000
1, 2, and 3	2,700,000	50,000	280,000	60,000	60,000
1, 2, 3, and 4	3,500,000	60,000	300,000	70,000	70,000

A 40-year life and no salvage value is assumed for earthwork dams. An interest rate of 4% is deemed appropriate for the investment. This rate is a good measure of the risk involved and is in line with the interest rate for bonds issued by the federal agency to finance public projects.

Based on B/C ratios, which of the four alternatives should be selected?

SOLUTION   The B/C ratio for the total values of each alternative is calculated from

$$\text{B/C ratio} = \frac{\text{Annual flood and fire savings} + \text{recreation benefits}}{\text{Equivalent annual construction costs} + \text{maintenance}}$$

where

$$\text{Equivalent annual construction cost} = \text{initial construction cost} \times (a/p)_{40}^4$$

The incremental B/C ratio is determined from the additional benefits returned by an increment of cost above the last acceptable alternative (B/C ratio > 1.0)

Dam sites	Annual benefits	Annual cost	Increments of Benefit	Increments of Cost	Total B/C ratio	Incremental B/C ratio
1	$250,000	$ 80,630			3.10	
			$ 10,000	$30,140		0.32
1 and 2	260,000	110,770			2.34	
			140,000	75,630		1.41
1, 2, and 3	400,000	186,400			2.14	
			40,000	50,420		0.79
1, 2, 3, and 4	440,000	236,820			1.85	

For an accurate evaluation the requirement that annual benefits must equal annual costs should be applied to each separable increment of project costs. Site 1 is compared to the alternative "no action" and yields a total B/C ratio = incremental B/C ratio = 3.10, which qualifies it as an acceptable alternative. The next increment that meets the B/C ratio standard is the location of dams at sites 1, 2, and 3 compared to a dam at site 1:

$$(\text{B/C})\,3 = \frac{\$10,000 + \$140,000}{\$30,140 + \$75,630} = 1.42$$

Adding another dam site fails to produce an acceptable B/C ratio:

$$(B/C)\,4 = \frac{\$40,000}{\$50,420} = 0.79$$

Therefore the third alternative should be selected.

Without an incremental analysis, the last alternative (four dams) might have been selected, because it does possess a total B/C ratio greater than 1.0 and offers the greatest total benefits. Another mistake would be to build only one dam at site 1 because it has the greatest total B/C ratio. The reasoning errors behind such conclusions are the same as those examined for incremental rates of return. The conclusion to accept the three-dam alternative based on the given data would also result from a rate-of-return or present-worth evaluation.

It is interesting to note the sensitivity of the selection to changes in the data. Using a required interest rate of 7% instead of 4% would change the choice to the first alternative (one dam) because all the added cost and benefit increments would produce B/C ratios less than unity. Including only the flood-control benefits would also make site 1 the only alternative with an acceptable B/C ratio. The number of multiple benefits to include in an analysis and the monetary rating given to the less tangible benefits can significantly influence decisions.

SELECTED REFERENCES

Baumol, W. J.: *Economic Theory and Operations Analysis*, 2nd ed., Prentice-Hall, Inc., Englewood Cliffs, N.J., 1965.

Bradley, J. F.: *Administrative Financial Management*, Holt, Rinehart and Winston, Inc., New York, 1964.

Colberg, M. R., W. C. Bradford, and R. M. Alt: *Business Economics*, 2nd ed., Richard D. Irwin, Inc., Homewood, Ill., 1965.

Davidson, R. K., V. L. Smith, and J. W. Wiley: *Economics: An Analytical Approach*, Richard D. Irwin, Inc., Homewood, Ill., 1958.

Dean, J.: *Capital Budgeting*, Columbia University Press, New York, 1951.

Doyle, L. A.: *Economics of Business Enterprise*, McGraw-Hill Book Company, New York, 1958.

Happel, J.: *Chemical Process Economics*, John Wiley & Sons, Inc., New York, 1958.

Lutz, F., and V. Lutz: *The Theory of Investment of the Firm*, Princeton University Press, Princeton, N.J., 1951.

Manne, A. S.: *Economic Analysis for Business Decisions*, McGraw-Hill Book Company, New York, 1961.

Teichroew, D.: *An Introduction to Management Science: Deterministic Models*, John Wiley & Sons, Inc., New York, 1964.

Valavanis, S.: *Econometrics*, McGraw-Hill Book Company, New York, 1959.

PROBLEMS

7.1 What is the maximum amount you could afford to bid for a $3000 (face value) bond with an annual rate of interest of 4% payable quarterly if your minimum attractive rate of return were 8% compounded quarterly? The bond matures in 5 years.

7.2 A sum of $200,000 has been invested in bonds which yield a return of 2% of the face value every 6 months. The bonds mature in 20 years. The dividends received from the bonds are invested at a rate of 10% compounded semiannually. What annual investment at 7% would be necessary to equal the returns in 20 years from the bond purchase with its reinvested dividends?

7.3 A $5000 bond matures in 10 years and pays 3% interest twice a year. If the bond sold for $5050, what is the actual investment rate?

7.4 A $2 million school-bond issue bearing interest at 3% payable annually and maturing in 25 years was sold at a price which provided a 4% rate of return to the investors. What amount was realized from the sale of the bond issue?

7.5 A corporation sold callable 10-year bonds with 5% semiannual interest payments (2½% per period). Each bond sold at the $500 face value was guaranteed a 10% premium if called before maturity. The extra $50 was added to the redemption value of the bonds bought back by the corporation 6 years from the time of the original issue. What was the yield to the bondholders of these bonds purchased at face value?

7.6 An individual in the 30% income-tax bracket purchased $10,000 worth of tax-exempt municipal bonds which mature in 15 years and pay $200 in interest twice a year. If the buyer remains in the same tax bracket, what effective interest rate would he have to receive on a taxable investment to equal the yield from the bond purchase?

7.7 A temporary water line is required to supplement the water supply at a plant until city water becomes available in a new industrial area. Three alternative pipe sizes with associated pumping facilities will satisfy water requirements:

Pipe size, in.	14	16	18
First cost	$18,000	$25,000	$34,000
Annual pumping cost	$6,400	$4,400	$2,800

The pipeline and pumping stations will be in the same location for any of the alternatives. The planning period is 5 years, and the pipe can be recovered at the end of the period. It is expected to yield 40% of its first cost when recovered, and the cost of recovery will be $2000 regardless of pipe size. Compare the rates of return for each alternative when a 9% return before taxes is desired.

7.8 An estimating service for contractors plans to provide an additional service for its customers. Besides the normal routine for making estimates, an additional follow-up service will be offered to review records of each project and compile actual costs versus estimated costs. Based on the expected workload for the next 3 years, the proposal could be conducted by

a Two secretaries with total direct and indirect wages of $10,000 per year using hand-operated equipment with an initial cost of $1400

b One secretary with total annual wages of $5000 using a bookkeeping machine which is priced at $8000 and has maintenance costs of $150 per month

c Subcontracting cost of the work at a monthly cost of $700 and hiring a part-time secretary for $2500 per year

Any investment must be written off in 3 years with no salvage value, and an 8% rate of return is required. Assuming all three alternatives provide work of equal quality, which one should be selected?

7.9 A company in the 40% income-tax bracket is considering the purchase of equipment which will eliminate a rental expense of $9000 per year. The equipment will cost $30,000 and have a zero salvage value at the end of its 8-year life. Maintenance and operating costs are estimated at $1800 per year. Insurance is 1% of the first cost. Straight-line depreciation is used for tax purposes. The company requires a 7% after-tax rate of return. Make a recommendation regarding the purchase of the equipment.

7.10 The owners of a prosperous partnership have profits of $40,000 they wish to invest outside their firm. One partner wants to invest in a venture which will yield a rate of return of 9%. The other partner wants to put $20,000 in bonds and the remainder in a venture for which the returns are difficult to estimate. The returns from the bonds (4% per year) are nontaxable, but other returns will be taxed at the partnership's 35% tax rate. Assuming that the risks involved are approximately the same, what rate of return must the other half of the bond venture earn in order to make the returns from the two alternatives equivalent?

7.11 Perpetual care for a small shrine in a cemetery can be assured by an investment of $10,000. The interest at 5% will cover all the expected upkeep and repair costs. If the capitalized cost is estimated at $15,000, what amount is anticipated for the first cost of the shrine?

7.12 A proposed mill in an isolated area can be furnished with power and water by a gravity-feed system. A stream high above the mill will be tapped to provide flow for water needs and power requirements by connecting it to the mill by a ditch and tunnel or by a wood-and-concrete flume. Either alternative will meet current and future water needs, and both will utilize the same power-generating equipment.

The ditch-and-tunnel system will cost $500,000, with annual maintenance of $2000. The flume has an initial cost of $200,000 and yearly maintenance costs of $12,000. In addition, the wood portion of the flume will have to be replaced every 15 years at a cost of $100,000.

a Compare the alternatives on the basis of capitalized costs with an interest rate of 6%.
b Compare the alternatives by calculating the rate of return based on a 60-year economic life.

7.13 Alternative A will produce direct-cost savings of $2800 per year more than alternative B. However, alternative B offers a more impressive layout than A. If the income-tax rate for the corporation is 38%, what is the implied worth of the prestige value of alternative B, assuming that it is selected in preference to alternative A?

7.14 A state-sponsored "forest protective association" is evaluating alternative routes for a new road into a formerly inaccessible region. Different routes for the road provide different benefits, as indicated in the following table:

Route	Construc-tion cost	Annual saving in fire damage	Recrea-tional benefits	Timber access	Annual mainte-nance cost
A	$185,000	$5000	$3000	$ 500	$1500
B	220,000	5000	6500	500	2500
C	310,000	7000	6000	2800	3000

The roads are assumed to have an economic life of 50 years, and the interest rate normally required is 3% per year.

a According to a B/C comparison, which route should be selected?

b Would the choice be changed if the interest rate were doubled?

c Would the choice be changed if annual maintenance costs were not included?

7.15 A cooperative which pays a 50% tax rate on gross profit made two investments which will have a total future value of $300,000 in 10 years. One of the investments (taxable) has a present worth of $50,500 and will yield before-tax returns of 16% compounded semiannually. The other investment is in nontaxable municipal bonds. One hundred bonds, each with a face value of $1000 and semiannual interest periods for 10 years, were purchased at a price to yield the same after-tax return as the other investment. What interest rate was stated for the bonds?

Section Three
Decisions
Recognizing Risk

Between the comfortable assumption of certainty and the unpleasant admission of uncertainty there are decision models recognizing risk. Whenever an "if" creeps into the statement of a solution, the condition of risk is implied. Informally, risk is included in most decision situations by doubts, second thoughts, or a questioning attitude.

A formal evaluation of risk is feasible when the likelihood of possible futures can be estimated and outcomes from alternative courses of action can be assessed. The required effort is an attempt to compensate for the inability to predict the future with certainty. Betting in poker is a decision under risk. By keeping track of the cards played and relating them to the known distribution of card values in a complete deck, a betting policy can be developed. However, any poker buff knows that one peek is more reliable than any probability calculation. Unfortunately, such perfect information is often not available, and we must turn to risk models to assist our choice of tactics and strategies. In this section we will consider probabilistic models such as expected utility, discounted-decision trees, queuing, and simulation.

Chapter Eight
Concepts
of Risk

In our previous considerations of resources and money we have based our calculations on the assumption that complete information was available and that any uncertainty connected with the analysis could be tolerated. Thus a resale value assigned today is expected to be valid 20 years hence. A positive cash flow of $1000 per year in our working model presupposes that exactly $1000 will become available each period on schedule. Unfortunately, real-world conditions do not always follow the models developed to represent them.

Variability is a recognized factor in most management and engineering studies. The properties of materials vary over time and from one source to another. Environmental factors are never constant, and the reactions of workers to different situations can seldom be anticipated. But recognition is easier than the task of coping with restrictions imposed by variability. Compensation for imperfect knowledge can take the form of safety factors or similar means of overdesign. In monetary decisions a high minimum attractive rate of return and short payback periods are expedients employed to deal with risk. In this chapter we will consider the use of probability estimates as another means of considering risk.

In selecting a method for analysis we must achieve a balance between realism and feasibility. The assumption of certainty is justified in most cases, because it leads to a reasonably satisfactory decision with less effort, and consequently lower expense, than more complex models. However, for some problems the use of explicit probabilities provides a basis for appraising the sensitivity of decisions. *The presence of significant risks which can be represented by the assignment of meaningful probabilities characterizes decisions under risk.*

As a nation, as members of industry, and as individuals, we are constantly making conjectures about the future. Conjectures of a predictive nature, as opposed to nebulous futuristic dreams, rank the likelihood of future events. In daily conversations we hear statements such as, "The chances are that . . . " and "Since that has happened, it's a good bet that . . . ." Though the language is not mathematically oriented, it is clear that the statements were provoked by some kind of probabilistic reasoning. By formalizing this type of reasoning we can make better use of available hints about future events. More reliable decisions are the usual result of a systematic analysis of properly organized information. We can examine such an approach in the study of probability.

SOURCE OF PROBABILITY ESTIMATES   The probability that an event will occur is the ratio of the chances favoring an event to the total number of chances for and against it. The first task in considering the future through the use of probabilities is to obtain estimates of likelihood of the events in which we are interested. The sources of these estimates may be either objective or subjective.

Objective evidence of probability is usually in the form of historical documentation or common experience. It is readily accepted that a coin has two sides and a die has six. A reasonable person would not question the assignment of a probability of 0.50 to the occurrence of a head on the flip of a coin or a probability of 1/6 for an ace from the roll of a die (assuming that both the coin and the die were fair or unbiased and that they were tossed or rolled in a fashion that assured an equal chance for all possible outcomes). This type of information is *prior* (also known as *a priori*) knowledge.

In practice we are seldom fortunate enough to have prior knowledge of probabilities. Most of the time we must look to past records of events and use this empirical knowledge as a basis for current probabilities. However, vigilance is required to determine the relationship of historical records to the present action. Seemingly unrelated events could influence each other, but the link should be definitive. On the other hand, the records of one machine can sometimes be used to predict the performance of a similar machine. Experimental and other measures which give us posterior (*a posteriori*) probabilities are necessarly approximate, but they can still provide a basis for practical decisions.

Subjective probability estimates are derived from opinions based on general experience and knowledge which pertains to the situation under consideration. An estimate of the situation can be made individually or collectively. In some ways it is a "guesstimate," but even an intuitive estimate often has surprising roots in fact when its lineage is probed.

DEFINITION OF TERMS Before venturing into the rules of probability, we must define some basic conditions. We shall use a well-shuffled standard deck of playing cards to illustrate the definitions. This "honest" deck is a known entity,[1] a condition which would be nearly impossible to duplicate in industrial practice, but it provides a secure approach to probability theory.

The selection of a single card is an *event*. All the different possible events, 52 of them in a deck of cards, taken together make up a *population*. The population can be divided into *sets*, such as the set of 13 hearts or the set of 4 queens.

A list of all the events, the 52 different cards, would

[1] An assumption of an "honest" or unbiased, thoroughly shuffled deck also presupposes an honest draw. That is, the selection of any card is equally possible. A card buff knows that the top card has a high probability of being chosen by a naïve subject because of its physical exposure. Conversely, the top card has a low probability of being selected by a sophisticated subject. These practical considerations, avoided here by assumption, are of the ever-present traps lurking in the background of a decision environment.

be termed *collectively exhaustive*. This condition exists when all possible outcomes are included in a list of probabilities for a given action. The sum of the probabilities from a collectively exhaustive list is 1.

Events can be either statistically independent or statistically dependent. Statistical dependence means that the probability of an outcome is dependent on or influenced by the occurrence of some other event. We will first consider independent events, events which are not affected by the occurrence of any other event.

Addition of probabilities   The probabilities of mutually exclusive events[1] can be added. The probability of drawing a queen from our honest deck of cards is the sum of the probabilities of all four queens in the deck. In functional notation this action would appear as

$$P(Q) = P(Q_S) + P(Q_H) + P(Q_D) + P(Q_C)$$
$$= 1/52 + 1/52 + 1/52 + 1/52 = 1/13$$

Intuitively, we could say that the probability of not drawing a queen is 1 minus the probability of drawing a queen

$$P(\emptyset) = 1 - P(Q) = 1 - (1/13) = 12/13$$

because the outcomes are mutually exclusive and collectively exhaustive. Mutually exclusive sets are also additive. The probability that a card will be either a spade or a heart is

$$P(S + H) = P(S) + P(H) = 13/52 + 13/52 = 1/2$$

EXAMPLE 8.1 Additive probabilities
The output of a machine has been classified into three grades: superior (A), passing (B), and failing (C). The items in each class from an output of 1000 are:

A	214
B	692
C	94

If the run from which the sample was taken were considered typical, the probability that the machine will turn out each grade of product would be

$$P(A) = 214/1000 = 0.214$$
$$P(B) = 692/1000 = 0.692$$
$$P(C) = 94/1000 = 0.094$$

[1]Events are mutually exclusive when one and only one outcome can occur in a single action. For instance, the action of flipping a coin results in either a head or a tail, but never both.

It could also be stated that the probability of making *at least* a passable product is

$$P(A + B) = P(A) + P(B) = 0.214 + 0.692 = 0.906$$

or

$$P(A + B) = P(\cancel{C}) = 1 - P(C) = 1 - 0.094 = 0.906$$

Multiplication of probabilities   The probability that two or more independent events will occur together or in succession is the product of all the individual probabilities. In terms of the deck of cards, the probability of drawing the queen of hearts twice in a row (provided the queen is reinserted in the deck and the deck is reshuffled) is

$$P(Q_H Q_H) = P(Q_H) P(Q_H) = 1/52 \times 1/52 = 1/2704$$

The same reasoning applies to drawing any predesignated cards in a predesignated order or to drawing the same predesignated cards simultaneously from more than one deck.

A probability tree provides a pictorial representation of sequential events. In the probability tree of Fig. 8.1 a new deck is used for each draw, and each suit is considered a set. The probability of drawing three hearts in a row is represented by the double line in the probability tree. By formula this action is equal to

$$P(H_1 H_2 H_3) = P(H_1) P(H_2) P(H_3)$$
$$= 0.25 \times 0.25 \times 0.25 = 0.015625$$

The same probability is evident for the sequence of drawing two hearts in a row and then drawing any predesignated suit on the third draw.

The probability of not drawing a heart in two consecutive draws is

$$P(\cancel{H})^2 = [1 - P(H)]^2 = (1 - 0.25)^2 = (0.75)^2 = 0.5625$$

and is shown in the tree by the sum of the probabilities in colored circles which end the paths containing no hearts. Then the probability of at least one heart in two draws is the sum of the probabilities in the light circles and is equal to 0.4375.

Binomial distribution   A probability tree is useful to illustrate permutations (changes in the order of events) and combinations (groups of events with different orders of arrangement), but it is an impractical calculation technique. As the size of the tree increases, the necessary enumerations become excessively tedious. As long as the probability of an event is known and each outcome is independent of previous outcomes, we can use the equation for the binomial distribution.

From the probability-tree example, we will let the outcome of a heart, $P(H)$, be known as p. The outcome of not drawing a heart, $P(\overline{H})$, is q, and $q = (1 - p)$. By the multiplication rule, the probability of drawing three

Figure 8.1 Probability tree for independent events

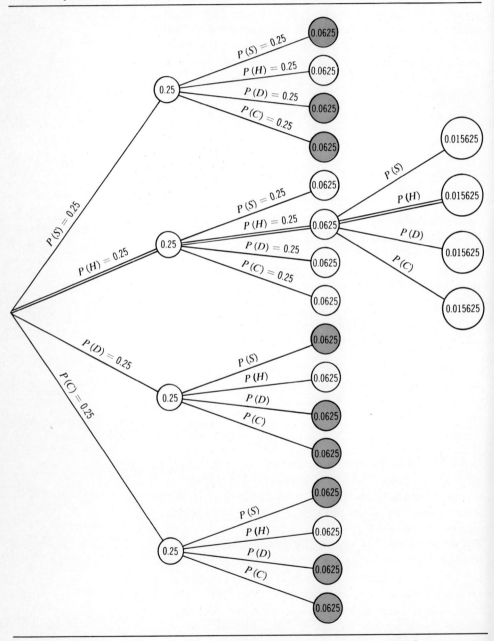

Draw 1   Draw 2   Draw 3

hearts in a row is

$$P(H_1H_2H_3) = ppp \quad \text{or} \quad p^d q^{n-d}$$
$$= 0.25 \times 0.25 \times 0.25 = (0.25)^3 \times (0.75)^{3-3}$$
$$= 0.015625$$

where n = number of trials (draws)

d = number of times probability p occurs

The draw of three straight hearts is only one of several combinations that could occur in three trials. All involve the outcome of a heart (p) appearing d times and the outcome of another suit (q) $n - d$ times. There are

$$\frac{n!}{d!\,(n-d)!} \quad \text{or} \quad \binom{n}{d} \quad \text{where } 0! = 1$$

ways to combine the occurrences. Thus the probability of *exactly* d outcomes of probability p in n trials is given by

$$P(d) = \frac{n!}{d!\,(n-d)!}\, p^d (1 - p)^{n-d}$$

Returning again to the probability-tree example, the probability of drawing exactly one heart in two draws is

$$P(1) = \frac{2!}{1!\,(2-1)!} \times (0.25)^1 \times (1 - 0.25)^{2-1}$$
$$= \frac{2 \times 1}{1\,(1)} \times 0.25 \times (0.75)^1$$
$$= 2 \times 0.25 \times 0.75 = 0.375$$

which can be confirmed by summing those paths on the probability tree that include only one heart in the first two branches.

The probability of obtaining *at least* d outcomes of probability p in n trials would be given by

$$\sum_{x=d}^{n} \frac{n!}{x!\,(n-x)!}\, p^x (1 - p)^{n-x}$$

and similarly, the probability of the event "*at most* d outcomes in n trials" is

$$\sum_{x=0}^{d} \frac{n!}{x!\,(n-x)!}\, p^x (1 - p)^{n-x}$$

In the example, the probability of obtaining at least two hearts in three draws would be

$$P(d \geq 2) = \sum_{x=2}^{3} \binom{3}{x} \times (0.25)^x \times (0.75)^{3-x}$$
$$= 3 \times (0.25)^2 \times (0.75)^1 + 1\,(0.25)^3 \times (0.75)^0$$
$$= 0.141 + 0.015 = 0.156$$

The probability of obtaining at most two hearts in three draws is then

$$P(d \leq 2) = \sum_{x=0}^{2} \binom{3}{x} \times (0.25)^x \times (0.75)^{3-x}$$

$$= 1 \times (0.25)^0 \times (0.75)^3 + 3(0.25)^1$$
$$\times (0.75)^2 + 3(0.25)^2 \times (0.75)^1$$

$$= 0.422 + 0.422 + 0.141 = 0.985$$

All the possible orderings for the occurrence of hearts in three draws and the formula relationships for each of them are given in Table 8.1.

Table 8.1

Combinations	n	d	$\dfrac{n!}{d!\,(n-d)!}$	$P(d)$
ppp	3	3	1	0.015
$pqp\ ppq\ qpp$	3	2	3	0.141
$pqq\ qpq\ qqp$	3	1	3	0.422
qqq	3	0	1	0.422

EXAMPLE 8.2 Binomial distribution

A series of samples from the output of a machine reveals that four items out of every 100 produced are defective. Thus $p = 0.04$. For an order of five items taken directly from the machine without preliminary inspection, the probability that the order will be filled without a defective item is

$$P(0) = \binom{5}{0} \times (0.04)^0 \times (0.96)^5$$
$$= (0.96)^5 = 0.81$$

The probability that the order has no more than one defective is

$$P(d \leq 1) = \sum_{x=0}^{1} \binom{5}{x} \times (0.04)^x \times (0.96)^{5-x}$$
$$= 0.81 + 5 \times (0.04)^1 \times (0.96)^4$$
$$= 0.81 + 0.14 = 0.95$$

DEPENDENT EVENTS An event is termed statistically dependent when its outcome is affected by the occurrence of another event. To illustrate dependent conditions, we will use two boxes, labeled X and Y, containing black and white balls. Box X contains three white and two black balls, while box Y holds one white and four black balls. This situation is depicted in the probability tree in Fig. 8.2.

The marginal probability of drawing a white ball in this situation is 0.4 [the sum of the probabilities of individual white balls, $P(W) = 1/2 \times 1/5 = 1/10$]. By marginal, we mean the probability of only one event. Even though two events may be related, a marginal probability refers to just one of the dependent events. From the probability tree in Fig. 8.2, it is clear that the probability of drawing a white ball is affected by the box from which it is drawn. Therefore the two events (drawing from one of the boxes and drawing a white ball) are related, but the marginal probability of drawing a white ball is still 0.4, because there are 10 balls with an equal probability of selection, and four of them are white.

Conditional probability   What is the probability that a black ball will be drawn from box Y? This condition can be expressed symbolically as $P(B\,|\,Y)$, where the vertical line is read "given." By inspecting the probability tree, we can see that there are four chances in five that a black ball will be selected from box Y. Expressed as

Figure 8.2 Population of balls

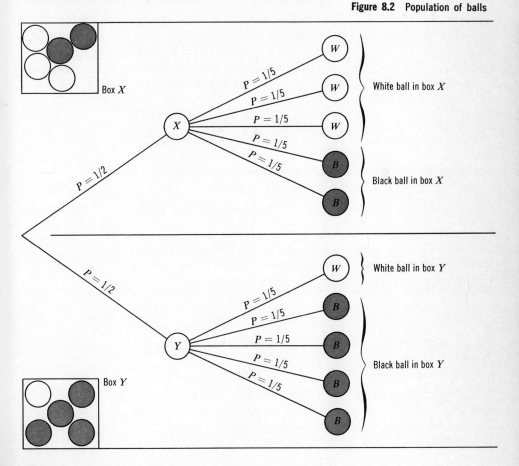

an equation, the conditional probability that a black ball will be drawn from box Y is equal to the probability that a black ball will occur in box Y divided by the probability that the draw will be made from box Y. Thus

$$P(B|Y) = \frac{P(BY)}{P(Y)} = \frac{0.4}{0.5} = 0.8$$

EXAMPLE 8.3 Conditional probability

The number of defective and acceptable items received in a shipment from two different companies is shown in the following table:

	Company C1	Company C2	Total
Defective	500	1,000	1,500
Acceptable	9,500	4,000	13,500
	10,000	5,000	15,000

The marginal probability of a defective item in the entire shipment is $1500/15,000 = 0.10$, but the conditional probability of a defective item, given that it was supplied by company $C1$, is 0.05. This result could be obtained logically by dividing the number of defective items D in the portion of the shipment supplied by company $C1$ (500) by the total number received from company $C1$ (10,000). It could also be calculated by formula:

$$P(D|C1) = \frac{P(DC1)}{P(C1)} = \frac{500/15,000}{10,000/15,000} = \frac{1}{20}$$

Joint probability   The joint probability that two dependent events will occur is given by the general equation

$$P(AB) = P(A|B) \times P(B) \qquad \text{or} \qquad P(B|A) \times P(A)$$

It is readily apparent that this is a restatement of the formula used to calculate conditional probabilities. In the illustration of black and white balls in boxes X and Y, the joint probability that a ball will be black and will come from box Y is

$$P(BY) = P(B|Y) \times P(Y) = 0.8 \times 0.5 = 0.4$$

Similar applications to other joint probabilities for this situation can be verified by referring to Fig. 8.2.

EXAMPLE 8.4 Joint probability

Records were kept for several years of the number of absentees in two offices of a firm. The average number of employees absent from work on each day of the workweek are summarized in the following table:

	M	T	W	Th	F	Total
Denver office	40	28	29	32	44	173
Miami office	26	21	20	22	28	117
	66	49	49	54	72	290

Knowing only that an employee of the firm was absent, we could say

The probability that he was absent on Friday is $P(F) = 72/290 = 0.248$

The probability that he worked in Denver is $P(D) = 173/290 = 0.6$

The probability that he was absent on Friday, given that he worked in Denver, is $P(F|D) = 44/173 = 0.255$

The probability he was absent on Friday *and* worked in Denver is

$$P(FD) = P(F|D) \times P(D) = 0.255 \times 0.6 = 0.15$$

or $\qquad P(DF) = P(D|F) \times P(F) = 44/72 \times 72/290 = 0.15$

COMPARISON OF INDEPENDENCE AND DEPENDENCE　　Under conditions of statistical dependence we have considered marginal, conditional, and joint probabilities. These same categories apply to situations involving independent events. A marginal probability has the same meaning under either dependency condition; it is the probability of a single event. When events are independent, $P(A|B)$ is just $P(A)$. That is,

$$P(A|B) = \frac{P(AB)}{P(B)} = \frac{P(A) \times P(B)}{P(B)} = P(A)$$

because the joint probability $P(AB)$ is the product of two independent events. Utilizing the illustration of a fair deck of cards, there is only one possible card that can be both a queen and a heart. Therefore $P(HQ) = 1/52$, and the probability of a heart draw is $1/4$. Substituting these values into the conditional probability equation, we have

$$P(Q|H) = \frac{P(HQ)}{P(H)} = \frac{1/52}{1/4} = 1/13$$

which confirms the known fact that there is only one queen in the heart suit, or that the likelihood of drawing a queen from the set of 13 hearts is simply the probability of the occurrence of the queen in the heart set.

The probability formulas pertaining to conditions of independence and dependence are summarized in Table 8.2.

Probability		Formulas for conditions of		Table 8.2
Type	Symbol	Independence	Dependence	
Marginal	$P(A)$	$P(A)$	$P(A)$	
Conditional	$P(A|B)$	$P(A)$	$P(AB)/P(B)$	
Joint	$P(AB)$	$P(A) \times P(B)$	$P(A|B) \times P(B)$	

REVISION OF PRIOR PROBABILITY ESTIMATES The opportunity to update and refine probability forecasts by taking advantage of additional information is a powerful analytic tool. Original objective or subjective probability assignments are developed from current knowledge to anticipate possible future outcomes. As time passes we often have access to new information about the events we are predicting. This additional information can be incorporated into our revised estimates of probability through the use of Bayes' theorem.

Bayesian analysis The concept of revising prior probability estimates to reflect new data is attributed to Thomas Bayes. His basic formula, $P(A|B) = P(AB)/P(B)$, was described previously in connection with the calculation of conditional probability. The routine followed in finding posterior probabilities is based on this basic formula. The sequence of operations follows the pattern that

given

$$P(AB) = P(B|A) \times P(A)$$

which can be rewritten as

$$P(BA) = P(A|B) \times P(B)$$

provides the equality

$$P(B|A) \times P(A) = P(A|B) \times P(B)$$

which can be converted to

$$P(B|A) = \frac{P(A|B) \times P(B)}{P(A)}$$

and the marginal probability of A is

$$P(A) = P(A|B_1) \times P(B_1) + \cdots + P(A|B_x)$$
$$\times P(B_x) + \cdots + P(A|B_n) \times P(B_n)$$
$$= \sum_x P(A|B_x) \times P(B_x)$$

The correct use of this routine allows an event B to be reevaluated when new information concerning the outcome of A becomes available.

Use of additional information The previous example of black and white balls in boxes X and Y (Fig. 8.2) will be adapted to illustrate a Bayesian analysis. Assume that the contents of each box is known but the identity of the boxes is unknown. This situation is equivalent to knowing the outcome of two possible futures without being certain which future will occur.

In this case we want to identify which box is X and which is Y. Since the two boxes are indistinguishable, there is an equal opportunity that either could be nominated as X or Y.

Event 1   The first event is a random selection of one of the boxes. The prior probability of this event is represented by the probability tree of Fig. 8.3.

Figure 8.3 Box selection

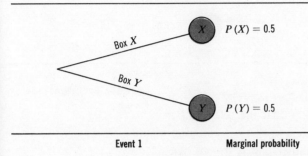

Box X — X — $P(X) = 0.5$

Box Y — Y — $P(Y) = 0.5$

Event 1   Marginal probability

Event 2   Next a ball is drawn from whichever box was picked in Event 1. We will assume that it is a black ball. Since we know the proportion of black to white balls in each box, we can calculate the probability of drawing a black ball, given that it came from a designated box. In box X three of the five balls are white, so the conditional probability for the top branch of an expanded probability tree is 0.6. The likelihood of drawing a ball of a given color from a given box is shown by the joint probability for each branch of the tree. The complete tabulation of joint probabilities (collectively exhaustive) totals to 1.0, but we are interested primarily in the probabilities relating to black balls, because our first draw was black. The sum of the probabilities pertaining to black balls is the marginal probability of drawing a black ball and is shown in the last column of Fig. 8.4.

The posterior probability of identifying the boxes, based on the additional information derived from the draw, is calculated by Bayes' basic formula. Box Y is arbitrarily used in the formula to give

$$P(Y|B) = \frac{P(YB)}{P(B)} = \frac{0.4}{0.6} = 0.67$$

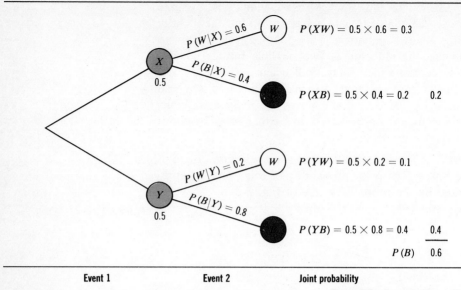

| Event 1 | Event 2 | Joint probability |

Figure 8.4 Box selection and first draw

Thus the added data have allowed us to revise our probability estimate from 0.5 to 0.67 that the selected box is indeed box Y.

Event 3   Now assume that another ball is drawn from the same box and is black. Conditional probabilities for this draw are calculated on the basis of the four balls remaining in the box after the first draw. Then the joint probabilities are determined for two successive black draws from either box. These procedures are depicted in the third section of the probability tree in Fig. 8.5.

A further revision of the likelihood that the chosen box is box Y now becomes

$$P(Y|B_1B_2) = \frac{P(B_1B_2Y)}{P(B)} = \frac{0.3}{0.35} = 0.857$$

Suppose the second draw had revealed a white rather than a black ball. This possibility is represented by the dotted lines in the probability tree. A format for revising the probability that the draws (B_1 and W_2) were from box Y is given in the following table:

Event 1	Event 2 = W_1	Event 3 = B_2	$P(E1E2E3)$
$P(X) = 0.5$	$P(W_1|X) = 0.6$	$P(B_2|W_1X) = 0.5$	$0.5 \times 0.6 \times 0.5 = 0.15$
$P(Y) = 0.5$	$P(W_1|Y) = 0.2$	$P(B_2|W_1Y) = 1.0$	$0.5 \times 0.2 \times 1.0 = \underline{0.10}$
			0.25

$$P(Y|W_1B_2) = \frac{0.10}{0.25} = 0.40$$

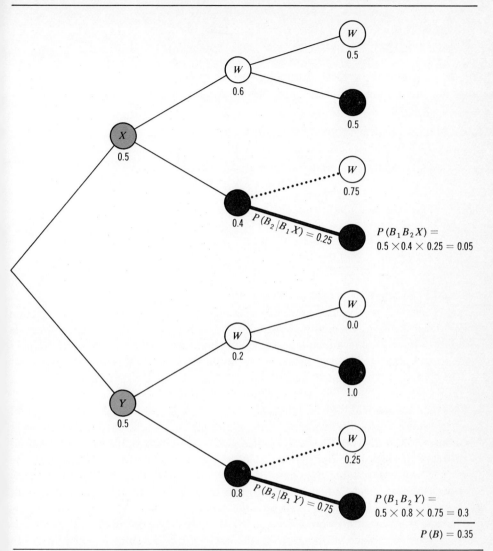

Event 1   Event 2   Event 3   Joint probability

Figure 8.5 Box selection and two draws

We would intuitively suspect that a reversed order of the draws (W_1 and B_2) would not alter our revised probability. This suspicion is confirmed by the following values:

Event 1	Event 2 $= B_1$	Event 3 $= W_2$	$P(E1E2E3)$
$P(X) = 0.5$	$P(B_1\mid X) = 0.4$	$P(W_2\mid B_1X) = 0.75$	$0.5 \times 0.4 \times 0.75 = 0.15$
$P(Y) = 0.5$	$P(B_1\mid Y) = 0.8$	$P(W_2\mid B_1Y) = 0.25$	$0.5 \times 0.8 \times 0.25 = \underline{0.10}$
			0.25

$$P(Y\mid B_1W_2) = \frac{0.10}{0.25} = 0.40$$

Event 4   As a final possibility, again assume that the first two balls drawn were black, and now a third black ball is picked from the same box. We have obviously been drawing from box Y, because box X originally contained only two black balls. Although formal calculations are unnecessary in this case, the conclusion is verified easily by recognizing that

$$P(3 \text{ black-ball draws} | \text{box } X) = 0.4 \times 0.25 \times 0.0$$

and

$$P(3 \text{ black-ball draws} | \text{box } Y) = 0.8 \times 0.75 \times 0.67$$
$$= 0.4$$

which makes the marginal probability of three successive black draws $0.0 + 0.4 = 0.4$, so

$$P(\text{box } Y | 3 \text{ black-ball draws}) = \frac{0.4 \times 0.5}{0.4 \times 0.5} = 1.0$$

EXAMPLE 8.5   Decision based on additional information

A complaint was received by company C from one of its wholesalers that a certain key part on appliances recently delivered by company C had often failed to operate properly. The company immediately stopped shipment on the remaining appliances made in the same production run as those supplied to the wholesaler. An investigation of similar malfunctions revealed that 70% of the time the trouble was caused by poor assembly and 30% was because of inferior materials. It was also determined that the probability of failure from incorrectly assembled parts was 0.40 and that failure probability from faulty materials was 0.90. If the material was bad, the whole part would have to be replaced, but if the trouble had been caused by improper assembling, the part could be readjusted to perform adequately. The only means of determining the cause of trouble was by destructive testing. A decision was made to test enough parts to determine with a probability of 0.95 that the trouble stemmed from one cause or the other.

The first five parts that were tested all failed because of poor materials. The company decided to replace all the parts on the basis of the following calculations:

Cause	$P(E1)$	$P(\text{failure} | \text{cause})$	$P(5 \text{ failures} | \text{cause})$	$P(5 \text{ failures})$
Material	0.3	0.90	$(0.9)^5 = 0.63$	0.189
Assembly	0.7	0.40	$(0.4)^5 = 0.01$	0.007
				0.196

$$P(\text{poor material} | 5 \text{ failures}) = \frac{0.189}{0.196} = 0.96$$

EXPECTED VALUE   Probabilities are assigned to possible consequences of alternative courses of action in order to compare proposals. In most cases a simple failure-or-success description is insufficient. Levels of success or failure expressed in monetary terms are the usual scales of value. A payoff table provides a convenient means of depicting the worth of alternatives in relation to possible futures.

Payoff tables   A payoff table is a format for organizing and displaying outcomes of alternative courses of action. The table allows the outcomes to be compared easily, and it helps assure that the alternatives are being evaluated on an equivalent basis.

In the payoff table below, the relative merits of two new products, A and B, are compared.

Product	Rejection	Acceptance	Dominate
A	$-\$50,000$	$\$200,000$	$\$500,000$
B	$-\$200,000$	$\$100,000$	$\$1,000,000$

The initial cost of developing product A is $50,000, and this amount would be lost if the product were rejected by consumers. If product A received average acceptance the expected gain would be $200,000, and if it dominated the market, the payoff would be $500,000. Product B would cost four times as much as product A to put into production, but if it became a best seller it would double A's profit. Because production costs for B are higher, an average demand would result in only half the payoff expected from A.

Some conclusions might be drawn from just the payoffs included in the table. For instance, a loss of $200,-000 could be considered disastrous to the company, while a loss of $50,000 would at least be tolerable. With such a severe penalty for failure, alternative B would practically be eliminated regardless of the potentially large payoff. However, even more meaningful observations can be made by including the relative likelihood of each outcome. The payoff table below has been modified to incorporate probability factors.

Product	Outcome and risk		
	$P(R) = 0.1$	$P(A) = 0.6$	$P(D) = 0.3$
A	$-\$50,000$	$\$200,000$	$\$500,000$
B	$-\$200,000$	$\$100,000$	$\$1,000,000$

It might have been necessary to assign probabilities to each outcome of each alternative, but we will assume that products A and B are similar enough to possess the same consumption pattern. In the example both products have a probability of 0.1 of rejection, 0.6 of normal demand, and 0.3 of booming acceptance. If all the possible futures are included, the sum of probabilities will equal 1.0.

Decision-making The expected value is a realistic and useful index for making decisions. It incorporates the effect of risk on potential outcomes by means of a weighted average. Each outcome of an alternative is multiplied by the probability that that outcome will occur. The sum of the products for each alternative can be entered in an "expected value" column of the payoff table. The general formula for the expected value E is

$$E(i) = \Sigma_j P_j O_{ij}$$

where P_j = probability for one column

O_{ij} = an outcome in the j column for alternative i

The expected values for alternatives A and B in the examples are

$$E(A) = 0.1 \times -\$50,000 + 0.6 \times \$200,000$$
$$+ 0.3 \times \$500,000$$
$$= \$265,000$$

$$E(B) = 0.1 \times -\$200,000 + 0.6 \times \$100,000$$
$$+ 0.3 \times \$1,000,000$$
$$= \$340,000$$

Alternative B appears to be more favorable unless the decision is subject to veto by overriding influences, such as the consequences of a \$200,000 loss described earlier. The degree of such influences can be expressed in terms of utility for purposes of analysis and will be discussed in the next section.

UTILITY

Once it has been established that a decision is best described in terms of risk, we must draw conclusions about the relative likelihood of possible futures and their monetary aspects. When a preponderance of historical or experimental evidence and representative opinions agree on the probability of future occurrences, we can state the alternatives with some feeling of security. This may amount to a false sense of security if the list of alternatives is incomplete, but we must have a starting point. Missing alternatives or gross bias in probability assignments are often recognized when the outcomes are evaluated for each state in the payoff table.

REACTION TO RISK   The value attached to an outcome (an element in the payoff table) for any alternative and a given future can vary among individuals or from one business enterprise to another. Response to risk is a very personal matter. It permeates our daily activities without causing particular awareness. Most pedestrians crossing a street probably know that their chances of being hit by an automobile are significantly greater than zero. Some apparently choose to ignore or consider insignificant the probability of an accident as they blithely jaywalk through a busy intersection. Others, by virtue of training or awareness of the value of safety, wait for the proper time to cross. A minority, because of an extreme sensitivity to the possibility of an accident, would wait until no cars at all were in sight before attempting to cross. With such divergent reactions to danger, it is logical that each of the three groups would place a different value on an insurance policy for pedestrians. The *utility* of the policy would be unique to each.

Not only does the utility vary among parties, it also varies with time. In the pedestrian example, either the jaywalker or the normally cautious street crosser might be converted to the hypercautious category after being an eyewitness to a serious accident. Putting the situation in monetary terms, we would anticipate that the witness would put a higher value on his insurance policy after viewing the accident. If he could buy protection, he would probably be willing to pay more for it after the accident, even though the probability that an accident will occur to him has not changed.

An individual or corporation places a value on an alternative which achieves a balance between the potential return and the probability of receiving those returns. Under common conditions a gamble may be attractive to one party, while a conservative approach is desirable to another. Later the positions could be reversed. Each party rates the anticipated returns of an alternative in relation to its chance of successful culmination in a manner that reflects their current economic status.

EXAMPLE 8.6   Reaction to risk

Suppose each of two university students was offered a proposition of putting up $100 for a double-or-nothing return on the throw of a single die. Each would win $100 if a 3, 4, 5, or 6 showed or would lose his ante if a 1 or a 2 turned up. Assume that both students have the same gambling instincts, but one is working his way through school and the other is the recent recipient of a large inheritance. The alternatives for acceptance or rejection of the proposition are expressed in the following payoff table:

	Win (2/3)	Lose (1/3)
Accept	$100	−$100
Reject	0	0

The two students would undoubtedly consider the proposition with different feelings. The lucky lad with ample resources would probably consider it a "good" bet. He might question the reason behind the odds or the fairness of the die. If the probabilities appeared true, he would be likely to accept the proposition because of the adventure aspects and because the consequence of the $100 loss would not be disastrous to his well-being. On the other hand, the working student would quite possibly reject the proposition because the chance loss of $100 would be a painful experience. He would appreciate the gain, but even with favorable odds, the potential reverse in his fortunes would outweigh the opportunity of winning. He might change his mind if the odds of winning were upped to 10 to 1, or if the original odds could be applied to a smaller sum, such as $10. His reaction to risk is a function of the degree of that risk to the importance of the gain or loss.

REFERENCE CONTRACT   The concept of a reference contract is a means of taking into account the unique value that individual parties place on different alternatives. To develop this reference contract we must determine the amount of money a party would demand or be willing to pay to be relieved of the obligation stated in a proposition. The fact that individuals are often inconsistent in stating their preferences for specified combinations of risk and the associated consequences necessitates a measure of caution in the analysis.

	S1 (0.5)	S2 (0.3)	S3 (0.2)
C	$80	0	−$40
T	$100	$40	−$100
N	0	0	0

Returning to the two students described in Example 8.6, consider their reactions to the opportunity of investing the money instead in campus services. The three alternatives are to invest in a food catering service C, or a tutoring service T, or to do nothing N. The payoff table shows the returns to be expected. The probability of success S in the ventures is based on enrollment in the university and the general state of the economy. We will assume the stated probabilities and the expected rewards are realistic. The outcomes are the returns from an investment of $100 over a year's period.

Let us look first at the preferences of the wealthy student, whom we will call Mr. Loaded. He is, at the time of the proposition, inclined to be a risk-taker. He feels that he will not be hurt by the consequences of a poor investment of this magnitude but will receive disproportionately high satisfaction from a success.

By asking him to relate the value he attaches to wins or losses associated with various probabilities, we hope to establish the cash equivalence of his preferences. We will consider a range of values from a gain of $100 to a loss of $100, although we could use any scale. The starting question could be, "What amount of cash would you be willing to accept in lieu of a contract that assures you (probability of 1.0) a gain of $100?" Any sensible person would ask at least $100, even though he might hope to receive more for it. Next we could ask what amount he would take in place of a contract that gave him an 80% chance of winning $100 and a 20% chance of losing $100. Since he is a risk-taker, he would probably ask for at least $80. This means he places an $80 value on the opportunity to win $100 at a probability of 0.8 with the associated 20% chance of losing $100. We could say he is indifferent to the two alternatives. By continuing this procedure through a selected range of discrete probabilities, we would obtain his reference contract or utility function as depicted in the following table:

Probability of $100 gain	Reference contract	
	Mr. Loaded	Mr. Broke
1.0	$100	$100
0.8	80	40
0.6	40	0
0.4	0	−40
0.2	−40	−70
0.0	−100	−100

The preferences for the working student, denoted as Mr. Broke in the table, could be determined by the same procedure. Because of his tight financial condition, we would expect him to try to avoid risk. His cautious nature is evident in his response to the offer of an 80% chance of a $100 gain versus a 20% chance of a $100 loss. He would be willing to accept $40 in place of the alternative. That is, he is indifferent to a sure gain of $40 in place of winning $100 with a probability of 0.8 or losing $100 with a probability of 0.2. The table continues to reflect his reluctance to incur a large debt. He would pay $40 to be relieved of a proposition that gave him only a 40% chance of winning and a 60% chance of losing $100.

TRANSLATED CONTRACT   Now that we have a utility index for each of the two students, we can personalize the original contract to indicate individual preferences. In the first statement of the payoffs the expected values of the alternatives were

$E(C) = \$80 \times 0.5 + 0 \times 0.3 + (-\$40) \times 0.2 = \$32$

$E(T) = \$100 \times 0.5 + \$40 \times 0.3 + (-\$100)$
$\qquad\qquad\qquad\qquad\qquad\qquad \times 0.2 = \$42$

$E(N) = 0 + 0 + 0 = \$0$

An immediate assumption is that a reasonable person would always choose the tutoring investment. However, by expressing the outcome in terms of the utility of each investment as expressed in the reference contract, we can see how conclusions would vary according to individual preferences. This is done by substituting the equivalent probability, or utility rating, of each return for the monetary outcome. Thus the dollar payoff table is translated to a utility payoff table.

Figure 8.6

	S1 (0.5)	S2 (0.3)	S3 (0.2)
C	$80	0	−$40
T	$100	$40	−$100
N	0	0	0

(a) Original payoff

	S1	S2	S3
C	0.8	0.4	0.2
T	1.0	0.6	0.0
N	0.4	0.4	0.4

(b) Mr. Loaded's utility payoff

	S1	S2	S3
C	0.96	0.6	0.4
T	1.0	0.8	0.0
N	0.6	0.6	0.6

(c) Mr. Broke's utility payoff

Then the expectation for the utility of each alternative is:

Mr. Loaded:

$E(C) = 0.5 \times 0.8 + 0.3 \times 0.4 + 0.2 \times 0.2 = 0.56$
$E(T) = 0.5 \times 1.0 + 0.3 \times 0.6 + 0.2 \times 0.0 = 0.68$
$E(N) = 0.40$

Mr. Broke:

$E(C) = 0.5 \times 0.96 + 0.3 \times 0.6 + 0.2 \times 0.4 = 0.74$
$E(T) = 0.5 \times 1.0 + 0.3 \times 0.8 + 0.2 \times 0.0 = 0.74$
$E(N) = 0.60$

Mr. Loaded, for instance, is indifferent to a sure reward of $80 and the probability of 0.8 of a $100 gain. Therefore we can substitute 0.8 for the $80 in his payoff table. This procedure is repeated for all the outcomes for each student and is shown in Fig. 8.6 along with the original payoff table.

If the goal is to maximize the expected utility, we see that Mr. Loaded would reasonably select an investment in the tutoring service, but Mr. Broke would be highly uncertain. Both investments appear to be equal if we assume that Mr. Broke has been consistent in his stated preferences and that neither investment is too much larger than the utility he places on doing nothing. He should obviously investigate the investment potentials further and assess the value of any other influencing factors.

EXAMPLE 8.7 Translated contracts

A small company is faced with the prospect that one of its products will shortly be outmoded by new developments achieved by a competitor. It would be possible to launch a crash program to develop a new version of the product that would be equal to or better than the competition. However, there is a better-than-even chance that neither the company's own new version nor the competitor's will receive significantly greater acceptance than the current model. A suggested compromise between doing nothing and developing a new model is to retain the present model but increase the sales budget. From a market survey on the likelihood of acceptance of the new product and the plant engineers' estimates of anticipated developmental costs, the following payoff table was obtained:

Alternative	New model Acceptance (0.4)	Rejection (0.6)	Expected value
Develop new model (A)	$300,000	−$200,000	0
Increase sales budget (B)	−$50,000	$100,000	$40,000
Retain present model (C)	−$100,000	0	−$40,000

Regardless of the reaction to risk, it is apparent that alternative C can be eliminated, because B is a more attractive choice in both possible futures. If the new product fails, B receives a reward of $100,000, compared with no gain for C, and if the new version succeeds, the expected loss from B will be $50,000 less than that for C. We can say that B *dominates* C. An alternative that is dominated by another can be eliminated from the decision process.

The next step is to consider the utility function of the company. It is a small but ambitious firm. It has made rapid growth and its products are well diversified. A loss of $200,000 would certainly be serious, but the other successful products could carry the company without too much hardship. The management feels that it needs a major accomplishment to build its reputation. A significant success would improve prestige and enlarge the horizons of the whole organization. The company has a proven engineering staff and is willing to gamble. The following utility index describes its current attitude:

Utility	Dollars
0.00	−400,000
0.06	−200,000
0.12	−100,000
0.16	−50,000
0.20	0
0.30	100,000
0.45	200,000
0.65	300,000
0.95	400,000

Judging just from the described attitude, we might guess that the company would decide to choose alternative A, even though the expected dollar value is zero. This is confirmed by converting the payoffs to utilities and calculating the expected value.

	New model		
Alternative	P (0.4)	P (0.6)	Expected value (utility)
A	0.65	0.06	0.296
B	0.16	0.30	0.244
C	0.12	0.20	0.168

We can make additional insights about utility functions by plotting the utilities of the money values involved in the decision. The shape of the curve in Fig. 8.7

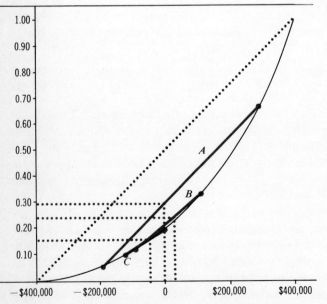

Figure 8.7 Utility function

typifies a risk-taker; it shows an increasing *marginal utility* for money. This means that as the rewards become higher, more value is placed on each additional dollar.

The alternatives can be shown by lines connecting the points on the utility curve which represent the outcomes. The dotted line to each chord shows the expected dollar value of each alternative. For A the expected dollar value is zero and the expected utility is about 0.3. C is shown in a similar manner and can be seen to have an expected loss of $40,000, with the corresponding utility rating of 0.17. The dollar expectation of B is greatest, but its utility is exceeded by that for A.

If the utility function for the company had been linear over its entire range, it would have appeared as the straight dotted line in the figure. Such a function shows the utility in proportion to the monetary value. In this case the expected value calculated from the dollar-payoff table would directly indicate the utility of each alternative.

PRACTICAL CONSIDERATIONS OF UTILITY   It is easier to manipulate utilities than it is to obtain them. Determining an individual's utility index is often a tedious and time-consuming task, but it can be even more difficult to obtain one that represents an organization's policy. While asking the series of questions necessary to establish a utility scale, side issues arising from the wording of the questions may cause distractions that show up as inconsistent responses. Then there is always the possibility that different responses would have been obtained on another day because of a change in mood or the temporary outlook of the person being questioned.

It should also be apparent that a utility function for a particular set of alternatives is not necessarily valid for another set of alternatives. Many intangible considerations fringe the choice of any specific rating. A manager might indicate a utility function which clearly shows a conservative approach in his attitudes toward industrial actions, but he might have an entirely different set of attitudes for gambling at a gaming table or in the stock market.

Under some conditions it is expedient to employ methods that retain the concepts of utility functions without the requirement of actually enumerating the full range of utilities.

An alternative can be deemed acceptable if it fulfills a minimum level of accomplishment. When applied to management, this principle is often called an *aspiration level*. It is essentially the same concept as that applied to operating systems, where it is called a *standard of performance*. In money decisions it commonly takes the form of a minimum level of profit that is acceptable or a level of cost which is not to be exceeded. Perhaps its most useful application is in decisions where the outcomes vary over periods of time. In a sales situation where bids on merchandise are received or made intermittently, as in offers made to a used-car dealer, an aspiration level is almost indispensable.

When the range of outcomes is relatively small, the expected dollar values can be used directly without introducing significant errors in preferences. A graph of a utility function is closely approximated by a straight line over a small range between maximum and minimum dollar returns. The question, "How small is small?" is a matter of judgment. A range of $500 may be trivial to a large corporation, but it could be a meaningful sum to a struggling business.

SELECTED REFERENCES

Chernoff, H., and L. E. Moses: *Elementary Decision Theory*, John Wiley & Sons, Inc., New York, 1959.

Feller, William: *An Introduction to Probability Theory and Its Application*, vol. 1, 2nd ed., John Wiley & Sons, Inc., New York, 1957.

Meier, R. C., and S. H. Archer: *An Introduction to Mathematics for Business Analysis*, McGraw-Hill Book Company, New York, 1960.

Mood, A. M., and F. A. Graybill: *Introduction to the Theory of Statistics*, McGraw-Hill Book Company, New York, 1963.

Moroney, M. J.: *Facts from Figures*, Penguin Books, Baltimore, Md., 1951.

Parzen, E.: *Modern Probability and its Applications*, John Wiley & Sons, Inc., New York, 1960.

Reichenbach, H.: *The Theory of Probability*, University of California Press, Berkeley, Calif., 1949.

Schlaifer, R.: *Probability and Statistics for Business Decisions*, McGraw-Hill Book Company, New York, 1959.

Shuchman, A.: *Scientific Decision Making in Business*, Holt, Rinehart and Winston, Inc., New York, 1963.

Stigler, G.: *The Theory of Price*, The Macmillan Company, New York, 1952.

PROBLEMS

8.1 Given a fair coin,

a What is the probability of at least one head in three tosses?

b What is the probability of flipping a tail, a head, and a head in that order?

c What is the probability of flipping at most two heads in three tosses?

8.2

drawing a queen was 1/13 and the probability of a heart was 1/4. The probability of drawing a queen *or* a heart is called a *union*, because the two sets overlap; they are not mutually exclusive. Therefore when the probabilities of the two sets are added the portion that overlaps must be subtracted. By this means we arrive at the formula for the probability of drawing a queen or a heart,

$$P(Q + H) = P(Q) + P(H) - P(QH)$$
$$= 1/13 + 1/4 - 1/52 = 4/13$$

a Show the union by a sketch of the overlapping heart and queen sets.

b Let three overlapping sets be A, B, and C. Sketch the sets and determine a formula for $P(A + B + C)$.

8.3 a Given the probability that 1 out of every 1000 tire valves are defective, what is the probability that two of the four tires on a car will have defective valves?

b In super-safety tires which have a separate inner tire, the valves for the inner tire are defective 1 time in 500. What is the probability that a tire will have both valves (see part (*a*)) defective?

8.4 When a machine is properly adjusted it will produce an acceptable product 9 times in 10. When it is out of adjustment the probability of an acceptable product is 0.4. The probability of the machine's being adjusted properly is 0.95.

a If the first part tested after an adjustment is not acceptable, what is the probability that the machine was correctly adjusted?

b If the first two parts were acceptable, what is the probability of a correctly adjusted machine?

8.5 There are 20 people in a room. What is the probability that at least two of them have the same birthday?

8.6 A shipment of parts contains 20 items, 8 of which are defective. Two of the items are randomly selected from the shipment and inspected.

a What is the probability that the first one selected is good?

b What is the probability that both are good?

c What is the probability that one is good and one is bad?

8.7 A data-processing firm mails 1000 bimonthly newsletters to present or potential clients. In one issue the firm announced a new service and asked that interested parties write for more information. The firm believed that one out of every two replies would come from one of its present customers. From past experience, it is estimated that the probability of a reply from noncustomers is 0.40. On the assumption that the mailing list includes the names of 300 present customers, how many replies can be expected?

8.8 New types of concrete mixes are tested in a laboratory by batching four test cylinders. The probability that a trial batch will yield the specified strength is 0.90 if the mix is properly prepared and tested. Occasionally, about once every 20 times, the trial batch will be improperly handled or the ingredients inaccurately measured. The probability that a poorly prepared mix will yield the specified strength is 0.20. If only one cylinder in a trial batch of four meets the specified strength, what is the probability that the mix was correctly prepared?

8.9 A Louisiana oil operator owns a $5 million oil rig. It costs $75,000 to pull his drills to safety and batten down the rig in anticipation of a bad storm. An uninsured average loss of $400,000 results from a bad storm when no precautionary measures are taken. A weather-forecasting service provides an assessment of the probability of a severe storm. Four out of five times that a severe storm is predicted with a probability of 1.0, it does occur. Only 1 severe storm in 100 arrives unpredicted. Should the rig owner pull his drills when the forecasting service predicts a storm at 1.0?

8.10 A manufacturer has three inspection plans: A, B, and C. The chance that a faulty unit will pass undetected is 2% in plan A, 5% in plan B, and 10% in plan C. The respective inspection costs per unit are $0.35, $0.10, and $0.01. A defective unit going undetected causes opportunity costs of $3.00.

a Which inspection plan should be used?
b Compare the plan selected in part (*a*) with a policy of no inspection.

8.11 A logging company must decide the most advantageous duration for a paving project. The beginning date of the project has been definitely set. A critical-path analysis has shown that three project durations are feasible. If the paving is completed in 4 months, the basic project cost will be $80,000. A 5-month duration will allow construction savings of $20,000, and it will cost an extra $40,000 over the basic cost to crash the project to 3 months. However, transportation expenses can be cut by $10,000 over the 4-month schedule if the paving is done in 3 months, and an extra transportation expense of $15,000 will be incurred for an extension of the paving time to 5 months.

Since the project must be completed during a period of expected foul weather, the extra expense due to possible weather conditions should also be considered. Weather records indicate that the probabilities for mild rain, heavy rain, and wind and rain are, respectively, 0.3, 0.5, and 0.2. The costs that must be included for these conditions are given in the following table:

Weather conditions	3 mo	4 mo	5 mo
Mild rain	$10,000	$15,000	$ 5,000
Heavy rain	10,000	40,000	60,000
Wind and rain	15,000	55,000	65,000

Which duration has the lowest expected total cost?

8.12 There are several methods available to discover defective welds. A company has investigated two methods. Method 1 costs $0.50 per inspection and detects defects 80% of the time. Method 2 costs $2.00 per test, but it always detects a defective weld. When a defective weld goes undetected, the estimated cost to the company is $30.00 for replacement and other incidental costs. The probability of a defective weld is 0.05. Using the expected-value criteria, determine whether method 1 or 2 should be used, or whether the company is better off with no inspection procedure.

8.13 Ninety percent of the fruit received at a cannery comes from local growers. The fruit from local sources averages 80% grade 1 and 20% grade 2. The fruit obtained from other sources averages 40% grade 1 and 60% grade 2. The markings on a shipment of bins full of fruit were lost. One bin was sampled, and from five pieces of fruit inspected, four were of grade 1. What is the probability that the bin came from a local grower?

8.14 Suppose you were notified that you were to receive a relatively small inheritance from a distant relative, but the exact amount had not yet been determined. Then someone offered to bet you double or nothing for the unknown sum on the flip of a fair coin. Make a payoff table to represent your alternative, letting I be the value of your inheritance. At what value of I would you be willing to accept the bet? What is the significance of this indifference point to your utility index?

8.15 What could be said about the individual with the utility function shown?

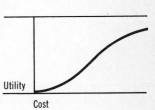

8.16 An individual decides that his utility rating for a loss of $20 is 0.10 and a gain of $100 is 0.60. In addition, he finds himself indifferent to the two alternatives in the payoff table below:
What is his utility rating for $50?

	P (0.3)	P (0.7)
A1	$50	$50
A2	-$20	$100

8.17 The company described in Example 8.7 has determined a new utility index since its decision to develop a refined version of its product.
a If this index had been applied to the decision to develop a refined product, what would the decision have been?
b What are some possibilities that could have influenced the altered utility index?
c At what probability would the expected utility of alternatives A and B be equal under the new utility scale?

Utility	Dollars
0.00	-400,000
0.40	-200,000
0.58	-100,000
0.65	-50,000
0.71	0
0.82	100,000
0.90	200,000
0.95	300,000
0.98	400,000

8.18 An investor is deciding whether to buy bonds or stocks. He estimates that the probabilities of inflation and recession are, respectively, 0.7 and 0.3. For his anticipated investment of $10,000, he believes his choice of stocks would gain 10% per year during a period of inflation and would lose 5% of their value in a recession. His selection of bonds would show a gain of 4% regardless of inflation or recession.
a Which alternative would he choose if his utility scale were $-\$1000 = 0.0$, $-\$500 = 0.2$, $\$0 = 0.4$, $\$400 = 0.6$, $\$800 = 0.8$, and $\$1000 = 1.0$? The scale shows the dollar values equated to an equivalent utility, and intermediate values can be obtained by straight-line interpolation.
b Which alternative would the investor choose if his utility scale were directly proportional to dollar values?
c At what probability of recession would he be indifferent to the two alternatives?

8.19 Another way of approaching a decision is temporarily to bypass specific assignments of the probabilities of possible futures by determining at what probability the decision-maker would be indifferent to each occurrence. Then he can make general observations about the future which can narrow his area of consideration. This is accomplished by finding the probabilities at which the utility of each strategy is equal; that is,

$$E(A1) = E(A2) = E(A3)$$

The payoff table below shows the utility a firm attaches to three alternative means of replacing obsolete equipment under the possible futures of a recession R, normal activity N, and inflation I.

a At what probabilities for R, N, and I would the firm be indifferent to alternatives $A1$, $A2$, or $A3$?

	R	N	I
A1	0.9	0.5	0.2
A2	0.7	1.0	0.1
A3	0.3	0.6	0.8

b What is the expected value of the utility?
c How could the firm use this information in narrowing the choice of alternatives?

8.20 Would it be accurate to say that one outcome is preferred to another because the utility of one is greater than another?

Chapter Nine
Evaluations
Recognizing
Risk

The distinguishing characteristic of decisions based on an analysis including risk considerations is the assessment of probable outcomes. All decision-making situations include the identification of alternative courses of action. In some cases it is most realistic to consider the alternatives are certain to occur. In other cases, several different alternative outcomes may be recognized, but it is difficult or impossible to rate their likelihood of occurrence. Between these limits lies a large class of decision situations in which it is appropriate and realistically possible to relate probability estimates to outcomes.

Although decision-making procedures were discussed in Chap. 1, a few additional comments should add meaning to problems involving risk. Every decision of any consequence has overtones of risk. Sometimes the risk

INCLUDING RISK IN THE DECISION ENVIRONMENT

is so remote that it can be disregarded as a factor. Even when risk is recognized, it may have to be ignored because of insufficient data for evaluation or because the evaluation would require too much time or money. Such secondary attention to risk factors is neither laziness nor stupidity; it is often a necessity. If every decision were subject to a searching appraisal of risk, management functions would grind along at an intolerably slow pace.

DEFINITION OF THE PROBLEM　The investigation leading to a problem definition should give strong hints as to the appropriateness of including risk considerations in the evaluation. Objectives that can be satisfied almost immediately are not as subject to chance variations that intrude over extended time periods. Narrow objectives bounded by limited means of accomplishment effectively exclude risk by confining the problem and solution to known quantities. Risk enters into the decision situation when current activities are projected into a distant future, and the resulting activities are subject to conditional influences.

COLLECTION OF DATA　Collecting data is a more demanding task when risk effects are to be considered. The first obstacle is the identification of possible alternatives. Both the obvious and the subtle warrant consideration. Creative effort is commonly considered a virtue in developing alternatives and is subordinated to statistical and accounting efforts in assessing outcomes. This is a mistaken belief. Both phases benefit from creativity and both rely on documentation. Moreover, the knowledge acquired in one phase is bound to contribute to other phases.

If we can compare the trunk of a tree to a problem, the main branches might be alternative solutions and the outcomes the secondary branches and twigs. Assessment of these outcomes includes (1) the identification of future states or condition, (2) the prediction of the probability of each state, and (3) the determination of returns associated with each state. Future states can be anticipated, but they cannot be controlled. Noncontrollable conditions may include weather, economic or technological developments, political legislation, world affairs, whims of buyers, and so forth. A key question is to decide which states are relevant to the problem objectives.

288

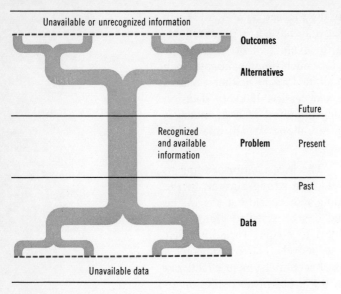

Unavailable or unrecognized information

Outcomes

Alternatives

Future

Recognized
and available
information

Problem

Present

Past

Data

Unavailable data

Figure 9.1 Problem-tree solution space

To continue the problem-tree analogy illustrated in Fig. 9.1, the roots of the tree or problem lie in the past and constitute the source material. We can get some information about the outcomes by investigating the roots. Other information is available from the structure of the limbs, or alternatives. The least promising alternatives can be pruned out, thereby reducing the effort required for outcome assessments to reasonable limits.

A shortage of pertinent information is a common handicap in risk evaluation. This condition is depicted in Fig. 9.1 by the perimeter line surrounding the problem tree. Lack of information may be due to a scarcity of historical data or the inability to decipher past trends in terms of future outcomes. Failure to identify promising alternatives can be traced to unavailability of data or to simply having overlooked a course of action that should have been apparent. Estimating distant outcomes is at best precarious with good information; without applicable data it becomes more heroic than rational.

FORMULATING THE MODEL   Many different model formats have been suggested in previous sections. More are offered in the following pages. Taken one at a time, they appear logical and directly applicable. Taken as a group, they may blend into a confusing spectrum of diverse solution paths. The question of which to use is a very real problem. A gross answer is that the data and objectives will indicate the most appropriate model. The effectiveness of this answer relies on extensive familiarity with available models.

Models have been divided into broad categories such as the certainty-risk-uncertainty and primary–minimum-cost–time-value classifications. The purpose of the divisions is to group models according to similar characteristics which serve as an index to solution methods. When the characteristics are matched to the decision situation, hopefully, the appropriate model is apparent.

EVALUATION   The selection of the most advantageous alternative can be compared with a simple weight balance. Each alternative is weighed. Rewards are balanced against outlays. Opportunity costs are compared to operating costs. The alternative that best meets the decision criteria on the economic balance is chosen.

Inclusion of risk factors does not automatically increase the accuracy of a study. Probabilities representing risk appear on both sides of the economic balance. Sometimes they can decidedly swing the balance to one side. The important point is to realize that some evaluations are trivial or misleading without risk considerations, while others will not benefit from the additional effort required to include risk. The ability to distinguish between the two comes from confidence nourished by familiarity and practice.

Including risk in an analysis can be likened to adding a small flashlight to a key ring; it can be a novelty and a conversation gambit, or it can be used for illumination.

DISCOUNTED-DECISION TREES

A decision-tree format has already been introduced for use in primary decisions and probability calculations. A related graphical format is utilized in this section to combine economic time values and probabilistic properties into one method of evaluation.

SUCCESSIVE DECISIONS   A discounted-decison tree shows decisions separated by time intervals and susceptible to external influencing factors.[1] Branches radiate from an initial decision point to indicate the primary alternatives. Each main branch is divided to show foreseeable outcomes associated with possible future events. Then the events are rated with respect to their probable oc-

[1] For additional details and examples see J. F. Magee, "Decision Trees for Decision Making," *Harvard Business Review*, July–August, 1964, and "How to Use Decision Trees in Capital Investment," *Harvard Business Review*, September–October, 1964.

currence. When gains can be maximized by introducing new alternatives at a future date, a second decision point is established. A succession of decision points can extend to the limit of forecasting ability. The time value of monetary outcomes is effected by discounting the outcomes to a common point in time.

The layout of a discounted-decision tree follows the extensive form employed for primary decisions. Again, decision points are represented by squares, and the circles symbolize outcomes. Dotted links represent courses of action, and solid links show possible consequences of these actions. Alternatives are evaluated on an equivalent basis by discounting receipts and disbursements of future occurrences back to a decision point. The decision criterion is the expected value of alternatives at each decision point.

SAMPLE APPLICATION OF DISCOUNTED-DECISION TREES   A warehousing problem of a small novelty-manufacturing company will serve to illustrate a decision tree for successive decisions. The company is relatively new and has captured a limited segment of the novelty market. It must have additional storage space to meet customer demands and to allow more flexible production scheduling. A primary decision has been made to secure additional inventory storage.

Alternatives   An initial investigation has revealed the availability of only one suitable rental warehouse, and it is available only if leased for 10 years. The warehouse has more space than is immediately required, but the company feels that some of the space could be sublet if desired. Estimates solicited from building contractors confirm that the construction of a new warehouse of equivalent size would amount to more than the $23,000-per-year lease cost.

Another alternative is to build a small warehouse now and enlarge it if future business activity warrants expansion. The owners feel that in 3 years they will know whether the company's growth will support the addition.

Forecasts   In order to evaluate the alternatives, estimates were made of possible business patterns and the likelihood of each. Their optimistic forecasts are shown in Table 9.1.

The owners feel the probability for increased growth during the next 3 years is $0.56 + 0.14 = 0.70$. If the growth materializes, they can use more room than is available in the anticipated small warehouse. Therefore,

Growth patterns	Probability
No increase in activity for 10 yr	0.15
No increase for 3 yr, but an expanded growth rate during the next 7 yr	0.15
Increasing growth for the next 3 yr, but no increase during the following 7 yr	0.14
Increasing activity for the full 10 yr	0.56

Table 9.1 Growth patterns

if they initially decide to build, they will have to make a decision in 3 years about whether to add to the small warehouse or find other means to obtain extra storage space. At that time the conditional probability that the company will continue to grow is $0.56/0.70 = 0.80$. The spectrum of forecasts and alternatives can be summarized in a decision tree as shown in Fig. 9.2.

Outcomes   The outcomes for the warehouse proposals are rated according to expected costs. Initial building costs for a small warehouse should be accurate, but the estimated price for an addition is less firm because of possible changes in building conditions at the time of construction. Yearly rental fees for the leased warehouse

Figure 9.2 Decision tree with alternatives and forecasts

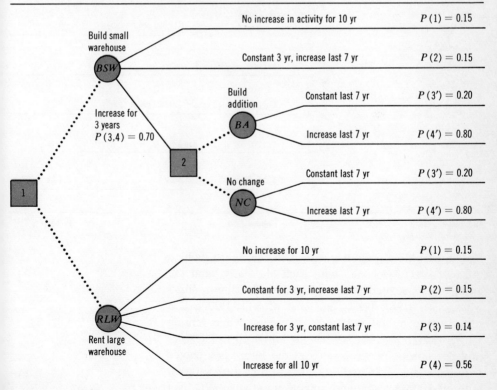

Build small warehouse **BSW** — No increase in activity for 10 yr		$P(1) = 0.15$
Constant 3 yr, increase last 7 yr		$P(2) = 0.15$
Increase for 3 years $P(3,4) = 0.70$ — **2** — Build addition **BA** — Constant last 7 yr		$P(3') = 0.20$
Increase last 7 yr		$P(4') = 0.80$
No change **NC** — Constant last 7 yr		$P(3') = 0.20$
Increase last 7 yr		$P(4') = 0.80$
RLW Rent large warehouse — No increase for 10 yr		$P(1) = 0.15$
Constant for 3 yr, increase last 7 yr		$P(2) = 0.15$
Increase for 3 yr, constant last 7 yr		$P(3) = 0.14$
Increase for all 10 yr		$P(4) = 0.56$

are a fixed amount. Other annual costs are less certain. Savings, denoted as negative costs in this example, will result if the entire capacity is not required for the company's inventory and the extra portion is rented. Conversely, additional costs are incurred when a lack of storage space forces production runs below the economical lot size or causes out-of-stock costs in supplying customers. Estimates of net annual costs for the outcomes of each alternative are tabulated in the decision tree of Fig. 9.3.

Figure 9.3 Costs associated with warehouse alternatives

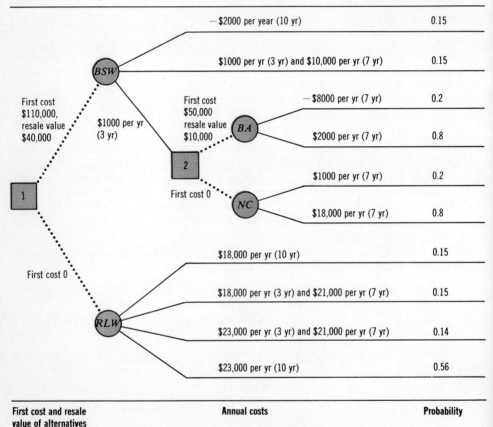

First cost and resale value of alternatives	Annual costs	Probability

The cash-flow estimates shown in the figure include the first costs associated with each alternative and the annual costs related to the outcomes. Building a small warehouse, *BSW*, has a first cost of $110,000 and a resale value of $40,000 after 10 years, while renting a large warehouse, *RLW*, has no initial cost. The second decision point three years in the future is a choice between building an addition, *BA*, at a cost of $50,000 with a $10,000 resale and making no change, *NC*. Net annual returns comprise repairs, taxes, insurance, leasing expense, and opportunity costs, as well as the negative costs of subletting when possible. The lease for the rental warehouse states an annual charge of $23,000, which includes taxes, insurance, and repairs. If there is no increase in the company's activities, this annual charge can be defrayed by $5000 from subletting extra space. Less rental income is anticipated when the company needs part or all of the space to handle its own increasing activity. The two periods of returns, 3 and 7 years, correspond to the original growth patterns indicated in Fig. 9.2.

Evaluation   Two types of calculations are involved in evaluating alternatives. The present value of receipts and expenditures are determined for each outcome and are then weighted according to their probability of occurrence. This procedure amounts to finding the expected value of the present worth of the outcomes. These expected values are compared at a decision point to select the most advantageous alternative.

Comparisons are made in a reverse chronological order. That is, the most distant decision point from time zero is evaluated first. The selected alternative from the first decision then becomes an input to the next decision. The backward pass through successive points is continued until the primary decision is resolved.

For the warehouse example, the discounting procedure begins at decision point 2. At this point in time, 3 years away from the primary decision, the company must decide whether to build an addition to the plant or make no change. The outcomes of each of these two alternatives depend on the level of business activity during the last 7 years of the study period. We will assume that the company uses an interest rate of 12%. The present worth of the four outcomes at decision point 2 is calculated as shown in Table 9.2.

Table 9.2 Present worth of outcomes at decision point 2

Alternative	First cost, resale, and annual costs discounted at 12% for 7 yr	Present worth
BA_{const}	$\$50,000 - \$10,000 \times 0.4523 - \$8000 \times 4.564$ $\quad\quad\quad\quad\quad (p/f)_7^{12} \quad\quad\quad\quad (p/a)_7^{12}$	$ 8,965
BA_{inc}	$\$50,000 - \$10,000 \times 0.4523 + \$2000 \times 4.564$	54,605
NC_{const}	$\$1,000 \times 4.564$ $\quad\quad (p/a)_7^{12}$	4,564
NC_{inc}	$\$18,000 \times 4.564$	82,152

To obtain the expected value we can use the payoff-table format.

Figure 9.4 Payoff table for decision point 2

Alternative	Company growth patterns		Expected value (costs)
	Constant (0.2)	Increase (0.8)	
BA	$8965	$54,605	$45,477
NC	$4564	$82,152	$66,634

Remembering that we are dealing with costs and that the minimum expected value is most attractive, we would select the alternative to build an addition, *BA*.

Decision point 1 also has two alternatives. Since we have already considered decision point 2, we will continue on this branch of the decision tree. The initial cost of building is $110,000, with an expected resale value of $40,000 after 10 years. Three outcomes may occur from this course of action. Company activity could increase or remain constant for the entire 10 years, or it could increase the first 3 years and then level off or continue to increase the remaining 7 years. The conditional decision made at point 2 was based on the possible outcomes of the last 7 years, *given* that activity increased during the first 3 years. This decision becomes an outcome of the primary alternative to build a warehouse. A comparison, assuming end-of-year returns and a 12% interest factor, is shown below.

Outcome	First cost, resale, and annual costs discounted at 12% for 10 yr	Present worth
BSW_{const}	$\$110,000 - \$40,000 \times \underset{(p/f)_{10}^{12}}{0.322} - \$2000 \times \underset{(p/a)_{10}^{12}}{5.65}$	$ 85,820
$BSW_{\text{const 3, inc 7}}$	$\$110,000 - \$40,000 \times \underset{(p/f)_{10}^{12}}{0.322} + \$1000 \times \underset{(p/a)_{3}^{12}}{2.402}$	
	$+ \$10,000 \times \underset{(p/a)_{7}^{12}}{4.564} \times \underset{(p/f)_{3}^{12}}{0.7118}$	132,009
$BSW_{\text{inc 3}}$	$\$110,000 - \$40,000 \times \underset{(p/f)_{10}^{12}}{0.322} + \$1000 \times \underset{(p/a)_{3}^{12}}{2.402}$	
	$+ 45,477 \times \underset{(p/f)_{3}^{12}}{0.7118}$	131,893

In a similar manner we can turn to the other branch of the tree and obtain the present worth of the annual costs associated with renting a large warehouse.

Outcome	Annual cost at 12% for 10 yr	Present worth
RLW_{const}	$\$18,000 \times \underset{(p/a)^{12}_{10}}{5.65}$	$\$101,700$
$RLW_{const\,3,\,inc\,7}$	$\$18,000 \times \underset{(p/a)^{12}_{3}}{2.402} + \$21,000 \times \underset{(p/a)^{12}_{7}}{4.564} \times \underset{(p/f)^{12}_{3}}{0.7118}$	$111,458$
$RLW_{inc\,3,\,const\,7}$	$\$23,000 \times \underset{(p/a)^{12}_{3}}{2.402} + \$21,000 \times \underset{(p/a)^{12}_{7}}{4.564} \times \underset{(p/f)^{12}_{3}}{0.7118}$	$123,468$
RLW_{inc}	$\$23,000 \times \underset{(p/a)^{12}_{10}}{5.65}$	$129,950$

Grouping these outcomes in a payoff table, we have Fig. 9.5.

Figure 9.5 Payoff table for decision point 1

	Company growth patterns				
Alternatives	Const. 10 yr (0.15)	Const. 3 yr, inc. 7 yr (0.15)	Inc. 3 yr, const. 7 yr (0.14)	Inc. 10 yr (0.56)	Expected value (cost)
BSW	$\$ 85,820$	$\$132,009$	$\$131,893$	$\$131,893$	$\$124,999$
RLW	$\$101,700$	$\$111,458$	$\$123,468$	$\$129,950$	$\$122,031$

From this analysis it is apparent that the most economical alternative is to sign the lease for renting the large warehouse. The margin of difference is $\$124,999 - \$122,031 = \$2968$.

VALUE OF ADDITIONAL INFORMATION The novelty company now has a quantitative base for making its decision. It may be satisfied with the information and proceed to sign the lease. It is also possible that some segment of management may not agree on the indicated course of action. There may be a disagreement as to estimated growth patterns or cost figures. Assuming that the need for some kind of storage facility is unanimously recognized, there is still another alternative available: the decision can be postponed. This alternative would be procrastination unless it were coupled with a firm desire to obtain more information about the problem. Such information could be provided by further intensive investigation by company personnel or by a study conducted by an independent agency.

The first step in considering the advisability of further research is to determine the worth of additional information. Securing new data costs money whether the investigation is conducted by company or outside investigators. This additional investment should be exceeded by the expected value of added profits or reduced costs realized from the information.

With *perfect* information the company would *know* which alternative would cost the least. From Fig. 9.5 we can see that the best alternative would be to build a small warehouse without an addition if we *knew* that the company would experience a constant growth pattern for 10 years. The cost of building ($85,820) is $15,880 less than leasing for this growth pattern. In a similar fashion we can determine the best alternative for each *known* future state. The expected value of such perfect foresight is calculated as shown in Fig. 9.6

Four future states were identified in the warehouse illustration. We have already observed that a small ware-

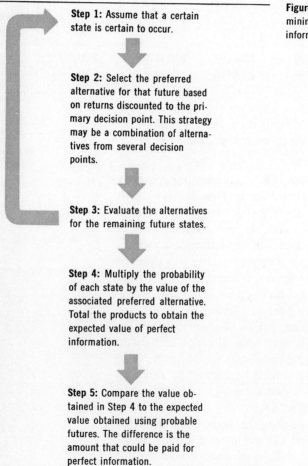

Figure 9.6 Flow chart for determining the value of perfect information

Step 1: Assume that a certain state is certain to occur.

Step 2: Select the preferred alternative for that future based on returns discounted to the primary decision point. This strategy may be a combination of alternatives from several decision points.

Step 3: Evaluate the alternatives for the remaining future states.

Step 4: Multiply the probability of each state by the value of the associated preferred alternative. Total the products to obtain the expected value of perfect information.

Step 5: Compare the value obtained in Step 4 to the expected value obtained using probable futures. The difference is the amount that could be paid for perfect information.

house should be built for a condition of constant growth for 10 years. The best alternative for 3 years of constant growth followed by 7 years of increasing activity is to lease. Figure 9.5 shows that the present worth of renting expense is $111,458 versus building costs of $132,009. The other two states are not so apparent from previous calculations.

From Table 9.2 we can see that it would be unwise to build an addition to the small warehouse *if we knew* that there would be an accelerated growth for 3 years followed by 7 years of level activity. The cost for no change in capacity was determined to be $4564. Discounting this value to the present and including the initial cost, resale, and annual costs for the first 3 years, we have

$$BSW_{inc\,3\,yr,\,const\,7\,yr} = \$110,000 - \$40,000 \times 0.322$$
$$+ \$1000 \times 2.402 + \$4564$$
$$\times 0.7118 = \$102,771$$

which is less than the lease expense of $123,468. By similar calculations we can determine that the building cost for 10 years of increasing activity is

$$\$110,000 - \$40,000 \times 0.322 + \$1000 \times 2.402$$
$$+ \$54,605 \times 0.7118 = \$138,390$$

which exceeds the rental costs of $129,950.

The expected value of the preferred alternatives is shown in Table 9.3.

Table 9.3 Expected value of perfect information

State	Preferred alternative	Cost	Proba-bility	Product
Constant 10 yr	*BSW*	$ 85,820	0.15	$ 12,873
Constant 3 yr, increase 7 yr	*RLW*	111,458	0.15	16,719
Increase 3 yr, constant 7 yr	*BSW-NG*	102,771	0.14	14,388
Increase 10 yr	*RLW*	129,950	0.56	72,772
		Expected value		$116,752

Comparison of the expected value of perfect information to the expected value of the best alternative obtained earlier (Fig. 9.5) indicates that the novelty company could afford to pay up to $122,031 − $116,752 = $5279 for a perfect forecast. Securing perfect information is at best a wild hope, but these figures do suggest that a significant savings could result from further study of the uncertainties in expected growth patterns.

In our previous considerations of economical order size and production quantity we assumed a condition of certainty. By this means we could pass directly to the basic properties of the problem. Now we will allow the influencing factors to vary. Demand and lead time are no longer fixed quantities; they are subject to fluctuations. By alloying the basic procedures with probability calculations, we can consider a wide range of inventory patterns.

INVENTORY FOR PERISHABLE PRODUCTS Some firms handle merchandise which has negligible utility if it is not sold almost immediately. Products in this category include newspapers, printed programs for special events, fresh produce, and other perishable commodities. Such items commonly have a high markup. The large difference between wholesale cost and retail price is due to the risk a vendor faces in stocking the item. He faces obsolescence costs on one hand and opportunity costs on the other.

In most cases a retailer cannot forecast exactly what his demand will be on a given day. He must balance the loss incurred from any unsold items left after their limited selling period against the loss in profit caused by unfilled orders. If he has records of past sales and believes that the pattern will not change appreciably in the future, he can calculate an order size which will permit him to make a maximum profit over an extended period of time.

Consider the case of a vendor who has an exclusive franchise to sell programs at a municipal coliseum. During the basketball season he orders programs in increments of 500. Using his records from the previous two seasons, he has developed the sales forecast shown in Table 9.4. It will be used to determine an ordering policy for typical games. Special attractions would require a separate forecast, because they have a different pattern from regular games.

The vendor purchases the programs for $0.15 each and sells them for $0.50. From his markup of $0.35 he must pay the commissions and fixed expenses. As a

Sales per game	Number of games sold	Probability of programs being sold	Table 9.4 Program sales
2500	4	0.10	
3000	6	0.15	
3500	10	0.25	
4000	16	0.40	
4500	4	0.10	
	40	1.0	

simplifying measure, we will call the $0.35 markup his profit.

His forecast does not tell him how many programs will be sold at a regular game, but it does tell him, for instance, that there is a 50% chance he will sell at least 3500 copies. It also indicates his profit outlook. If he orders 4000 programs but sells only 3500, his profit will be $3500 \times \$0.35 - 500 \times \$0.15 = \$1150$. In an extreme case of misjudgment, he could order 4500 and sell 2500. This calamity would result in the minimum profit of $2500 \times \$0.35 - 2000 \times \$0.15 = \$575$. A maximum profit of $1575 would result from ordering and selling 4500 programs.

Between $575 and $1575 is a range of possible profits. These are conditional profits. That is, each is the profit that will result from a possible demand, given that a certain number of programs have been ordered. The range of possible profits is determined by the range of possible sales. There is no need to extend the range, because all past performances are included. All the conditional profits are tabulated in Table 9.5.

Table 9.5 Conditional profit

Possible order supply	Possible demand				
	2500	3000	3500	4000	4500
2500	$875	$ 875	$ 875	$ 875	$ 875
3000	800	1050	1050	1050	1050
3500	725	975	1225	1225	1225
4000	650	900	1150	1400	1400
4500	575	825	1075	1325	1575

The vendor's profit status can be further refined by analyzing his sales history in combination with his conditional profits. This combination takes the form of an expected-value table. The future states are the possible sales levels. Associated with each state is the probability of its occurrence, derived from sales records. The alternatives are the various order sizes and the outcomes are the conditional profits.

Alternative (order size)	State of demand					Expected profit
	2500 (0.10)	3000 (0.15)	3500 (0.25)	4000 (0.40)	4500 (0.10)	
2500	$875	$ 875	$ 875	$ 875	$ 875	$ 875.00
3000	800	1050	1050	1050	1050	1025.00
3500	725	975	1225	1225	1225	1137.50
4000	650	900	1150	1400	1400	1187.50
4500	575	825	1075	1325	1575	1047.50

Figure 9.7 Expected profit from program sales

The vendor can expect to make the most profit by ordering 4000 programs each time. By following this policy he will average $1187.50 profit for each game, provided the actual demand follows the pattern of past sales. He is not guaranteed this amount for a given game, but any other quantity will leave him with less *average* profit.

After studying the calculations reported in Fig. 9.7 the vendor might ponder the possibility of improving his operation. Perhaps he could use weather forecasts to anticipate the size of the crowd at a game. Maybe he could devise a program which would retain its appeal for postgame sales. The amount he could afford to pay to develop improvements is the difference between the expected profit calculated in Fig. 9.7 and the profit he could make if he possessed perfect information. Table 9.6 shows that the maximum possible profit is $1268.75. Therefore he could afford $1268.75 − $1187.50 = $81.25 to develop means to avoid accumulating obsolete programs.

Program sales	Preferred alterna- tive	Profit	Probability of demand	Expected profit from perfect data
2500	2500	$ 875	0.10	$ 87.50
3000	3000	1050	0.15	157.50
3500	3500	1225	0.25	306.25
4000	4000	1400	0.40	560.00
4500	4500	1575	0.10	157.50
			Maximum profit	$1268.75

Table 9.6 Maximum profit with perfect information

INVENTORY FOR PRODUCTS WITH A SALVAGE VALUE   Many products which are subject to a limited selling period still retain a salvage value after the period is over. Style changes, the end of a holiday season, technological advances, and many other factors may limit a sales period. In most cases some value can be realized from the outdated products. Such circumstances are analyzed by measures similar to those employed for perishable products.

Bakery products are a familiar illustration of products with a limited selling period and a subsequent salvage value. In this case we will look at a production quantity instead of an order size. Day-old goods are sold at a fraction of their original price. Assume that a dozen sweetrolls sell for $1.50 the day they are baked and return $0.60 after the first day. The direct cost of baking a dozen rolls is $0.48. The difference between direct cost and selling price will again be termed "profit."

The manager of the bakery could develop a sales pattern from records of past performance. He would probably make separate forecasts for midweek days and preholiday or preweekend days. Unless all the day-old goods were sold, he would also have to determine the number of rolls that have no salvage value. Conditional profits for one batch size would be calculated according to

$$
\begin{aligned}
\text{Conditional profits} =\ & \text{no. sold on first day} \times \text{profit} (\$1.50 - \$0.48) \\
+\ & \text{no. sold after first day} \times \text{profit} (\$0.60 - \$0.48) \\
-\ & \text{no. unsold} \times \text{cost} (\$0.48)
\end{aligned}
$$

It is apparent that this formula is the same as the one used for perishable products, with one term added to account for the profit obtained from the items sold later. The remaining calculations required to determine the batch size for the greatest expected profit are identical to those followed for perishable products.

INCREMENTAL ANALYSIS   A comparison of the gain versus the cost per unit change in level of activity is the crux of an incremental analysis. In previous inventory problems we compared total gain to total cost. The same solutions are achieved by comparing incremental gains and incremental costs. In some cases an incremental analysis is more revealing and can be applied more directly than a total-value analysis.

In Chap. 2 we found that maximum profit occurs when the incremental gain (marginal revenue) from producing one more unit equals the incremental cost (marginal cost) of producing that unit. We also observed that the optimum order quantity is the inventory level at which annual holding costs are equal to yearly order costs (page 68). The logical extension of these concepts is to conclude that when the savings from an additional increment of inventory equal to the additional costs incurred from holding that stock level, the optimal inventory policy is identified.

Expressed as a formula, the optimum order quantity occurs when

$$\text{Incremental gain} = \text{incremental cost}$$
$$\Delta_G = \Delta_C$$

When we include risk in the analysis, the relationship becomes

Expected value of incremental gain
$$= \text{expected value of incremental cost}$$
$$E(\Delta_G) = E(\Delta_C)$$

which can be expanded to

$$H - [S\ P(D)] = O[1 - P(D)]$$

where

$P(D) =$ probability that fewer than D units will be demanded

$H =$ holding costs per unit per period (often this is the purchase price)

$S =$ Salvage value per unit of unused inventory

$O =$ Opportunity cost per unit demanded but not available (often this is the selling price)

Rearranging to solve for the limiting probability $P(D)$, we have

$$O\ P(D) - S\ P(D) = O - H$$
$$(O - S)P(D) = O - H$$
$$P(D) = \frac{O - H}{O - S}$$

which indicates the cumulative probability of demand associated with the stock level that equates incremental gain to incremental cost. In other words, *the best inven-*

tory policy is to stock enough units to meet the highest demand that has a probability of occurrence equal to or less than P (D).

Applying this approach to the program vendor's data from Table 9.4, we find that if

| Program sales per game, D | = 2500 | 3000 | 3500 | 4000 | 4500 |

then

| Probability of fewer than D sales per game, $P(D)$ | = 0.0 | 0.10 | 0.25 | 0.50 | 0.90 |

and from the description of the problem,

$H = \$0.15$, the vendor's purchase cost for one program

$S = 0$, out-of-date programs are worthless

$O = \$0.50$, amount received for each program sold

Then the limiting probability is

$$P(D) = \frac{O - H}{O - S} = \frac{\$0.50 - \$0.15}{\$0.50 - 0} = \frac{\$0.35}{\$0.50} = 0.70$$

The largest stock level with a probability not exceeding $P(D) = 0.70$ is 4000 programs. This solution agrees with the conclusion derived from expected profits in Fig. 9.7.

EXAMPLE 9.1 Inventory policy by incremental analysis

A garden-supply store buys its entire supply of 2-year old evergreen shrubs from a nursery for $4.00 per doz at the beginning of the planting season. Each shrub is then priced at $1.00. In addition, profit from related sales lost by not having demanded shrubs available is estimated to be $2.00 per doz. During the annual 3-month planting season, the yearly frequency distribution of sales for these shrubs follows the pattern shown:

| Doz of shrubs sold, $D =$ | 120 | 150 | 180 | 210 | 240 | 270 |
| Probability of selling $D =$ | 0.20 | 0.40 | 0.15 | 0.10 | 0.10 | 0.05 |

If all the shrubs ordered are not sold during the planting season, the nursery will buy the remaining shrubs back for $1.50 per doz. The average cost of handling, storage, and care is $0.25 per shrub. How many shrubs should be ordered at the beginning of the season to maximize profit?

SOLUTION

$$H = \text{holding costs} = 12 \times \$0.25 + \$4 = \$7 \text{ per doz per season}$$
$$S = \text{salvage value} = \$1.50 \text{ per doz}$$

$$O = \text{opportunity cost} = \text{sales price plus lost related sales}$$
$$= 12 \times \$1 + \$2 = \$14 \text{ per doz}$$
$$P(D) = \frac{\$14 - \$7}{\$14 - \$1.50} = \frac{\$7}{\$12.50} = 0.56$$

The probability of selling fewer than 150 doz shrubs is 0.20 and the probability of selling fewer than 180 doz shrubs is 0.60. Therefore, the optimum stocking policy is to order 150 doz shrubs at the beginning of the season.

VARIABLE LEAD TIME AND DEMAND RATE   Variations in lead time and demand rate are largely responsible for many opportunity costs. These conditions are depicted in Fig. 9.8. Receiving an order a week later than anticipated may cause an interruption in production or a loss of sales. An unexpected increase in demand may cause

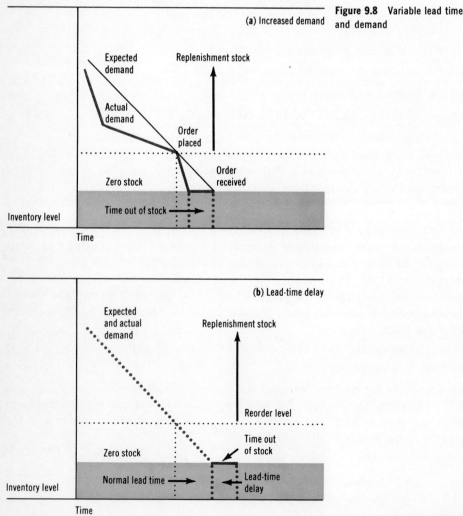

Figure 9.8   Variable lead time and demand

a stockout of merchandise or supplies. Such risks are relieved by carrying a reserve inventory, or *safety stock*.

Safety stock acts as a buffer between anticipated and actual inventory levels. In Fig. 9.8, safety stock would appear as a minus $(-)$ inventory in the colored section below the zero-stock level, where it serves to eliminate or reduce the out-of-stock time. Reducing stockouts reduces opportunity costs, but it increases holding costs. A very large safety stock could completely eliminate the chance of stockouts, and correspondingly, it would substantially raise insurance, damage, interest, and other holding costs. The problem is to determine a safety-stock level which will provide adequate protection from stockouts at reasonable holding costs.

Variable Lead Times   A manufacturing plant uses special chemicals in its finishing department. The chemicals must be stored under a controlled environment. Because the chemicals deteriorate with age, the producer must make a new batch for each delivery. This leads to a considerable variation between the time an order is placed and the time at which it is received.

The distribution of lead times is shown in Table 9.7. The minimum delivery time is 7 days. By cumulating the lead times we can see there is a probability of 0.50 that a delivery will take at least 10 days. In order to evaluate the significance of the lead-time distribution, we must know more about the costs and usage rate of the chemicals.

Many factors in the problem are known with relative certainty. Continuous production entails an annual demand for 1150 cylinders used at a constant rate through the year. Each cylinder costs $40, in addition to the order and inspection costs of $55 per order for a typical order size. Holding costs are 25% of the value of the average inventory in storage.

Disregarding stockout costs for a moment, we can determine an order size based on known conditions. Costs and demand are substituted into the economic-lot-size formula developed for conditions of certainty to obtain

Table 9.7   Lead time

Lead time, days	Relative frequency
6	0.00
7	0.04
8	0.08
9	0.38
10	0.24
11	0.12
12	0.09
13	0.03
14	0.02
	1.00

$$Q = \sqrt{\frac{2OD}{H}}$$
$$= \sqrt{\frac{2 \times 55 \times 1150}{10}}$$
$$= 113 \text{ cylinders}$$

where O = order costs = \$55 per order

D = annual usage rate = 1150 cylinders

H = holding costs = $0.25 \times \$40 = \$10$ per cylinder-yr

Knowing Q, we can calculate the number of orders per year as

$$\text{Orders per year} = \frac{D}{Q} = \frac{1150}{113} = 10.1$$

Assuming 230 working days per year, we have the time between orders as

$$\text{Order interval} = \frac{230}{10.1} = 23 \text{ days}$$

and a daily usage rate of

$$D_{\text{daily}} = \frac{1150}{230} = 5 \text{ cylinders per day}$$

Now we can determine the effect of lead-time distribution on the basic inventory plan. For a fixed lead time of 7 days the company would place an order whenever the inventory fell to $7 \times 5 = 35$ cylinders. Under conditions of certainty there would be no chance of late delivery and therefore no danger of running out of chemicals. However, from the table of lead times it is apparent that a 7-day lead time occurs with a probability of only 0.04. This indicates that the chances of running out of stock for at least one day are 96 out of 100 if an order is not placed until the inventory level reaches 35. Ordering when the stock level is higher than 35 reduces the chance of a stockout, but adds the costs of holding a safety stock. Both holding and opportunity costs must be included in the economic-lot-size calculations to achieve a minimum-cost inventory policy.

Figure 9.9a shows the effect of each ordering alternative (amount of lead time provided). The colored portion indicates the shortage that will occur for each day of delay from the lead time provided. The lower portion shows the incremental size of safety stock which will be accumulated by providing more lead time than is required. If orders are based on a 7-day lead time, there will never be old stock on hand when a new order arrives. At the other extreme, an order policy based on a lead time of 14 days assures the company that it will never run out of stock, although as many as 35 cylinders could be in storage when a new supply is delivered.

The opportunity cost of running out of stock is estimated to be $40 per cylinder. This cost accrues from the disruption of production. The manufacturing plant would sustain a loss of $5 \times \$40 = \$200$ per day for late deliveries based on a daily usage of five cylinders. By multiplying the stock deficiencies in Fig. 9.9a by $40 and the excess stock by the $10-per-cylinder holding costs, we can develop the expected-value table of Fig. 9.9b.

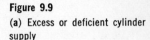

Figure 9.9
(a) Excess or deficient cylinder supply

Lead time provided	Lead time required								
	7	8	9	10	11	12	13	14	
7		−5	−10	−15	−20	−25	−30	−35	
8	5		−5	−10	−15	−20	−25	−30	
9	10	5		−5	−10	−15	−20	−25	Number of
10	15	10	5		−5	−10	−15	−20	cylinders
11	20	15	10	5		−5	−10	−15	not supplied
12	25	20	15	10	5		−5	−10	
13	30	25	20	15	10	5		−5	
14	35	30	25	20	15	10	5		

Number of cylinders stored

(b) Expected costs of lead-time alternatives

Lead time provided	Lead time required, wk								Expected value	
	7 (0.04)	8 (0.08)	9 (0.38)	10 (0.24)	11 (0.12)	12 (0.09)	13 (0.03)	14 (0.02)	HC	OC
7	$ 0	$200	$400	$600	$800	$1000	$1200	$1400	$ 0	$562
8	50	0	200	400	600	800	1000	1200	2	370
9	100	50	0	200	400	600	800	1000	8	194
10	150	100	50	0	200	400	600	800	33	94
11	200	150	100	50	0	200	400	600	70	42
12	250	200	150	100	50	0	200	400	113	14
13	300	250	200	150	100	50	0	200	161	4
14	350	300	250	200	150	100	50	0	210	0

In Fig. 9.9b the alternatives are the lead times provided, and the future states are lead times that could occur. The outcomes result from two types of costs: holding costs and opportunity costs. These two costs affect the ordering policy in different ways. Opportunity costs occur only when an order takes longer to arrive than the lead time that was allowed. Since this cost is associated with the order interval, it can be treated like an ordering expense or a setup cost. Holding costs are annual expenses and reflect the extra inventory or safety stock that is held in storage. We can calculate an expected value for each of these costs by separating outcome costs by type in the table.

The expected-value column on the right of the table has two divisions. One applies to holding costs for an alternative and the other to the opportunity costs. Both are calculated from pertinent outcome costs. When the lead time provided coincides with the actual lead time required, the outcome is a zero cost. Obviously, one zero outcome must occur for each alternative. The costs to the left of the zero outcome arise from holding costs, while those to the right are opportunity costs. Each type is multiplied by the likelihood of its occurrence, and the sum of the products is entered in the appropriate expected-value column. Thus a 7-day lead time shows no holding costs and a 14-day lead time has no opportunity costs. For a lead-time alternative of 11 days we have

$$E(HC_{11}) = \$200 \times 0.04 + \$150 \times 0.08 + \$100 \\ \times 0.38 + \$50 \times 0.24$$
$$= \$8 + \$12 + \$38 + \$12$$
$$= \$70$$

where HC = holding costs of safety stock, and

$$E(OC_{11}) = \$200 \times 0.09 + \$400 \times 0.03 \\ + \$600 \times 0.02$$
$$= \$18 + \$12 + \$12$$
$$= \$42$$

where OC = opportunity costs. The expected values for the other alternatives are obtained in a similar manner.

Each lead-time alternative provides a different economic lot size because of different opportunity costs. By adding the expected value of the opportunity costs to the other costs, we can apply the same economic-lot-size formula used previously. For a 7-day lead time,

$$Q_i = \sqrt{\frac{2(O + OC)D}{H}}$$
$$= \sqrt{\frac{2 \times (55 + 562) \times 1150}{10}}$$
$$= 383$$

All the lot sizes are shown in the accompanying table.

The final step is to determine which lot size will allow

Lead time provided	Economic lot size
7	383
8	314
9	239
10	186
11	150
12	126
13	117
14	113

the lowest total cost. Assuming that the purchase price of cylinders is not subject to quantity discounts, price-breaks will not affect the ordering policy. Then the total cost becomes the sum of annual ordering costs and holding costs. The ordering costs include both the cost of placing an order and the opportunity cost. Holding costs are composed of the storage expense due to the order size, H, and the additional storage expense incurred from providing a safety margin for delivery delays, HC. This latter cost is the expected value of the holding cost for each lead-time alternative in Fig. 9.9b. Total costs are calculated from the formula

$$C_{LT} = \frac{(O + OC)D}{Q} + \frac{HQ}{2} + HC$$

This yields the total cost for a 7-day lead time as

$$C_7 = \frac{(55 + 562) \times 1150}{383} + \frac{10 \times 383}{2} + 0$$
$$= \$3770$$

and an 8-day-lead-time total cost of

$$C_8 = \frac{(55 + 370) \times 1150}{314} + \frac{10 \times 314}{2} + 2$$
$$= \$3130$$

From the complete tabulation of costs shown here in the total-cost table, we can see that the most economical policy is to allow a 13-day lead time. An order should be placed whenever the stock level declines to $13 \times 5 = 80$ cylinders. By following this policy the company should expect to run out of chemicals twice in every 100 order periods.

Sensitivity Opportunity costs are considered more difficult to estimate than holding costs. It is interesting to observe the sensitivity of the lead-time calculations to different opportunity-cost estimates. Total annual costs for the cylinder-inventory problem with four different opportunity costs are shown in Table 9.9. All other factors in the problem are unchanged. It is apparent that estimates of the same general magnitude will not change the results significantly. Consequently, there should not be too much concern if opportunity costs cannot be estimated with the desired degree of accuracy.

Variable demand rates Variations in demand or usage rates produce situations similar to variable lead times. If the lead time is fixed, the risk of a stockout is dependent on

Table 9.8

Lead time	Total cost
7	$3770
8	3130
9	2402
10	1884
11	1564
12	1373
13	1326
14	1335

Table 9.9

Opportunity cost	Lead time	Total cost
$10	12	$1272
20	13	1305
30	13	1314
40	13	1326

the actual demand exceeding the anticipated demand. Holding a safety stock reduces the risk. The problem then becomes one of selecting a safety-stock size which balances the expense of holding the safety stock against the cost of a stock shortage.

Consider a maintenance section which receives deliveries of spare parts from a distributing firm. Deliveries are made regularly a week after an order is placed. The ordering policy has been to reorder class 2 parts whenever the inventory level dips to 200 parts. A series of stockouts has indicated that the policy should be reviewed. It was decided to retain the same lot size, but a safety stock could be carried for certain parts. Part No. 323 has the usage rate depicted by the histogram in Fig. 9.10. It shows the relative frequency of demand for a 1-week period. Annual holding costs for the part are $2, and the stock is replenished about six times a year. Opportunity costs, estimated to be $1 per week, are the result of special ordering procedures and inconveniences caused by the part's being required but unavailable.

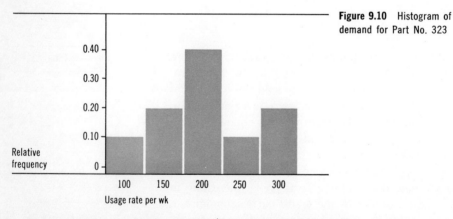

Figure 9.10 Histogram of demand for Part No. 323

Before seeking a solution to this inventory situation, let us inspect the conditions carefully. Here we have a fixed order size and a fixed lead time. A stockout can occur only if the demand increases during the lead time. The solution space has been limited to the investigation of an appropriate safety stock for certain parts. These conditions considerably simplify the calculations. Without a fixed order size, we would follow the same general approach to a solution as that used for variable lead times. A zero safety stock would be associated with a 200-part reorder point. This is equivalent to decreasing the reorder point, and it would be a reasonable alternative if storage space is limited or if negligible inconvenience results from stockouts. In turn, altering the reorder point would affect the order quantity by increasing costs associated with the order interval. But with the fixed order interval, we need only consider the effect of adding a buffer stock to the accepted reorder level.

A reorder level of 200 parts will lead to a stockout 30% of the time. Holding an extra 50 parts would limit running out of parts to a probability of 0.20, and a 100-part cushion would completely eliminate the chances of a stockout if the demand pattern remains unchanged. The expected value of the opportunity costs for each of these alternatives is shown in Fig. 9.11. Each outcome is the product of the cost of a shortage and the number of times a shortage would occur in a year.

Figure 9.11 Expected value of opportunity costs

Parts provided	Reorder point	Safety stock	Safety stock required		Expected value OC
			50 (0.10)	100 (0.20)	
200	200	0	$50 \times \$1 \times 6 = \$300$	$110 \times \$1 \times 6 = \$600$	$150
250	250	50	0	$50 \times \$1 \times 6 = \$300$	$ 60
300	300	100	0	0	0

The total cost of each of the alternatives is the sum of the opportunity costs and the holding costs. No additional holding costs are incurred for a zero safety stock. For each safety-stock increment of 50 parts the annual holding cost is $50 \times \$2 = \$100$. From the totals in Table 9.10, it appears that the original ordering policy was sound and the reorder point should remain at 200 for Part No. 323.

Table 9.10 Total-cost table for Part No. 323

Safety stock provided	Opportunity costs	Holding costs	Total cost
0	$150	0	$150
50	60	$100	160
100	0	200	200

SIMULATION   When both the lead time and demand rate vary significantly from average values, the task of determining a satisfactory safety stock is considerably more complicated. No direct mathematical techniques are generally available to handle this situation, but we can consider the net effect of the interaction between fluctuating demand and lead time by simulation. With this technique, often called Monte Carlo simulation, a model is developed which duplicates the actual situation as closely as possible. Then the model is manipulated to produce data representative of the real world.

One procedure for generating simulated experience

is utilization of random numbers. An abbreviated tabulation of random numbers is offered in Fig. 9.12.[1] These groups of numbers follow no pattern or special order; they are randomly distributed. The main concern a user should have is to avoid imposing a pattern by repeatedly using the same set in a consistent order. The figures can be read in any manner desired – by rows or columns, diagonally, up or down, etc.

Figure 9.12   Random numbers

32867	53017	22661	39610	03796	43693	18752
43111	28325	82319	65589	66048	04944	61691
38947	60207	70667	39843	60607	63948	49197
71684	74859	76501	93456	95714	87291	19436
15606	13543	09621	68301	69817	39143	64893
82244	67549	76491	09761	74484	91307	64222
55847	56155	42878	23708	97999	40131	52360
94095	95970	07826	25991	37584	56966	68623
11751	69469	25521	44097	07511	88976	30122
69902	08995	27821	11758	64989	61902	32131

For an example of simulation, the pie charts in Fig. 9.13 may be assumed to represent the relative frequency of lead times and usage rates for a commodity. The relative size of the slices in the "pies" corresponds to the chance occurrence of each increment of lead time or demand. Thus possible lead times are 8, 9, 10, and 11 days, occurring with respective relative frequencies of 0.20, 0.20, 0.30, and 0.30.

Figure 9.13   Relative frequency of lead times and usage rates

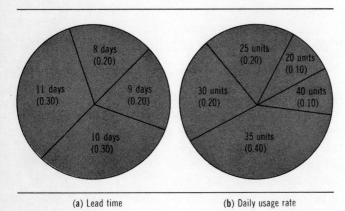

(a) Lead time   (b) Daily usage rate

[1] Taken from *Table of 105,000 Random Decimal Digits*, issued as Statement 4914, File 261-A-1, by the U.S. Interstate Commerce Commission, May, 1949.

The simulation of stock movement is conducted by randomly selecting both a lead time and a usage rate. This could be done by mounting spinners on the two pies. A spin on the lead-time pie might show 9 days, and the associated spin on the usage pie could point to 30 units. The two spins are combined to indicate one level of total demand that could occur after an order has been placed.

A random-number table would commonly be used in place of spinners. In a group of 10 numbers, any digit from 0 to 9 is equally likely to occur. By letting each digit be equal to 10%, we can assign certain digits to each increment of lead time and usage according to its likelihood of occurrence. An arbitrary assignment might be

Lead time		Usage rate per day	
Days	Digits	Units	Digits
8	0 and 1	20	0
9	2 and 3	25	1 and 2
10	4, 5, and 6	30	3 and 4
11	7, 8, and 9	35	5, 6, 7, and 8
		40	9

Then each pair of numbers in the random-number table could represent a lead-time duration and the number of units used per day during that duration. Using the first two numbers in the first column of Fig. 9.12, the inventory pattern would take the shape shown in Table 9.11. The reorder level is based on an average lead time of 10 days and an average usage rate of 30 units per day. A typical order is placed when the stock on hand falls to $10 \times 30 = 300$ units.

If the simulation procedure started in Table 9.11 is

Table 9.11 Simulation of five reordering periods

Random number	Lead time (1)	Usage rate (2)	Demand during lead time, (1) × (2) (3)	Average reorder level (4)	Stock on hand when order arrives, (4) − (3) (5)
32	9	25	225	300	+75
43	10	30	300	300	0
38	9	35	315	300	−15
71	11	25	275	300	+25
15	8	35	280	300	+20

continued, a distribution can be determined for expected stock levels at the time of delivery. From this distribution an inventory policy can be developed which establishes a minimum-cost balance between holding and opportunity costs. The computations would be similar to those followed for a variable-lead-time inventory policy. A more direct tactic would be to set a tolerable limit for stockouts per year and hold a safety stock which conforms to this limit.

It is logical that the greater the number of trials, the more closely the simulation will correspond to the actual inventory pattern. Computers are frequently used for simulation because actual distributions usually cover a far greater range than those used in the examples, and a relatively large number of trials is required to give reliable information.

MAINTENANCE-REPLACEMENT POLICY

Maintenance costs were influencing factors in long-term replacement decisions made under assumed certainty, and they are equally significant in short-term replacement decisions which include risk. The short-term effect of wear often follows a consistent pattern. After the pattern has been identified, a user has the alternative of dealing with each item as it fails or following a policy of collective remedial action before failure. Preventive maintenance is a well-known example of the latter alternative.

Maintenance policies are extremely varied in practice. They depend on the characteristics of the items, available maintenance facilities, and relevant costs. We will consider a basic model which may be adapted to fit the circumstances of a particular situation. It includes the factors common to most situations: probable life pattern, alternative courses of preventive action, and outcome costs for the alternatives. The objective is to find the interval at which preventive action is most suitable, and then compare this with the alternative of remedial action to decide which is more economical.

To illustrate a maintenance policy, assume that a factory has 30 similar machines, which exhibit the probability distribution of failures shown in the accompanying table. The cost of remedial action after a breakdown averages $100, and the cost of providing preventive maintenance is $30 per machine.

The total cost of a preventive-maintenance program is the sum of servicing expense for all the machines each

Mo after maintenance	Probability of failure
1	0.2
2	0.1
3	0.1
4	0.2
5	0.4

maintenance period (30 machines $\times$ $30 per machine = $900) and the cost of breakdowns occurring between services. For a *monthly* preventive-maintenance policy, *PM*1, the cost is $900 plus $100 for each breakdown expected in the first month after servicing. This amounts to

$$PM1 = \$900 + \$100 \times 30 \times 0.20 = \$1500 \text{ per mo}$$

A *bimonthly* policy must again include the $900 basic group-servicing cost and the cost of individual breakdowns. In the first month of the period $30 \times 0.20 = 6$ machines are expected to break down. During the second month $30 \times 0.10 = 3$ machines serviced at the regular period are likely to break down, and 20% of the individual breakdowns treated during the first month will *again* fail. These calculations are depicted in Fig. 9.14, where a modified expected-value table is utilized.

Figure 9.14 Expected failures for two *PM* periods

PM periods	Individual failures during mo		Expected value	
	1 (0.2)	2 (0.1)	Individual	Cumulative
1	30	0	6	6
2	6	30	4.2	10.2

The first alternative in the table represents a monthly preventive-maintenance policy. The expected value of this alternative is six machines treated each month, which agrees with our previous calculations. The second line of outcomes depicts the failures of the second month. The total number of expected breakdowns in 2 months is the cumulative value for both months ($6 + 4.2 = 10.2$ machines). The cost of a bimonthly policy is

$$PM2 = \$900 + \$100 \times 10.2 = \$1920$$

which makes the cost per month equal to $1920/2 = $960.

A policy of servicing all the machines every 3 months would lead to the expected failure record shown in Fig. 9.15. Now a pattern can be observed. Some of the original group of 30 machines continue to break down each month, and some of those repaired fail again individually. The repairs made each month start a new cycle which must follow the failure distribution. Thus the expected number of breakdowns from one month is always the first outcome (0.20 probability of failure) for the next month. Similarly, the expected value 2 months ago is the second outcome for the current month and the cumulative value is the total number of expected breakdowns for a cycle of so many months. A 3-month cycle would have a total cost of

$$PM3 = \$900 + \$100 \times 14.64 = \$2364$$

or a monthly cost of $\$2364/3 = \$788$.

PM periods	Individual failures during mo			Expected value	
	1 (0.20)	2 (0.10)	3 (0.10)	Individual	Cumulative
1	30	0	0	6	6
2	6	30	0	4.2	10.2
3	4.2	6	30	4.44	14.64

Figure 9.15 Expected failures for three *PM* periods

Figure 9.15 can be converted to costs and expanded to include all the necessary calculations for the cost of every preventive-maintenance alternative. The outcomes are converted from units of machines to dollar values by multiplying the number of machines by the individual remedial cost (\$100). Columns are added to account for the cyclic group *PM* costs, the sum of individual and group costs, and the prorated monthly costs. The completed table in Fig. 9.16 displays the same recurring pattern of outcomes described previously.

Figure 9.16 Expected cost of preventive-maintenance alternatives

PM period	Individual failure costs during mo					Expected value		PM cost	Total cost	Monthly cost
	1 (0.20)	2 (0.10)	3 (0.10)	4 (0.20)	5 (0.40)	Ind.	Cum.			
1	$3000	0	0	0	0	$ 600.00	$ 600	$900	$1500	$1500
2	600	$3000	0	0	0	420.00	1020	900	1920	960
3	420	600	$3000	0	0	444.00	1464	900	2364	788
4	444	420	600	$3000	0	791.00	2255	900	3155	789
5	791	444	420	600	$3000	1564.60	3819	900	4719	944

The last step is to determine the costs associated with a policy of performing no preventive maintenance; machines are serviced whenever they break down. We can calculate the expected period between breakdowns from the original failure distribution. The expected period is

1 mo $\times$ 0.2 + 2 mo $\times$ 0.1 + 3 mo $\times$ 0.1 + 4 mo
$\times$ 0.2 + 5 mo $\times$ 0.4 = 3.5 mo between breakdowns

Then, with the cost of servicing individual breakdowns pegged at $100 per breakdown, we have a remedial-action-policy cost of

$$\frac{30 \text{ machines} \times \$100 \text{ per machine service}}{3.5 \text{ mo per service}} = \$857 \text{ per mo}$$

A comparison of the $857 monthly cost for the remedial-action alternative with the minimum monthly cost of a preventive-maintenance policy from Fig. 9.16 ($788) indicates that the latter alternative is preferable. Both the 3-month and 4-month preventive-maintenance periods show a lower expected cost than that for dealing with machines only after they fail.

This approach can be applied to a variety of situations. The items being evaluated could fail completely, like electric light bulbs or electronic tubes. Failures may represent personnel who are no longer available owing to transfers or retirement, and replacement could be the recruiting or training policy. There are also numerous modifications which fit special maintenance and repair situations.

WAITING-TIME POLICY

Whenever waiting lines form in an industrial system there is reason to question the situation. A lineup means congestion. The cost of congestion may be directly observable, as trucks waiting to be unloaded, or the costs may be more subtle, as when a potential customer leaves a line that has formed at a sales counter. But there is also a cost associated with relieving congestion. Providing more services — more loading crews or sales clerks — eliminates congestion at the risk of creating excess service capacity. Surplus capacity merely transfers idle time to the service facility. The objective must be to minimize the sum of congestion and service costs.

Two methods are available to reduce total costs: schedule and control the flow of arrivals into the system and/or provide the correct service capacity. The preferred approach depends on whether the input flow or service facilities (or both) can be altered suitably. In this section we will primarily consider improving service capabilities.

In order to evaluate a waiting-time situation we must know the characteristics of the system. The input to the system is defined by an *arrival rate A* in units per time period. The units may be human or inanimate. They arrive in a pattern described by a probability distribution of time between arrivals. After arriving, they are subject to an order in which they are served, such as "first come, first served." They receive service at a designated *number of servicing stations N*. Each station has the capacity for a certain *number of services per unit time, S,* and a distribution of service times.

Figure 9.17 Waiting-line (queue) characteristics

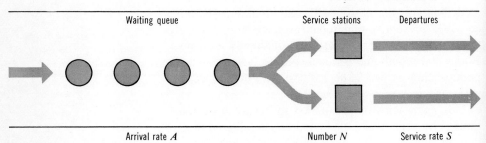

Waiting queue	Service stations	Departures
Arrival rate A	Number N	Service rate S

DISTRIBUTION OF ARRIVALS AND SERVICE TIMES   Constant arrival and service rates are the easiest to evaluate but are rare in practice. An automatic machine feeding arrivals to another automatic machine exemplifies a constant pattern if no breakdowns occur. In such cases the second machine will process the products without delay as long as its service rate $S2$ is equal to or shorter than the arrival rate from the first machine, $A1$. A waiting line forms when $S2$ is greater than $A1$. In this "explosive" case the waiting line increases indefinitely with time.

Random arrival and service rates are much more common than a uniform pattern. With random rates it is possible for new arrivals to be forced to wait even though the service time is actually less than the average time between arrivals. This condition exists because arrivals may be bunched together. In the period between bunches the service facility can reduce or eliminate the queue, but the temporary waiting time may still be a source of significant costs.

SIMULATED QUEUES   Simulation methods are appropriate means of evaluating the effect of waiting time. This general approach can be used regardless of the distribution of arrivals or service times. The techniques involved are the same as those described for inventory simulation. In a waiting-time application we have the objective of determining a service policy which will minimize the total cost of idleness within the system.

Machine breakdowns in a factory could be considered as arrivals to a repair (servicing) facility. Breakdowns are randomly distributed, with an average arrival rate of 40 minutes. The cost of an idle machine awaiting repair is estimated at $12 per hour. A repairman hired at a wage of $5 per hour can repair machines according to the distribution of service times shown in Table 9.12. The service rate for two men working together is also shown. Should a one- or a two-man crew be employed?

Table 9.12 Distribution of service times

1 repairman ($S1$), at $5 per hr		2 repairmen ($S2$), at $10 per hr	
Time, min	Probability	Time, min	Probability
10	0.10	5	0.10
20	0.10	10	0.10
30	0.30	15	0.20
40	0.30	20	0.20
50	0.20	30	0.30
		35	0.10
34 min av.		21 min av.	

Arrivals One way of simulating random arrivals with random numbers is to select one digit to represent a breakdown. This digit will average one appearance in a group of 10 random numbers. Then, for this example, each group of 10 digits represents 40 minutes of factory time. The number of times the selected digit appears in each group of 10 numbers indicates how many breakdowns occurred in that 40-minute period. The number of breakdowns will vary from zero in a period to the remotely possible maximum of 10.

A more definitive arrival simulation could be used if more information were available. A detailed probability distribution of periods between breakdowns would specify the breakdown pattern more precisely. In this example we are assuming that at most 10 breakdowns could possibly occur in a 40-minute period, and we must arbitrarily set the pattern within the period for multiple breakdowns. We will assume that:

If two occur, one is at the beginning of minute 21 and the other is at the end of the period.

If three occur, one will be at the start of the period, one at the end, and one at the beginning of minute 21. If more occur, they will follow a similar periodic arrangement.

Servicing Service-time simulation is accomplished by assigning digits in proportion to the frequency of each repair time. For the distribution of service times with one repairman, we could let digit $0 = 10$ minutes, $1 = 20$ minutes, 2, 3, and $4 = 30$ minutes, 5, 6, and $7 = 40$ minutes, and 8 and $9 = 50$ minutes.

Letting digit 0 be an arrival, a table of waiting times for a single repairman could appear as shown in Table 9.13. The random numbers are from Fig. 9.12.

Table 9.13 Waiting-time simulation for one repairman

Arrivals				Service				Queue (machine waiting time)
Work period, min	Random no.	Arrival no.	Break-down time	Ran-dom no.	Service period	Service begins	Service ends	
0–40	3961003796	1	20	1	20	20	40	0
		2	40	8	50	40	90	0
40–80	6658966048	3	80	7	40	90	130	$90 - 80 = 10$
80–120	3984360607	4	100	5	40	130	170	$130 - 100 = 30$
		5	120	2	30	170	200	$170 - 120 = 50$
120–160	9345695714	...	...	...	...	...	...	...
160–200	6830169817	6	200	6	40	200	240	0

Costs The tabulations in Table 9.13 are just a beginning. Many more samples would be required before legitimate conclusions could be drawn, but the same procedures would be followed. For each arrival (breakdown) a service time is simulated. The difference between the time a breakdown occurs and the time a service man can begin repairs is the waiting time per machine. The total waiting time divided by the number of machines repaired is the average waiting time per machine. In an 8-hour day (480 minutes) the average number of breakdowns is

$$\frac{480 \text{ min per day}}{40 \text{ min per machine}} = 12 \text{ machines per day}$$

and the total daily cost of waiting time plus servicing is calculated from

$$\frac{\text{Repair costs}}{\text{day}} = \frac{\text{no. of}}{\text{repairmen}} \times \frac{\text{daily}}{\text{wage}}$$
$$+ \frac{\text{av. no. of breakdowns}}{\text{day}} \times \frac{\text{av. waiting time (hr)}}{\text{breakdown}} \times \frac{\text{hourly cost of}}{\text{idle machines}}$$

For the simulated data from Table 9.13 this amounts to

$$\text{Repair costs} = 1 \times (8 \times \$5)$$
$$+ 12 \times \frac{10 + 30 + 50}{60 \times 6} \times \$12$$
$$= \$40 + \$36$$
$$= \$76$$

The same simulation procedure is followed for each alternative waiting-time policy. For the example situation we would next determine the total repair costs with a two-man crew. Repair costs are then compared for each alternative to decide which policy is most suitable.

MATHEMATICAL QUEUING MODELS A more direct calculation method is available for some types of waiting-line (queuing) problems. We can use formulas developed for special cases without going into the underlying statistical foundations if we recognize the restrictions on their applications. Basic assumptions of the mathematical queuing models are as follows:

1. Arrivals follow a Poisson distribution. A histogram of this distribution displays a range of values from zero to infinitely large, with higher relative frequencies occurring toward the lower end of the scale. Many practical situations are well approximated by a Poisson arrival rate.

2. Arrivals are not affected by the length of the queue or any previous experience with the waiting line. This means a long queue will not discourage arrivals, and disgruntled arrivals will not leave the queue after spending time in a waiting line.

3. Arrivals are served on a "first come, first served" basis. No special priority or emergency provisions are included.

4. Service times follow an exponential distribution. This distribution, which shows continually decreasing relative frequencies from a zero value, is a good model of service time associated with Poisson arrivals. Theo-

retically, an infinitely long waiting line could develop, but we will consider only reasonable relationships between arrival and servicing rates.

Single service facility   When the above assumptions are valid conditions for an actual situation, we can apply established equations to evaluate the system. For example, assume that logging trucks arriving at a lumber mill follow a Poisson distribution of arrival times. An average of three trucks per hour arrive at the log pond for unloading. The trucks are unloaded at an exponential rate averaging four per hour.

With just the arrival A and servicing rates S we can investigate several aspects of the system. The equation for the average number of trucks in a waiting line is

$$\text{Length of queue} = \frac{A^2}{S(S - A)}$$

and for the example,

$$\frac{(3)^2}{4 \times (4 - 3)} = \frac{9}{4} = 2.25 \text{ trucks in the waiting line}$$

To find the average waiting time for the trucks in the queue (including trucks which are served immediately), we can use the equation

$$\text{Waiting time in queue} = \frac{A}{S(S - A)}$$

which yields

$$\frac{3}{4 \times (4 - 3)} = \frac{3}{4} = 0.75 \text{ hr in line per truck}$$

When service time is included with the waiting time, the formula for total unloading time is

$$\text{Waiting time} = \frac{1}{S - A}$$

and for the logging trucks the average time spent at the unloading dock is

$$\frac{1}{4 - 3} = \frac{1}{1} = 1 \text{ hr for unloading}$$

The proportion of arrival times a trucker can expect to find the service facility busy is A/S, or 3/4 of his trips to the mill. Conversely, the proportion of time the unloading facility is idle is $1 - A/S$, or 1/4 of the time.

The lumber mill is considering the replacement of its present log dump with a new unloading facility which is expected to provide an exponential service rate of six trucks per hour. The initial cost will be $200,000, with no salvage value at the end of its 10-year life. The cost of an idle truck is $20 per hour and is composed of overtime pay and contract carrier charges for additional log deliveries to meet mill requirements. With money valued at 10% and no salvage expected from the present facility, should the investment be made?

Annual costs for lost transportation time are based on a 40-hour week with 50 working weeks per year ($40 \times 50 = 2000$ hours per year). Then the annual waiting-time cost for the *present* facility is

Unloading cost per yr

$$= A \times W \times \text{opportunity cost per hr} \times \text{hr per yr}$$
$$= 3 \times 1 \times \$20 \times 2000$$
$$= \$120,000$$

The servicing costs of the *new* facility will be

$$\text{Unloading cost per yr} = 3 \times \frac{1}{6-3} \times \$20 \times 2000$$
$$= \$40,000$$

Expected annual savings for the new unloader are, then, $120,000 - $40,000 = $80,000.

The new facility has no extra operating costs compared to the present method. Judging from the expected savings, we would surmise that the new investment would be profitable even without converting the initial cost to annual costs for comparative purposes. This suspicion is confirmed by

$$\text{Annual cost of new unloader} = \text{initial cost} \times (a/p)_{10}^{10}$$
$$= \$200,000 \times 0.16275$$
$$= \$32,550$$

Alternatives   Although the lumber company may be satisfied with its plan to replace the present log-dump facility, it should also give consideration to other means of improving its unloading capabilities. General alternatives and specific considerations include:

Changing the arrival rate   An appointment system or a priority rating could be initiated. Trucks could be dispatched from logging areas according to a schedule, but this arrangement would have to be coordinated with the woods crew. Incentives can occasionally be instigated, such as cheaper rates at certain hours, to alter the arrival distribution.

Changing service conditions   Service rates could be altered by adding stations or by redesigning existing facilities. Special arrangements for periods of congestion can often be provided. The logging company should consider adding a smaller, less expensive unloader to the present facilities. This would allow the use of two service stations on an as-required basis.

Changing queue discipline   Arrivals requiring a short service time could be served first, or arrivals could be assigned to the most appropriate service station when multiple stations are available. Trucks with the longest hauls could be given service priority in order to reduce overtime resulting from adverse starting times for roundtrip cycles.

Formulas are available for a number of these alternatives, but care must be exercised to assure that the assumptions made in developing the formulas pertain to the actual system. It is just as necessary to be sure the data used in simulation are descriptive of the real-life situation. Whenever models are used, it is advisable to give particular attention to the most sensitive characteristics. In queuing models the total cost is highly influenced by small changes in arrival and service rates.

INVESTMENTS TO AVOID RISK

An investment made to avoid the consequences of risk may provide self-protection or insurance. An outlay which effectively reduces the cause or risk of the penalty associated with it is self-protection. The purchase of insurance transfers the burden of risk to another party. In either case the objective is to minimize the effect of a disaster.

PENALTY ESTIMATES: INTANGIBLE CONSIDERATIONS   The cost of avoiding a disaster can be very high. The price is most commonly accepted in projects dealing with public safety. When human lives are involved, designers invariably strive to include an ample safety factor. The question is how large is ample? Before we can answer this question we must know the value of human life. So many intangible considerations surround the value that we would probably receive a different estimate from each person questioned. A crude yardstick can be developed from previous safety efforts. If $100,000 has been spent in a given area to reduce the probability of a fatal accident from 0.001 to 0.0001, the consequent value implied for a life is

$$\frac{\$100,000}{0.001 - 0.0001} = \$111,111,111$$

Although this method is not too precise in that it recognizes no other contributory factors, it does provide a reference level for difficult or intangible considerations.

The same approach can assist in the often difficult estimate of opportunity costs. An idea of the magnitude of these costs can frequently be obtained by investigating a present level of investment committed to risk reduction. For example, if a standby generator costs $300 per year to maintain and is used on the average of once a year, the value placed on an electrical outage is

$$\frac{\$300}{1/365} = \$109,500$$

Then $109,500 could be used as an estimate of opportunity costs for evaluation of other investments to reduce risks from a similar source.

SELF-PROTECTION An adequate investment can essentially eliminate risk in unique cases. Ski resorts can make provisions for artificial snow in anticipation of a dry winter. Investments are made in massive irrigation projects to eliminate the dangers of drought. On a smaller scale, the selection by a city engineer of a storm drain sized to handle the maximum expected runoff is an attempt to nullify risk.

A more typical response in avoiding risk is a compromise. Even if the cause or penalty associated with a risk can conceivably be eliminated, the cost may be prohibitive. Yet the effects of risk often can be limited to a tolerable level by a reasonable expenditure. We have already dealt with this compromise when we considered safety-stock levels for an inventory policy. Similarly, the city engineer could select a storm-drain size which balances the extra costs of larger-diameter sewers against damages that could occur in exceptional storms.

QUALITY CONTROL A quality-control program balances the cost of passing defective items against the cost of an inspection procedure capable of detecting inferior quality. Consider the case of a company which receives a contract to build 3000 new type precision instruments. The terms of the contract strongly suggest an inspection system to avoid the risk of supplying defective instruments; the penalty clause states damages of $300 per faulty unit.

Inspection equipment which would limit undetected faulty units to 0.5% could be purchased for $19,000. It would have no value after termination of the 3-year contract. A trained operator for the testing equipment would have to be paid $7000 per year, and operating costs would amount to $1000 annually. Assuming a desired rate of return of 10%, the annual cost of inspection would be

Testing machine: $19,000 \, (a/p)_3^{10}$

	$19,000 \, (0.40211)$	$ 7,640
Operator		7,000
Operation		1,000
Total cost of investment		$15,640

In addition to the investment costs, there is still a penalty for the few defective instruments which pass undetected and adjustment or reworking costs for the detected faulty instruments:

$$\text{Annual cost of penalty} = \frac{3000 \text{ instruments}}{3 \text{ yr}} \times 0.005$$
$$\times \$300 \text{ per instrument}$$
$$= \$1500$$

Annual adjustment, reworking, and
scrap costs $= X - 0.005 \times 1000$ instruments per yr
$$\times C_{av} \text{ per instrument}$$

where

X = percentage of defective instruments produced
C_{av} = average cost of reworking a defective instrument to enable it to pass inspection

Then the total cost of the inspection program is the sum of inspection, penalty, and reworking costs. Setting the cost of reworking at $C_{av} = \$50$ per instrument, we have

$$\text{Total cost} = \$15,640 + \$1500 + (X - 0.005)$$
$$\times 1000 \times \$50$$
$$= \$17,140 + (X - 0.005) \times \$50,000$$

By equating the cost of the inspection program to the penalty cost of no inspections, we get

$$\text{Cost of vigilance} = \text{cost of error}$$
$$\$17,140 + (X - 0.005) \times \$50,000 = X \times 1000$$
$$\times \$300$$
$$X = 6.8\%$$

X represents the percentage of defective units produced at which the two costs are equal. If the production capabilities can limit the percentage of defective instruments to 6.8% or less, the investment in this inspection program is unwarranted from strictly a cost viewpoint. However, reputation and other intangible considerations should influence the decision. It would also be wise to explore other inspection programs which are not so precise in detecting errors, but are less expensive investments.

INSURANCE   The dichotomy of risk costs is again apparent in the use of an insurance program which transfers the burden of risk. Paying a premium to an insurer is an investment made to avoid the consequences of a specific disaster. The amount of the premium should reflect the potential magnitude of the disaster in proportion to the probability of its occurrence (plus administrative costs and profit). For a disaster which could cause damages of \$100,000 with a probability of 0.001 per year, it would be reasonable to expect an annual premium cost of at least $\$100,000 \times 0.001 = \$100$.

The reason insurance programs are so prevalent is that they spread the cost of protection over a period of time and transfer the risk of a financial calamity to a group better prepared to meet the payment. Just because the chance of a disaster is one in a thousand, it cannot be stated in exactly what year it will occur or even that it could not occur 2 years in a row. Premiums prorate the disaster shock to the pooled assets of the absorbing insurance company.

A program of self-insurance is followed by some companies for specific risks. Such a policy presumes sufficient resources to cover potential damages and is usually limited to minor risks. Accident liability is a popular area for self-insurance.

Investments may be made to reduce premiums for a group insurance policy or to reduce the probability of risk for a self-insurance policy. Annual investments in a plant safety program are aimed at reducing the probability of accidents. They should result in less damage payment for the self-insured or lower premiums for group insurance.

A feasible amount to spend for a risk-reduction investment can be estimated from insurance rates. Companies which sell insurance normally have a great deal of experience to draw on in setting rates. These rates may be used as estimates of risk for related situations as described in the following example.

The owners are considering an automatic sprinkling system for a warehouse. The company insuring the warehouse will reduce the annual $1200 fire-insurance premium by one-third if the system is installed. The owners estimate opportunity costs incurred as a result of a serious fire, such as relocation expenses, disruption of deliveries, and loss of reputation, would amount to one-half the value of the warehouse. Using the insurance company's evaluation for the extent of risk reduction, the expected value of annual savings in opportunity costs from the installation would be $1200 \times 1/2 \times 1/3 =$ $200.

If annual taxes and maintenance costs for the sprinklers are $100, the life of the proposed system is 20 years, and capital is worth 15%, a feasible price for the sprinkler system could be determined from the following equality:

$$(a/p)_{20}^{15} = \begin{matrix} \text{premium} \\ \text{reduc-} \\ \text{tion} \end{matrix} + \begin{matrix} \text{opportunity-} \\ \text{cost} \\ \text{reduction} \end{matrix} - \begin{matrix} \text{annual} \\ \text{taxes and} \\ \text{maintenance} \end{matrix}$$

$$= \frac{\$1200 \times 1/3 + \$200 - \$100}{0.1598} = \$3141$$

SELECTED REFERENCES

Buchan, J., and E. Koenigsberg: *Scientific Inventory Management*, Prentice-Hall, Inc., Englewood Cliffs, N.J., 1963.

Dean, B. V., M. W. Sasieni, and S. K. Gupta: *Mathematics for Modern Management*, John Wiley & Sons, Inc., New York, 1963.

Duncan, A. J.: *Quality Control and Industrial Statistics*, 3rd ed., Ricard D. Irwin, Inc., Homewod, Ill., 1964.

Goode, H. H., and R. E. Machol: *System Engineering*, McGraw-Hill Book Company, New York, 1959.

Grant, E. L.: *Statistical Quality Control*, McGraw-Hill Book Company, New York, 1952.

Holt, C. C., F. Modigliani, J. F. Muth, and H. A. Simon: *Planning Production, Inventories and Work Force*, Prentice-Hall, Inc., Englewood Cliffs, N.J., 1960.

Magee, J. F.: *Production Planning and Inventory Control*, McGraw-Hill Book Company, New York, 1958.

Morse, P. M.: *Queues, Inventory, and Maintenance*, John Wiley & Sons, Inc., New York, 1958.

Naddor, F.: *Inventory Systems*, John Wiley & Sons, Inc., New York, 1966.

Peck, L. G., and R. N. Hazelwood: *Finite Queueing Tables*, John Wiley & Sons, Inc., New York, 1958.

Pratt, J. W., H. Raiffa, and R. Schlaifer: *Introduction to Statistical Decision Theory*, McGraw-Hill Book Company, New York, 1965.

Saaty, T. L.: *Elements of Queueing Theory*, McGraw-Hill Book Company, New York, 1961.

Sasieni, M., A. Yaspan, and L. Friedman: *Operations Research: Methods and Problems*, John Wiley & Sons, Inc., New York, 1959.

Starr, M., and D. W. Miller: *Inventory Control: Theory and Practice*, Prentice-Hall, Inc., Englewood Cliffs, N.J., 1962.

Wagner, H. M.: *Statistical Management of Inventory Systems*, John Wiley & Sons, Inc., New York, 1962.

PROBLEMS

9.1 For the decision situation depicted in the decision tree below, where capital is valued at 8%,

a What is the expected profit at decision point 2?

b Which alternative should be selected at decision point 1 and what is its present value?

c How much could be paid for perfect information?

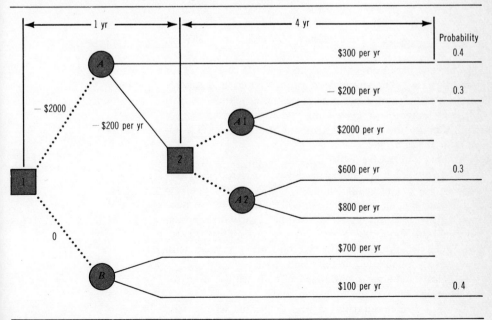

9.2 A small foundry has had trouble with its old arc furnace. This furnace has been completely depreciated for accounting purposes, but it could currently be sold for $6000. The immediate alternatives are to overhaul and modify the old machine or to buy a current model which has many desirable features that could not be incorporated in the modification of the old machine. The plans are complicated by the general opinion in the industry that a breakthrough could be made in furnace technology in the near future.

The best estimate the foundry owners can make is that there is a 40% chance that a radically improved furnace will be available in about 3 years. If it is developed, the probability that it will make present models noncompetitive is 0.90 and that it will be only a minor improvement is 0.10.

The cost of modifying the old machine is $8000, and the cost of a new, current-model machine is $25,000. Expected savings and resale values are given in the accompanying table based on the following three possible future states:

$S1$ = no technological breakthrough

$S2$ = furnace developed which provides significant savings

$S3$ = furnace developed which provides minor savings

Possible outcomes	Buy new		Modify	
	Savings per yr	Resale at 8 yr	Savings per yr	Resale at 8 yr
$S1$	$6000	$8000	$2000	$4000
$S2$	2000	2000	1000	2000
$S3$	3000	4000	1000	3000

The table is based on a study period and life of 8 years for both furnaces. The sharp decrease in savings and salvage in the states 2 and 3 occur because the development of a radically different or even improved furnace would probably cut into the foundry's demand and its general competitive position.

Another alternative exists for the foundry. If the new type of furnace is developed in 3 years, the modified furnace could be sold at that time for $9000 and the new one purchased for an estimated $45,000. This new furnace would provide a savings of $13,000 per year with a probability of 0.90 and $8000 per year with a probability of 0.10. It will be worth $20,000 or $15,000 after 5 years with respective probabilities of 0.90 and 0.10.

If a new machine is purchased now, it will be used for 8 years regardless of new developments.

Using a discounted-decision tree, determine whether the

old furnace should be modified or a new, current model should be purchased. Interest is 10%.

9.3 A firm has produced a new product which was unusually successful, and in order to meet the unexpectedly high demand it will be necessary to add additional production facilities. The troubling question is whether the high demand will continue, increase, or decrease. Plan *A* provides a permanent capacity increase and will be more profitable if the demand continues to increase. Plan *B* is a stopgap measure which can be converted to permanent capacity by a supplementary investment, *B'*, after 3 years, when the demand pattern is better known. For a steady or lower demand, plan *B* is more profitable than plan *A*. The estimated future outcomes for an 8-year study period are as indicated: Initial cost estimates are

Plan *A*	$100,000
Plan *B*	70,000
Plan *B'*	45,000

First 3 yr	Last 5 yr	Probability
High	High	0.40
High	Low	0.20
Low	High	0.30
Low	Low	0.10

The supplementary investment in plan *B*, *B'*, will take place after the demand is known for the first 3 years.

Annual income estimates are as follows:

Plan *A* with a high demand will yield a cash flow of $40,000 per year.

Plan *A* with a low demand will yield $5000 per year.

Plan *B* with a high demand will yield $30,000 per year in the first 3 years and $20,000 annually in the last 5 years.

Plan *B* combined with *B'* will yield $40,000 per year with high demand.

Plan *B* combined with *B'* will yield $10,000 per year with low demand.

Plan *B* with a low demand will yield $30,000 per year.

With interest at an annual rate of 8%, determine which plan or combination of plans appears most attractive.

9.4 The owners of the novelty company described in the chapter disagree as to the solution of their storage problem. There is a minority feeling that more research should be given to the question. One member of the minority group is anxious to do such a study. He estimates that it would cost about $5000 and would take approximately 6 months to complete. The company could limp through this period with existing inventory facilities. Although the other owners have faith in the person who would make the study, they feel that he is overconservative. Because of this attitude they estimate (1) that if company activity in the next 6 months is very strong, the probability that the sudy will indicate a continuation of increasing growth will be 0.60, and (2) that if the next 6 months' activity is relatively constant, the chance of a forecast for increasing growth will be 0.10. On the basis of these estimates an engineer in the company is asked to calculate:

a The probability that the study will indicate increasing growth

b If the study indicates increasing growth, the probability of continued increase and the chance of leveling off

c If the study indicates no increase, the probability of increase and the chance of level activity

Carry out the engineer's assignment and show the results in a decision-tree format without costs. (*Hint*: You must use the original estimates disclosed in the chapter example in conjunction with those in the problem. The decision tree has three primary alternatives.)

9.5 Engineering Service, a large consulting firm, is considering the acquisition of a computer to lower its project accounting and control costs. It can rent a large computer for $180,000 per year on a noncancellable but renewable 3-year lease. The other alternative is to buy a smaller computer at a cost of $200,000.

There is a probability of 0.70 for a high service demand in the next 3 years. If the demand is large the first 3 years, the probability that it will continue large is 0.60. Expected annual net savings during a period of high demand are $300,000 from a large computer and $170,000 from a smaller model. If demand is low, the large computer will permit a saving of $140,000 per year, and the smaller computer's net annual savings will be $110,000. The probability of a continuously low demand for the 6-year study period is 0.27.

After 3 years the lease on the large computer could be terminated and a smaller, used computer could be purchased for $120,000. Either purchased computer would have a negligible salvage value at the end of the 6-year period. Also, after 3 years the smaller computer could be sold for $120,000 and a large one could be leased for the remaining 3 years for $200,000 per year.

Assume that all receipts and disbursements are end-of-year payments and the acceptable interest rate is 8% before taxes. Using a decision tree, determine the most attractive alternative for Engineering Services.

9.6 An automobile dealer has kept a record of the lead time for delivery of new cars from the factory. He estimates that the opportunity cost of lost sales averages $60 for each car not on display when it might have been. His sales are relatively uniform at seven per week. Ordering costs average $20 per order and holding costs are $120 per year for each car in stock. What ordering policy should the dealer use?

Delivery lead times, wk	Probability
2	0.1
3	0.2
4	0.3
5	0.3
6	0.1

9.7 Compute the reorder point for the following situation:

Average lead time	5 days
Holding costs per unit per yr	$2
Optimum order interval	2 mo
Cost of stockouts per order interval	$20
Average demand rate	15 units per day

Demand during lead time	Probability
60	0.05
65	0.05
70	0.15
75	0.40
80	0.20
85	0.10
90	0.05

9.8 A small plant uses wood chips as a raw material for one of its products. Chips are delivered in units of railway cars. The average demand is four cars per month, but the demand varies according to the accompanying table.

Since special unloading equipment is rented when a delivery arrives, it is desirable to have large orders. Space is available to store any size of order, but stored inventory is subject to weather damage. The costs associated with wood-chip inventory are

Holding costs	$60 per yr for each unit
Order costs	$300 per order (includes rental of unloading equipment)
Opportunity costs	$80 per unit (includes altering production schedules)
Lead time	1 mo (4 wk)

What safety stock should be carried?

Demand	Probability
6	0.10
5	0.20
4	0.50
3	0.20

9.9 The Able Company places an order for 300 gal of paint (the EOQ when opportunity costs are not considered) 25 times each year. The average lead time is 7 calendar days. The usage rate is 20 gal per day 60% of the time. The probability of 15, 25, and 30 gal usage is, respectively, 0.10, 0.20, and 0.10. If the order costs are $30 per order and the cost of being out of stock is $20 per gal, what safety stock should be carried? Develop an expected-cost table and determine the total cost for each safety-stock alternative.

9.10 A florist with an airport concession makes up fresh leis and garlands of flowers every 2 days. The flowers on display are discarded if not sold. $1.50 is the average cost to make one floral piece. Handling costs are $0.40 per piece. Opportunity costs are believed to be about $1.00 for each unfilled demand. The probable demand for floral pieces is as shown:

If the demand =	2	4	6	8	10	12	14	16
Probability =	0.05	0.15	0.20	0.20	0.15	0.10	0.10	0.05

a Determine the optimal stock level.
b Determine the expected cost for the best stocking policy.
c How much change can be allowed in the estimate of "O" before the stock level should be changed (consider both upper and lower levels)?
d Based on (c), what conclusions can be made about the sensitivity of operating costs?

9.11 During vacation periods a restaurant sends "traveling cafes" to nearby beaches. Meals are prepackaged and kept warm in specially fitted trucks. For the average meal preparation costs are $0.60 and the food plus packaging materials amounts to $1.30. If a meal is not sold during the day, it is thrown away. Loss in revenue and other opportunity costs are estimated at $2.00 for a meal demanded but unavailable. The demand varies considerably. It is equally likely that any number of meals from 74 through 92 will be sold by one truck in one day. On days when crowds are small, no trucks are dispatched. There are five trucks serving areas with similar demand patterns. How many meals should be packaged on a day when good crowds are expected?

9.12 Supplies to an Alaskan mining camp are delivered by boat and truck during the summer. In the winter supplies can be delivered only by airplane. It costs four times as much to deliver a pound of supplies by air as by water and road. The amount of supplies used varies, and the period that the road is closed because of snow also varies from season to season. The cost of storage for holding a period of supplies over an entire winter period (when roads are closed) is equal to one-half the cost of transportation by boat and truck. The probability of using more than 20,000 lb of supplies during a winter lasting 7 months is 0.4, and the probability that the roads will be closed longer than 7 months is 0.2. Based on the worst conditions, should more or less than 20,000 lb of supplies be stored at the beginning of winter?

9.13 Because of a shortage of wood chips, the lead time for the small plant orders given in Prob. 9.8 can no longer be considered fixed. The estimated lead-time distribution is shown in the table. The costs and demand rate from Prob. 9.8 still pertain. Determine by simulation the size of the safety stock the company should hold.

Lead time, wk	Probability
1	0.1
2	0.1
3	0.3
4	0.5

9.14 A machinery supply and service company advertises that orders received by 8:00 A.M. will be delivered that day or a customer will only have to pay half-price for his order. The amount of an average order is $124. The number of orders received before the deadline varies according to the following pattern:

Orders per day:	16	17	18	19	20	21	22	23
Probability:	0.05	0.10	0.10	0.20	0.25	0.15	0.10	0.05

Each order is delivered by van. The fixed cost of a van is $10 for a normal 8-hour working day. Van variable costs depend on the length of time required to deliver an order. The daily average order-time distribution and the associated variable costs are as shown:

Average hr per order during 1 day	Variable cost	Probability
½	$ 3.50	0.40
1	7.00	0.30
1½	10.50	0.20
2	14.00	0.10

How many vans should the company operate?

9.15 It has been suggested to a data-processing firm that they adopt a policy of periodically replacing all the tubes in certain pieces of equipment. A given type of tube is known to have the mortality distribution shown in the table. There are approximately 1000 tubes of this type in all the combined equipment. The cost of replacing the tubes on an individual basis is estimated to be $1.00 per tube, and the cost of a group-replacement policy averages $0.30 per tube. Compare the cost of preventive versus remedial replacement.

Tube failures per wk	Probability of failure
1	0.3
2	0.1
3	0.1
4	0.2
5	0.3

9.16 A vending-machine operator has machines in 40 locations. There is an equal probability each day during a 10-day period that the machines in one location will be emptied. After 10 days all the machines will be empty. The cost to individually replenish the machines at one location (travel and working time) is $18. The loss in profit from idle machines in one location is $10 per day. Replenishments may be made individually as requested when the machines in one location are empty, or they may be made all at one time with a total cost to service the 40 locations of $250. What is the lowest-cost replenishment policy?

9.17 An automobile dealer has used cars which need reconditioning before they can be sold. They have a Poisson arrival rate which averages four per week. The dealer is going to hire one of two men to clean up his cars. The first is capable of reconditioning cars at the rate of seven per week, but it would cost the dealer $100 per week to hire him. The alternative is to hire a less efficient man for $65 per week, but he is capable of reconditioning only five cars per week. The dealer estimates the cost of holding a car off the used-car lot at $45 per week. Which man should he hire? Assume the cars are reconditioned at an exponential rate.

9.18 Referring to the waiting-time example in the chapter, suppose the lumber company could equip its trucks with special equipment which would make all the unloading times constant rather than exponentially distributed. The average unloading time is 10 minutes per truck while all the other conditions remain the same. The special equipment has a life of 10 years with no salvage value. What is the maximum amount that could be spent on refitting the trucks to make this alternative comparable to providing a new unloader? [*Hint*: Waiting time $= A/2S(S - A)$ applies to constant service time.]

9.19 Simulate a waiting-time situation by using two dice to represent an arrival distribution. The total number of points on a toss of the two dice represents the time between arrivals. Let a single die represent the service times. Each time an arrival occurs, throw a die to determine how long that arrival spends in the service station.

a What is the average arrival rate?
b What is the average service time?
c What is the average length of the queue?
d What is the average waiting time in the queue?
e Compare the answers from (*c*) and (*d*) above to the same questions answered by using a Poisson arrival distribution and an exponential service rate. Comment on your results.
f Reverse the distribution for arrival and service rates described in the problem statement. How many service stations are required to limit the average waiting time to that determined in (*d*)?

9.20 Machines break down in a factory at an average rate of four per day. Breakdowns occur in a manner which closely follows a Poisson time distribution. An idle machine costs the company $30 per day. The current method of servicing follows an exponential repair rate averaging six per day. The cost of this facility is $60 per day. By purchasing diagnostic equipment for $12,000, the capacity of this facility will be doubled while still following an exponential repair-time distribution. The diagnostic equipment will last 10 years and the operating costs will be $35 per day. A minimum rate of return of 12% is expected on all new investments. There are 250 working days per year. Should the equipment be purchased?

9.21 A resident engineer on a construction project has been troubled with parts received from a supplier. Eight percent of the parts have been defective. The scrap and reworking costs for each item averages $6. At least 2000 parts will be used over the next 2 years. Two methods have been suggested to reduce the risk of defective parts:

a Visual inspection by part-time labor would reduce the risk by half. The labor cost would be $250 per year.
b Only 0.5% defective parts would be accepted if gages were purchased for $90 and a worker were trained to use them. The training cost would be $30, and an annual wage for the inspection time would total $350.

Which of the three alternatives should be adopted if a 10% rate of return is considered acceptable?

9.22 An assembly line has 30 identical machines. The pattern of breakdowns is shown in the accompanying table. Breakdowns can usually be fixed in a short period, but the disruption of the production line creates considerable expense. One way to eliminate this disruption is to provide standby machines. The daily cost of keeping a standby machine is estimated to be $12. The cost of an out-of-order machine is $150 per day. How many standby machines should be provided?

No. of machines out of order at one time	Probability
0	0.5
1	0.2
2	0.1
3	0.1
4	0.1

9.23 A private golf course lies in a hollow beside a river. Every other year the river rises to a level that prohibits play. The loss of revenue and damage to the course averages $8000 each time the river rises to this level. A new clubhouse has been constructed on higher ground, but flood data indicate a 1/20 chance the river will reach a level which will inundate the facility. The owners estimate that a flood of this magnitude would cause $40,000 damage to the clubhouse.

a How much could the course owners afford to pay for a levee that would protect them from the biennial damage? The required rate of return is 8% and economic life of the levee is expected to be 30 years.

b What would be a reasonable annual premium for a full-coverage flood insurance policy on the clubhouse?

c Compare the premium in (b) to a self-insurance policy the owners could follow of laying $1/20 \times \$40,000 = \$2000$ per year aside in anticipation of a major flood.

Section Four
Decisions
Admitting
Uncertainty

The step into the unknown beyond risk is the condition of uncertainty. Here we can recognize different potential outcomes, but we cannot confidently estimate their probability of occurrence. This is an undesirable but often unavoidable decision situation.

We have a choice of essentially two ways to view the future. We can consider it to be hostile or indifferent. Hostility presupposes that an intelligent opponent is capable of limiting our gains to a minimum. This condition is analyzed according to game theory. Indifference may be evaluated from a pessimistic or an optimistic viewpoint, depending on how conservative we want to be in a given decision situation. Neither treatment offers a neat, precise solution, but both at least provide a better understanding of the problem. The concepts presented in this section introduce principles of choice applicable to decisions rendered under the difficult condition of uncertainty.

Chapter Ten
Concepts
of
Uncertainty

No one enjoys an admission that his problem is subject to unknown forces, yet such situations do occur and decisions still have to be made. A problem falls in the uncertainty category when probabilities cannot be assigned to outcomes. Under assumed *certainty*, a future outcome is considered to have a probability of occurrence of 1.0. Under *risk*, each outcome is assigned a probability and the sum of all these probabilities is 1.0. Under *uncertainty*, the alternatives are identified and the outcomes are estimated, but their relative likelihood of occurrence is unknown. This means the decision criteria developed for certainty and risk situations are no longer appropriate. Therefore we must resort to other methods which are perhaps less definitive but do guide the decision-maker's choice.

In this chapter we will consider two types of uncertainty problems. The first type includes situations essentially subject to chance. These are often termed decisions against nature. The second type is a competitive decision situation in which an opponent or opponents are capable of using counterstrategy to limit our gains. The distinction between the two types is one of intent. Nature is assumed never to actively oppose our strategy, while competitors do strive to defeat our objectives.

A decision situation labeled *noncompetitive* may appear trivial or unimportant. If so, the impression is deceptive. The term "noncompetitive" refers to the treatment of outcomes for any alternative. Each course of action has several possible outcomes. We do not know the probability associated with each outcome, but we do know that a probability exists and that it will not change as a result of our choice of a certain alternative. There is no active opposition controlling the likelihood of outcomes. Thus our objectives may be competitive in the financial sense, but the competition is neutral or isolated from any cause-and-effect reactions.

Nature is a good example of a neutral opponent. Man is continuously in competition with nature. He suffers the inconvenience of carrying an umbrella to guard against rain or alters his plans to "beat the weather." He purchases insurance to soften the loss from storms and launches tremendous research efforts to discover the "secrets" of nature. In each case nature is the opponent. Yet nature makes no willful effort to thwart our actions. Carrying an umbrella neither increases nor decreases the chance of rain. The probability of storms is not a function of the amount of insurance carried. Even though researchers may swear nature tries to frustrate their experiments, there is no evidence to support their claims. Nature is neutral.

Nature pervades social and economic situations as well as physical problems. All men are under the same handicap in determining probabilities for future states. Weather forecasting seeks to foretell coming meteorological states, and public-opinion polls try to forecast social behavior; neither is completely reliable. Probing or spying is unproductive, because nature fails to react to the stimulus of our effort. Even records of past performance, such as stock-market or weather charts, often give false clues because only a portion of the influenc-

ing factors are identified. As a result, when unidenti-
fied factors exert unknown influences on future states,
we turn to decision criteria attuned to our personal
philosophies.

PROBLEM CHARACTERISTICS   A problem under uncertainty
is treated initially like a problem under risk. Different
alternative solutions are developed. The possible futures
or states of nature are identified as completely as feasible. Then outcomes are estimated for each alternative
under the assumption that each future state is certain to
occur. The resulting figures are entered in a payoff matrix. Similarities and differences between certainty, risk,
and uncertainty decisions are illustrated by the typical
formats in Fig. 10.1.

Figure 10.1   Problem formats
for conditions of certainty,
risk, and uncertainty

	$P(1.0)$
A	O_i
B	O_i

(a) Certainty. Solution:
greatest profit

	$P(0.7)$	$P(0.3)$
A	O_{ij}	O_{ij}
B	O_{ij}	O_{ij}

(b) Risk. Solution: highest expected
value

State of nature

	$N1$	$N2$
A	O_{ij}	O_{ij}
B	O_{ij}	O_{ij}

(c) Uncertainty. Solution:
preferred strategy

Payoff matrix   A payoff matrix under uncertainty closely
resembles that used for problems under risk. There can
be any number of alternative courses of action. It is important to identify all the pertinent states of nature
$(N1, N2, \ldots , Nn)$. Omitting states of nature is equivalent to neglecting states of risk, but it is easier to detect
an omission under risk, because the associated probabilities would sum to less than 1. Sometimes related
states of nature are lumped together because their effect
on alternatives is the same. The check for using composite states comes when estimating outcomes (O_{ij}). If
one payoff for each alternative accurately measures the
effect of every condition implied by the composite state,
the combination is valid.

Dominance   After the payoff matrix has been developed,
the next step is to check for dominance. The problem
objective is to select the best-paying alternative. If one
alternative produces a greater payoff than another alternative for *every* state of nature, then a rational decision-
maker would never select the lower-paying course of
action. The higher-paying alternative is said to dominate

the lower one.[1] In Fig. 10.2 alternative A dominates alternative C. Consequently, the dominated alternative, C, may be dropped from the matrix. An early check for dominance avoids unnecessary calculations by reducing the size of the problem matrix.

DECISION CRITERIA   The most difficult aspect of noncompetitive problems under uncertainty is to decide what type of criteria to use for making a decision. In essence, we must determine the criteria for the criterion. The choice should be consistent with management philosophy. Is the current management outlook optimistic or pessimistic, conservative or adventurous? Certain criteria are compatible only with certain management views. Thus it is necessary to understand both management policy and the principles of choice before selecting a decision criterion.

Minimum-maximum criterion   A conservative approach to a decision is to look at the worst possible outcome for each alternative and select the course of action which assures the best results for the worst conditions. The underlying viewpoint is that nature is malicious. If things can go wrong, they will. This pessimistic philosophy dictates that attention be focused only on the most damaging outcomes in order to limit the damage as much as possible.

The words minimax and maximin are derived from the measures taken to identify the limiting loss or the guaranteed gain. A *minimax* decision minimizes the maximum loss. The *maximin* principle is associated with positive payoffs, where it maximizes the minimum gain or profit. For either criterion the smallest payoff (or greatest loss) for each alternative is noted. Then the alternative having the most favorable of the collected worst payoffs is selected.

Maximax criterion   A maximax philosophy is one of optimism and adventure. Nature is considered to be benevolent, so greatest gains are highlighted. The principle of choice is to identify the maximum gain possible for each alternative and then choose the course of action with the greatest maximum gain.

Hurwicz criterion   A moderate outlook between the ex-

Figure 10.2 Dominance relationship

State of nature

	$N1$	$N2$	$N3$	$N4$
A	10	1	3	6
B	6	2	5	3
C	7	0	2	4

[1]When *all* payoffs for one alternative are better than those of a second alternative, a condition called "strict dominance" exists. However, an alternative is still dominant when its payoffs are *equal to or greater than* the corresponding payoffs of another alternative.

tremes of optimism and pessimism is allowed by the Hurwicz criterion. The degree of optimism is established by a coefficient called alpha (α), which may take any value between 0 and 1.0, with the following interpretation:

Coefficient of optimism (α):	0.0		1.0
Decision-maker's philosophy:	Pessimistic	$\rightarrow$	optimistic

After deciding the value of α which measures the decision-maker's degree of optimism, maximum and minimum gains are identified for each alternative. Then the maximum payoffs are multiplied by α and the minimum payoffs by $1 - \alpha$. The two products for each alternative are added and the alternative with the largest sum is chosen.

The minimax-maximin and maximax criteria are special cases of the Hurwicz criterion. When $\alpha = 1$ only the maximum payoffs are included in the final alternative selection, because the minimum payoffs have been eliminated by zero multiplication. The opposite is true for $\alpha = 0$, a completely pessimistic outlook. Any value of α other than 1 or 0 is a compromise opinion about the hostility or benevolence of nature.

EXAMPLE 10.1 Different degrees of optimism

Two sons and their father own and operate an import shop in a medium-sized city. They have been successful enough to be in a position to expand their operations. Three courses of action are deemed most desirable: (1) expand their present operations by opening a store in a nearby city, (2) start a catalog business from their present location, or (3) invest their extra money in real estate and rentals. Each alternative will utilize about the same amount of capital and will require equivalent management. They recognize that the returns from each of these investments depend on the national economy (inflation versus recession) and on the local economy (growth versus stagnation). However, they have no consensus opinion of the probability of what the future conditions will be.

Outcomes for each of the alternatives have been developed for four possible levels of business activity: very high (VH), high (H), medium (M), and low (L). The payoffs shown below are the estimated percentage returns on invested capital for expanding E, starting a catalog service C, or investing in property P:

State of nature

	VH	H	M	L
E	20	12	8	4
C	26	10	4	-4
P	10	8	7	5

The youngest son is an optimist and a risk-taker. The father is conservative and the other son is midway between his father and brother. Which alternative would probably appeal to each member of the family?

SOLUTION   The younger son, being an optimist, would use the maximax criterion. By so doing he would limit his selection area to the *VH* level of business activity, where the largest gains occur. From the possible gains of 20, 26, and 10% he would naturally select the highest, which results from opening a catalog store.

The conservative father would lean toward the maximin criterion, where he could be assured a minimum gain of 5% [the maximum gain under the worst condition of low (*L*) business activity] by choosing to invest in real estate and rentals.

The other son might use the Hurwicz criterion with a coefficient of optimism (α) of 0.5. The consequent calculations reveal that his choice would be to expand the import business to the nearby town.

Alternative	$\max O_i \times \alpha + \min O_i \times 1 - \alpha$	= total	
E	$20 \times 0.5 + 4 \times (1 - 0.5)$	= 12	maximum
C	$26 \times 0.5 + (-4) \times (1 - 0.5)$	= 11	
P	$10 \times 0.5 + 5 \times (1 - 0.5)$	= 7.5	

The relationship of the three philosophies can be better interpreted by plotting the maximum and minimum gains from each as a function of α. As shown in Fig. 10.3, the topmost lines indicate the alternative that would be selected for different levels of optimism. At $\alpha = 0$ the maximin criterion is in effect, and property appears to be the most attractive investment. Property continues to be favored until the less pessimistic attitude of $\alpha = 0.09$ is attained. The next switchpoint occurs at the intersection of the lines representing expand and catalog. Using the equation for the return expected from these two alternatives, the value of α at which a decision-

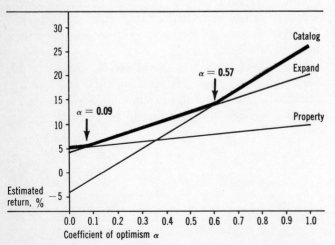

Figure 10.3 Sensitivity of alternatives to the decision-maker's degree of optimism

maker is indifferent to the choice between the two is calculated as

$$20\alpha + 4 \times (1 - \alpha) = 26\alpha + (-4) \times (1 - \alpha)$$
$$16\alpha + 4 = 30\alpha - 4$$
$$\alpha = 0.571$$

Mapping the alternatives gives an indication of their sensitivity with respect to the degree of optimism of the decision-maker. The property alternative is quite sensitive because its selection requires a very pessimistic attitude. The remaining alternatives are relatively insensitive because each would be chosen over a considerable range of α values. The apparent range of attitudes which favor each alternative could aid the father and sons in a search for a compromise solution.

Minimax-regret criterion Opportunity costs have been used in previous chapters to express the loss incurred by not selecting the best alternative. The minimax-regret criterion is based on similar costs. The opportunity costs are determined for each state of nature by subtracting the largest payoff in each column from all other payoffs in the column.[1] The absolute value of each subtraction is the amount of "regret" that results from not selecting the best alternative for the occurrence of a given state. This procedure converts the original matrix to a regret matrix.

A rational decision-maker attempts to minimize his "regret." By applying the minimax principle, the alternative with the minimum maximum (lowest value of the worst regret for each row) is selected. The minimax regret procedure applied to the data from Example 10.1 is shown in Fig. 10.4. The indicated preference is for the expand alternative. In general, the minimax regret criterion tends toward a conservative viewpoint.

Original payoff matrix

	VH	H	M	L
E	20	12	8	4
C	26	10	4	-4
P	10	8	7	5

Regret matrix

	VH	H	M	L	Worst regret
E	6	0	0	1	6
C	0	2	4	9	9
P	16	4	1	0	16

Figure 10.4 Original and regret matrix

Equal-likelihood criterion When it is possible to assign probabilities to future states we use the expected-value cri-

[1]When the original payoff matrix is written in terms of loss rather than gain, the lowest-cost alternative in each column of the regret matrix will be zero. Then the minimax criterion is applied to the regret matrix.

terion to select a preferred alternative. An extension of this approach is the basis of the equal-likelihood criterion. Under uncertainty we admit that we cannot reasonably estimate outcome probabilities. Therefore, since we have no excuse to believe otherwise, why not treat each outcome as the same? The rationale behind this theory is that there is insufficient reason to believe one state of nature more probable than another, so each should be assigned an equal probability of occurrence.

The equal-likelihood criterion is certainly the simplest to apply. Under the assumption that each future is equally likely to occur, the expected value of an alternative becomes its average outcome. The alternative with the largest average payoff is preferred. As applied to the data from Example 10.1, we have

$$E(E) = 20 \times 1/4 + 12 \times 1/4 + 8 \times 1/4$$
$$+ 4 \times 1/4 = 11$$
$$E(C) = 26 \times 1/4 + 10 \times 1/4 + 4 \times 1/4$$
$$- 4 \times 1/4 = 10$$
$$E(P) = 10 \times 1/4 + 8 \times 1/4 + 7 \times 1/4$$
$$+ 5 \times 1/4 = 7.5$$

which again leads to the decision to expand.

EXAMPLE 10.2 Application of decision criteria
Given the payoff matrix below, which alternative would be selected under each of the noncompetitive decision criteria? Assume that the coefficient of optimism is 0.375 ($\alpha = 3/8$) for the Hurwicz criterion.

	N1	N2	N3	N4
A	2	2	2	2
B	1	5	1	0
C	1	4	1	1
D	1	3	1	4
E	3	4	3	0

SOLUTION The procedures followed for each criterion reduce the original matrix to a single column of outcomes from which the desired value is selected. The results and preferences indicated by applying all the criteria are as shown on page 347.

It should not be too surprising that each criterion indicates a different preferred alternative. Each criterion has a slightly distinctive underlying principle. The key is to decide which criterion best fits the decision environment for each specific application.

Alternative	Maximin (pessimist)	Maximax (optimist)	Hurwicz ($\alpha = 3/8$)	Minimax regret	Equal likelihood
A	2	2	2	3	2.0
B	0	5	15/8	4	1.75
C	1	4	17/8	3	1.75
D	1	4	17/8	2	2.25
E	0	4	12/8	4	2.5

EVALUATION OF CRITERIA   Several different criteria for making noncompetitive decisions under uncertainty have been offered because no one criterion is unanimously preferred. Each one has certain weaknesses. Often one criterion is more intuitively appealing than the others. This appeal seems to vary among individuals and to vary with time or circumstances. As there is no universal preference, a sound recourse is to investigate the criteria limitations in order to select the principle which accommodates a given decision environment.

Partial-optimist principle   The key factor in applying the Hurwicz criterion is the choice of a value for α. An arbitrary choice defeats the intent of portraying an individual outlook. A deliberate choice is a forced judgment often based on slim evidence. However, the judgment does allow a measure of added knowledge, even though it is undefined, to be included in the decision. This additional knowledge could be described as "a feel for the problem" or an "educated guess." Until methods are developed to determine α objectively, its value will remain uniquely individual.

Pure optimism and pessimism are special cases of the Hurwicz criterion. Since these are extreme outlooks, they often leave a decision-maker uncomfortable in applying them to special situations. For instance, the maximin criterion applied to

	N1	N2	Minimum
A	$0.01	$0.01	$0.01 maximin
B	0	$100	0

would indicate that alternative A should be selected, yet most people would be inclined to choose B. In the same vein, the maximax criterion applied to the matrix below would lead to the choice of B; most decision-makers would express a decided preference for alternative A.

	N1	N2	Maximum
A	$99	$99	$99
B	0	$100	$100 maximax

By selecting a value for α other than 1 or 0, a more moderate outlook is achieved. However, the criterion still possesses some dissatisfying aspects. According to the criterion, the two alternatives in the following matrix are considered equivalent, because attention is given only to the best and worst outcomes:

	N1	N2	N3	N4	N5	N6
A	$100	$100	$100	$100	$100	0
B	0	0	0	0	0	$100

Many people faced with this choice would cast a strong vote in favor of A over B.

There is also another difficulty. Some critics object to a decision criterion that changes preferences when a constant is added to all the outcomes in one column. Such a criterion is said to lack the property of "column linearity." To illustrate, the Hurwicz criterion would indicate a preference for alternative B at α values less than 0.5 when applied to Fig. 10.5a. The outcomes in both matrices are the same, with the exception of 100

	N1	N2
A	0	100
B	50	50

(a)

	N1	N2
A	100	100
B	150	50

(b)

Figure 10.5 Column linearity

added to both alternatives under $N1$ in Fig. 10.5b. Such an exception could be caused by a discovery that a bonus payoff would result from the occurrence of state $N1$ regardless of which alternative were selected. The disturbing feature is that although the bonus has the same effect on both alternatives, it changes the preference from B to A for the same α values.

Opportunity-loss principle   The minimax-regret criterion is plagued by many of the same defects as the Hurwicz criterion. Attention is focused on only the largest opportunity costs, with a resultant disregard for other payoffs. It also lacks the property of column linearity.

A further argument against the minimax-regret criterion is that the addition of irrelevant information to the matrix can switch the alternative preferences. From the payoff matrix,

	N1	N2	N3
A	100	125	25
B	25	125	75

the resulting regret matrix is

	N1	N2	N3	Worst regret
A	0	0	50	50 minimax
B	75	0	0	75

which leads to the choice of alternative A. Now an additional, rather unattractive, course of action is included in the matrix as

	N1	N2	N3
A	100	125	25
B	25	125	75
C	25	25	125

The addition, alternative C, changes the regret matrix to

	N1	N2	N3	Worst regret
A	0	0	100	100
B	75	0	50	75 minimax
C	75	100	0	100

which indicates that alternative B rather than A should be selected. Although the switch caused by irrelevant information may seem disturbing, it can also be argued that the additional alternative is not necessarily "irrelevant," because it can reveal more information about the states of nature, such as the change in the maximum possible payoff for N3.

Average-outcome principle   Most of the doubts raised for the other criteria are not applicable to the equal-likelihood criterion. It has column linearity, it includes all the outcomes in an evaluation, and the addition of an unattractive alternative cannot switch an earlier preference. However, it also has one serious defect: the selection is very sensitive to the number of future states identified for a problem.

Consider the problem faced by a company that is bidding on a contract. They can build special low-operating-cost equipment which will be ready if they get the contract, or they can buy higher-operating-cost equipment after they know they have won the bidding. The payoffs, in thousands of dollars, are shown in the accompanying matrix.

	No contract	Win contract	Average outcome
Build	−50	125	37.5
Buy	0	100	50.0 maximum

When the future states are limited to winning or losing the one contract, the equal-likelihood criterion shows a preference for buying the equipment. If other future states, such as the possibilities of winning two more similar contracts, are included, the same criterion indicates a preference for building the equipment.

	No contract	Win contract 1	Win contract 2	Win contract 3	Average outcome
Build	−50	125	125	125	81.25 maximum
Buy	0	100	100	100	75.0

Beginning with an exhaustive list of futures will eliminate the chance of a preference change. If one state is subdivided into substates such that the sum of the probabilities for the substates is equal to the probability of the original state, the problem is also avoided. However, each of these methods presumes some knowledge of the future that contradicts the assumption of uncertainty upon which the criterion is based.

Application of principles   None of the criteria is perfect. None can take the place of an accurate forecast. They should be considered guidelines which will help in the interpretation and consideration of possible choices.

It should be noted that most of the reservations about the criteria were more intuitive than deductive. Perhaps the adoption of a certain criterion must also rely to some degree upon intuition, because such insight is often a function of knowledge not yet formalized into distinct views. Nevertheless, the decision-maker must understand the characteristics of each principle to be able to select the one which corresponds most closely to his attitude toward uncertainty.

COMPETITIVE DECISIONS

In competitive decision-making two or more decision-makers are pitted against each other. Both are considered to be equally informed and intelligent. They are referred to as *players*, and their conflicts are called *games*. The rationale of their competion is the basis of *game theory*.[1]

Some of the terms associated with game theory need a special explanation. The generic term "game" in no way implies that game theory is limited to parlor games or similar entertainment contests. The players could be nations maneuvering on the brink of war, labor and management negotiating to ward off a strike on their own terms, or gasoline-station owners seeking a strategy to end a price war with an acceptable compromise.

In a game context, alternative courses of action are *strategies*. There is a subtle difference between alternatives in games of skill (akin to conditions of certainty), games of chance (risk), and games of strategy. In the last category the best course of action for a player depends on what his adversaries can do. Thus an optimum strategy in a competitive environment may be always to use one alternative or to mix alternatives — that is, to use different alternatives for successive plays. The considerations inherent in determining strategies make game theory a rich source of fundamental ideas for decision-making.

PROBLEM CHARACTERISTICS   In our treatment of game theory we will limit attention to games involving two players. Allowing more than two players greatly increases mathematical complication without a corresponding accrual of basic logic. Multiplayer games rely on essentially the same type of inductive and deductive

[1] The publication of *Theory of Games and Economic Behavior* by von Neumann and Morgenstern in 1947 laid the framework and stirred subsequent interest in game theory.

reasoning as two-person games. Actually, the two-player limitation is not as restrictive as a first impression might seem. Strategy for one side in a conflict is often designed to counter the aims of the most dangerous member of an opposing team. In other cases a player may view the entire array of business competitors as a single opponent (a viewpoint similar to treating nature as hostile) and thereby reduce the conflict to a two-person contest.

Payoff matrix   In two-person games the rows of the payoff matrix contain the outcomes for one player and the columns show the outcomes for the other player. The outcomes are written in terms of the player on the left, player A in Fig. 10.6. The alternatives for player A are $A1$, $A2$, $A3$, and $A4$. Player B also has four possible courses of action, $B1$, $B2$, $B3$, and $B4$. If player A selects alternative $A1$ and player B uses $B1$, the outcome is a loss of 1 for A and the gain of 1 for B. At $A1, B4$ the outcome is a gain of 5 for A and a corresponding loss of 5 for B. Thus a positive number is always a gain for A and a negative number is a gain for B. Because the sum of the payoffs for any choice of alternatives is zero (when A wins, B loses), the game described by Fig. 10.6 is called a zero-sum game.

Player B

		$B1$	$B2$	$B3$	$B4$
Player A	$A1$	-1	-2	4	5
	$A2$	-1	4	-3	-2
	$A3$	0	3	1	2
	$A4$	-2	-3	3	1

Figure 10.6 Two-person zero-sum game

Several assumptions are implied for a conflict situation represented by a two-person zero-sum payoff matrix:
1. The conflict is between only two opponents.
2. Each opponent has a finite number of alternatives.
3. Both players know all the alternatives available.
4. All gains or losses can be quantified to a single number.
5. Both players know all the outcomes (numbers).
6. The sum of the payoffs for each outcome is zero.

Dominance   The first step in analyzing a game matrix is to check for dominance. In previous matrices we had to compare only the rows for dominance. In competitive decisions the columns as well as the rows represent alternatives. Therefore it is necessary to check both horizontally and vertically for dominance. Furthermore, the discovery of one dominant relationship may reveal another dominant condition that was previously indistinguishable.

A sequential dominance relationship can be observed in Fig. 10.6. A check of the columns, the alternatives available to player B, shows that no one alternative is better for every outcome than any of the other alternatives. For instance, $B3$ is preferred to $B4$ for all outcomes except those in the bottom row, $A4$.

Turning to the alternatives available to player A, we see that $A1$ is always preferred to $A4$. Eliminating $A4$ from the matrix, we have

	$B1$	$B2$	$B3$	$B4$
$A1$	-1	-2	4	5
$A2$	-1	4	-3	-2
$A3$	0	3	1	2

Now, from the viewpoint of player B, $B3$ is always preferable to $B4$. A further check reveals no additional dominant relationships.

The assumption that allows two-way dominance checks is that both players are intelligent. Thus B would recognize that A would never use $A4$, which means he would never have a use for his $B4$. Viewed from either side, the end result would be the same 3×3 matrix (three alternatives for each player) shown in Fig. 10.7.

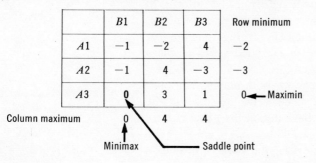

Figure 10.7 Saddle point for the reduced matrix

Saddle point When a player uses the same alternative every time he plays, we say he follows a *pure strategy*. If it is advantageous for both players to use pure strategy, a saddle point is present. A *saddle point* is identified by an outcome which is *both* the smallest number in its row *and* the largest number in its column. In Fig. 10.7 the smallest numerical values for each row are listed to the right of the matrix and the largest numerical values for the columns are shown below the matrix. The outcome 0 at $A3, B1$ satisfies the requirements for a saddle point.

The significance of a saddle point develops from an investigation of the player's motives. Alternatives $A1$ and $A2$ are attractive to A because they allow a potential gain of four units. However, B can be as sure that A will lose one unit (-1) by using $B1$ whenever A chooses to utilize $A1$ or $A2$. A would also be attracted to $A3$ because no negative outcomes can occur from this alternative. Again B can thwart gains by A through the use of $B1$. Since A is astute enough to observe the advantage $B1$ affords B, he would select the alternative that minimizes his opponent's gain from following the pure $B1$ strategy. This alternative is $A3$. Therefore both players would use pure strategy, with A always employing alternative $A3$ and B always using $B1$. The result is a standoff, where neither side gains an advantage.

The underlying principle of choice for the players is maximin-minimax. B seeks the least of his maximum losses, minimax; A identifies the least of his minimum gains, maximin. This conservative viewpoint acknowledges that each player is capable of selecting the strategy which will satisfy his objective to maximize gain or minimize loss.

Value of a game The return from playing one game is the amount each player nets from the ensuing outcome. For instance, if one player gets a return of $+5$ after each has followed a certain course of action, the other player gets -5 in a zero-sum game. The average winnings or losses per play taken over an extended series of plays is called the *value* of the game.

When the optimal strategy for both players is a pure strategy, the value of the game is the outcome at the saddle point. In Fig. 10.7 the value of the game is zero; neither player wins nor loses.

When no saddle point exists, the players turn to a policy called *mixed strategy*. This means that different alternatives are used for a fixed proportion of the plays, but the alternative employed for each play is a random choice from those available. The value of the game is the average return resulting from each player's having followed his optimal mixed strategy.

SOLUTION METHODS FOR MIXED-STRATEGY ZERO-SUM GAMES Several different methods have been developed to solve zero-sum games. Every two-person zero-sum game with a finite number of alternatives can be transformed into a linear programming problem and solved accordingly. In addition, there are special methods appropriate to certain conditions. Often these special methods are much less demanding than the general approach. A different solution method is offered in each of the following sections for games of different sizes. Other methods are available from the references at the end of the chapter.

2 × 2 games A game with only two alternatives for each player readily reveals the wisdom of mixed strategy. Referring to Fig. 10.8, we see that all the payoffs are positive. Therefore player A is bound to be a winner. The objective of B is to limit his losses (A's gains) as much as possible. To do so he cannot use a pure strategy.

A quick check shows that there is no dominance among the alternatives and no saddle point. The absence of a saddle point means that the players should rely on mixed strategy. Sometimes player A will use $A1$ and other times $A2$. Similarly, B switches randomly between $B1$ and $B2$. The problem is to determine the proportion of time each player will use each of his alternatives.

There is a very simple method for solving 2 × 2 games. The procedural steps are listed in Fig. 10.9 and illustrated by application to the matrix of Fig. 10.8.

Step 1: Obtain the absolute value of the difference in payoff for each row and column.

Step 2: Add the values obtained in Step 1 for the rows and columns. The sum of the column differences should equal the sum of the row differences.

Step 3: Form a fraction associated with each row and column by using the values obtained in Step 1 as the numerator and the number obtained in Step 2 as the denominator.

Figure 10.8 2 × 2 matrix

	B1	B2
A1	1	5
A2	3	2

Figure 10.9 Solution steps for 2 × 2 games

	B1	B2	Payoff difference
A1	1	5	$4 = 5 - 1$
A2	3	2	$1 = 3 - 2$
Payoff difference	2	3	

	B1	B2	
A1	1	5	4
A2	3	2	1
	2 +	3	= 5

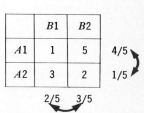

	B1	B2	
A1	1	5	4/5
A2	3	2	1/5
	2/5	3/5	

Step 4: Interchange each pair (row and column) of fractions obtained in Step 3. The fraction now associated with each alternative is the proportion of plays that that alternative should be used for an optimal mixed strategy.

	B1	B2	
A1	1	5	1/5
A2	3	2	4/5
	3/5	2/5	

The indicated strategy is that A should use his first alternative 20% of the time and his other alternative for 80% of the plays. B should play B1 60% of the time and B2 the other 40 percent.

The strategies appear intuitively sound when we remember the conservative viewpoint inherent in game theory. A would use A2 more often because of its higher minimum gain (two units instead of one). B would rely on B1 more than B2 because of the lower minimum and maximum losses. The validity of the strategies becomes even more apparent by considering the value of the game.

The long-run game return is the expected value of all the outcomes to one player. In order to calculate the probability of each outcome we must know how often each player plans to follow a strategy which includes the outcome. This information is provided by the optimal mixed strategy. Figure 10.9 shows the strategies determined for the sample-problem data. The cells of the matrix in Fig. 10.10 contain the probable occurrence of each outcome in the original payoff matrix (Fig. 10.8). The cell values are the product of the probabilities for each row and column. The sum of these joint probabilities must equal 1.0. From Fig. 10.10,

$$3/25 + 2/25 + 12/25 + 8/25 = 25/25 = 1.0$$

By multiplying each outcome by the probability of its occurrence and adding them together, we have the expected value of the game. In terms of player A, the value of the game is

$$3/25 \times 1 = 3/25 \qquad 2/25 \times 5 = 10/25$$
$$12/25 \times 3 = 36/25 \qquad 8/25 \times 2 = 16/25$$

$$E(A) = 3/25 + 10/25 + 36/25 + 16/25$$
$$= 65/25 = \underline{2.6 \text{ units}}$$

which means A can expect an average payoff of 2.6 units per play over a large number of plays. Since we are

Figure 10.10 Probability of outcomes

	B1 (3/5)	B2 (2/5)
A1 (1/5)	3/25	2/25
A2 (4/5)	12/25	8/25

dealing with a zero-sum game, we would expect B's loss to be equal to A's gain. This is confirmed by

$$E(B) = 3/25 \times (-1) + 2/25 \times (-5)$$
$$+ 12/25 \times (-3) + 8/25 \times (-2)$$
$$= (-3/25) + (-10/25) + (-36/25)$$
$$+ (-16/25)$$
$$= -2.6 \text{ units}$$

The best B can do is an average loss of 2.6 units.

If B tried to improve his position by changing strategy, say to a pure $B1$ strategy, A would soon recognize the pattern and switch accordingly to a pure $A2$ strategy. The value of the game would then change to 3, the outcome of $A2, B1$. If A continued his optimal mixed strategy while B switched to pure $B1$ strategy, the value of the game for A would remain unchanged:

$$E(A) = 1/5 \times 1 + 4/5 \times 3 = 13/5$$
$$= 2.6 \text{ units}$$

	B1 (1.0)
A1 (1/5)	1/5
A2 (4/5)	4/5

From this result, we can observe that in 2×2 games one player can assure the value of the game by using his optimal strategy, regardless of what his opponent does.

EXAMPLE 10.3 2×2 matching contest

Two prudent but impoverished gamblers were matching dimes. One player, Al, won both dimes when two heads or two tails occurred. The other player, Bob, won both dimes when the coins did not match. After a long series of flips, both players were tired, bored, and nonwinners. Then Bob offered a suggestion: "Let's stop flipping coins and just turn up whichever face we want. To make it interesting, you win the dime if we both show heads, I win a nickel if we don't match, and neither of us wins if we both show tails. It's a fair game, because you have one chance of winning a dime while I have two chances of winning a nickel."

Al stopped to think. He visualized the game in matrix form and recognized it as a two-person zero-sum game. With no saddle point, it had to be mixed strategy. Calculating his optimal strategy, he found that he should turn up a head one-fourth of the time and a tail three-fourths of the time. After calculating Bob's strategy, he found his value of the game to be

$$E(\text{Al}) = 1/16 \times \$0.10 + 3/16 \times (-\$0.05) + 3/16 \times (-\$0.05) + 9/16 \times 0$$
$$= -\$0.0125$$

		Bob	
		H (1/4)	T (3/4)
Al	H (1/4)	$0.10	−$0.05
	T (3/4)	−$0.05	0

After cogitating a bit, he said to Bob: "Your game sounds like fun, but we don't have any nickels to use as payoffs, so let's use only dimes. I'll give you four dimes if we both show heads and one dime for two tails. You give me two dimes if I show a head while you turn up a tail and three dimes if I have a tail and you have a head. Since both our total payoffs come to 50 cents, the game is just as fair as the one you suggested."

Now Bob stopped to think. He mentally pictured the payoff matrix, determined the strategies, and calculated his expected return:

Bob

		H	T
Al	H	−4	2
	T	3	−1

E (Bob) $= 0.3 \times 0.4 \times \$0.40 + 0.3 \times 0.6 \times (-\$0.30) + 0.7 \times 0.4 \times (-\$0.20)$
$\qquad + 0.7 \times 0.6 \times \$0.10 = \$0.048 - \$0.054 - \$0.056 + \$0.042$
$\qquad = -\$0.02$

Bob

		H (0.3)	T (0.7)
Al	H (0.4)	−$0.40	$0.20
	T (0.6)	$0.30	−$0.10

Noting his negative average payoff, he replied: "This takes too much thinking. Let's go back to flipping coins."

$2 \times n$ and $n \times 2$ games   When the number of alternatives increased beyond two, the method used to solve 2×2 games is not directly applicable. However, through the use of a graphical technique we can convert a $2 \times n$ or $n \times 2$ game to a 2×2 game. The obvious limitation is that one of the players still has to have only two alternatives.

To introduce the graphical method, we can apply it to the 2×2 game already solved in the previous section and shown again in Fig. 10.11. The data from the pay-

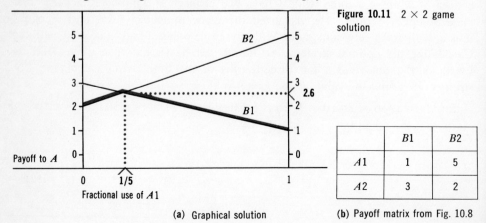

Figure 10.11 2×2 game solution

(a) Graphical solution

	B1	B2
A1	1	5
A2	3	2

(b) Payoff matrix from Fig. 10.8

off matrix is entered on a graph which shows payoffs on the ordinates and mixed strategy on the abscissa. The vertical scale must accommodate the largest payoff, and the horizontal scale runs from 0 to 1.0.

Figure 10.11 represents player A's interests. Alternative $A1$ is depicted by the abscissa, and the ordinates are A's payoffs. If A used pure $A2$ (left vertical scale), he could expect to win two or three units, depending on B's strategy. The right vertical scale shows the possible payoffs from a pure $A1$ strategy. The lines connecting points on the two vertical scales represent B's alternatives. They serve to constrain the payoffs to A as indicated by the solid colored line, the minimum possible gains by A. Since A uses the maximin criterion, he selects the strategy which gives him the best of the minimum payoff. This payoff is the value of the game (2.6) and is indicated by the intersection of lines $B1$ and $B2$. The point on the horizontal scale directly below the intersection designates the fraction of the time A should use $A1$.

The graphical method contributes little to the solution of a 2×2 game; it was applied above only to illustrate the technique. Its value lies in identifying the two limiting alternatives among several possessed by one player. As will be observed later, when one opponent has only two alternatives, the other player can advantageously play only two of his alternatives even though he has several others available. This condition[1] allows the game to be reduced to 2×2 and solved accordingly, once the limiting alternatives are known.

A 3×4 payoff matrix is shown in Fig. 10.12b. The first step in its solution is to check for dominance and a saddle point. The dominance of $A2$ over $A3$ reduces the matrix to a 2×4, which allows a graphical approach. The scales of the graph always represent the player with only two alternatives. Letting the abscissa denote $A1$, each of B's alternatives are plotted with $A2$ payoffs (0 use of $A1$) on the left and $A1$ payoffs on the right.

After the graph has been completed, there are two ways to determine the mixed strategies and value of the game. The first is to read the value of the game and the strategy for A directly from the graph. If the scale

[1]An exception occurs when one player has an optimal pure strategy. Problem 10.10 at the end of the chapter illustrates this condition.

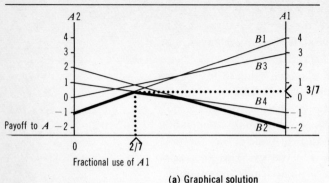

(a) Graphical solution

Figure 10.12 2 × 4 game solution

	B1	B2	B3	B4
A1	4	−2	3	−1
A2	−1	2	0	1
A3	−2	1	−2	0

(b) Payoff matrix

were sufficiently large for accurate readings, the value of the game could be taken from Fig. 10.12a as 3/7 and the strategy for A as 2/7 $A1$ and 5/7 $A2$. The value of the game is the maximum amount A can gain if B uses his optimal strategy. This strategy is defined by the intersection of $B1$ and $B4$ at the highest point of A's minimum gains. Knowing the value of the game and the payoffs for each of B's limiting alternatives, we can set up the relations

$$x \times 4 + (1 - x) \times (-1) = 3/7$$
$$x \times (-1) + (1 - x) \times 1 = 3/7$$

where $x =$ fractional use of $B1$
$1 - x =$ fractional use of $B4$

Then, solving for x,

$$4x + x - 1 = -x - x + 1$$
$$7x = 2$$
$$x = 2/7$$

we find that B should use $B1$ two-sevenths of the time and $B4$ five-sevenths of the time. $B2$ and $B3$ are never used. The validity of this strategy can be interpreted from the graph and confirmed by calculating the value of the game for any other strategy.

The other way to calculate the optimal mix of strategies is to let the graph just point out the two limiting alternatives and solve the evident 2 × 2 game. This method of solution for the sample problem is shown in Fig. 10.13.

$$E(A) = 2/7 \times 2/7 \times 4 + 2/7 \times 5/7 \times (-1) + 5/7 \times 2/7 \times (-1) + 5/7 \times 5/7 \times 1$$
$$= 3/7 \text{ units}$$

Figure 10.13 Solution of a graphically reduced payoff matrix

	B1*	B4*
A1	4	−1
A2	−1	1

*Limiting alternatives are selected graphically

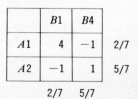

	B1	B4	
A1	4	−1	2/7
A2	−1	1	5/7
	2/7	5/7	

The solution of an $n \times 2$ game is analogous to that used for $2 \times n$ games. The payoff scales on the graph represent the player with two alternatives (by our previous notation, this would be player B). Then the alternatives are plotted for the other player. Since the payoffs are written in terms of A, the player with two alternatives (B) seeks to minimize his maximum losses. *Therefore the solution plane lies along the topmost set of lines.* The minimax solution is the lowest point on the plane. The lines intersecting at this point indicate the limiting alternatives for A. An $n \times 2$ game is illustrated in the following example.

EXAMPLE 10.4 Competitive selling efforts

A new restaurant, Anton's, has opened in a city where the main competition is from Blue's restaurant. Anton's management has observed that Blue's promotional effort varies between reduced prices, $B1$, on certain nights and special menus, $B2$, on other nights. To attract customers from Blue's, Anton's can also reduce prices, $A1$, serve special meals, $A2$, or emphasize a takeout service, $A3$.

Both restaurants use the same advertising media to promote one special attraction each week. Because of differences in physical facilities and experience, each restaurant excels in certain specialties. Payoffs, the percentages of gain or loss in net revenue, have been estimated by Anton's management for the different outcomes:

Blue's

Anton's

	B1	B2
A1	−3%	6%
A2	2%	−6%
A3	−1%	5%

What strategy should Anton's follow in scheduling its weekly specials?

SOLUTION

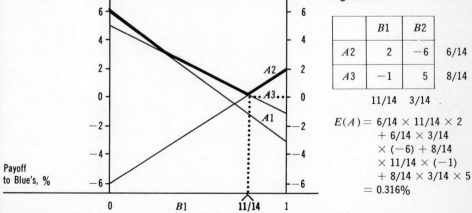

Figure 10.14

	B1	B2	
A2	2	−6	6/14
A3	−1	5	8/14
	11/14	3/14	

$$E(A) = 6/14 \times 11/14 \times 2$$
$$+ 6/14 \times 3/14$$
$$\times (-6) + 8/14$$
$$\times 11/14 \times (-1)$$
$$+ 8/14 \times 3/14 \times 5$$
$$= 0.316\%$$

Anton's can expect a slight gain of 0.316% in revenue by serving special menus 44% of the time and featuring takeout meals 56% of the time.

n × *n* **games**   When a game matrix has more than two alternatives per player, the first effort should be a check for dominance and a saddle point. If these steps fail to produce a solution or a matrix reduced to two alternatives, an exact solution by linear programming or other methods can be undertaken. These measures can be very tedious. There is also an approximation method which avoids mathematical complications and provides good estimates of strategy and the value of the game.

The approximation method is based on a series of fictitious plays of the game. In this respect it resembles the simulation methods we applied to queuing and inventory problems. The difference between the two methods is that the game returns are not a function of chance. When one player makes a play, the other player reacts by selecting the course of action which minimizes the gain of his opponent. In this way both players act under the assumption that past plays offer the best guide to the future. At each play an optimal pure strategy is selected according to the mixture of outcomes which represent all the opponent's past plays.

Detailed procedures for fictitious play can best be described by a sample application. A normal payoff matrix represents the contest. There can be any number of alternatives for either player. The sample problem shown in Fig. 10.15 is a two-person, zero-sum, 3 × 3 game.

Figure 10.15

Step 1: One of player *A*'s alternatives is arbitrarily selected for use in the first play. We will choose *A*1. The payoffs for *A*1 are then entered directly below the bottom row of the matrix.

	*B*1	*B*2	*B*3
*A*1	4	2	0
*A*2	2	0	3
*A*3	2	4	1
	4	**2**	**0**

Step 2: The response of player *B* to *A*1 is to select and play an alternative which minimizes the gain to *A*. Therefore the smallest payoff, 0, is selected (boldface) to indicate that *B*3 is *B*'s best counter to *A*'s use of *A*1.

	*B*1	*B*2	*B*3
*A*1	4	2	0
*A*2	2	0	3
*A*3	2	4	1
	4	2	**0**

Step 3: Now B's first play, the use of $B3$, is entered to the right of the matrix. The best pure strategy for A against the use of $B3$ is $A2$. The largest number in the column, 3, indicates this choice.

	B1	B2	B3	
A1	4	2	0	0
A2	2	0	3	3
A3	2	4	1	1
	4	2	0	

Step 4: Add the payoff from the alternative selected in Step 3 ($A2$) to the last play by A as shown below:

```
4  2  0    First play
2  0  3    Second play
6  2  3    Cumulative payoff
```

Enter the cumulative payoff as the next row. Again select the smallest number (2).

	B1	B2	B3	
A1	4	2	0	0
A2	2	0	3	3
A3	2	4	1	1
	4	2	0	
	6	2	3	

Step 5: Add the payoff from the indicated column ($B2$ from Step 4) to the last column on the right of the matrix. Enter the payoff sums as a new column and indicate the largest number.

	B1	B2	B3		
A1	4	2	0	0	2
A2	2	0	3	3	3
A3	2	4	1	1	5
	4	2	0		
	6	2	3		

Step 6: For each successive play the boldface number designates the row or column alternative to be added to the cumulative payoff. When a tie for high or low payoffs exists, any consistently applied rule may be used to select the next number. In the sample problem, to break a tie we will designate an alternative different from the one last chosen. The number of plays is continued until a desired accuracy is obtained. Figure 10.16 shows 20 iterations for the sample game.

The value of the game is estimated by dividing the boldface payoff at each play by the number of that play. In Fig. 10.16 the tenth play for A shows a payoff of 22 and the tenth play for B shows 18. Therefore the average payoff at the tenth play is $22/10 = 2.2$ for A and $18/10 = 1.8$ for B. The value of the game lies between the *highest* average payoff to B (maximum loss or minimum gain) and the *lowest* average payoff to A. From the sample problem, the value of the game lies between 1.9 (occurring at play 20 for B) and 2.0, which occurs several times for A.

	B1	B2	B3	3.0	2.5	2.0	2.5	2.2	2.0	2.14	2.13	2.0	2.2	2.09	2.0	2.08	2.07	2.0	2.12	2.06	2.0	2.05	2.05		Av payoff
A1	4	2	0	0	2	2	4	4	4	6	6	8	8	8	8	10	10	12	12	12	12	14	0	
A2	2	0	3	3	3	6*	6	9	12*	15	15	18*	18	21	24*	27	27	30*	30	33	36*	39	39	10	Response by A
A3	2	4	1	1	5	6	10	11	12	13	17	18	22	23	24	25	29	30	34	35	36	34	41	10	
0.0	4	2	0	1	2	3	4	5	6	7	8	9	10	11	12	13	14	15	16	17	18	19	20		Play

	B1	B2	B3	Play	
0.0	4	2	0	1	
1.0	6	2	3	2	
1.33	8	6	4	3	**Value of game between 1.9 and 2.0**
1.5	10	6	7	4	**Results of ficticious play** — Strategy for A:
1.6	12	10	8	5	A1 A2 A3
1.5	14	14	9	6	0 10/20 10/20
1.72	16	14	12	7	
1.75	18	14	15	8	Strategy for B:
1.78	20	18	16	9	B1 B2 B3
1.8	22	18	19	10	0 7/20 13/20
1.82	24	22	20	11	
1.75	26	26	21	12	
1.85	28	26	24	13	**Value of game 2.0**
1.86	30	26	27	14	**Exact solution** — Mixed strategies:
1.87	32	30	28	15	A1 A2 A3 B1 B2 B3
1.88	34	30	31	16	0 1/2 1/2 0 1/3 2/3
1.88	36	34	32	17	
1.83	38	38	33	18	
1.89	40	38	36	19	
1.90	42	38	39	20	
	0	7	13		
Av payoff	Response by B		Play	

*Ties broken by avoiding the last used alternative

Figure 10.16 $n \times n$ approximation method carried out for 20 fictitious plays

The optimal strategy is approximated by the number of times each alternative is used during fictitious play. In our illustration, A2 and A3 were each used half the time, while B2 and B3 were used, respectively, for 7/20 and 13/20 of the plays. The proximity of the exact values to the approximate values are indicated in Fig. 10.16.

The approximation method is a powerful tool for very large games. Its iterative nature makes it a natural candidate for machine computations. If there are several optimal solutions to a game, fictitious play will approximate one of them. It can be shown that the approximate solutions will converge on the actual solution with continued playing.

NONZERO-SUM GAMES   Many, if not most, real-life games are nonzero-sum games. In a conflict between nations neither side completely wins; if anything, both sides in a war are losers, regardless of which side surrenders. On the other hand, in labor-management negotiations both sides may be winners; labor can win an increase in wages, while the company wins increased productivity. Perhaps there is collusion in the game by the two players, labor and management, against an unrepresented but respected third party, the consumers.

Bargaining positions occur in nonzero-sum games because different players place different values on the same outcomes. A conciliation offer by a food processor to farmers might be less than either side wanted, but it could be accepted to avoid consequences both sides fear. In a compromise each side gives up certain alternatives on the basis that the other side will not take advantage of the reduced game.

Unfortunately, there is no generally acceptable solution method for nonzero-sum games. However, the concepts of pure and mixed strategies, decision criteria, matrix representation, and game values provide considerable assistance in analyzing any conflict situation.

EXAMPLE 10.4   Analysis of a two-person nonzero-sum game

Two large shopping centers are competing for the same market. The Alpha company attracts customers by staging contests, $A1$, and by special sales or loss leaders, $A2$. The other firm, Beta, also uses contests, $B1$, and special bargains, $B2$. In addition, Beta has the exclusive franchise in the area for trading stamps, $B3$. Both firms periodically change advertising emphasis on their promotions. During these periods the entire advertising budget is spent exclusively on only one of the promotional alternatives.

The estimated gains and losses for each possible outcome are shown in the accompanying payoff matrix. The payoffs represent the net daily change in revenue resulting from competing promotional activities.

		Beta		
		$B1$	$B2$	$B3$
Alpha	$A1$	−$100	0	$100
	$A2$	$400	$200	−$300

Alpha is a new, locally owned firm. The company's utility for money is directly proportional to the amount gained or lost. Beta is one store of a large chain which has a conservative management philosophy. The utility each firm places on changes in daily revenue is indicated by the following utility functions:

If net change,

in dollars ($)	= 500	400	300	200	100	000	−100	−200	−300	−400	−500
then Alpha (U) =	1.0	0.9	0.8	0.7	0.6	0.5	0.4	0.3	0.2	0.1	0.0
and Beta (U) =	1.0	0.95	0.9	0.85	0.8	0.7	0.6	0.5	0.3	0.2	0.0

If the monetary payoffs are converted to utility payoffs, the game matrix takes the values shown, where the first payoff in each cell is the utility of that outcome to Alpha and the second number is Beta's utility payoff for the same outcome. Analyze the position of the two competitors.

	B1	B2	B3
A1	4,8	5,7	6,6
A2	9,2	7,5	2,9

SOLUTION The usual check for dominance and a saddle point is unrewarding. Considerable insight can be gained by plotting graphs for both the utility payoffs. The resulting 3 × 2 games are then solved in terms of each player's utility function. From the first graph in Fig. 10.17 it appears that Alpha can expect an average payoff of 5.11 utiles by using A1 seven-ninths of the time. The second graph indicates that this strategy for Alpha will allow a value of the game for Beta of 6.667 if Beta uses one-third B1 and two-thirds B3. If Beta decides to use maximum strategy for his own utility payoffs, the value of the game for Alpha would not be changed:

$$E(A) = 7/27 \times 4 + 14/27 \times 6 + 2/27 \times 9 + 4/27 \times 2$$
$$= 5.11$$

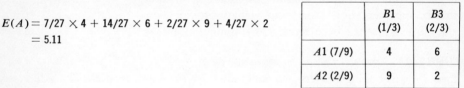

	B1 (1/3)	B3 (2/3)
A1 (7/9)	4	6
A2 (2/9)	9	2

Figure 10.17

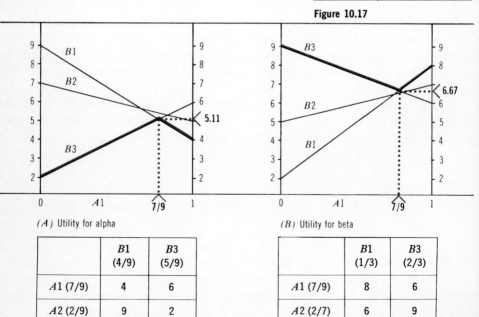

(A) Utility for alpha

(B) Utility for beta

	B1 (4/9)	B3 (5/9)
A1 (7/9)	4	6
A2 (2/9)	9	2

	B1 (1/3)	B3 (2/3)
A1 (7/9)	8	6
A2 (2/7)	6	9

Therefore both firms should be quite pleased with their mixed strategy; Alpha receives a slight cash gain ($11.11 per play), and Beta's concern for maintaining the status quo (as implied by its utility function) is satisfied by the high utility payoff.

The competition might include other factors that could lead to collusion, conciliation, or compromise. Perhaps both firms consider contests too expensive and difficult to administer. Alpha might avoid using contests if Beta would agree to use $B2$ 70% of the time and $B3$ 30%. This strategy would allow an average utility for Alpha of $0.7 \times 7 + 0.3 \times 2 = 5.5$, and Beta's utility would be $0.7 \times 5 + 0.3 \times 9 = 6.2$.

If Beta wanted to stop staging contests and special bargains ($B1$ and $B2$), it might get Alpha to agree to use only $A1$. This compromise would allow both firms an equal utility payoff, 6. Beta would be giving Alpha an increase in average payoff for the privilege of administering only trading stamps. There are many such bargaining positions that can be established in nonzero-sum games.

EVALUATION OF GAME THEORY   Game theory is not a panacea for decision-makers, nor is it a purely theoretical exercise in logic. While few practical industrial applications have been realized, it must be remembered that game theory is still a relatively new approach to decision-making. Proponents of game theory believe continued research and development will make it more applicable to realistic problems. Some of the main difficulties preventing more widespread usage are:

1. Assigning meaningful payoffs
2. Solving very large matrices
3. Handling nonzero-sum and multiplayer games
4. Taking into consideration the possibility of collusion, conciliation, irrational players, and conditions which do not conform to the conventional game assumptions

Despite the difficulties, there is much to be gained from just an awareness of the reasoning behind game theory. It forces attention to an opponent's strategy as well as our own. Payoffs have to be quantified, ranked, or otherwise evaluated. The potential of mixed strategy is stressed. It suggests a philosophy for dealing with human conflict, an area where decision-makers have long needed assistance.

SELECTED REFERENCES

Blackwell, D., and M. A. Girschik: *Theory of Games and Statistical Decisions*, John Wiley & Sons, Inc., New York, 1954.

Buchanan, J. M., and G. Tullock: *The Calculus of Consent*, University of Michigan Press, Ann Arbor, Mich., 1962.

Karlin, S.: *Math Methods and Theory in Games, Programming and Economics*, Addison-Wesley Publishing Company, Reading, Mass., 1954.

Luce, R. D., and H. Raiffa: *Games and Decisions*, John Wiley & Sons, Inc., New York, 1957.

McDonald, J.: *Strategy in Poker, Business and War*, McGraw-Hill Book Company, New York, 1953.

McKinsey, J. C. C.: *Introduction to the Theory of Games*, McGraw-Hill Book Company, New York, 1953.

Schelling, T. C.: *The Strategy of Conflict*, Harvard University Press, Cambridge, Mass., 1960.

Shubik, M.: *Game Theory and Related Approaches to Social Behavior*, John Wiley & Sons, Inc., New York, 1964.

Siegel, S., and L. E. Fouraker: *Bargaining and Group Decision Making*, McGraw-Hill Book Company, New York, 1960.

von Neuman, J., and O. Morgenstern: *Theory of Games and Economic Behavior*, Princeton University Press, Princeton, N.J., 1944.

Williams, J. D.: *The Compleat Strategyst* rev. ed., McGraw-Hill Book Company, New York, 1966.

PROBLEMS

10.1 The profit expected from four alternative courses of action, *A, B, C,* and *D,* under four states of nature, is given below:

	1	2	3	4
A	7	9	5	2
B	8	1	10	4
C	6	6	6	6
D	5	7	9	8

a Which alternative would be selected by applying each of the following criteria: maximax, maximin, regret, and equal likelihood?

b Subtract 12 from each number in the matrix and multiply the resulting difference by 3. Apply the criteria from part (*a*) to the modified payoffs. What do the results indicate?

c Suppose the states of nature are colors of girls' hair: brown, black, blonde, and red. A payoff will be made according to the color of hair of the next girl that passes. You do not know which state applies to each hair coloring. Which alternative would you choose if the numbers in the matrix represented $1000 bills? If the numbers in the matrix represented $1 bills? Which criterion do the above choices resemble?

d Add 10 to each number in the first column of the original matrix. Apply the same criteria as in part (a). What do the results indicate?

10.2 Apply the Hurwicz criterion to the matrix below and show how different degrees of optimism will affect the selection of a preferred alternative:

	V	W	X	Y	Z
A	−8	6	2	−5	4
B	4	−2	−3	3	2
C	0	1	2	1	0
D	6	11	−10	4	−7

If each payoff represented years added to or subtracted from your life expectancy, which alternative would you choose?

10.3 An enterprising young man read about a national Nature Club meeting to be held in a remote desert setting. He visualizes a great potential for the sale of ice-cream products during their meeting in the hot desert. He can carry up to 3000 ice-cream bars in a rented refrigeration truck. The bars will be sold for $.50 each and cost only $.05. Any bars he fails to sell will have no salvage value because of melting and refreezing. His only problem is that he does not know how many will attend the meeting or how many of those that do attend will buy his products. A rough guess is that 750 people will attend, and his expenses, exclusive of the cost of ice-cream bars, would be $125 to make the trip. What criterion would you suggest he use to help decide whether or not to go and how many bars to take? Why? What preference is indicated? Assume that his alternatives are increments of 500 bars.

10.4 Figure 9.9b gave the expected costs of lead-time alternatives for a chemical-inventory problem. The solution to the problem was based on an estimated distribution of possible lead times. Now assume that nothing is known about the expected lead times except that they will vary from

7 to 14 days. Apply the minimax and equal-likelihood criteria to select a safety-stock size. Base your conclusion on the direct-holding and opportunity costs, without regard to economic lot size.

10.5 The expected rates of return for investment in securities and investment in expanded plant facilities are estimated below for two levels of future business activity:

	Recession	Inflation
Securities	5	7
Expansion	1	15

a The company is undecided as to the likelihood of each of the future conditions. It has been suggested that each future be considered equally likely. Then the probability of each future at which the two alternatives are equivalent can be calculated. These are "indifference probabilities." The decision rule would be to select the alternative which has the highest return for the future state that has the greatest difference between the equal-likelihood probability and the indifference probability. Apply this decision rule and comment on the results.

b Consider the states of business activity as being controlled by an intelligent opponent. What strategy should the company use under this assumption?

10.6 Determine the optimal strategies and value of the following 2×2 two-person zero-sum games:

a
−1	6
7	2

b
4	6
−1	3

c
−11	0
−1	−4

d
8	2
6	1

10.7 Determine the optimal strategies and value of the following $2 \times n$ and $n \times 2$ two-person zero-sum games:

a
−3	4	1	−3
5	0	6	−5

b
−8	−1	−7
−2	6	9

c
4	0	1	7
2	8	4	2

d
7	1
3	0
4	8

e
−6	9
−10	−10
8	−4

f
7	2
8	0
4	7

g
6	−4
−1	3
4	−2

10.8 Determine the optimal strategies and value of the following $n \times n$ two-person zero-sum games:

a

8	4	2	−1
9	2	4	3
4	−5	3	0
3	−1	5	2
7	3	0	−3

b

2	−4	3
5	0	−2
4	1	0
−2	3	1

c

1	6	3	−4	0
−2	7	−1	1	2
3	2	5	−2	4

d

4	−1	−7	2
−2	0	3	4
1	2	−1	−6

e

400	100	200	0	−500
0	−100	300	−200	−400
500	0	300	0	−100
400	200	−100	100	100
200	100	300	100	−100

f

1	−2	3
−2	3	−4
3	−4	5

10.9 Abner devised a new card game to play with Berty during the long winter months. The new game uses only eight playing cards: the ace, king, queen, and jack of spades and hearts. Each player has four different face cards in one suit. At each play a particular card is selected by each player from the four available. Each player shows the other his selected card at the same time. Then they turn to the matrix below to see how many points were scored.

Berty

		A	K	Q	J
Abner	A	−2	3	4	−1
	K	4	1	−1	0
	Q	−3	−2	3	−2
	J	3	0	−3	−4

What strategy should each player use? Did Abner set up the game for his benefit?

10.10 What strategy should Abel and Baker use for the game described below? What is the value of the game?

	B1	B2	B3
A1	−$1000	$3000	$1000
A2	$4000	0	$1000

10.11 Two ruthless but modern underworld gangs are competing in the same city. Once a month they must make a decision as to where to set up their illegal gambling operations to minimize police interference. Some locations are more profitable than others. The outcomes of the competing alternatives are indicated in the matrix below, where the payoffs are in thousands of dollars:

Bandits

		B1	B2	B3
Angels	A1	−5	8	6
	A2	4	−3	2
	A3	−10	7	−2

Suppose the Angel gang were able to place a spy in the Bandit gang. What amount could the Angels afford to pay the spy for perfect information about where the Bandits plan to stage each new operation?

10.12 A hotel has 100 rooms that rent for an average of $12 per day. The fixed cost per room is $5 per day and the variable cost is $2 per day. The hotel policy is to accept more reservations than there are rooms available during rush periods. They have found that between 0 and 8% of those reserving rooms will fail to claim them. A disgruntled customer who has reserved a room but finds none available is estimated to cost the hotel $20 in loss of future business. Analyze the situation as a competitive and noncompetitive problem. How many rooms should be rented under each condition? Assume that no deposit is required with a reservation.

10.13 Two very large firms with big government contracts have a serious shortage of technical people. Both firms attempt to fill their personnel needs by recruiting in colleges and by pirating from other firms. Company B has a very desirable location and pays excellent extra benefits. The other company, A, is not so well situated but is known for its enlightened management and superb working conditions. Because of their respective reputations, B appeals to recent college graduates and A is more attractive to people with industrial experience.

Both companies have several teams scouring the country for workers. In any given locality a team can attempt to (1) recruit or (2) pirate, but not both at one time because of time and personnel limitations. Often teams from both companies meet in one locality, which sets up the conflict situation shown in the following matrix:

	B1	B2
A1	−4,−1	0,0
A2	−1,0	−1,−3

The payoffs denote extra thousands of dollars beyond an average annual salary required to hire a man under the conditions of each outcome. The first number in each cell refers to A's payoff, and the second to B's.

a Analyze the problem and suggest independent solutions for each company.

b Comment on the possibility of collusion. Which company has the strongest bargaining position? Suggest a possible compromise solution.

10.14 Two companies compete in a relatively small market with very similar products. Ajax is the larger of the two and sells approximately twice as many units as Besta. Since the products sold by Ajax and Besta serve the same purpose with about equal efficiency, each company attempts to elevate its product through consumer-oriented promotional plans. Three basic promotions are currently in vogue: (1) Television and magazine advertising, (2) Special packaging with bonus "gifts," and (3) Short-term price reductions advertised in stores and local newspapers. Alternatives 2 and 3 tend to differentiate the two brands of product, but alternative 1 tends to increase the general awareness of the buying public to the product type without regard to the manufacturer. Thus a strong advertising policy by Ajax would also increase the sales of Besta. Since Ajax is larger and works with a bigger budget, it benefits proportionately less from Besta's advertising than Besta does from Ajax's. Other alternatives also show a carryover effect between the gains registered by each company.

Ajax has developed the payoff estimates for the most commonly used alternatives of the two companies. The values are in percent of net gain or increased increment of profit expected from the following various alternatives during one quarter. The payoffs for Ajax from advertising by television and magazines ($A1$) depend on the extent of advertising conducted; the values for Besta are based on an extrapolation of historical data:

Besta

		B1	B2	B3
Ajax	A1	$x,12$	$y,21$	$z,18$
	A2	$-6,4$	$26,-12$	$-12,-20$
	A3	$4,0$	$9,9$	$-6,0$

a What strategy should Ajax follow to maximize gains if x, y, and z are respectively, 14, 8, and 12? Discuss the pros and cons of the alternatives open to Ajax.

b Based on the values of x, y, and z given in (a), what is the best strategy for Besta?

c Ajax recognizes that Besta benefits from an advertising campaign conducted by Ajax, but the reciprocal is not true. Ajax believes that its advertising budget can be manipulated from the level given in (a) so that for every 2% reduction in profit for Ajax, Besta's profit will decrease 3%. However, if advertising is increased by Ajax, Besta will gain 3% for every 1% increase. The maximum and minimum payoffs possible for Ajax are 20% and 0. What strategy combined with what advertising policy will be most advantageous for Ajax?

Appendix
Compound-Interest Factors

½%

	To find F, given P: $(1+i)^n$	To find P, given F: $\dfrac{1}{(1+i)^n}$	To find A, given F: $\dfrac{i}{(1+i)^n-1}$	To find A, given P: $\dfrac{i(1+i)^n}{(1+i)^n-1}$	To find F, given A: $\dfrac{(1+i)^n-1}{i}$	To find P, given A: $\dfrac{(1+i)^n-1}{i(1+i)^n}$	
n	$(f/p)^{\frac{1}{2}}_n$	$(p/f)^{\frac{1}{2}}_n$	$(a/f)^{\frac{1}{2}}_n$	$(a/p)^{\frac{1}{2}}_n$	$(f/a)^{\frac{1}{2}}_n$	$(p/a)^{\frac{1}{2}}_n$	n
1	1.005	0.9950	1.00000	1.00500	1.000	0.995	1
2	1.010	0.9901	0.49875	0.50375	2.005	1.985	2
3	1.015	0.9851	0.33167	0.33667	3.015	2.970	3
4	1.020	0.9802	0.24183	0.25313	4.030	3.950	4
5	1.025	0.9754	0.19801	0.20301	5.050	4.926	5
6	1.030	0.9705	0.16460	0.16960	6.076	5.896	6
7	1.036	0.9657	0.14073	0.14573	7.106	6.862	7
8	1.041	0.9609	0.12283	0.12783	8.141	7.823	8
9	1.046	0.9561	0.10891	0.11391	9.182	8.779	9
10	1.051	0.9513	0.09777	0.10277	10.228	9.730	10
11	1.056	0.9466	0.08866	0.09366	11.279	10.677	11
12	1.062	0.9419	0.08107	0.08607	12.336	11.619	12
13	1.067	0.9372	0.07464	0.07964	13.397	12.556	13
14	1.072	0.9326	0.06914	0.07414	14.464	13.489	14
15	1.078	0.9279	0.06436	0.06936	15.537	14.417	15
16	1.083	0.9233	0.06019	0.06519	16.614	15.340	16
17	1.088	0.9187	0.05615	0.06151	17.697	16.259	17
18	1.094	0.9141	0.05323	0.05823	18.786	17.173	18
19	1.099	0.9096	0.05030	0.05530	19.880	18.082	19
20	1.105	0.9051	0.04767	0.05267	20.979	18.987	20

n	$(f/p)^{1/2}_n$	$(p/f)^{1/2}_n$	$(a/f)^{1/2}_n$	$(a/p)^{1/2}_n$	$(f/a)^{1/2}_n$	$(p/a)^{1/2}_n$	n
21	1.110	0.9006	0.04528	0.05028	22.084	19.888	21
22	1.116	0.8961	0.04311	0.04811	23.194	20.784	22
23	1.122	0.8916	0.04113	0.04613	24.310	21.676	23
24	1.127	0.8872	0.03932	0.04432	25.432	22.563	24
25	1.133	0.8828	0.03767	0.04265	26.559	23.446	25
26	1.138	0.8784	0.03611	0.04111	27.692	24.324	26
27	1.144	0.8740	0.03469	0.03969	28.830	25.198	27
28	1.150	0.8697	0.03336	0.03836	29.975	26.068	28
29	1.156	0.8653	0.03213	0.03713	31.124	26.933	29
30	1.161	0.8610	0.03098	0.03598	32.280	27.794	30
31	1.167	0.8567	0.02990	0.03490	33.441	28.651	31
32	1.173	0.8525	0.02889	0.03389	34.609	29.503	32
33	1.179	0.8482	0.02795	0.03295	35.782	30.352	33
34	1.185	0.8440	0.02706	0.03206	36.961	31.196	34
35	1.191	0.8398	0.02622	0.03122	38.145	32.035	35
40	1.221	0.8191	0.02265	0.02765	44.159	36.172	40
45	1.252	0.7990	0.01987	0.02487	50.324	40.207	45
50	1.283	0.7793	0.01765	0.02265	56.645	44.143	50
55	1.316	0.7601	0.01548	0.02084	63.126	47.981	55
60	1.349	0.7414	0.01433	0.01933	69.770	51.726	60
65	1.383	0.7231	0.01306	0.01806	76.582	55.377	65
70	1.418	0.7053	0.01197	0.01697	83.566	58.939	70
75	1.454	0.6879	0.01102	0.01602	90.727	62.414	75
80	1.490	0.6710	0.01020	0.01520	98.068	65.802	80
85	1.528	0.6545	0.00947	0.01447	105.594	69.108	85
90	1.567	0.6383	0.00883	0.01383	113.311	72.331	90
95	1.606	0.6226	0.00825	0.01325	121.222	75.476	95
100	1.647	0.6073	0.00773	0.01273	129.334	78.543	100

1%

n	To find F, given P: $(1 + i)^n$	To find P, given F: $\dfrac{1}{(1 + i)^n}$	To find A, given F: $\dfrac{i}{(1 + i)^n - 1}$	To find A, given P: $\dfrac{i(1 + i)^n}{(1 + i)^n - 1}$	To find F, given A: $\dfrac{(1 + i)^n - 1}{i}$	To find P, given A: $\dfrac{(1 + i)^n - 1}{i(1 + i)^n}$	n
	$(f/p)^1_n$	$(p/f)^1_n$	$(a/f)^1_n$	$(a/p)^1_n$	$(f/a)^1_n$	$(p/a)^1_n$	
1	1.010	0.9901	1.00000	1.01000	1.000	0.990	1
2	1.020	0.9803	0.49751	0.50751	2.010	1.970	2
3	1.030	0.9706	0.33002	0.34002	3.030	2.941	3
4	1.041	0.9610	0.24628	0.25628	4.060	3.902	4

n	$(f/p)_n^1$	$(p/f)_n^1$	$(a/f)_n^1$	$(a/p)_n^1$	$(f/a)_n^1$	$(p/a)_n^1$	n
5	1.051	0.9515	0.19604	0.20604	5.101	4.853	5
6	1.062	0.9420	0.16255	0.17255	6.152	5.795	6
7	1.072	0.9327	0.13863	0.14863	7.214	6.728	7
8	1.083	0.9235	0.12069	0.13069	8.286	7.652	8
9	1.094	0.9143	0.10674	0.11674	9.369	8.566	9
10	1.105	0.9053	0.09558	0.10558	10.462	9.471	10
11	1.116	0.8963	0.08645	0.09645	11.567	10.368	11
12	1.127	0.8874	0.07885	0.08885	12.683	11.255	12
13	1.138	0.8787	0.07241	0.08241	13.809	12.134	13
14	1.149	0.8700	0.06690	0.07690	14.947	13.004	14
15	1.161	0.8613	0.06212	0.07212	16.097	13.865	15
16	1.173	0.8528	0.05794	0.06794	17.258	14.718	16
17	1.184	0.8444	0.05426	0.06426	18.430	15.562	17
18	1.196	0.8360	0.05098	0.06098	19.615	16.398	18
19	1.208	0.8277	0.04805	0.05805	20.811	17.226	19
20	1.220	0.8195	0.04542	0.05542	22.019	18.046	20
21	1.232	0.8114	0.04303	0.05303	23.239	18.857	21
22	1.245	0.8034	0.04086	0.05086	24.472	19.660	22
23	1.257	0.7954	0.03889	0.04889	25.716	20.456	23
24	1.270	0.7876	0.03707	0.04707	26.973	21.243	24
25	1.282	0.7798	0.03541	0.04541	28.243	22.023	25
26	1.295	0.7720	0.03387	0.04387	29.526	22.795	26
27	1.308	0.7644	0.03245	0.04245	30.821	23.560	27
28	1.321	0.7568	0.03112	0.04112	32.129	24.316	28
29	1.335	0.7493	0.02990	0.03990	33.450	25.066	29
30	1.348	0.7419	0.02875	0.03875	34.785	25.808	30
31	1.361	0.7346	0.02768	0.03768	36.133	26.542	31
32	1.375	0.7273	0.02667	0.03667	37.494	27.270	32
33	1.391	0.7201	0.02573	0.03573	38.869	27.990	33
34	1.403	0.7130	0.02484	0.03484	40.258	28.703	34
35	1.417	0.7059	0.02400	0.03400	41.660	29.409	35
40	1.489	0.6717	0.02046	0.03046	48.886	32.835	40
45	1.565	0.6391	0.01771	0.02771	56.481	36.095	45
50	1.645	0.6080	0.01551	0.02551	64.463	39.196	50
55	1.729	0.5785	0.01373	0.02373	72.852	42.147	55
60	1.817	0.5504	0.01224	0.02224	81.670	44.955	60
65	1.909	0.5237	0.01100	0.02100	90.937	47.627	65
70	2.007	0.4983	0.00993	0.01993	100.676	50.169	70
75	2.109	0.4741	0.00902	0.01902	110.913	52.587	75
80	2.217	0.4511	0.00822	0.01822	121.672	54.888	80
85	2.330	0.4292	0.00752	0.01752	132.979	57.078	85
90	2.449	0.4084	0.00690	0.01690	144.863	59.161	90
95	2.574	0.3886	0.00636	0.01636	157.354	61.143	95
100	2.705	0.3697	0.00587	0.01587	170.481	63.029	100

1½%

	To find F, given P: $(1 + i)^n$	To find P, given F: $\dfrac{1}{(1 + i)^n}$	To find A, given F: $\dfrac{i}{(1 + i)^n - 1}$	To find A, given P: $\dfrac{i(1 + i)^n}{(1 + i)^n - 1}$	To find F, given A: $\dfrac{(1 + i)^n - 1}{i}$	To find P, given A: $\dfrac{(1 + i)^n - 1}{i(1 + i)^n}$	
n	$(f/p)_n^{1\frac{1}{2}}$	$(p/f)_n^{1\frac{1}{2}}$	$(a/f)_n^{1\frac{1}{2}}$	$(a/p)_n^{1\frac{1}{2}}$	$(f/a)_n^{1\frac{1}{2}}$	$(p/a)_n^{1\frac{1}{2}}$	n
1	1.015	0.9852	1.00000	1.01500	1.000	0.985	1
2	1.030	0.9707	0.49628	0.51128	2.015	1.956	2
3	1.046	0.9563	0.32838	0.34338	3.045	2.912	3
4	1.061	0.9422	0.24444	0.25944	4.091	3.854	4
5	1.077	0.9283	0.19409	0.20909	5.152	4.783	5
6	1.093	0.9145	0.16053	0.17553	6.230	5.697	6
7	1.110	0.9010	0.13656	0.15156	7.323	6.598	7
8	1.126	0.8877	0.11858	0.13358	8.433	7.486	8
9	1.143	0.8746	0.10461	0.11961	9.559	8.361	9
10	1.161	0.8617	0.09343	0.10843	10.703	9.222	10
11	1.178	0.8489	0.08429	0.09930	11.863	10.071	11
12	1.196	0.8364	0.07668	0.09168	13.041	10.908	12
13	1.214	0.8240	0.07024	0.08524	14.237	11.732	13
14	1.232	0.8118	0.06472	0.07972	15.450	12.543	14
15	1.250	0.7999	0.05994	0.07494	16.682	13.343	15
16	1.269	0.7880	0.05577	0.07077	17.932	14.131	16
17	1.288	0.7764	0.05208	0.06708	19.201	14.908	17
18	1.307	0.7649	0.04881	0.06381	20.489	15.673	18
19	1.327	0.7536	0.04588	0.06088	21.797	16.426	19
20	1.347	0.7425	0.04325	0.05825	23.124	17.169	20
21	1.367	0.7315	0.04087	0.05587	24.471	17.900	21
22	1.388	0.7207	0.03870	0.05370	25.838	19.621	22
23	1.408	0.7100	0.03673	0.05173	27.225	19.331	23
24	1.430	0.6995	0.03492	0.04992	28.634	20.030	24
25	1.451	0.6892	0.03325	0.04826	30.063	20.720	25
26	1.473	0.6790	0.03173	0.04673	31.514	21.399	26
27	1.495	0.6690	0.03032	0.04532	32.987	22.068	27
28	1.517	0.6591	0.02900	0.04400	34.481	22.727	28
29	1.540	0.6494	0.02778	0.04278	35.999	23.376	29
30	1.563	0.6398	0.02664	0.04164	37.539	24.016	30
31	1.587	0.6303	0.02557	0.04057	39.102	24.646	31
32	1.610	0.6210	0.02458	0.03958	40.688	25.267	32
33	1.634	0.6118	0.02364	0.03864	42.229	25.879	33
34	1.659	0.6028	0.02276	0.03776	43.933	26.482	34
35	1.684	0.5939	0.02193	0.03693	45.592	27.076	35
40	1.814	0.5513	0.01843	0.03343	54.268	29.916	40
45	1.954	0.5117	0.01572	0.03072	63.614	32.552	45

n	$(f/p)_n^{1\frac{1}{2}}$	$(p/f)_n^{1\frac{1}{2}}$	$(a/f)_n^{1\frac{1}{2}}$	$(a/p)_n^{1\frac{1}{2}}$	$(f/a)_n^{1\frac{1}{2}}$	$(p/a)_n^{1\frac{1}{2}}$	n
50	2.105	0.4750	0.01357	0.02857	73.683	35.000	50
55	2.268	0.4409	0.01183	0.02683	84.530	37.271	55
60	2.443	0.4093	0.01039	0.02539	96.215	39.380	60
65	2.632	0.3799	0.00919	0.02419	108.803	41.338	65
70	2.835	0.3527	0.00817	0.02317	122.364	43.155	70
75	3.055	0.3274	0.00730	0.02230	136.973	44.842	75
80	3.291	0.3039	0.00655	0.02155	152.711	46.407	80
85	3.545	0.2821	0.00589	0.02089	169.665	47.861	85
90	3.819	0.2619	0.00532	0.02032	187.930	49.210	90
95	4.114	0.2431	0.00482	0.01982	207.606	50.462	95
100	4.432	0.2256	0.00437	0.01937	228.803	51.625	100

2%

	To find F, given P: $(1 + i)^n$	To find P, given F: $\dfrac{1}{(1 + i)^n}$	To find A, given F: $\dfrac{i}{(1 + i)^n - 1}$	To find A, given P: $\dfrac{i(1 + i)^n}{(1 + i)^n - 1}$	To find F, given A: $\dfrac{(1 + i)^n - 1}{i}$	To find P, given A: $\dfrac{(1 + i)^n - 1}{i(1 + i)^n}$	
n	$(f/p)_n^2$	$(p/f)_n^2$	$(a/f)_n^2$	$(a/p)_n^2$	$(f/a)_n^2$	$(p/a)_n^2$	n
1	1.020	0.9804	1.00000	1.02000	1.000	0.980	1
2	1.040	0.9612	0.49505	0.51505	2.020	1.942	2
3	1.061	0.9423	0.32675	0.34675	3.060	2.884	3
4	1.082	0.9238	0.24262	0.26262	4.122	3.808	4
5	1.104	0.9057	0.19216	0.21216	5.204	4.713	5
6	1.126	0.8880	0.15853	0.17853	6.308	5.601	6
7	1.149	0.8706	0.13451	0.15451	7.434	6.472	7
8	1.172	0.8535	0.11651	0.13651	8.583	7.325	8
9	1.195	0.8368	0.10252	0.12252	9.755	8.162	9
10	1.219	0.8203	0.09133	0.11133	10.950	8.983	10
11	1.243	0.8043	0.08216	0.10218	12.169	9.787	11
12	1.268	0.7885	0.07456	0.09456	13.412	10.575	12
13	1.294	0.7730	0.06812	0.08812	14.680	11.348	13
14	1.319	0.7579	0.06260	0.08260	15.974	12.106	14
15	1.346	0.7430	0.05783	0.07783	17.293	12.849	15
16	1.373	0.7284	0.05365	0.07365	18.639	13.578	16
17	1.400	0.7142	0.04997	0.06997	20.012	14.292	17
18	1.428	0.7002	0.04670	0.06670	21.412	14.992	18
19	1.457	0.6864	0.04378	0.06378	22.841	15.678	19
20	1.486	0.6730	0.04116	0.06116	24.297	16.351	20
21	1.516	0.6598	0.03878	0.05878	25.783	17.011	21

n	$(f/p)_n^2$	$(p/f)_n^2$	$(a/f)_n^2$	$(a/p)_n^2$	$(f/a)_n^2$	$(p/a)_n^2$	n
22	1.546	0.6468	0.03663	0.05663	27.299	17.658	22
23	1.577	0.6342	0.03467	0.05467	28.845	18.292	23
24	1.608	0.6217	0.03287	0.05287	30.422	18.914	24
25	1.641	0.6095	0.03122	0.05122	32.030	19.523	25
26	1.673	0.5976	0.02970	0.04970	33.671	20.121	26
27	1.707	0.5859	0.02829	0.04829	35.344	20.707	27
28	1.741	0.5744	0.02699	0.04699	37.051	21.281	28
29	1.776	0.5631	0.02578	0.04578	38.792	21.844	29
30	1.811	0.5521	0.02465	0.04465	40.568	22.396	30
31	1.848	0.5412	0.02360	0.04360	42.379	22.938	31
32	1.885	0.5306	0.02261	0.04261	44.227	23.468	32
33	1.922	0.5202	0.02169	0.04169	46.112	23.989	33
34	1.961	0.5100	0.02082	0.04082	48.034	24.499	34
35	2.000	0.5000	0.02000	0.04000	49.994	24.999	35
40	2.208	0.4529	0.01656	0.03656	60.402	27.355	40
45	2.438	0.4102	0.01391	0.03391	71.893	29.490	45
50	2.692	0.3715	0.01182	0.03182	84.579	31.424	50
55	2.972	0.3365	0.01014	0.03014	98.587	33.175	55
60	3.281	0.3048	0.00877	0.02877	114.052	34.761	60
65	3.623	0.2761	0.00763	0.02763	131.126	36.197	65
70	4.000	0.2500	0.00667	0.02667	149.978	37.499	70
75	4.416	0.2265	0.00586	0.02586	170.792	38.677	75
80	4.875	0.2051	0.00516	0.02516	193.772	39.745	80
85	5.383	0.1858	0.00456	0.02456	219.144	40.711	85
90	5.943	0.1683	0.00405	0.02405	247.157	41.587	90
95	6.562	0.1524	0.00360	0.02360	278.085	42.380	95
100	7.245	0.1380	0.00320	0.02320	312.232	43.098	100

$2\frac{1}{2}\%$

n	To find F, given P: $(1 + i)^n$	To find P, given F: $\dfrac{1}{(1 + i)^n}$	To find A, given F: $\dfrac{i}{(1 + i)^n - 1}$	To find A, given P: $\dfrac{i (1 + i)^n}{(1 + i)^n - 1}$	To find F, given A: $\dfrac{(1 + i)^n - 1}{i}$	To find P, given A: $\dfrac{(1 + i)^n - 1}{i (1 + i)^n}$	n
	$(f/p)_n^{2\frac{1}{2}}$	$(p/f)_n^{2\frac{1}{2}}$	$(a/f)_n^{2\frac{1}{2}}$	$(a/p)_n^{2\frac{1}{2}}$	$(f/a)_n^{2\frac{1}{2}}$	$(p/a)_n^{2\frac{1}{2}}$	
1	1.025	0.9756	1.00000	1.02500	1.000	0.976	1
2	1.051	0.9518	0.49383	0.51883	2.025	1.927	2
3	1.077	0.9386	0.32514	0.35014	3.076	2.856	3
4	1.104	0.9060	0.24082	0.26582	4.153	3.762	4

n	$(f/p)_n^{2\frac{1}{2}}$	$(p/f)_n^{2\frac{1}{2}}$	$(a/f)_n^{2\frac{1}{2}}$	$(a/p)_n^{2\frac{1}{2}}$	$(f/a)_n^{2\frac{1}{2}}$	$(p/a)_n^{2\frac{1}{2}}$	n
5	1.131	0.8839	0.19025	0.21525	5.256	4.646	5
6	1.160	0.8623	0.15655	0.18155	6.388	5.508	6
7	1.189	0.8413	0.13250	0.15750	7.547	6.349	7
8	1.218	0.8207	0.11447	0.13947	8.736	7.170	8
9	1.249	0.8007	0.10046	0.12546	9.955	7.971	9
10	1.280	0.7812	0.08926	0.11426	11.203	8.752	10
11	1.312	0.7621	0.08011	0.10511	12.483	9.514	11
12	1.345	0.7436	0.07249	0.09749	13.796	10.258	12
13	1.379	0.7254	0.06605	0.09105	15.140	10.983	13
14	1.413	0.7077	0.06054	0.08554	16.519	11.691	14
15	1.448	0.6905	0.05577	0.08077	17.932	12.381	15
16	1.485	0.6736	0.05160	0.07660	19.380	13.055	16
17	1.522	0.6572	0.04793	0.07293	20.865	13.712	17
18	1.560	0.6412	0.04467	0.06967	22.386	14.353	18
19	1.599	0.6255	0.04176	0.06676	23.946	14.979	19
20	1.639	0.6103	0.03915	0.06415	25.545	15.589	20
21	1.680	0.5954	0.03679	0.06179	27.183	16.185	21
22	1.722	0.5809	0.03465	0.05965	28.863	16.765	22
23	1.765	0.5667	0.03270	0.05770	30.584	17.332	23
24	1.809	0.5529	0.03091	0.05591	32.349	17.885	24
25	1.854	0.5394	0.02928	0.05428	34.158	18.424	25
26	1.900	0.5262	0.02777	0.05277	36.012	18.951	26
27	1.948	0.5134	0.02638	0.05138	37.912	19.464	27
28	1.996	0.5009	0.02509	0.05009	39.860	19.965	28
29	2.046	0.4887	0.02389	0.04889	41.856	20.454	29
30	2.098	0.4767	0.02278	0.04778	43.903	20.930	30
31	2.150	0.4651	0.02174	0.04674	46.000	21.395	31
32	2.204	0.4538	0.02077	0.04577	48.150	21.849	32
33	2.259	0.4427	0.01986	0.04486	50.354	22.292	33
34	2.315	0.4319	0.01901	0.04401	52.613	22.724	34
35	2.373	0.4214	0.01821	0.04321	54.928	23.145	35
40	2.685	0.3724	0.01484	0.03984	67.403	25.103	40
45	3.038	0.3292	0.01227	0.03727	81.516	26.833	45
50	3.437	0.2909	0.01026	0.03526	97.484	28.362	50
55	3.889	0.2572	0.00865	0.03365	115.551	29.714	55
60	4.400	0.2273	0.00735	0.03235	135.992	30.909	60
65	4.978	0.2009	0.00628	0.03128	159.118	31.965	65
70	5.632	0.1776	0.00540	0.03040	185.284	32.898	70
75	6.372	0.1569	0.00465	0.02965	214.888	33.723	75
80	7.210	0.1387	0.00403	0.02903	248.383	34.452	80
85	8.157	0.1226	0.00349	0.02849	286.279	35.096	85
90	9.229	0.1084	0.00304	0.02804	329.154	35.666	90
95	10.442	0.0958	0.00265	0.02765	377.664	36.169	95
100	11.814	0.0846	0.00231	0.02731	432.549	36.614	100

3%

	To find F, given P: $(1 + i)^n$	To find P, given F: $\dfrac{1}{(1 + i)^n}$	To find A, given F: $\dfrac{i}{(1 + i)^n - 1}$	To find A, given P: $\dfrac{i(1 + i)^n}{(1 + i)^n - 1}$	To find F, given A: $\dfrac{(1 + i)^n - 1}{i}$	To find P, given A: $\dfrac{(1 + i)^n - 1}{i(1 + i)^n}$	
n	$(f/p)_n^3$	$(p/f)_n^3$	$(a/f)_n^3$	$(a/p)_n^3$	$(f/a)_n^3$	$(p/a)_n^3$	n
1	1.030	0.9709	1.00000	1.03000	1.000	0.971	1
2	1.061	0.9426	0.49261	0.52261	2.030	1.913	2
3	1.093	0.9151	0.32353	0.35353	3.091	2.829	3
4	1.126	0.8885	0.23903	0.26903	4.184	3.717	4
5	1.159	0.8626	0.18835	0.21835	5.309	4.580	5
6	1.194	0.8375	0.15460	0.18460	6.468	5.417	6
7	1.230	0.8131	0.13051	0.16051	7.662	6.230	7
8	1.267	0.7894	0.11246	0.14246	8.892	7.020	8
9	1.305	0.7664	0.09843	0.12843	10.159	7.786	9
10	1.344	0.7441	0.08723	0.11723	11.464	8.530	10
11	1.384	0.7224	0.07808	0.10808	12.808	9.253	11
12	1.426	0.7014	0.07046	0.10046	14.192	9.954	12
13	1.469	0.6810	0.06403	0.09403	15.618	10.635	13
14	1.513	0.6611	0.05853	0.08853	17.086	11.296	14
15	1.558	0.6419	0.05377	0.08377	18.599	11.938	15
16	1.605	0.6232	0.04961	0.07961	20.157	12.561	16
17	1.653	0.6050	0.04595	0.07595	21.762	13.166	17
18	1.702	0.5874	0.04271	0.07271	23.414	13.754	18
19	1.754	0.5703	0.03981	0.06981	25.117	14.324	19
20	1.806	0.5537	0.03722	0.06722	26.870	14.877	20
21	1.860	0.5375	0.03487	0.06487	28.676	15.415	21
22	1.916	0.5219	0.03275	0.06275	30.537	15.937	22
23	1.974	0.5067	0.03081	0.06081	32.453	16.444	23
24	2.033	0.4919	0.02905	0.05905	34.426	16.936	24
25	2.094	0.4776	0.02743	0.05743	36.459	17.413	25
26	2.157	0.4637	0.02594	0.05594	38.553	17.877	26
27	2.221	0.4502	0.02456	0.05456	40.710	18.327	27
28	2.288	0.4371	0.02329	0.05329	42.931	18.764	28
29	2.357	0.4243	0.02211	0.05211	45.219	19.188	29
30	2.427	0.4120	0.02102	0.05102	47.575	19.600	30
31	2.500	0.4000	0.02000	0.05000	50.003	20.000	31
32	2.575	0.3883	0.01905	0.04905	52.503	20.389	32
33	2.652	0.3770	0.01816	0.04816	55.078	20.766	33
34	2.732	0.3660	0.01732	0.04732	57.730	21.132	34
35	2.814	0.3554	0.01654	0.04654	60.462	21.487	35
40	3.262	0.3066	0.01326	0.04326	75.401	23.115	40
45	3.782	0.2644	0.01079	0.04079	92.720	24.519	45

n	$(f/p)^3_n$	$(p/f)^3_n$	$(a/f)^3_n$	$(a/p)^3_n$	$(f/a)^3_n$	$(p/a)^3_n$	n
50	4.384	0.2281	0.00887	0.03887	112.797	25.730	50
55	5.082	0.1968	0.00735	0.03735	136.072	26.774	55
60	5.892	0.1697	0.00613	0.03613	163.053	27.676	60
65	6.830	0.1464	0.00515	0.03515	194.333	28.453	65
70	7.918	0.1263	0.00434	0.03434	230.594	29.123	70
75	9.179	0.1089	0.00367	0.03367	272.631	29.702	75
80	10.641	0.0940	0.00311	0.03311	321.363	30.201	80
85	12.336	0.0811	0.00265	0.03265	377.857	30.631	85
90	14.300	0.0699	0.00226	0.03226	443.349	31.002	90
95	16.578	0.0603	0.00193	0.03193	519.272	31.323	95
100	19.219	0.0520	0.00165	0.03165	607.288	31.599	100

4%

	To find F, given P: $(1 + i)^n$	To find P, given F: $\dfrac{1}{(1 + i)^n}$	To find A, given F: $\dfrac{i}{(1 + i)^n - 1}$	To find A, given P: $\dfrac{i(1 + i)^n}{(1 + i)^n - 1}$	To find F, given A: $\dfrac{(1 + i)^n - 1}{i}$	To find P, given A: $\dfrac{(1 + i)^n - 1}{i(1 + i)^n}$	
n	$(f/p)^4_n$	$(p/f)^4_n$	$(a/f)^4_n$	$(a/p)^4_n$	$(f/a)^4_n$	$(p/a)^4_n$	n
1	1.040	0.9615	1.00000	1.04000	1.000	0.962	1
2	1.082	0.9246	0.49020	0.53020	2.040	1.886	2
3	1.125	0.8890	0.32035	0.36035	3.122	2.775	3
4	1.170	0.8548	0.23549	0.27549	4.246	3.630	4
5	1.217	0.8219	0.18463	0.22463	5.416	4.452	5
6	1.265	0.7903	0.15076	0.19076	6.633	5.242	6
7	1.316	0.7599	0.12661	0.16661	7.898	6.002	7
8	1.369	0.7307	0.10853	0.14853	9.214	6.733	8
9	1.423	0.7026	0.09449	0.13449	10.583	7.435	9
10	1.480	0.6756	0.08329	0.12329	12.006	8.111	10
11	1.539	0.6496	0.07415	0.11415	13.486	8.760	11
12	1.601	0.6246	0.06655	0.10655	15.026	9.385	12
13	1.665	0.6006	0.06014	0.10014	16.627	9.986	13
14	1.732	0.5775	0.05467	0.09467	18.292	10.563	14
15	1.801	0.5553	0.04994	0.08994	20.024	11.118	15
16	1.873	0.5339	0.04582	0.08582	21.825	11.652	16
17	1.948	0.5134	0.04220	0.08220	23.698	12.166	17
18	2.026	0.4936	0.03899	0.07899	25.645	12.659	18
19	2.107	0.4746	0.03614	0.07614	27.671	13.134	19
20	2.191	0.4564	0.03358	0.07358	29.778	13.590	20
21	2.279	0.4388	0.03128	0.07128	31.969	14.029	21

n	$(f/p)_n^4$	$(p/f)_n^4$	$(a/f)_n^4$	$(a/p)_n^4$	$(f/a)_n^4$	$(p/a)_n^4$	n
22	2.370	0.4220	0.02920	0.06920	34.248	14.451	22
23	2.465	0.4057	0.02731	0.06731	36.618	14.857	23
24	2.563	0.3901	0.02559	0.06559	39.083	15.247	24
25	2.666	0.3751	0.02401	0.06401	41.646	15.622	25
26	2.772	0.3607	0.02257	0.06257	44.312	15.983	26
27	2.883	0.3468	0.02124	0.06124	47.084	16.330	27
28	2.999	0.3335	0.02001	0.06001	49.968	16.663	28
29	3.119	0.3207	0.01888	0.05888	52.966	16.984	29
30	3.243	0.3083	0.01783	0.05783	56.085	17.292	30
31	3.373	0.2965	0.01686	0.05686	59.328	17.588	31
32	3.508	0.2851	0.01595	0.05595	62.701	17.874	32
33	3.648	0.2741	0.01510	0.05510	66.210	18.148	33
34	3.794	0.2636	0.01431	0.05431	69.858	18.411	34
35	3.946	0.2534	0.01358	0.05358	73.652	18.665	35
40	4.801	0.2083	0.01052	0.05052	95.026	19.793	40
45	5.841	0.1712	0.00826	0.04826	121.029	20.720	45
50	7.107	0.1407	0.00655	0.04655	152.667	21.482	50
55	8.646	0.1157	0.00523	0.04523	191.159	22.109	55
60	10.520	0.0951	0.00420	0.04420	237.991	22.623	60
65	12.799	0.0781	0.00339	0.04339	294.968	23.047	65
70	15.572	0.0642	0.00275	0.04275	364.290	23.395	70
75	18.945	0.0528	0.00223	0.04223	448.631	23.680	75
80	23.050	0.0434	0.00181	0.04181	551.245	23.915	80
85	28.044	0.0357	0.00148	0.04148	676.090	24.109	85
90	34.119	0.0293	0.00121	0.04121	827.983	24.267	90
95	41.511	0.0241	0.00099	0.04099	1012.785	24.398	95
100	50.505	0.0198	0.00081	0.04081	1237.624	24.505	100

5%

n	To find F, given P: $(1+i)^n$	To find P, given F: $\dfrac{1}{(1+i)^n}$	To find A, given F: $\dfrac{i}{(1+i)^n - 1}$	To find A, given P: $\dfrac{i(1+i)^n}{(1+i)^n - 1}$	To find F, given A: $\dfrac{(1+i)^n - 1}{i}$	To find P, given A: $\dfrac{(1+i)^n - 1}{i(1+i)^n}$	n
	$(f/p)_n^5$	$(p/f)_n^5$	$(a/f)_n^5$	$(a/p)_n^5$	$(f/a)_n^5$	$(p/a)_n^5$	
1	1.050	0.9524	1.00000	1.05000	1.000	0.952	1
2	1.103	0.9070	0.48780	0.53780	2.050	1.859	2
3	1.158	0.8638	0.31721	0.36721	3.153	2.723	3
4	1.216	0.8227	0.23201	0.28201	4.310	3.546	4

n	$(f/p)_n^5$	$(p/f)_n^5$	$(a/f)_n^5$	$(a/p)_n^5$	$(f/a)_n^5$	$(p/a)_n^5$	n
5	1.276	0.7835	0.18097	0.23097	5.526	4.329	5
6	1.340	0.7462	0.14702	0.19702	6.802	5.076	6
7	1.407	0.7107	0.12282	0.17282	8.142	5.786	7
8	1.477	0.6768	0.10472	0.15472	9.549	6.463	8
9	1.551	0.6446	0.09069	0.14069	11.027	7.108	9
10	1.629	0.6139	0.07950	0.12950	12.578	7.722	10
11	1.710	0.5847	0.07039	0.12039	14.207	8.306	11
12	1.796	0.5568	0.06283	0.11283	15.917	8.863	12
13	1.886	0.5303	0.05646	0.10646	17.713	9.394	13
14	1.980	0.5051	0.05102	0.10102	19.599	9.899	14
15	2.079	0.4810	0.04634	0.09634	21.579	10.380	15
16	2.183	0.4581	0.04227	0.09227	23.657	10.838	16
17	2.292	0.4363	0.03870	0.08870	25.840	11.274	17
18	2.407	0.4155	0.03555	0.08555	28.132	11.690	18
19	2.527	0.3957	0.03275	0.08275	30.539	12.085	19
20	2.653	0.3769	0.03024	0.08024	33.066	12.462	20
21	2.786	0.3589	0.02800	0.07800	35.719	12.821	21
22	2.925	0.3418	0.02597	0.07597	38.505	13.163	22
23	3.072	0.3256	0.02414	0.07414	41.430	13.489	23
24	3.225	0.3101	0.02247	0.07247	44.502	13.799	24
25	3.386	0.2953	0.02095	0.07095	47.727	14.094	25
26	3.556	0.2812	0.01956	0.06956	51.113	14.375	26
27	3.733	0.2678	0.01829	0.06829	54.669	14.643	27
28	3.920	0.2551	0.01712	0.06712	58.403	14.898	28
29	4.116	0.2429	0.01605	0.06605	62.323	15.141	29
30	4.322	0.2314	0.01505	0.06505	66.439	15.372	30
31	4.538	0.2204	0.01413	0.06413	70.761	15.593	31
32	4.765	0.2099	0.01328	0.06328	75.299	15.803	32
33	5.003	0.1999	0.01249	0.06249	80.064	16.003	33
34	5.253	0.1904	0.01176	0.06176	85.067	16.193	34
35	5.516	0.1813	0.01107	0.06107	90.320	16.374	35
40	7.040	0.1420	0.00828	0.05828	120.800	17.159	40
45	8.985	0.1113	0.00626	0.05626	159.700	17.774	45
50	11.467	0.0872	0.00478	0.05478	209.348	18.256	50
55	14.636	0.0683	0.00367	0.05367	272.713	18.633	55
60	18.679	0.0535	0.00283	0.05283	353.584	18.929	60
65	23.840	0.0419	0.00219	0.05219	456.798	19.161	65
70	30.426	0.0329	0.00170	0.05170	588.529	19.343	70
75	38.833	0.0258	0.00132	0.05132	756.654	19.485	75
80	49.561	0.0202	0.00103	0.05103	971.229	19.596	80
85	63.254	0.0158	0.00080	0.05080	1245.087	19.684	85
90	80.730	0.0124	0.00063	0.05063	1594.607	19.752	90
95	103.035	0.0097	0.00049	0.05049	2040.694	19.806	95
100	131.501	0.0076	0.00038	0.05038	2610.025	19.848	100

6%

	To find F, given P: $(1 + i)^n$	To find P, given F: $\dfrac{1}{(1 + i)^n}$	To find A, given F: $\dfrac{i}{(1 + i)^n - 1}$	To find A, given P: $\dfrac{i(1 + i)^n}{(1 + i)^n - 1}$	To find F, given A: $\dfrac{(1 + i)^n - 1}{i}$	To find P, given A: $\dfrac{(1 + i)^n - 1}{i(1 + i)^n}$	
n	$(f/p)_n^6$	$(p/f)_n^6$	$(a/f)_n^6$	$(a/p)_n^6$	$(f/a)_n^6$	$(p/a)_n^6$	n
1	1.060	0.9434	1.00000	1.06000	1.000	0.943	1
2	1.124	0.8900	0.48544	0.54544	2.060	1.833	2
3	1.191	0.8396	0.31411	0.37411	3.184	2.673	3
4	1.262	0.7921	0.22859	0.28859	4.375	3.465	4
5	1.338	0.7473	0.17740	0.23740	5.637	4.212	5
6	1.419	0.7050	0.14336	0.20336	6.975	4.917	6
7	1.504	0.6651	0.11914	0.17914	8.394	5.582	7
8	1.594	0.6274	0.10104	0.16104	9.897	6.210	8
9	1.689	0.5919	0.08702	0.14702	11.491	6.802	9
10	1.791	0.5584	0.07587	0.13587	13.181	7.360	10
11	1.898	0.5268	0.06679	0.12679	14.972	7.887	11
12	2.012	0.4970	0.05928	0.11928	16.870	8.384	12
13	2.133	0.4688	0.05296	0.11296	18.882	8.853	13
14	2.261	0.4423	0.04758	0.10758	21.015	9.295	14
15	2.397	0.4173	0.04296	0.10296	23.276	9.712	15
16	2.540	0.3936	0.03895	0.09895	25.673	10.106	16
17	2.693	0.3714	0.03544	0.09544	28.213	10.477	17
18	2.854	0.3503	0.03236	0.09236	30.906	10.828	18
19	3.026	0.3305	0.02962	0.08962	33.760	11.158	19
20	3.207	0.3118	0.02718	0.08718	36.786	11.470	20
21	3.400	0.2942	0.02500	0.08500	39.993	11.764	21
22	3.604	0.2775	0.02305	0.08305	43.392	12.042	22
23	3.820	0.2618	0.02128	0.08128	46.996	12.303	23
24	4.049	0.2470	0.01968	0.07968	50.816	12.550	24
25	4.292	0.2330	0.01823	0.07823	54.865	12.783	25
26	4.549	0.2198	0.01690	0.07690	59.156	13.003	26
27	4.822	0.2074	0.01570	0.07570	63.706	13.211	27
28	5.112	0.1956	0.01459	0.07459	68.528	13.406	28
29	5.418	0.1846	0.01358	0.07358	73.640	13.591	29
30	5.743	0.1741	0.01265	0.07265	79.058	13.765	30
31	6.088	0.1643	0.01179	0.07179	84.802	13.929	31
32	6.453	0.1550	0.01100	0.07100	90.890	14.084	32
33	6.841	0.1462	0.01027	0.07027	97.343	14.230	33
34	7.251	0.1379	0.00960	0.06960	104.184	14.368	34
35	7.686	0.1301	0.00897	0.06897	111.435	14.498	35
40	10.286	0.0972	0.00646	0.06646	154.762	15.046	40
45	13.765	0.0727	0.00470	0.06470	212.744	15.456	45

n	$(f/p)_n^6$	$(p/f)_n^6$	$(a/f)_n^6$	$(a/p)_n^6$	$(f/a)_n^6$	$(p/a)_n^6$	n
50	18.420	0.0543	0.00344	0.06344	290.336	15.762	50
55	24.650	0.0406	0.00254	0.06254	394.172	15.991	55
60	32.988	0.0303	0.00188	0.06188	533.128	16.161	60
65	44.145	0.0227	0.00139	0.06139	719.083	16.289	65
70	59.076	0.0169	0.00103	0.06103	967.932	16.385	70
75	79.057	0.0126	0.00077	0.06077	1300.949	16.456	75
80	105.796	0.0095	0.00057	0.06057	1746.600	16.509	80
85	141.579	0.0071	0.00043	0.06043	2342.982	16.549	85
90	189.465	0.0053	0.00032	0.06032	3141.075	16.579	90
95	253.546	0.0039	0.00024	0.06024	4209.104	16.601	95
100	339.302	0.0029	0.00018	0.06018	5638.368	16.618	100

7%

	To find F, given P: $(1+i)^n$	To find P, given F: $\dfrac{1}{(1+i)^n}$	To find A, given F: $\dfrac{i}{(1+i)^n-1}$	To find A, given P: $\dfrac{i(1+i)^n}{(1+i)^n-1}$	To find F, given A: $\dfrac{(1+i)^n-1}{i}$	To find P, given A: $\dfrac{(1+i)^n-1}{i(1+i)^n}$	
n	$(f/p)_n^7$	$(p/f)_n^7$	$(a/f)_n^7$	$(a/p)_n^7$	$(f/a)_n^7$	$(p/a)_n^7$	n
1	1.070	0.9346	1.00000	1.07000	1.000	0.935	1
2	1.145	0.8734	0.48309	0.55309	2.070	1.808	2
3	1.225	0.8163	0.31105	0.38105	3.215	2.624	3
4	1.311	0.7629	0.22523	0.29523	4.440	3.387	4
5	1.403	0.7130	0.17389	0.24389	5.751	4.100	5
6	1.501	0.6663	0.13980	0.20980	7.153	4.767	6
7	1.606	0.6227	0.11555	0.18555	8.654	5.389	7
8	1.718	0.5820	0.09747	0.16747	10.260	5.971	8
9	1.838	0.5439	0.08349	0.15349	11.978	6.515	9
10	1.967	0.5083	0.07238	0.14238	13.816	7.024	10
11	2.105	0.4751	0.06336	0.13336	15.784	7.499	11
12	2.252	0.4440	0.05590	0.12590	17.888	7.943	12
13	2.410	0.4150	0.04965	0.11965	20.141	8.358	13
14	2.579	0.3878	0.04434	0.11434	22.550	8.745	14
15	2.759	0.3624	0.03979	0.10979	25.129	9.108	15
16	2.952	0.3387	0.03586	0.10586	27.888	9.447	16
17	3.159	0.3166	0.03243	0.10243	30.840	9.763	17
18	3.380	0.2959	0.02941	0.09941	33.999	10.059	18
19	3.617	0.2765	0.02675	0.09675	37.379	10.363	19
20	3.870	0.2584	0.02439	0.09439	40.995	10.594	20
21	4.141	0.2415	0.02229	0.09229	44.865	10.836	21

n	$(f/p)_n^7$	$(p/f)_n^7$	$(a/f)_n^7$	$(a/p)_n^7$	$(f/a)_n^7$	$(p/a)_n^7$	n
22	4.430	0.2257	0.02041	0.09041	49.006	11.061	22
23	4.741	0.2109	0.01871	0.08871	53.436	11.272	23
24	5.072	0.1971	0.01719	0.08719	58.177	11.469	24
25	5.427	0.1842	0.01581	0.08581	63.249	11.654	25
26	5.807	0.1722	0.01456	0.08456	68.676	11.826	26
27	6.214	0.1609	0.01343	0.08343	74.484	11.987	27
28	6.649	0.1504	0.01239	0.08239	80.698	12.137	28
29	7.114	0.1406	0.01145	0.08145	87.347	12.278	29
30	7.612	0.1314	0.01059	0.08059	94.461	12.409	30
31	8.145	0.1228	0.00980	0.07980	102.073	12.532	31
32	8.715	0.1147	0.00907	0.07907	110.218	12.647	32
33	9.325	0.1072	0.00841	0.07841	118.923	12.754	33
34	9.978	0.1002	0.00780	0.07780	128.259	12.854	34
35	10.677	0.0937	0.00723	0.07723	138.237	12.948	35
40	14.974	0.0668	0.00501	0.07501	199.635	13.332	40
45	21.002	0.0476	0.00350	0.07350	285.749	13.606	45
50	29.457	0.0339	0.00246	0.07246	406.529	13.801	50
55	41.315	0.0242	0.00174	0.07174	575.929	13.940	55
60	57.946	0.0173	0.00123	0.07123	813.520	14.039	60
65	81.273	0.0123	0.00087	0.07087	1146.755	14.110	65
70	113.989	0.0088	0.00062	0.07062	1614.134	14.160	70
75	159.876	0.0063	0.00044	0.07044	2269.657	14.196	75
80	224.234	0.0045	0.00031	0.07031	3189.063	14.222	80
85	314.500	0.0032	0.00022	0.07022	4478.576	14.240	85
90	441.103	0.0023	0.00016	0.07016	6287.185	14.253	90
95	618.670	0.0016	0.00011	0.07011	8823.854	14.263	95
100	867.716	0.0012	0.00008	0.07008	12381.662	14.269	100

8%

	To find F, given P: $(1 + i)^n$	To find P, given F: $\dfrac{1}{(1 + i)^n}$	To find A, given F: $\dfrac{i}{(1 + i)^n - 1}$	To find A, given P: $\dfrac{i(1 + i)^n}{(1 + i)^n - 1}$	To find F, given A: $\dfrac{(1 + i)^n - 1}{i}$	To find P, given A: $\dfrac{(1 + i)^n - 1}{i(1 + i)^n}$	
n	$(f/p)_n^8$	$(p/f)_n^8$	$(a/f)_n^8$	$(a/p)_n^8$	$(f/a)_n^8$	$(p/a)_n^8$	n
1	1.080	0.9259	1.00000	1.08000	1.000	0.926	1
2	1.166	0.8573	0.48077	0.56077	2.080	1.783	2
3	1.260	0.7938	0.30803	0.38803	3.246	2.577	3
4	1.360	0.7350	0.22192	0.30192	4.506	3.312	4

n	$(f/p)^8_n$	$(p/f)^8_n$	$(a/f)^8_n$	$(a/p)^8_n$	$(f/a)^8_n$	$(p/a)^8_n$	n
5	1.469	0.6806	0.17046	0.25046	5.867	3.993	5
6	1.587	0.6302	0.13632	0.21632	7.336	4.623	6
7	1.714	0.5835	0.11207	0.19207	8.923	5.206	7
8	1.851	0.5403	0.09401	0.17401	10.637	5.747	8
9	1.999	0.5002	0.08008	0.16008	12.488	6.247	9
10	2.159	0.4632	0.06903	0.14903	14.487	6.710	10
11	2.332	0.4289	0.06008	0.14008	16.645	7.139	11
12	2.518	0.3971	0.05270	0.13270	18.977	7.536	12
13	2.720	0.3677	0.04652	0.12652	21.495	7.904	13
14	2.937	0.3405	0.04130	0.12130	24.215	8.244	14
15	3.172	0.3152	0.03683	0.11683	27.152	8.559	15
16	3.426	0.2919	0.03298	0.11298	30.324	8.851	16
17	3.700	0.2703	0.02963	0.10963	33.750	9.122	17
18	3.996	0.2502	0.02670	0.10670	37.450	9.372	18
19	4.316	0.2317	0.02413	0.10413	41.446	9.604	19
20	4.661	0.2145	0.02185	0.10185	45.762	9.818	20
21	5.034	0.1987	0.01983	0.09983	50.423	10.017	21
22	5.437	0.1839	0.01803	0.09803	55.457	10.201	22
23	5.781	0.1703	0.01642	0.09642	60.893	10.371	23
24	6.341	0.1577	0.01498	0.09498	66.765	10.529	24
25	6.848	0.1460	0.01368	0.09368	73.106	10.675	25
26	7.396	0.1352	0.01251	0.09251	79.954	10.810	26
27	7.988	0.1252	0.01145	0.09145	87.351	10.935	27
28	8.627	0.1159	0.01049	0.09049	95.339	11.051	28
29	9.317	0.1073	0.00962	0.08962	103.966	11.158	29
30	10.063	0.0994	0.00883	0.08883	113.283	11.258	30
31	10.868	0.0920	0.00811	0.08811	123.346	11.350	31
32	11.737	0.0852	0.00745	0.08745	134.214	11.435	32
33	12.676	0.0789	0.00685	0.08685	145.951	11.514	33
34	13.690	0.0730	0.00630	0.08630	158.627	11.587	34
35	14.785	0.0676	0.00580	0.08580	172.317	11.655	35
40	21.725	0.0460	0.00386	0.08386	259.057	11.925	40
45	31.920	0.0313	0.00259	0.08259	386.506	12.108	45
50	46.902	0.0213	0.00174	0.08174	573.770	12.233	50
55	68.914	0.0145	0.00118	0.08118	848.923	12.319	55
60	101.257	0.0099	0.00080	0.08080	1253.213	12.377	60
65	148.780	0.0067	0.00054	0.08054	1847.248	12.416	65
70	218.606	0.0046	0.00037	0.08037	2720.080	12.443	70
75	321.205	0.0031	0.00025	0.08025	4002.557	12.461	75
80	471.955	0.0021	0.00017	0.08017	5886.935	12.474	80
85	693.456	0.0014	0.00012	0.08012	8655.706	12.482	85
90	1018.915	0.0010	0.00008	0.08008	12723.939	12.488	90
95	1497.121	0.0007	0.00005	0.08005	18701.507	12.492	95
100	2199.761	0.0005	0.00004	0.08004	27484.516	12.494	100

9%

	To find F, given P: $(1 + i)^n$	To find P, given F: $\dfrac{1}{(1 + i)^n}$	To find A, given F: $\dfrac{i}{(1 + i)^n - 1}$	To find A, given P: $\dfrac{i(1 + i)^n}{(1 + i)^n - 1}$	To find F, given A: $\dfrac{(1 + i)^n - 1}{i}$	To find P, given A: $\dfrac{(1 + i)^n - 1}{i(1 + i)^n}$	
n	$(f/p)_n^9$	$(p/f)_n^9$	$(a/f)_n^9$	$(a/p)_n^9$	$(f/a)_n^9$	$(p/a)_n^9$	n
1	1.090	0.9174	1.00000	1.09000	1.000	0.917	1
2	1.188	0.8417	0.47847	0.56847	2.090	1.759	2
3	1.295	0.7722	0.30505	0.39505	3.278	2.531	3
4	1.412	0.7084	0.21867	0.30867	4.573	3.240	4
5	1.539	0.6499	0.16709	0.25709	5.985	3.890	5
6	1.677	0.5963	0.13292	0.22292	7.523	4.486	6
7	1.828	0.5470	0.10869	0.19869	9.200	5.033	7
8	1.993	0.5019	0.09067	0.18067	11.028	5.535	8
9	2.172	0.4604	0.07680	0.16680	13.021	5.995	9
10	2.367	0.4224	0.06582	0.15582	15.193	6.418	10
11	2.580	0.3875	0.05695	0.14695	17.560	6.805	11
12	2.813	0.3555	0.04965	0.13965	20.141	7.161	12
13	3.066	0.3262	0.04357	0.13357	22.953	7.487	13
14	3.342	0.2992	0.03843	0.12843	26.019	7.786	14
15	3.642	0.2745	0.03406	0.12406	29.361	8.061	15
16	3.970	0.2519	0.03030	0.12030	33.003	8.313	16
17	4.328	0.2311	0.02705	0.11705	36.974	8.544	17
18	4.717	0.2120	0.02421	0.11421	41.301	8.756	18
19	5.142	0.1945	0.02173	0.11173	46.018	8.950	19
20	5.604	0.1784	0.01955	0.10955	51.160	9.129	20
21	6.109	0.1637	0.01762	0.10762	56.765	9.292	21
22	6.659	0.1502	0.01590	0.10590	62.873	9.442	22
23	7.258	0.1378	0.01438	0.10438	69.532	9.580	23
24	7.911	0.1264	0.01302	0.10302	76.790	9.707	24
25	8.623	0.1160	0.01180	0.10181	84.701	9.823	25
26	9.399	0.1064	0.01072	0.10072	93.324	9.929	26
27	10.245	0.0976	0.00973	0.09973	102.723	10.027	27
28	11.167	0.0895	0.00885	0.09885	112.968	10.116	28
29	12.172	0.0822	0.00806	0.09806	124.135	10.198	29
30	13.268	0.0754	0.00734	0.09734	136.308	10.274	30
31	14.462	0.0691	0.00669	0.09669	149.575	10.343	31
32	15.763	0.0634	0.00610	0.09610	164.037	10.406	32
33	17.182	0.0582	0.00556	0.09556	179.800	10.464	33
34	18.728	0.0534	0.00508	0.09508	196.982	10.518	34
35	20.414	0.0490	0.00464	0.09464	215.711	10.567	35
40	31.409	0.0318	0.00296	0.09296	337.882	10.757	40
45	48.327	0.0207	0.00190	0.09190	525.859	10.881	45

n	$(f/p)^9_n$	$(p/f)^9_n$	$(a/f)^9_n$	$(a/p)^9_n$	$(f/a)^9_n$	$(p/a)^9_n$	n
50	74.358	0.0134	0.00123	0.09123	815.084	10.962	50
55	114.408	0.0087	0.00079	0.09079	1260.092	11.014	55
60	176.031	0.0057	0.00051	0.09051	1944.792	11.048	60
65	270.846	0.0037	0.00033	0.09033	2998.288	11.070	65
70	416.730	0.0024	0.00022	0.09022	4619.223	11.084	70
75	641.191	0.0016	0.00014	0.09014	7113.232	11.094	75
80	986.552	0.0010	0.00009	0.09009	10950.556	11.100	80
85	1517.948	0.0007	0.00006	0.09006	16854.444	11.104	85
90	2335.501	0.0004	0.00004	0.09004	25939.000	11.106	90
95	3593.513	0.0003	0.00003	0.09003	39917.378	11.108	95
100	5529.089	0.0002	0.00002	0.09002	61422.544	11.109	100

10%

	To find F, given P: $(1+i)^n$	To find P, given F: $\dfrac{1}{(1+i)^n}$	To find A, given F: $\dfrac{i}{(1+i)^n-1}$	To find A, given P: $\dfrac{i(1+i)^n}{(1+i)^n-1}$	To find F, given A: $\dfrac{(1+i)^n-1}{i}$	To find P, given A: $\dfrac{(1+i)^n-1}{i(1+i)^n}$	
n	$(f/p)^{10}_n$	$(p/f)^{10}_n$	$(a/f)^{10}_n$	$(a/p)^{10}_n$	$(f/a)^{10}_n$	$(p/a)^{10}_n$	n
1	1.100	0.9091	1.00000	1.10000	1.000	0.909	1
2	1.210	0.8264	0.47619	0.57619	2.100	1.736	2
3	1.331	0.7513	0.30211	0.40211	3.310	2.487	3
4	1.464	0.6830	0.21547	0.31547	4.641	3.170	4
5	1.611	0.6209	0.16380	0.26380	6.105	3.791	5
6	1.772	0.5645	0.12961	0.22961	7.716	4.355	6
7	1.949	0.5132	0.10541	0.20541	9.487	4.868	7
8	2.144	0.4665	0.08744	0.18744	11.436	5.335	8
9	2.358	0.4241	0.07364	0.17364	13.579	5.759	9
10	2.594	0.3855	0.06275	0.16275	15.937	6.144	10
11	2.853	0.3505	0.05396	0.15396	18.531	6.495	11
12	3.138	0.3186	0.04676	0.14676	21.384	6.814	12
13	3.452	0.2897	0.04078	0.14078	24.523	7.103	13
14	3.797	0.2633	0.03575	0.13575	27.975	7.367	14
15	4.177	0.2394	0.03147	0.13147	31.772	7.606	15
16	4.595	0.2176	0.02782	0.12782	35.950	7.824	16
17	5.054	0.1978	0.02466	0.12466	40.545	8.022	17
18	5.560	0.1799	0.02193	0.12193	45.599	8.201	18
19	6.116	0.1635	0.01955	0.11955	51.159	8.363	19
20	6.727	0.1486	0.01746	0.11746	57.275	8.514	20
21	7.400	0.1351	0.01562	0.11562	64.002	8.649	21

n	$(f/p)_n^{10}$	$(p/f)_n^{10}$	$(a/f)_n^{10}$	$(a/p)_n^{10}$	$(f/a)_n^{10}$	$(p/a)_n^{10}$	n
22	8.140	0.1228	0.01401	0.11401	71.403	8.772	22
23	8.954	0.1117	0.01257	0.11257	79.543	8.883	23
24	9.850	0.1015	0.01130	0.11130	88.497	8.985	24
25	10.835	0.0923	0.01017	0.11017	98.347	9.077	25
26	11.918	0.0839	0.00916	0.10916	109.182	9.161	26
27	13.110	0.0763	0.00826	0.10826	121.100	9.237	27
28	14.421	0.0693	0.00745	0.10745	134.210	9.307	28
29	15.863	0.0630	0.00673	0.10673	148.631	9.370	29
30	17.449	0.0573	0.00608	0.10608	164.494	9.427	30
31	19.194	0.0521	0.00550	0.10550	181.943	9.479	31
32	21.114	0.0474	0.00497	0.10497	201.138	9.526	32
33	23.225	0.0431	0.00450	0.10450	222.252	9.569	33
34	25.548	0.0391	0.00407	0.10407	245.477	9.609	34
35	28.102	0.0356	0.00369	0.10369	271.024	9.644	35
40	45.259	0.0221	0.00226	0.10226	442.593	9.779	40
45	72.890	0.0137	0.00139	0.10139	718.905	9.863	45
50	117.391	0.0085	0.00086	0.10086	1163.909	9.915	50
55	189.059	0.0053	0.00053	0.10053	1880.591	9.947	55
60	304.482	0.0033	0.00033	0.10033	3034.816	9.967	60
65	490.371	0.0020	0.00020	0.10020	4893.707	9.980	65
70	789.747	0.0013	0.00013	0.10013	7887.470	9.987	70
75	1271.895	0.0008	0.00008	0.10008	12708.954	9.992	75
80	2048.400	0.0005	0.00005	0.10005	20474.002	9.995	80
85	3298.969	0.0003	0.00003	0.10003	32979.690	9.997	85
90	5313.023	0.0002	0.00002	0.10002	53120.226	9.998	90
95	8556.676	0.0001	0.00001	0.10001	85556.760	9.999	95
100	13780.612	0.0001	0.00001	0.10001	137796.123	9.999	100

12%

	To find F, given P: $(1 + i)^n$	To find P, given F: $\dfrac{1}{(1 + i)^n}$	To find A, given F: $\dfrac{i}{(1 + i)^n - 1}$	To find A, given P: $\dfrac{i(1 + i)^n}{(1 + i)^n - 1}$	To find F, given A: $\dfrac{(1 + i)^n - 1}{i}$	To find P, given A: $\dfrac{(1 + i)^n - 1}{i(1 + i)^n}$	
n	$(f/p)_n^{12}$	$(p/f)_n^{12}$	$(a/f)_n^{12}$	$(a/p)_n^{12}$	$(f/a)_n^{12}$	$(p/a)_n^{12}$	n
1	1.120	0.8929	1.00000	1.12000	1.000	0.893	1
2	1.254	0.7972	0.47170	0.59170	2.120	1.690	2
3	1.405	0.7118	0.29635	0.41635	3.374	2.402	3
4	1.574	0.6355	0.20923	0.32923	4.779	3.037	4

n	$(f/p)_n^{12}$	$(p/f)_n^{12}$	$(a/f)_n^{12}$	$(a/p)_n^{12}$	$(f/a)_n^{12}$	$(p/a)_n^{12}$	n
5	1.762	0.5674	0.15741	0.27741	6.353	3.605	5
6	1.974	0.5066	0.12323	0.24323	8.115	4.111	6
7	2.211	0.4523	0.09912	0.21912	10.089	4.564	7
8	2.476	0.4039	0.08130	0.20130	12.300	4.968	8
9	2.773	0.3606	0.06768	0.18768	14.776	5.328	9
10	3.106	0.3220	0.05698	0.17698	17.549	5.650	10
11	3.479	0.2875	0.04842	0.16842	20.655	5.938	11
12	3.896	0.2567	0.04144	0.16144	24.133	6.194	12
13	4.363	0.2292	0.03568	0.15568	28.029	6.424	13
14	4.887	0.2046	0.03087	0.15087	32.393	6.628	14
15	5.474	0.1827	0.02682	0.14682	37.280	6.811	15
16	6.130	0.1631	0.02339	0.14339	42.753	6.974	16
17	6.866	0.1456	0.02046	0.14046	48.884	7.120	17
18	7.690	0.1300	0.01794	0.13794	55.750	7.250	18
19	8.613	0.1161	0.01576	0.13576	63.440	7.366	19
20	9.646	0.1037	0.01388	0.13388	72.052	7.469	20
21	10.804	0.0926	0.01224	0.13224	81.699	7.562	21
22	12.100	0.0826	0.01081	0.13081	92.503	7.645	22
23	13.552	0.0738	0.00956	0.12956	104.603	7.718	23
24	15.179	0.0659	0.00846	0.12846	118.155	7.784	24
25	17.000	0.0588	0.00750	0.12750	133.334	7.843	25
26	19.040	0.0525	0.00665	0.12665	150.334	7.896	26
27	21.325	0.0469	0.00590	0.12590	169.374	7.943	27
28	23.884	0.0419	0.00524	0.12524	190.699	7.984	28
29	26.750	0.0374	0.00466	0.12466	214.582	8.022	29
30	29.960	0.0334	0.00414	0.12414	241.333	8.055	30
31	33.555	0.0298	0.00369	0.12369	271.292	8.085	31
32	37.582	0.0266	0.00328	0.12328	304.847	8.112	32
33	42.091	0.0238	0.00292	0.12292	342.429	8.135	33
34	47.142	0.0212	0.00260	0.12260	384.520	8.157	34
35	52.800	0.0189	0.00232	0.12232	431.663	8.176	35
40	93.051	0.0107	0.00130	0.12130	767.091	8.244	40
45	163.988	0.0061	0.00074	0.12074	1358.230	8.283	45
50	289.002	0.0035	0.00042	0.12042	2400.018	8.305	50

15%

	To find F, given P: $(1 + i)^n$	To find P, given F: $\dfrac{1}{(1 + i)^n}$	To find A, given F: $\dfrac{i}{(1 + i)^n - 1}$	To find A, given P: $\dfrac{i(1 + i)^n}{(1 + i)^n - 1}$	To find F, given A: $\dfrac{(1 + i)^n - 1}{i}$	To find P, given A: $\dfrac{(1 + i)^n - 1}{i(1 + i)^n}$	
n	$(f/p)_n^{15}$	$(p/f)_n^{15}$	$(a/f)_n^{15}$	$(a/p)_n^{15}$	$(f/a)_n^{15}$	$(p/a)_n^{15}$	n
1	1.150	0.8696	1.00000	1.15000	1.000	0.870	1
2	1.322	0.7561	0.46512	0.61512	2.150	1.626	2
3	1.521	0.6575	0.28798	0.43798	3.472	2.283	3
4	1.749	0.5718	0.20027	0.35027	4.993	2.855	4
5	2.011	0.4972	0.14832	0.29832	6.742	3.352	5
6	2.313	0.4323	0.11424	0.26424	8.754	3.784	6
7	2.660	0.3759	0.09036	0.24036	11.067	4.160	7
8	3.059	0.3269	0.07285	0.22285	13.727	4.487	8
9	3.518	0.2843	0.05957	0.20957	16.786	4.772	9
10	4.046	0.2472	0.04925	0.19925	20.304	5.019	10
11	4.652	0.2149	0.04107	0.19107	24.349	5.234	11
12	5.350	0.1869	0.03448	0.18448	29.002	5.421	12
13	6.153	0.1625	0.02911	0.17911	34.352	5.583	13
14	7.076	0.1413	0.02469	0.17469	40.505	5.724	14
15	8.137	0.1229	0.02102	0.17102	47.580	5.847	15
16	9.358	0.1069	0.01795	0.16795	55.717	5.954	16
17	10.761	0.0929	0.01537	0.16537	65.075	6.047	17
18	12.375	0.0808	0.01319	0.16319	75.836	6.128	18
19	14.232	0.0703	0.01134	0.16134	88.212	6.198	19
20	16.367	0.0611	0.00976	0.15976	102.444	6.259	20
21	18.821	0.0531	0.00842	0.15842	118.810	6.312	21
22	21.645	0.0462	0.00727	0.15727	137.631	6.359	22
23	24.891	0.0402	0.00628	0.15628	159.276	6.399	23
24	28.625	0.0349	0.00543	0.15543	184.168	6.434	24
25	32.919	0.0304	0.00470	0.15470	212.793	6.464	25
26	37.857	0.0264	0.00407	0.15407	245.711	6.491	26
27	43.535	0.0230	0.00353	0.15353	283.569	6.514	27
28	50.066	0.0200	0.00306	0.15306	327.104	6.534	28
29	57.575	0.0174	0.00265	0.15265	377.170	6.551	29
30	66.212	0.0151	0.00230	0.15230	434.745	6.566	30
31	76.143	0.0131	0.00200	0.15200	500.956	6.579	31
32	87.565	0.0114	0.00173	0.15173	577.099	6.591	32
33	100.700	0.0099	0.00150	0.15150	664.664	6.600	33
34	115.805	0.0086	0.00131	0.15131	765.364	6.609	34
35	133.176	0.0075	0.00113	0.15113	881.170	6.617	35
40	267.863	0.0037	0.00056	0.15056	1779.090	6.642	40
45	538.769	0.0019	0.00028	0.15028	3585.128	6.654	45
50	1083.657	0.0009	0.00014	0.15014	7217.716	6.661	50

n	To find F, given P: $(1 + i)^n$	To find P, given F: $\dfrac{1}{(1 + i)^n}$	To find A, given F: $\dfrac{i}{(1 + i)^n - 1}$	To find A, given P: $\dfrac{i(1 + i)^n}{(1 + i)^n - 1}$	To find F, given A: $\dfrac{(1 + i)^n - 1}{i}$	To find P, given A: $\dfrac{(1 + i)^n - 1}{i(1 + i)^n}$	n
	$(f/p)_n^{20}$	$(p/f)_n^{20}$	$(a/f)_n^{20}$	$(a/p)_n^{20}$	$(f/a)_n^{20}$	$(p/a)_n^{20}$	
1	1.200	0.8333	1.00000	1.20000	1.000	0.833	1
2	1.440	0.6944	0.45455	0.65455	2.200	1.528	2
3	1.728	0.5787	0.27473	0.47473	3.640	2.106	3
4	2.074	0.4823	0.18629	0.38629	5.368	2.589	4
5	2.488	0.4019	0.13438	0.33438	7.442	2.991	5
6	2.986	0.3349	0.10071	0.30071	9.930	3.326	6
7	3.583	0.2791	0.07742	0.27742	12.916	3.605	7
8	4.300	0.2326	0.06061	0.26061	16.499	3.837	8
9	5.160	0.1938	0.04808	0.24808	20.799	4.031	9
10	6.192	0.1615	0.03852	0.23852	25.959	4.192	10
11	7.430	0.1346	0.03110	0.23110	32.150	4.327	11
12	8.916	0.1122	0.02526	0.22526	39.581	4.439	12
13	10.699	0.0935	0.02062	0.22062	48.497	4.533	13
14	12.839	0.0779	0.01689	0.21689	59.196	4.611	14
15	15.407	0.0649	0.01388	0.21388	72.035	4.675	15
16	18.488	0.0541	0.01144	0.21144	87.442	4.730	16
17	22.186	0.0451	0.00944	0.20944	105.931	4.775	17
18	26.623	0.0376	0.00781	0.20781	128.117	4.812	18
19	31.948	0.0313	0.00646	0.20646	154.740	4.843	19
20	38.338	0.0261	0.00536	0.20536	186.688	4.870	20
21	46.005	0.0217	0.00444	0.20444	225.025	4.891	21
22	55.206	0.0181	0.00369	0.20369	271.031	4.909	22
23	66.247	0.0151	0.00307	0.20307	326.237	4.925	23
24	79.497	0.0126	0.00255	0.20255	392.484	4.937	24
25	95.396	0.0105	0.00212	0.20212	471.981	4.948	25
26	114.475	0.0087	0.00176	0.20176	567.377	4.956	26
27	137.371	0.0073	0.00147	0.20147	681.853	4.964	27
28	164.845	0.0061	0.00122	0.20122	819.223	4.970	28
29	197.813	0.0051	0.00102	0.20102	984.068	4.975	29
30	237.376	0.0042	0.00085	0.20085	1181.881	4.979	30
31	284.851	0.0035	0.00070	0.20070	1419.257	4.982	31
32	341.822	0.0029	0.00059	0.20059	1704.108	4.985	32
33	410.186	0.0024	0.00049	0.20049	2045.930	4.988	33
34	492.223	0.0020	0.00041	0.20041	2456.116	4.990	34
35	590.668	0.0017	0.00034	0.20034	2948.339	4.992	35
40	1469.772	0.0007	0.00014	0.20014	7343.858	4.997	40
45	3657.258	0.0003	0.00005	0.20005	18281.331	4.999	45
50	9100.427	0.0001	0.00002	0.20002	45497.191	4.999	50

Index